VIRTUE, EMOTION AND IMAGINATION IN LAW AND LEGAL REASONING

What is the role and value of virtue, emotion and imagination in law and legal reasoning? These new essays, by leading scholars of both law and philosophy, offer striking and exploratory answers to this neglected question. The collection takes a holistic approach, inquiring as to the connections and relations between virtue, emotion and imagination. In addition to the principal focus on adjudication, essays in the collection also engage with a variety of different legal, political and moral contexts: eg criminal law sentencing, the Black Lives Matter movement and professional ethics. A number of different areas of the law are addressed (eg criminal law, constitutional law and tort law) and the issues explored include: the benefits and limits of empathy in legal reasoning; the role of attention and perception in judicial reasoning; the identification of judicial virtues (such as compassion and humility) and judicial vices (such as callousness and partiality); the values and dangers of certain imaginative devices (eg personification); and the interactive and social dimensions of virtue, emotion and imagination.

Virtue, Emotion and Imagination in Law and Legal Reasoning

Edited by
Amalia Amaya
and
Maksymilian Del Mar

•HART•
OXFORD • LONDON • NEW YORK • NEW DELHI • SYDNEY

HART PUBLISHING

Bloomsbury Publishing Plc

Kemp House, Chawley Park, Cumnor Hill, Oxford, OX2 9PH, UK

1385 Broadway, New York, NY 10018, USA

HART PUBLISHING, the Hart/Stag logo, BLOOMSBURY and the Diana logo are trademarks of Bloomsbury Publishing Plc

First published in Great Britain 2020

A catalogue record for this book is available from the British Library.

Library of Congress Cataloging-in-Publication data

Names: Amaya, Amalia, editor. | Del Mar, Maksymilian, 1979- editor.

Title: Virtue, emotion and imagination in law and legal reasoning / Amalia Amaya, Maksymilian Del Mar.

Description: Chicago : Hart Publishing, an imprint of Bloomsbury Publishing, 2020. | Includes bibliographical references and index.

Identifiers: LCCN 2019044099 (print) | LCCN 2019044100 (ebook) | ISBN 9781509925131 (hardback) | ISBN 9781509925148 (Epub)

Subjects: LCSH: Law—Methodology. | Law—Philosophy. | Virtue. | Emotions (Philosophy) | Imagination.

Classification: LCC K212 .V569 2020 (print) | LCC K212 (ebook) | DDC 340/.1—dc23

LC record available at https://lccn.loc.gov/2019044099

LC ebook record available at https://lccn.loc.gov/2019044100

ISBN: HB: 978-1-50992-513-1
ePDF: 978-1-50992-515-5
ePub: 978-1-50992-514-8

Typeset by Compuscript Ltd, Shannon
Printed and bound in Great Britain by TJ International Ltd, Padstow, Cornwall

To find out more about our authors and books visit www.hartpublishing.co.uk. Here you will find extracts, author information, details of forthcoming events and the option to sign up for our newsletters.

CONTENTS

List of Contributors ... vii

1. *New Horizons for the Study of the Legal Mind: Relating Virtue, Emotion and Imagination* ... 1
   Amalia Amaya and Maksymilian Del Mar

PART I
VIRTUE – AND EMOTION, IMAGINATION

2. *Admiration, Exemplarity and Judicial Virtue* ... 25
   Amalia Amaya

3. *Impartiality and Legal Reasoning* ... 47
   Catherine Z Elgin

4. *Austerity, Compassion and the Rule of Law* ... 59
   Benjamin C Zipursky

5. *All Judges on the Couch? On Iris Murdoch and Legal Decision-Making* ... 77
   Iris van Domselaar

PART II
EMOTION – AND VIRTUE, IMAGINATION

6. *On Emotions and the Politics of Attention in Judicial Reasoning* ... 101
   Emily Kidd White

7. *'Black Lives Matter': Moral Frames for Understanding the Police Killings of Black Males* ... 121
   Lawrence Blum

8. *Suffering and Punishment* ... 139
   Michael S Brady

9. *Empathy and Negative Intimacy* ... 157
   Olbeth Hansberg

PART III
IMAGINATION – AND EMOTION, VIRTUE

10. *Empathy, Imagination and the Law* 179
Amy Kind

11. *Imagining Motives* 199
Adam Morton

12. *The Legal Imagination in Historical Perspective* 217
Simon Stern

13. *The Legal Imagination: Individual, Interactive and Communal* 235
Maksymilian Del Mar

Index 261

LIST OF CONTRIBUTORS

Amalia Amaya is British Academy Global Professor at Edinburgh Law School and Research Professor at the Institute for Philosophical Research at the National Autonomous University of Mexico. She works primarily in philosophy of law, with a particular focus on the epistemology of legal proof, theories of legal reasoning, and judicial ethics. She is the author of *Law, Virtue and Justice* (co-edited with Ho Hock Lai) (Hart Publishing, 2012) and *The Tapestry of Reason: An Inquiry into the Nature of Coherence and its Role in Legal Argument* (Hart Publishing, 2015).

Lawrence Blum is Emeritus Distinguished Professor of Liberal Arts and Education and Professor of Philosophy at the University of Massachusetts Boston. He specialises in race studies, moral philosophy, philosophy of education, and moral and political philosophy. He is the author of five books in these areas, most recently *High Schools, Race, and America's Future: What Students Can Teach Us About Morality, Diversity, and Community* (2012).

Michael S Brady is Professor of Philosophy at the University of Glasgow. His research interests focus on emotion, epistemology and ethics. His monograph *Emotional Insight: The Epistemic Role of Emotional Experience* was published by Oxford University Press (OUP) in 2013. A second monograph – *Suffering & Virtue* – was published by OUP in 2018.

Maksymilian Del Mar is Professor of Legal Theory in the School of Law, Queen Mary University of London. Most recently, he is the author of *Artefacts of Legal Inquiry: The Value of Imagination in Adjudication* (Hart/Bloomsbury), and editor (with Simon Stern and Bernadette Meyler) of *The Oxford Handbook of Law and Humanities.*

Catherine Z Elgin is professor of the philosophy of education at Harvard Graduate School of Education. Her writing lies at the intersection of epistemology, aesthetics and the philosophy of science. Her most recent book is *True Enough* (MIT Press).

Olbeth Hansberg is a research professor at the Institute for Philosophical Research at the National Autonomous University of México (UNAM). Her main subject is the Philosophy of Mind, with a special interest in the study of the emotions. She is the director of the University Seminar on Affectivity and the emotions (SUAFEM) at UNAM.

Amy Kind is the Russell K. Pitzer Professor of Philosophy at Claremont McKenna College. She is the editor of *The Routledge Handbook of Philosophy of Imagination* and *Philosophy of Mind in the Twentieth and Twenty-First Centuries* (Routledge), and the co-editor of *Knowledge Through Imagination* (Oxford University Press). She has also authored the textbook *Persons and Personal Identity* (Polity Press).

Adam Morton writes on epistemology, the philosophy of mind, and occasionally on ethics. His most recent books are *Bounded Thinking* and *Emotion and Imagination*.

Simon Stern is Professor of Law and English at the University of Toronto. His recent publications include articles on the history of obscenity, legal aesthetics, and the 'reasonable person'. He is co-editor, with Robert Spoo, of the *Law and Literature* series for Oxford University Press, and has co-edited (with Maks Del Mar and Bernadette Meyler) *The Oxford Handbook of Law and Humanities*. He is currently working on a book-length study of the history and theory of legal fictions in the common law.

Iris van Domselaar is an Associate Professor in legal philosophy and legal ethics at the University of Amsterdam and director of the Amsterdam Centre on the Legal Professions. She writes about virtue ethics and legal decision-making, tragedy and law, and legal ethics for (corporate) lawyers.

Emily Kidd White is an Assistant Professor at Osgoode Hall Law School. She works on questions of legal argumentation. She is the author of *Emotions in Judicial Reasoning* (Oxford Legal Philosophy Series, Oxford University Press, forthcoming), and co-editor of *The Research Handbook on Law and Emotion* (Edward Elgar Press, forthcoming).

Benjamin C Zipursky is Professor of Law at Fordham Law School, where he holds the James H. Quinn '49 Chair in Legal Ethics and has twice served as Associate Dean (2001–03; 2010–13). He has taught as a visiting professor at Columbia Law School, Harvard Law School, Vanderbilt Law School, and New York University's Department of Philosophy. Professor Zipursky is a leading scholar in torts, jurisprudence and legal ethics, and has published more than sixty articles and chapters on subjects ranging from punitive damages and conflicts of interest in mass tort litigation to the place of compassion in jurisprudence and the varieties of pragmatism within legal philosophy.

1

New Horizons for the Study of the Legal Mind: Relating Virtue, Emotion and Imagination

AMALIA AMAYA AND MAKSYMILIAN DEL MAR*

I. Introduction

This collection aims to examine the relevance of virtue, emotion and imagination to legal reasoning and, more generally, to legal theory. The twelve chapters collected here bring to light the various ways in which these elements contribute to legal argument and explore the connections that there exist among them. The study of the interlocking roles that virtue, emotion and imagination play in law and legal reasoning is critical to developing a complex and nuanced account of the kinds of patterns of inquiry and deliberation that are involved in reasoning and decision-making in legal contexts. This book seeks to contribute to current work on virtue, emotion and imagination in legal contexts. It does so by foregrounding the relations between virtue, emotion and imagination, and thus treating them not in isolation, but as elements that jointly contribute to the development of a theory of legal reasoning that results in sound legal judgement. Before giving an account of the structure and content of the book, we shall place the present volume in the context of existing legal scholarship on virtue, emotion and imagination. We do so in four sections, exploring: (1) virtue, (2) emotion, (3) imagination, and (4), briefly commenting on relations between them. Following these sections, we then present an overview of the chapters in this collection and finish the introduction with suggestions for future research.

* We would like to express our thanks to the British Academy and the Newton Fund for funding this project, including the conference where almost all of the chapters in this volume were first presented. We also thank our respective universities – the National Autonomous University of Mexico and Queen Mary University of London – for their support of the project and its events.

II. Virtue, Legal Reasoning and Legal Theory

An exciting development in legal scholarship in recent years has been the development of virtue jurisprudence.[1] Virtue jurisprudence places the notion of virtue at the centre of legal analysis. The turn to virtue is not idiosyncratic of legal studies; rather, a vindication of virtue has taken place across different disciplines, most prominently, ethics, epistemology and political theory.[2] Virtue jurisprudence draws upon and feeds into a broader transdisciplinary movement that aims to recognise and study the different ways in which matters of character are key to a broad range of normative issues. A central feature of virtue theory – as much in law as everywhere else – is an inversion of the direction of analysis. Virtue theorists seek to explain the normative properties of beliefs, decisions, plans or actions in terms of the virtues (or their lack thereof) of agents, rather than the other way around. From this point of view, the question of which kind of agents we are and want to be becomes most important, for it provides the ground upon which one may begin to develop an account of which beliefs, decisions, plans or actions are to be positively assessed.

In recent decades, virtue theory has begun to establish itself as a main normative framework, alongside traditional deontological and consequentialist accounts. It has also progressively diversified as virtue theorists have begun to explore different views on virtue – in addition to the vastly influential Aristotelian theory – and have applied a number of virtue-based tools to address an increasing variety of problems. Similarly, virtue jurisprudence has gained both in relevance and visibility within legal scholarship; it has enlarged its scope of application as a growing number of fields of substantive law have been subjected to virtue analysis, and a great diversity of perspectives on virtue have begun to be employed in legal studies. The relevance of character to sound judicial reasoning has been one of the issues that has benefited the most from a virtue-based analysis. Judicial reasoning is also the main focus of the essays in this volume that primarily discuss virtue – as well as its connections with the judge's emotional dispositions and imaginative capacities.

The book makes a number of distinctive contributions to virtue jurisprudence, and especially to virtue-oriented work on judicial reasoning. First, the time has come for virtue jurisprudence to move from designing its general architecture to developing in detail specific aspects of the theory. An important way in which this may be done is by examining individual juridical virtues and vices. The chapters by Zipursky, Amaya and Elgin contribute to this aspect of theory development by analysing compassion, impartiality, humility, magnanimity and austerity. The analysis of individual virtues and vices is not only an important (and necessary)

[1] For a brief introduction to virtue jurisprudence, see Cimino (2018) and Solum (2015). The essays contained in Farrely and Solum (2008); Amaya and Ho (2012); and Amaya and Michelon (2018) may give a good sense of the kind of work done and the breadth of virtue-based approaches to law.

[2] See Snow (2018a) for an overview.

step towards developing a more thorough virtue-based theory of law and adjudication; it may also have a significant impact on virtue theory in domains other than law, where the investigation of individual virtues and vices is a growing area of research.

Second, a central topic for investigation in virtue jurisprudence (and virtue theory, more broadly) is the structure of virtue. How could virtue be more plausibly conceived? A number of competing models of virtue have been advanced in the literature. Prominent among those is the perceptual account of virtue, according to which virtue is first and foremost a highly refined perceptual capacity.[3] Regardless of the merits and drawbacks that this model might have in ethics, where it has been more forcefully defended, it faces severe objections as an account of judicial virtue, given the constraints of publicity and accessibility of reasons that have to be satisfied in the public domain. However, even if a thoroughgoing perceptual model may be in conflict with important legal commitments, perceptual abilities are still a core element of a virtuous judicial character. Chapters by Elgin, van Domselaar and White examine the perceptual dimensions of judicial virtue as well as some of the worries that may be raised against giving perception a broad role in legal argument.

Third, (neo-)Aristotelian virtue theory is the most influential approach in contemporary virtue theory across disciplines. However, in recent years, increasing attention has been paid to other varieties of virtue theory within Western philosophy as well as to Eastern perspectives on virtue. Likewise, in virtue jurisprudence, the resources of traditions of virtue theories other than Aristotelian ethics have been recently explored, most prominently, Plato's theory of virtue, Confucian views on virtue, sentimentalist virtue theory, as well as natural law approaches.[4] The chapters by van Domselaar and Amaya contribute to this trend towards enlarging the philosophical landscape of virtue jurisprudence by examining the relevance of Murdoch's ethics and exemplarist virtue ethics, respectively, to judicial decision-making.

Fourth, a thriving area of research in contemporary virtue theory is virtue education. An attractive feature of this body of work is that it is highly interdisciplinary, as it engages philosophers, psychologists and scholars working in education theory. Law, however, has not yet fully joined this movement towards virtue education. The training of character is a topic that has received far too little attention in both virtue jurisprudence and legal education scholarship.[5] Kind's, van Domselaar's and Amaya's chapters emphasise the importance of the cultivation of virtue and contribute to the examination of the developmental aspects of judicial virtue as well as the different educational strategies that might be employed to inculcate

[3] See Snow (2018b).

[4] See Annas (2018); Wang and Solum (2012); Slote (2012); Solum (2012); and Amaya (forthcoming).

[5] There are, of course, some exceptions – but generally, much more work remains to be done. See Scharffs (2001); McGinnis (2011); and see Sherletics (2017) and the references therein.

virtuous traits of character within the judiciary. The literature on virtue education intersects with work on professional role ethics. Thus, a focus on virtue acquisition in legal scholarship may also open up a productive collaboration among scholars working in virtue jurisprudence and legal education, as well as in legal ethics.

Finally, virtue jurisprudence has some features that seem problematic such as its focus on agents – and their inner psychology – rather than on (external) actions; the blurring of the distinction between the private and the public realm; the centrality of the notion of virtue, which, in some views, is highly dependent on culture; its reliance (in the dominant Aristotelian version) on a concept of the good life; the fuzziness of the guidelines for action it provides; and its emphasis on a fine-tuned situational appreciation as a critical element for good judgment. These characteristics give rise to doubts as to whether virtue jurisprudence is a framework that is compatible with current liberal legal orders – which are committed not to trespass into the private realm, to responsiveness to the facts of value pluralism, to neutrality among conceptions of the good, and to respectfulness of the rule of law and principle-of-legality virtues, like certainty, publicity and generality. Several chapters in the volume (see the chapters by Elgin, Zipursky, van Domselaar and Kind) discuss the tensions between virtue jurisprudence and the main tenets of liberal legal orders, thereby contributing to addressing the foregoing concerns.

III. Law, Emotion and the Affective Sciences

An important body of literature aims to explore the impact on law of the affective sciences, which have experienced spectacular growth in the last decades.[6] Within contemporary legal theory, law and emotion scholarship began to form as a distinct field of inquiry in the mid-1990s.[7] The aim, at first, was to challenge deep-rooted assumptions about emotions being forces that are contrary to reason and ought not to play a role in law and legal reasoning. The next phase of inquiry moved from examining the legitimacy of emotions in law, to the analysis of which kinds of emotions operate in legal contexts and what roles they play. Later work has engaged in a more normative type of analysis, exploring the dynamics of the relationship between law and emotion – how the emotions bestow law with value, as well as the ways in which the law may channel, shape and transform the emotions of individuals and groups. In very recent years, the literature has expanded rapidly to cover a wider range of areas of substantive law and including a rich number of perspectives in the affective sciences. It is also a very active area of scholarship within legal history.

[6] See for an overview Abrams and Keren (2010).

[7] Of course, reflections on relations between law and emotion stretch much further back, especially within the rhetorical tradition. In addition, some important and neglected work on law and emotion was done by early legal realists, eg Leon Petrazycki.

Despite the theoretical work already done in legal scholarship, the dichotomised picture of reason and emotion, together with the view of law and legal reasoning as a purely cognitive enterprise that should be divested from any emotional influence, still has a strong hold among legal practitioners and scholars.[8] This attitude is out of keeping with findings in psychology, neuroscience, sociology and other relevant disciplines, which show the pivotal contribution of the emotions to reasoning and rationality. The project that law and emotion scholars have ahead is, as Abrams and Keren have argued, threefold.[9] First, it seeks to illuminate the assumptions about emotions upon which law relies. Second, it aims to determine the accuracy of these assumptions in light of relevant empirical findings. And, finally, an important objective of law and emotion scholarship is to advance a number of normative goals: the proposal of doctrinal revisions, the development of institutional design, and the advancement of policies that are responsive to the best available knowledge we have about the nature and role of emotions.

This volume aims to contribute to challenge what has proved to be a highly sticky conception of legal rationality as impervious to emotion, and to show that emotions are not only ineliminable but also a vital component of a sound theory of law and legal reasoning. On Maroney's useful taxonomy, law and emotion scholarship falls under six main categories: an *emotion-centred approach*, which seeks to analyse specific emotions and their impact in law; an *emotional phenomenon approach*, which centres on analysing particular emotion-driven phenomena, such as empathy or affective forecasting, in the law; an *emotion-theory approach*, which focuses on a given theory of emotion and its potential applicability to the legal domain; a *legal doctrine approach*, which seeks to analyse how an area of law incorporates the emotions; a *theory-of-law approach*, which examines the relationship between theories of emotion and different theories of law; and a *legal-actor approach*, which explores how emotions influence or should inform assigned legal functions.[10] This volume advances law and emotion scholarship by making a number of contributions to these different theoretical approaches.

The *emotion-centred approach* has mostly focused on analysing 'negative' emotions, such as shame, disgust, fear and anger, but it is important to explore the role that a wider range of emotions play in law. White's and van Domselaar's chapters emphasise the relevance of positive emotions, such as wonder, curiosity and awe, to judicial decision-making and Amaya's chapter discusses in detail the relevance of the positive emotion of admiration to the development of judicial virtue.

Empathy has been a key topic in the *emotional phenomenon approach*, and it is also a central theme in this volume. The book contributes to the understanding of empathy and its relevance to law by examining the connections between empathy

[8] See Maroney (2018).
[9] Abrams and Keren (2010).
[10] See Maroney (2006).

and attention (in White's chapter), empathy and intimacy (in Hansberg's chapter), empathy, sympathy and compassion (in Hansberg and Zipursky's chapters), and empathy and imagination (in Kind's chapter) as well as by analysing the role of empathy in a number of constitutional law cases (Zipursky's chapter). In addition to empathy, the book also advances the *emotional phenomenon approach* by discussing (in Morton's chapter) the legal implications of the difficulties associated with the attribution of mental states, such as affective states and motives.

While there is no attempt in this volume to articulate and/or defend a particular theory of emotion for the law, the volume advances the *theory of emotion approach* insofar as it discusses a range of ways in which emotions may be evaluated, communicated and nurtured, which are only plausible under the view that emotions include an important cognitive component.

Brady's chapter on the role of emotions in the justification of punishment, as well as Morton's chapter on the ascriptions of states of mind, including emotions, contribute to a core research field in the *legal doctrine approach*, namely, criminal law, and it also expands the scope of this area of study by discussing emotion-related problems that are relevant to constitutional law (in Zipursky's and Kind's chapters) as well as family law and medical law (in Hansberg's chapter).

The *theory-of-law approach* is advanced in this volume by exploring the connections between virtue and emotion and thus the important synergies that there are between virtue jurisprudence and the law and emotion movement.

Finally, most work in the *legal-actor approach* has focused primarily on juries; judge's emotions have comparatively received less attention. Several chapters in this volume focus on judicial reasoning, with an emphasis on the emotional capacities that may improve the quality of their decisional processes and outputs (see the chapters by van Domselaar, White, Elgin, Kind and Zipursky). Particular attention is paid to the epistemic, motivational and expressive roles that emotions may play in judicial decision-making. In addition, the contributions to this volume also broaden the repertoire of relevant legal actors by examining the appropriateness of the police's emotional outlooks (Blum), educational strategies for training the emotions of law students (Amaya), as well as the emotional engagement that is distinctive of intimacy relationships that are relevant to law, such as lawyer-client, doctor-patient and victim-victimiser relationships (Hansberg).

IV. Imagination, Language and History

As with the other key concepts in this collection, the history of theoretical reflection on imagination is rich and deeply contested. Perhaps even more so than virtue and emotion, imagination has swung from being presented as foundational for the mind – it is enough to mention Aristotle, Hume and Kant to get a sense of the historical variety and sweep of such a claim – to it being said to be the very obstacle to and the very enemy of reason and knowledge. Telling a history of the scholarship on imagination is further complicated by the entanglement of many issues concerning imagination with certain features of language, including what are often called figurative or rhetorical features. Finally, any such history is also complicated – though, in turn, enriched too – by being spread across a whole range of different disciplines, extending considerably beyond philosophy to include psychology, literary theory and history, philosophy and history of science, and much else besides.

In the legal context, although some attention has been paid to imagination – especially amongst twentieth century scholarship in law and literature (James Boyd White's *The Legal Imagination* being, of course, the pioneering and stand-out example)[11] – it is only relatively recently that the imagination has attracted more sustained theoretical attention. There is, certainly, a long and rich tradition of rhetorical theories of law and legal language, and, given the close relationship between certain features of language and processes of imagination, this is highly relevant and important. Work on rhetoric, for instance, has included theorising the role of mental imagery – including the quality of vividness that characterises certain experiences of seeing with the 'mind's eye'.[12] Further, and, as one would expect from the rhetorical tradition, this attention to imagination, and certain related qualities of language, is combined with sophisticated treatment of the relations between advocacy, the audience and judgement. It is often within the rhetorical tradition, rather than in philosophical work, that one encounters the most subtle analyses of, for example, the uses by advocates and effects on audiences of metaphor, metonymy, synecdoche, parable and personification.[13] In addition, given the importance of both virtue and emotion to the rhetorical tradition, there is much to mine within this tradition for examining relations between the three key concepts in this book. Finally, there have been some important studies on the relations between rhetoric and reasoning in particular areas of legal practice, most especially equity.[14]

As important, and underestimated in contemporary legal theory, as the rhetorical tradition is,[15] those who pursue systematic philosophical treatment of imagination may not always find what they are looking for there. Apart from reference to rhetoric, and related work in law and literature – which has often been connected to work on the moral imagination, as for instance in Martha Nussbaum's body of scholarship – the other domain within legal scholarship that has contributed to theorising imagination is cognitive legal studies. Recent decades have seen a burst of legal scholarship in this vein, and much of it is highly relevant to any student of the legal imagination. Some of this scholarship began on the back of the

[11] White (1973).

[12] Eg, see Webb (2009).

[13] See eg Perelman and Olbrechts-Tyteca (1969).

[14] See Watt (2009) and Eden (1986).

[15] With some exceptions, of course: eg generally the work of Peter Goodrich (eg Goodrich, 1987); see also Lowrie and Ludemann (2015).

rise of interest in metaphor and metaphorical cognition, thanks especially to Mark Johnson and George Lakoff's *Metaphors We Live By*.[16] A standout example within legal scholarship in this respect is Steven Winter's *A Clearing in the Forest: Law, Life and Mind*.[17] Further important work in cognitive legal studies has been done by Jerome Bruner, Ellen Spolsky and Linda Berger.[18] This work is important, in part, because, as with all second-generation cognitive studies, it pays close attention to the relations between mind and body, and thus investigates the embodied character of the imagination. In doing so, it also often relates imagination and emotion together.

In addition to the above, there has been important work in the legal context on particular kinds of processes of imagination, with their related features of language. A good deal of this has focused on metaphor and narrative.[19] However, some scholars have also looked at personification, and the use of imaginary figures in legal thought (as one would expect, there is an especially large literature on the Reasonable Person).[20] In addition, there is the scholarship on legal fictions, and, more broadly, fictionality in legal discourse and legal reasoning.[21] What perhaps is missing from this wealth of literature is systematic theoretical reflection on imagination in a legal context. Just what is common to all these processes – for example in metaphorical or figural cognition? Why do these processes – if they do – all deserve to be placed under the canopy of imagination?

Here, legal scholars may find it helpful – as some already have (see eg the chapters by Stern and Del Mar in this volume) – to draw on the recent burst of philosophical interest in imagination. One of the pioneers here has been Amy Kind, who also contributes to this volume. Through her own writing, but also editorially,[22] Kind has done much to revive this topic on the contemporary philosophical agenda. Another contemporary pioneer – though via a different philosophical tradition and connecting also to the important work on the role of imagination in science[23] – is Catherine Elgin, who has also contributed to this volume. Important contemporary philosophical work has also been done on the relations between imagination and emotion – and two philosophers who have been leading this debate, Adam Morton and Michael Brady, are also included in this volume. There are, however, a great many more connections to be made, for instance, by reference to the flowering of work on thought experiments in philosophy,[24] as well as to more general treatments of the structure or architecture of imagination.[25]

[16] See Lakoff and Johnson (1980).
[17] See Winter (2001).
[18] See Bruner (1986); Spolsky (2015); and Berger and Stanchi (2018).
[19] See, recently, Hanne and Weisberg (2018).
[20] See Moran (2003).
[21] See eg Petroski (2019); Del Mar and Twining (2015).
[22] See Kind and Kung (2016); Kind (2016); as well as her blog (*The Junkyard of the Mind*).
[23] See Godfrey-Smith and Levy (forthcoming).
[24] See, recently, Stuart, Fehige and Brown (2017).
[25] See Currie and Ravenscroft (2002); Nichols (2006).

There are many ways to cut the cake of theoretical issues on imagination. Here, we shall mention only three, which also connect strongly to what is examined in this volume: first, the value and danger of the imagination; second, the social character of imagination; and, third, the importance of theorising imagination historically.

A number of the chapters in this volume directly confront issues concerning the role and value, but also the dangers and risks, of imagination in the legal context. Of course, as noted above, attacks on imagination are not new and come in various shapes and sizes: one of them is that imagination belongs on the discovery side of the traditional divide between discovery and justification (see eg Elgin's chapter in this volume). It is then said that, as important as it might be to discovery, imagination does not contribute to the practices of justification. This view also results in a certain division of labour – imagination can be studied by psychologists, who are interested in the causes of judicial decision-making, but is not especially relevant to philosophers, who are more interested in reasons than in causes. On this view, although there is some role and value of imagination, it is a very restricted one. This is an important issue for anyone confronting the topic of imagination in legal scholarship. What is the connection between reason-giving and imagination? Or, is that the wrong question, and ought we instead to loosen the hold of the traditional conceptual divide, with related division of labour, between contexts of discovery and justification? For instance, when Elgin in this volume speaks of using imagination to broaden one's 'conception of what qualifies as someone's home', why is this not closely related to the practice of reason-giving – at least more closely than a strict divide between discovery and justification might suggest? Similarly with the uses of personification examined by Morton and Stern in this volume – are the imaginary figures in legal thought not also part of the legal tests for liability, and thus used by judges as justifications for decisions? Do judges not say that such-and-such a defendant is negligent because the defendant did not do what the Reasonable Person would have done? In what sense is this not a justification – or a practice of reason-giving? As Del Mar argues in his chapter, similar challenges to the orthodox view (which make imagination irrelevant, or marginal, to justification) can be made via the use of legal fictions, metaphors and scenarios (or hypothetical narratives).

Even if, however, one does defend the view that there is a closer relation between imagination and justification than has been previously thought, one might still think there are certain dangers and risks of the imagination. As Morton discusses in his chapter, we may not be especially good at imagining – for instance, the experiences of others (a topic that arises across many chapters of this volume, including in van Domselaar's, Blum's, Zipursky's, Kind's and Hansberg's). Imagination is replete with biases, as with all cognition, but one could ask: does imagining actually enhance the prospects of persons being biased, or does it decrease it? Are there better or worse uses of imagination? If so, what does it mean to imagine well? A lot may be said to hang on these questions for the status of imagination in legal scholarship.

A second issue is that of the social character of the imagination. Arguably, imagination is most commonly approached as a matter for individual minds. However this is further specified – as the process of, say, constructing mental imagery without immediate sensory feedback, or of supposing something is so (as in so-called propositional imagining), or of simulating another person's perspective and experience (how they might have felt in such-and-such a situation), or constructing counter-factual alternatives to what happened – imagination is routinely identified with processes in individual minds. However, when one looks more closely – and this is perhaps especially evident in the legal context, within the pragmatics of adjudication – imagining is something that persons often do together. Thus, for example, advocates and judges engage together, interactively, with hypothetical narratives or with the counterfactual actions of imaginary figures. If we keep in view the relations between imagination and certain features of language, then we can see that imagining is often spread out over time and distributed across a much wider range of persons. After all, to give just one example, the use of metaphor (and metaphorical cognition) is often not a one-off occasion but is instead alive within legal discourse for considerable periods of time, being imagined and re-imagined on multiple occasions, by multiple audiences. In this volume, Del Mar, and to an extent also Stern, make the argument that we need to examine the legal imagination at multiple levels: the individual one remains important, but this alone is insufficient; we need also to pay attention to the interactive and communal dynamics of imagining and its related uses of language.

A final, third, issue is that of the importance of theorising imagination historically. This is most explicitly prominent in Stern's contribution to this volume. In part, the importance of the historical view connects to the above-mentioned point as to the social dimensions of imagination and associated features of legal language. As Stern shows, once introduced, the device of personification is copied and imitated by other legal actors: the prudent man, for instance, travels across many areas of the law – from commercial law (eg the law of bailment) to criminal law and beyond. These are travels across time, and thus any sophisticated engagement with any process of imagining and any related feature of language will track not only the degree of popularity of those processes and features, but also how they change over time (even if one sticks to surface-level descriptions, these can be fascinating, eg the shift in language from the 'prudent man' to the 'reasonable person'). Certain dynamics may only come into view when looked at historically: for example the politics of imagining, with its gender and racial dimensions, may be best seen over time.[26] Further, there are clearly important links between practices of imagination and the general culture: for example with respect to the reasonable person, there are fascinating connections to be mined between such devices in legal thought and their uses in literary production (ie in the history

[26] See eg Robin Stacey's (2018) work on imagination in medieval Wales, with attention, eg to the politics of relations between England and Wales.

of personhood, agency and character in works of literature).[27] Devices like the reasonable person are often said to be some of the most public-facing aspects of legal language and legal thought – indeed, some of them (like the reasonable person) may have been introduced with the public literally in mind (ie as devices that are jury-friendly). It is likely, then, that there is much to explore here as to the historical links between the legal and the popular imagination.

V. Virtue, Emotion and Imagination in Law and Legal Reasoning

A key theme of this collection is that virtue, emotion and imagination are not isolated from each other in legal argument but are instead elements that mutually reinforce each other. There are important connections between all three elements, some of which are highlighted in the chapters contained in this volume.

First, virtue and emotion are closely related dimensions of legal argument. Virtue is both a way of acting and a way of feeling. Virtue requires one not only to act in an appropriate way but also to have the right sort of emotional response. Emotional engagement is thus critical to virtuous legal deliberation. The constitutive link that there is between virtue and emotion (and which is discussed in several chapters of this volume) also obtains between vice and emotion. As argued by Blum in this book, some vices are partly constituted by emotions (or their lack thereof). In addition, emotional involvement is also essential to enhance the perceptual abilities that virtue partly consists of. Both emotional and perceptual capacities are at the core of virtuous behaviour, but these two elements are not isolated. Rather, the perceptions of the virtuous judge are emotionally loaded; emotions improve the quality of the deliverances of the fine-tuned perceptual abilities that are the mark of virtue. They are also central to bringing about the kind of focused attention that results in virtuous legal reasoning and judgement (on this, see van Domselaar's, Brady's and Kind's chapters). Finally, emotions are not only constitutively linked to virtue, but there is also a developmental link, as discussed by Amaya, between them. Virtue education requires nurturing appropriate emotional dispositions, and some emotions, like admiration, play a central role in the acquisition of virtue.

Second, there are close connections between emotion and imagination as well. Imagination is linked to emotion in that part of what is distinctive about some feelings (what it is like to feel them) is that they involve certain sort of imaginings (eg what we imagine about those whom we are scared of or love is part of our feeling scared or in love). There is also a causal relationship between emotion and imagination, as imaginative engagement triggers the generation of emotions.

[27] See eg Frow (2014); Zittoun and Glaveanu (2018).

Imagining certain sorts of emotional objects and events gives rise to a range of corresponding emotions – a point that is of consequence to discussions on criminal punishment, as argued in Brady's chapter in this volume. Imagination is also key to some emotional phenomena like empathy. Empathy can be understood as requiring the sharing of feelings and the embracement of a perspective oriented towards the other, both of which crucially depend on the empathiser's capacity to imagine the other person's subjective experience (see Hansberg's chapter). The capacity to imagine others' emotional reactions is also an important tool for the education of the emotions.[28]

Third, imagination is also intimately connected with virtue. To begin with, the development of imaginative abilities goes hand-to-hand with the acquisition of virtue. Virtue is most efficiently inculcated by imitation, and the process of emulation, as discussed in Amaya's chapter in this volume, critically involves the exercise of imagination. The imaginative participation in the exemplar's ethical experience is necessary for successful imitation. One needs to be able to put oneself in the situation of the exemplar in order to understand how she behaved the way she did, what motivations she had, what her attitudes and feelings were, and what she was responding to. Only after has one gained an adequate understanding of the exemplar's character, is one able to grasp what virtue requires in new circumstances. Thus, imagination is central to fully comprehending exemplary characters and putting that understanding into practice. In addition, imagination is also central in virtuous legal deliberation. When deliberating in the legal context, one needs to rehearse in imagination various competing possible decisions and how the different alternatives are likely to impact the development of the law as well as the parties involved (as Del Mar notes in his chapter, this can be done, for instance, via hypothetical narratives). Virtuous deliberation critically requires a detailed description of the situation of choice faced by the legal decision-maker, prior to any decision that she might take. The exercise of imagination, as argued in van Domselaar's chapter, is necessary for correctly undertaking the description of cases that, from a virtue perspective is a critical part of legal reasoning. A number of the chapters in this volume suggest that there is a close relationship between imagination and the construction and re-construction of the significance and relevance of facts and patterns of facts (see the chapters by Elgin, Kind, Del Mar and Stern). Finally, it might even be the case – as Kind and Morton suggest – that imagination may be profitably understood as a judicial virtue, this being a tighter connection that deserves to be more thoroughly explored.

Thus, virtue, emotion and imagination are mutually reinforcing elements, rather than independent contributors to legal argument. Virtuous judgement requires emotional involvement and imaginative engagement. A central aim of this volume is to provide an analysis of the ways in which these three elements relate to each other within a full-blown theory of legal reasoning. In order to

[28] See Maxwell and Reichenbach (2007).

accomplish this aim, the volume employs a variety of methodological tools and sources beyond those of conceptual analysis that are traditionally used in the field of legal theory, such as literature and the arts (as in Amaya and van Domselaar's chapters), history (see Del Mar and Stern's chapters) and mass media communication (in Blum's chapter).

In addition, this collection deploys a highly interdisciplinary methodology. The development of a theory of legal reasoning that includes virtue, emotion and imagination as main components raises questions and overlaps with the concerns of other fields of philosophical inquiry, such as ethics and epistemology, as well as with topics dealt with in contemporary work on the affective sciences, social psychology, education theory, and cognitive science. Thus, several chapters in this volume draw on bodies of literature and use methods other than those that are the landmark of contemporary analytic jurisprudence. As a result, this volume, we hope, can also show the ways in which the recognition and study of allegedly peripheral elements in law and legal reasoning, such as virtue, emotion and imagination, may also have an impact on legal scholarship at a methodological level, expanding the modes of analysis employed in legal theory and contributing to the cross-fertilisation between law and other disciplines.

VI. Plan of the Book

This book has three parts. Each of these parts includes chapters that focus on one of the target elements of this volume – virtue, emotion or imagination – while keeping the other two elements in the background and examining relations between them in the course of the argument.

The first part 'Virtue – and Emotion, Imagination' contains four chapters that contribute to virtue jurisprudence as well as advance the knowledge of how virtue connects to emotion and imagination. The first chapter, 'Admiration, Exemplarity and Judicial Virtue' by **Amalia Amaya**, explores the relevance of the emotion of admiration to the development of judicial virtue. A critical venue for the development of the traits of character that are virtues in the context of the judicial role is the imitation of exemplary judges. Admiration, argues Amaya, plays a central role in this process as it disposes those who admire to emulate the exemplar in the admired respect. In addition to triggering a process of emulation that results in the acquisition of judicial virtue, admiration also brings with it a number of beneficial social effects for the judiciary at both the individual and the collective level. The chapter concludes by vindicating the importance of cultivating a virtuous disposition to admire in legal education.

The second chapter, 'Impartiality and Legal Reasoning' by **Catherine Elgin**, argues for an understanding of legal judgment as an 'impartial judgment'. Unlike impersonal judgments and virtuous judgements, impartial judgements, claim Elgin, satisfy two core principles that any viable legal system should respect, namely, the principles of consistency and publicity. Virtue, emotion and imagination are valuable elements in judicial decision-making, but their role, contends Elgin, should be constrained by consistency and publicity.

In 'Austerity, Compassion and the Rule of Law' **Benjamin Zipursky** claims that austerity, that is, a cultivated dispassionateness, sometimes conflicts with the requirements imposed by the rule of law. His argument for this claim relies on a detailed analysis of the US Supreme Court decision in *PLIVA v Mensing*, which eliminated 'failure to warn' claims for all generic prescription drugs. The analysis of this case provided in the minority opinion, written by Justice Sotomayor, often regarded as an empathetic and compassionate judge, was, argues Zipursky, strongly supported by principle-of-legality virtues. This shows, according to Zipursky, that compassion – and the emotional dispositions it involves – is not only in tension with the rule of law, but may in fact sometimes enable better compliance with the values it embeds and protects.

The last chapter in this part, 'All Judges on the Couch? On Iris Murdoch and Legal Decision-Making', by **Iris van Domselaar**, puts forward a Murdochian approach of judicial reasoning. Central to this account is the idea that the judge's vision and her perceptual capacities play a critical role in judicial decision-making. Such perception is affectively-loaded: good judging requires, on this view, an emotional maturity on the part of the judge as well as an attitude of loving kindness and empathy towards the parties. After describing the main features of a Murdochian approach to legal reasoning and the vision-based account of judicial virtue which it underwrites, van Domselaar discusses a number of problems that need to be further explored in order to show the feasibility and legitimacy of this account in a liberal legal order.

Part II, 'Emotion – and Virtue, Imagination', revolves around the place of emotion in law and legal reasoning and its connections with virtue and imagination. The first chapter, 'On Emotions and the Politics of Attention' by **Emily Kidd White**, argues that judges must practice a certain politics of attention, that is to say, a conscious effort to pay attention and distribute it in a principled way. Emotions, claims White, play critical roles in motivating and facilitating this kind of attention, of which empathy is a facet. White identifies a number of ways in which judicial efforts at paying attention to the claimant may go wrong. When seeking to pay attention, judges may obscure, co-opt, selectively empathise with the claimant, or claim the space that is rightfully theirs. Despite these tendencies towards error, argues White, there are important reasons for judges to cultivate a politics of attention. Legal commitments to equality and respect require a practice of judicial reasoning that properly reflects such politics.

In '"Black Lives Matter": Moral Frames for Understanding the Police Killings of Black Males', **Lawrence Blum** examines the absence, amongst police officers, of a particular emotional attitude, namely caring about the life of a human being unknown personally to oneself. Looking closely at five killings of black males in the US, and especially at failure by police officers to come to the aid of subjects after they were shot or taken down, Blum emphasises the importance of attending to the affective dimension of the moral failures in question. These moral failures, he argues, are not captured by, for instance, reference to stereotyping, implicit bias, or failure to recognise the right of black people. Neither is it sufficient to examine simply the behaviour of police of officers. Rather, what is required is a sophisticated approach to the emotions involved, which were so markedly, and tragically, absent in the police officers in the cases above. There is, Blum insists, an irreducible 'vice of emotional character' in failing to value (black) lives. This vice, he adds, is not solely an individual one: it is also one that can, and ought to, be studied as a social and cultural phenomenon.

The next chapter, 'Suffering and Punishment', by **Michael Brady** continues Blum's examination of the affective dimensions of crime. It focuses specifically on judicial practices of punishment of criminal offenders. Here, Brady argues in defence of the imposition of suffering (in the form of hard treatment) by the judiciary. Words, he says, may not be enough for censure and condemnation – what may be required for punishment (when, of course, it is considered appropriate) is that the offender actually experiences suffering. Wrongdoing, Brady says, merits a certain emotional response from the state, but mere words will often not be effective enough. Defending, in particular, Antony Duff's communicative theory of punishment against objections from Matt Matravers, Brady argues that this theory can explain how the imposition of suffering (in the form of hard treatment) by the state can be legitimate. Brady, then, contributes further to this volume's interest in the social – including institutional – contexts of the emotions.

The last chapter of this part, 'Empathy and Negative Intimacy', by **Olbeth Hansberg**, zooms in on one of the most discussed, and contested, concepts in this volume, namely empathy. Hansberg examines this concept in the particular context of intimate relations. Hansberg's general claim is that empathy is necessary for intimate relations, in part because it is necessary, in intimate relations, to see the other as 'minded'. The principal focus of the chapter is what is meant by empathy in this context. Here, Hansberg helpfully distinguishes empathy from nearby emotional states – such as sympathy and compassion – and also shows how certain empathy-related process, such as emotional contagion, emotional matching and imitation, are not quite fully fledged forms of empathy. Although empathy – understood in its more fully-fledged character as a cognitive and affective-imaginative process – may not always be positive, it is nevertheless necessary for intimate relations.

The third part of the book, 'Imagination – and Emotion, Virtue' examines the role of imagination in law and legal reasoning and its relations to virtue and emotion. The first chapter, 'Empathy, Imagination and the Law', by **Amy Kind** connects neatly to the final chapter of the second part, by also confronting the concept of empathy. Ultimately, Kind argues that empathy may not be the best concept for an inquiry into judicial decision-making. Rather, Kind says, we should work with the concept of imagination. In developing and defending this argument, Kind addresses the highly-charged debate in the US context as to models of the judicial role. The two models that have featured in this debate are the umpire model and the empathy model. For Kind, however, neither of these two models appropriately captures what are the admirable and desirable qualities amongst judges. It is not, says Kind, empathy, or empathic resonance, that we want judges to exhibit, but instead understanding, which is best cultivated by what Kind calls 'imaginative projection'.

Adam Morton's chapter, 'Imagining Motives', confronts some of the dangers and risks of imagining. In particular, as his title suggests, Morton is concerned with the abilities of persons to imagine the motives of others. Morton is generally sceptical about these abilities – although persons may be good at some aspects of imagining the motives of others (eg whether someone is inclined to help or not), persons are generally not good at, say, 'matching combinations and compromises between all the potential motives' within the actions performed by others. Most attributions of the motives of others is the result of 'shallowly conceptualised expectations of what a person will do and how they might react to what oneself does', and these expectations often mislead us about, for instance, depression, social panic, or the long-term effects of damaging experiences. Given the frequency with which persons in the legal context need to imagine the motives of others, this scepticism about our abilities to imagine them raises serious questions – for instance, as to the impartiality of legal systems.

In 'The Legal Imagination in Historical Perspective', **Simon Stern** is also concerned with how, in the legal context, the actions of others are understood and evaluated. Stern pursues this interest by examining the history of personification – the invention of imaginary figures, whose actions are imagined as part of the application of certain legal tests. Stern's focus is on the introduction of the figure of the reasonable man in the nineteenth century, and especially on one neglected chapter in this story, ie its unsuccessful spell in the law of negotiable instruments. Stern theorises the device of personification – and its related processes of imagining – historically, and he therefore asks: why was it introduced in the first place? How was it deployed over time? Why was it eventually rejected? Stern's analysis is not confined to the area of the law of negotiable instruments; helpfully, he also shows how the device was copied and how it thus travelled across different areas of the law. By examining these travels – some more successful than others – one can also better see the limits of the utility of certain devices and related processes of imagination. And this, in turn, better helps us appreciate the various constraints under which imagination operates in the legal context.

The last chapter, 'The Legal Imagination: Individual, Interactive and Communal', by **Maksymilian Del Mar**, turns to another arguably neglected aspect of theories of the legal imagination, namely its social dimension. Del Mar recognises the importance of the individual level of imagination, and he discusses how, at that level, imagination has an important role to play, including making a contribution to the practices of justification in legal decision-making. However, the role and value of imagination is not limited to the individual level. Imagining is something that people often do together, both interactively in the course of a trial, as well as collectively and over time. Paying attention also to the relations between processes of imagination and certain features of language, Del Mar offers four examples that, he argues, to be appreciated, ought to be examined at all three levels, ie the individual, the interactive and the communal. These four examples are: fictions, metaphors, figures and scenarios. Some of the role and value of these can, at each level, be expressed via their relations with emotion and virtue (including the affective dynamics of interaction, or collective epistemic virtues).

We hope that this volume will stimulate further research on the ways in which virtue, emotion and imagination may jointly contribute to sound legal argument. In the next section, we suggest some lines for future research.

VII. Future Research

A first area of research that would greatly advance the study of the role that virtue, emotion and imagination play in legal argument is the investigation of vice, rather than virtue, its associated emotions, and the way in which vices may impinge on the legal imagination. In this collection, Zipursky discusses the vice of austerity; Amaya's chapter also briefly touches upon the vices of obsequiousness and arrogance, and Blum examines unconcern and indifference towards other's suffering as a kind of vice that is partly emotional in nature. Important progress could be made by thoroughly investigating the traits of character that are vicious in different legal roles. It would also be necessary to clarify the conditions under which emotions are vicious or which kind of emotional dispositions are involved in vice. In his discussion of indifference, Blum argues that the vice in question consists in a lack of the appropriate emotions, rather than the presence of distinct vicious emotions. Careful analysis of the relationships that may be established between vice and emotional dispositions (or their lack thereof) would advance the understanding of the relevance of character and emotions to sound legal judgement. There is scope here, too, for relating vices with not only emotion, but also imagination. For instance, the absence of imagination – or the inability or unwillingness to imagine something (ie imaginative resistance), for example the suffering of another – is a good example of a vice that matters greatly to adjudication. If one thinks that certain kinds of language – for example metaphorical – are better than others in inviting persons to imagine, and if, again, one thinks that the absence of imagination can be a vice in adjudication, then one can also argue that legal language ought to contain more qualities that invite legal reasoners to imagine.

As mentioned earlier, most work in law and emotion focuses on negative emotions. The emotional register that is relevant to law and legal reasoning is, however, much richer. The emotion of admiration, as a positive emotion, is discussed in detail in this collection, and some attention is paid to other positive emotions, such as awe, satisfaction and pride, as well as to epistemic emotions, like wonder, curiosity and surprise.[29] A lot of work needs to be done with a view to exploring the role that emotions other than negative ones play in law and legal argument. Such research will greatly benefit and contribute to current research on social and epistemic emotions, which is a growth area in both emotion studies and (virtue) epistemology. Central to the analysis of the variety of emotions that are relevant in law is the study of how they contribute to virtuous legal inquiry and deliberation as well as the way in which they enhance and are bolstered by artefacts of legal imagination. There is, indeed, a potentially very close relationship between certain artefacts of legal language, related processes of imagination, and certain epistemic emotions. Arguably, part of the affective phenomenology of metaphorical imagining is a mixture of wonder (at, say, the semantic incongruity set up by a metaphor), as well as desire to resolve that incongruity. Put more strongly, it is difficult to see how one could properly investigate the role of epistemic emotions without attention to imagination.

Work on virtue, emotion and imagination, as much as the broader field of legal reasoning, focuses on the individual, rather than on the social dimensions of legal argument. The last years have witnessed an increasing attention to the social aspects of the production of knowledge and the processes of reasoning and decision-making. Likewise, a social turn would be necessary in the study of virtue, emotion and imagination in legal contexts. As far as virtue is concerned, there is an array of important questions, some of which are posed in Del Mar's chapter, that are in need of further study: which traits of character improve the quality of social interactions in legal settings? Which virtues foster genuine and productive group deliberations? Do groups and institutions, such as the jury, a multi-member court or an agency, possess virtues? Similarly, the social dimensions of emotions give rise to a host of interesting questions, some of which are only touched upon in this volume. Amaya discusses the social effects within the judiciary of the emotion of admiration; Brady argues for the possibility of attributing emotions to groups and collectives, such as the state; and van Domselaar, White and Hansberg examine the emotional texture of social relationships in legal contexts – such as intimate relationships, relationships between the judge and the parties, and relationships between the judge and counsel. A detailed examination of emotions and its impact on the social dynamics in law would draw from and contribute to current work on the social psychology of emotions. Finally, collective processes of imagination in the legal domain are still largely unexplored – although there is some important work on social imaginaries in philosophy and sociology, little of it has made its way into legal scholarship. When this is tackled, it would be important that the communal imagination is investigated by reference to its relations to the social dimensions of virtue and emotion (as urged, in a preliminary way, in Del Mar's chapter).

[29] See eg Brun, Doguoglo and Kuenzle (2008).

An important aspect that will deserve to be carefully investigated in the future is the impact that social structures, more importantly, legal institutional structures, have on fostering processes of decision-making that are virtuous, emotionally engaged, and enhanced by imagination. As suggested in Blum's chapter, social structures are at the origin of some (individual) vices and vicious sentiments and their remedy depends not only on individual transformation but also in social reform. How do social structures – especially legal institutions – influence, hinder or promote virtue among the different legal actors? Which kinds of emotional demeanour and, more broadly, emotional communication, are encouraged, banned or accepted in legal settings? How could legal institutions and legal culture be transformed so that they can benefit from more genuine and open forms of emotional expression, which would importantly affect the moral quality of the decision-making processes? How could legal institutions best channel and shape the emotions that are likely to be present in legal contexts? And how may legal deliberations be structured, and legal rules and procedures designed, so that they may put in motion the powers of imagination that lie in both individuals, in interactive dynamics, and in communities? Which architectural and spatial designs foster the engagement of virtue, emotion and imagination in legal decision-making? Further work on virtue, emotion and imagination that is responsive to the institutional structure in which these elements operate in legal settings is likely to have a significant impact on legal institutional design and reform.

Another important practical implication of work on virtue, emotion and imagination in law and legal argument is legal education. A principal objective of this book has been the vindication of the critical role that these three elements play in legal reasoning, thereby also contributing to dismantling some deep-seated assumptions in this field. Virtue is not merely a desirable feature for legal actors to have, but is instead an indispensable element in sound legal reasoning; the emotions are not forces contrary to reason, but ineliminable and valuable elements in legal cognition; and imagination, far from being an element alien to law, is a fertile resource for legal argument. If, as argued in this book, virtue, emotion and imagination are core elements in law and legal reasoning, then it seems imperative to rethink and revise the core curricula at the law schools and professional legal training with a view to inculcating virtuous traits of character among law students and practitioners, educate their emotional dispositions, and cultivate their imaginative capacities. Although some important work has been done – especially within law and literature scholarship – on the vital role of imagination in law schools,[30] and some also on the importance of affective pedagogy in legal contexts,[31] there is much that awaits further research.

One final possible topic for future research would begin with recognising the many varieties of imagination and seek to then explore connections between

[30] See, recently, van Klink, van Rossum and de Vries (2019).
[31] See Maughan and Maharg (2011).

these different varieties and virtue and emotion. Philosophers have proposed, for example, distinctions between sensory and cognitive imagination, with the latter not requiring the construction of any mental imagery, but being restricted to say, supposing, conceiving or entertaining something.[32] Others have proposed a distinction between dramatic and hypothetical imagination, with the emphasis in the first being on rehearsal of possibilities, also including the simulation of affect and mental imagery, and being much more self-involving, with the second not involving any such simulation or self-involvement.[33] As Richard Moran says, 'different kinds of imagining involve different kinds of effort, draw on different kinds of resources within the person, and thus may require such things as being receptive in the right way, or having had certain experiences'.[34] Moran also suggests that there may be different standards as to what it is to imagine well in different kinds of imagining. Further, recently, philosophers have been questioning whether the above distinctions are so straightforward, and in particular considering whether there are connections between cognitive (also called propositional) or hypothetical imagining and our affects. Thus, for example, Margherita Arcangeli argues that supposition – which she includes under the canopy of imagination – does connect to our affects, even if less strongly and not as directly as with sensory or dramatic imagination.[35] Whether one accepts these distinctions or not, there is considerable scope here for further interdisciplinary work on varieties of imagining in legal thought, including exploring the connections between these and emotion and virtue. After all, legal thought appears to require both sensory (or dramatic) and propositional (or hypothetical) imagining, and possibly also kinds of imagining in between (such as supposition).

Work on these, among other topics, will only advance legal studies if undertaken in a highly interdisciplinary fashion. As most work on virtue, emotion and imagination in domains other than law shows, understanding how these notions contribute to reasoning and rationality requires a collaborative effort among experts from different disciplines. Broadening the horizon of legal reasoning – and thereby putting forward a complex view of what legal reasoning involves, which appropriately recognises the roles of virtue, emotion and imagination – requires expanding the kind of methods that may be profitably used in legal analysis and embracing an inclusive academic community that trespasses disciplinary frontiers. The collaboration between philosophers and legal scholars that this book is a result of is, we hope, a first step in the direction of integrating work on law, the humanities, and sciences that will further elucidate the interplay of the characterial, affective and imaginative dimensions of legal argument.

[32] For a recent overview, see Stuart (2019).
[33] See Moran (2017).
[34] Ibid, 13.
[35] See Arcangeli (2018).

References

Abrams, L and Keren, H (2010) 'Who's Afraid of Law and the Emotions?' 94 *Minnesota Law Review* 1997.

Amaya, A (forthcoming) 'Virtue and Natural Law' in J Crowe and CY Lee (eds) *Research Handbook on Natural Law Theory* (Cheltenham, Edward Elgar Publishing).

Amaya, A and Ho, HL (2012) *Law, Virtue and Justice* (Oxford, Hart Publishing).

Amaya, A and Michelon, C (eds) (2018) 'Virtue and Law' 9 *Jurisprudence*.

Annas, J (2018) *Virtue and Law in Plato and Beyond* (Oxford, Oxford University Press).

Arcangeli, M (2018) *Supposition and the Imaginative Realm* (London, Routledge).

Berger, L and Stanchi, K (2018) *Legal Persuasion: A Rhetorical Approach to the Science* (New York: Routledge).

Brun, G, Doguoglo, U and Kuenzle, D (eds) (2008) *Epistemology and Emotions* (Aldershot, Ashgate).

Bruner, J (1986) *Actual Minds, Possible Worlds* (Cambridge, Harvard University Press).

Cimino, C (2018) 'Virtue Jurisprudence' in N Snow (ed) *The Oxford Handbook of Virtue* (Oxford, Oxford University Press) 359.

Currie, G, and Ravenscroft, I (2002) *Recreative Minds* (Oxford, Clarendon Press).

Del Mar, M and Twining, W (eds) (2015) *Legal Fictions in Theory and Practice* (Dordrecht, Springer).

Eden, K (1986) *Poetic and Legal Fiction in the Aristotelian Tradition* (Princeton, Princeton University Press).

Farrely, C and Solum, L (2008) *Virtue Jurisprudence* (eds) (New York, Plagrave MacMillan).

Frow, J (2014) *Character and Person* (Oxford, Oxford University Press).

Godfrey-Smith, P and Levy, A (eds) (forthcoming) *The Scientific Imagination* (Oxford, Oxford University Press).

Goodrich, P (1987) *Legal Discourse: Studies in Linguistics, Rhetoric and Legal Analysis* (Houndmills, Palgrave Macmillan).

Hanne, M and Weisberg, R (eds) (2018) *Narrative and Metaphor in the Law* (Cambridge, Cambridge University Press).

Kind, A (ed) (2016) *The Routledge Handbook of the Philosophy of Imagination* (London, Routledge).

Kind, A and Kung, P (eds) (2016) *Knowledge Through Imagination* (Oxford, Oxford University Press).

Lakoff, G and Johnson, M (1980) *Metaphors We Live By* (Chicago, Chicago University Press).

Lowrie, M and Ludemann, S (eds) (2015) *Exemplarity and Singularity: Thinking Through Particulars in Philosophy, Literature, and Law* (Abingdon, Routledge, 2015).

Maroney, T (2006) 'Law and Emotion: A Proposed Taxonomy of an Emerging Field' 30 *Law and Human Behavior* 119.

Maroney, T (2018) 'Judicial Emotion as Vice or Virtue: Perspectives Both Ancient and New' in L Huppes-Cluysenaer and N Coelho (eds) *Aristotle on Emotions in Law and Politics* (Dordrecht, Springer) 11.

Maughan, C and Maharg, P (2011) *Affect and Legal Education: Emotion in Learning and Teaching the Law* (London, Routledge).

Maxwell, B and Reichenbach, R (2007) 'Educating Moral Emotions: A Praxiological Analysis' 26(2) *Studies in Philosophy and Education* 147.

McGinnis, M (2011) 'Virtue Ethics, Earnestness, and the Deciding Lawyer: Human Flourishing in a Legal Community' 87 *North Dakota Law Review* 19.
Moran, M (2003) *Rethinking the Reasonable Person: An Egalitarian Reconstruction of the Objective Standard* (Oxford, Oxford University Press).
Moran, R (2017) *The Philosophical Imagination* (Oxford, Oxford University Press).
Nichols, S (ed) (2006) *The Architecture of the Imagination: New Essays on Pretence, Possibility and Fiction* (Oxford, Oxford University Press).
Perelman, C and Olbrechts-Tyteca, L (1969) *The New Rhetoric: A Treatise on Argumentation* (Indiana, University of Notre Dame Press).
Petroski, K (2019) *Fiction and the Languages of Law* (New York, Routledge).
Scharffs, B (2001) 'Law as Craft' 54(6) *Vanderbilt Law Review* 2245.
Sherletics, A (2017) 'The Role of Virtues in Legal Education' 7(8) *Oñati Socio-legal Series* 1679.
Slote, M (2012) 'Empathy, Law and Justice' in A Amaya and HL Ho (eds) *Law, Virtue and Justice* (Oxford, Hart Publishing).
Snow, N (ed) (2018a) *The Oxford Handbook of Virtue* (Oxford, Oxford University Press).
Snow, N (2018b) 'Models of Virtue' in N Snow (ed), *The Oxford Handbook of Virtue* (Oxford, Oxford University Press).
Solum, L (2015) 'Law and Virtue' in L Besser-Jones and M Slote (eds) *The Routledge Companion to Virtue Ethics* (New York, Routledge).
Spolsky, E (2015) *Contracts of Fiction: Cognition, Culture, Community* (Oxford, Oxford University Press).
Stacey, R (2018) *Law and the Imagination in Medieval Wales* (Philadelphia, Pennsylvania University Press).
Stuart, M (2019) 'Towards a Dual Process Epistemology of Imagination' *Synthese* 1.
Stuart, M, Fehige, Y and Brown, J (eds) (2017) *The Routledge Companion to Thought Experiments* (London, Routledge).
Van Klink, B, van Rossum, H and de Vries, B (eds) (2019) 'Active Learning and Teaching in Legal Education', Special Issue, *Law & Method*. Available at http://www.lawandmethod.nl/tijdschrift/lawandmethod/2019/2/lawandmethod-D-19-00003.
Wang, L and Solum, L (2012) 'Confucian Virtue Jurisprudence' in A Amaya and HL Ho (eds) *Law, Virtue and Justice* (Oxford, Hart Publishing).
Watt, G (2009) *Equity Stirring: The Story of Justice Beyond the Law* (Oxford, Hart Publishing).
Webb, R (2009) *Ekphrasis, Imagination and Persuasion in Ancient Rhetorical Theory and Practice* (Farnham, Ashgate).
White, JB (1973) *The Legal Imagination* (Chicago, Chicago University Press).
Winter, S (2001) *A Clearing in the Forest: Law, Life and Mind* (Chicago, Chicago University Press).
Zittoun, T and Glaveanu, V (eds) (2018) *Handbook of Imagination and Culture* (Oxford, Oxford University Press).

PART I

Virtue – and Emotion, Imagination

2

Admiration, Exemplarity and Judicial Virtue

AMALIA AMAYA*

I. Introduction

A principal venue for the development of judicial virtue is the imitation of exemplars. Exemplary judges are those judges who have a large share of the judicial virtues.[1] This virtue-based view of exemplarity is importantly different from a highly influential view according to which admirability is the key to exemplarity. In this view, exemplary judges would be those who are most admirable. The concept of virtue is claimed to be derivative from the concept of admiration: it is a trait of character that we admire in an exemplar.[2] The thesis according to which judgements of exemplarity depend on judgements of admirability – articulated and most forcefully defended by Linda Zagzebski – faces serious problems. Most importantly, it seems to have things backwards: it is not that a judge is exemplary because we admire her, but rather, we admire her because she is exemplary. It is the possession and display of virtuous traits of character that grounds judgments of admirability, not the other way around.[3] The rejection of the claim that admiration is the foundation upon which exemplarity rests does not, however, amount to denying the important role that admiration plays within an exemplarist theory. Admiration is pivotal in the process of emulation of exemplars that results in the acquisition of judicial virtue and it is also instrumental to the realisation of a number of social functions that exemplary judges are called to perform.

In this chapter, I shall discuss the central – albeit non-foundational – role that the emotion of admiration plays in a virtue-based theory of judicial exemplarity.

* I am very grateful to Maksymilian Del Mar for detailed and valuable comments on an earlier draft.

[1] I have developed a virtue-based approach to judicial exemplarity and given an account of the role that exemplary judges play in the development of judicial virtue in Amaya (2013) and (2018a).

[2] See Zagzebski (2017), 105.

[3] I have developed in more detail this critique of Zagzebski's admiration-based exemplarist theory in Amaya (2013).

In the first section, I will examine the emotion of admiration, drawing on both philosophical approaches to the study of this emotion as well as work on the psychology of admiration. The second section examines the role that admiration plays in the process of emulation of exemplary judges that results in the acquisition of virtuous traits of character. I will also discuss a number of ways in which this process may go wrong, and which provide some additional reasons why it is advisable to refrain from identifying exemplarity with admirability. In the third section, I will examine a number of social benefits associated to admiration, which enable exemplars to perform important social functions within the judiciary. I will conclude the chapter by discussing some educational implications of vindicating the importance of the emotion of admiration for virtue exemplarism. Given the relevance of the emotion of admiration for the development of judicial virtue and the realisation of the social functions that may be plausibly attributed to exemplary judges, it seems critical that legal education should aim to cultivate virtuous admiration.

II. Admiration for Virtue

Admiration is an emotion and, as such, it has an intentional object, an affective component, and a characteristic motivational profile.[4] Admiration involves an intentional object, that is to say, it is directed as something or someone. We may admire someone's acute sense of humour, an extraordinary ballet performance, a student who volunteers in his community, the elegance of a mathematical theorem, the exceptional skill of a craftsman, a loving and dedicated school teacher, the moral commitment of a political activist, a hero who risks his life to save others, the perseverance of a scientist, and a person who devotes his life to improving the life conditions of an indigenous community. Despite the diversity of objects of admiration (more on this later), admiration, like other emotions, is always directed at a particular person or act, rather than it being felt in general.[5] It is also important to note that, in a way also similar to other emotions, the emotion of admiration may or may not fit its object, ie, just as what we fear may be harmless, what we admire may not be admirable.

The affective component of admiration is its characteristic feeling or distinctive physical sensation. It feels different admiring a person or a person's action than to love him, to envy him, or to be angry at him. Admiration combines feelings of surprise and wonder with feelings of approval and appreciation.[6] According to research done by Haidt and collaborators, the phenomenology and physiology of

[4] See Zagzebski (2017), 32–33.

[5] See Wilson (2019). That the motivation to imitate an admirable model is triggered by its particularity is also argued by Compaijen (2017), 584.

[6] See Archer (2019) and Schilder et al (2013), 87.

admiration vary depending on the object of admiration. Whereas chills are most characteristic of admiration for skill and talent, moral excellence elicits a warm feeling of dilation or opening in the chest as well as the feeling that one has been uplifted or elevated.[7]

Finally, admiration, like other emotions, is a motivating force. Most importantly, admiration moves us to emulate the person in the admired respect.[8] Another significant motivational output of admiration is inspiration, which may or may not involve emulation of the exemplar.[9] Yet other responses to admiration include a motivation to enhance the reputation of the person admired, to praise her and extol her virtues to others, and to promote the values admired in the object of admiration.[10] These responses, as we will see later, are central for admiration to perform critical social functions. However, a desire to emulate remains central to the motivational profile of admiration.

Admiration is a 'positive' emotion. According to Frederickson, positive emotions 'broaden one's perspective and motivate one to do things that will build skills or resources for the future'.[11] In contrast, 'negative' emotions, 'narrow and focus one's attention on the matter at hand to solve a problem'.[12] Positive emotions may not lead to immediate changes in behaviour (unlike, for example, the 'fight or flight' that is triggered by the emotion of fear) but, according to Frederickson's 'broaden and build' proposal, they 'change people's cognitions and motivations in ways that make it easier for them to build relationships and skills'.[13] Positive emotions thus have effects in the long run in one's behaviours mediated by fundamental changes at both the cognitive and the affective levels. There are different families within the group of the positive emotions, and there is some variation on the issue of how to best classify the emotion of admiration.[14] On Algoe and Haidt's view, admiration belongs, together with elevation and gratitude, to the family of the 'other praising' emotions, which arise from witnessing other's exemplary actions.[15]

[7] See Algoe and Haidt (2009), 124.

[8] See Zagzebski (2017), 33. See also Velleman (2002), 101. That there is a natural connection between admiration and emulation is a point that is widely accepted in both the philosophical and the psychological literature. Nonetheless, there are several complications (some of which will be discussed in section III) as several factors may interfere and prevent admiration from motivating emulation.

[9] See Haidt and Seder (2009). Admirable others may inspire one to become like them (by emulating them) or they might inspire us to improve, and yet not trigger a motivation to emulate them if such emulation, given the distance between one's own capacities and those of the model, is likely to be ineffective. The inspiration that admiration gives rise to may also be decoupled from emulation when witnessing the excellence in others motivates improvement in domains other than the specific domain in which the model excels.

[10] Archer has argued against what he calls 'the emulation view' according to which, in prototypical cases, admiration motivates one to emulate and has proposed replacing this view by a 'value promotion view', which states that admiration prototypically motivates one to promote the values admired in the object of admiration, with emulation being one way of promoting these values. See Archer (2019).

[11] See Algoe and Haidt (2009), 105 (discussing Frederickson (1998)).

[12] Ibid.

[13] Ibid, 123.

[14] See Onu, Kessler and Smith (2016).

[15] See Algoe and Haidt (2009), 105.

Smith includes admiration in the category of the 'upward assimilative emotions' like optimism and inspiration.[16] Ortony and collaborators place admiration within the family of the 'appreciation' emotions, such as awe, appreciation, esteem and respect.[17] The differences and similarities between admiration and other (more or less closely related emotions, depending on the taxonomy used) such as awe, adoration, gratitude and elevation have been the object of some studies, but more work is needed to further illuminate the distinctive psychology of admiration.[18]

Different kinds of admiration may be distinguished depending on the object of admiration. According to Zagzebski, a main division among objects of admiration is that between natural versus acquired excellences.[19] There are three main differences between admiration for natural talent and admiration for acquired talent. First, they feel different, as Haidt's research, mentioned above, has shown. Second, whereas I can imitate a person with an acquired talent, a natural talent cannot be the object of imitation – even if one might imitate the perseverance, determination, hard work and courage of the people who reach extraordinary levels of artistic, physical or intellectual excellence.[20] More moderately, one might say that exemplars of natural talent may not propel us to emulate, as such emulation is thought to be ineffective, even if they can still inspire us to improve.[21] Third, whereas contempt is a fitting emotional response to an acquired defect, it is an inappropriate emotion to have toward a person who lacks an inborn talent.

Haidt makes a related distinction between admiration for non-moral excellence, ie admiration for skill and talent, and admiration for moral excellence, which he terms 'elevation', on the grounds that there are differences at the phenomenological level (chills vs warm feelings as mentioned earlier) and the behavioural level (whereas admiration energises people to work harder towards their own goals, elevation leads to emulation of the admired model).[22] Two main differences between Zagzebski's and Haidt's study of admiration (or elevation, in his terminology) should, however, be noted. On Zagzebski's account, acquired talents include both intellectual and moral virtues, which are admired in the same way; whereas Haidt's research on elevation is restricted to moral virtue. In addition, Zagzebski and Haidt have different views on the kind of emotion that is opposed to admiration: contempt (or scorn and disdain) and disgust, respectively.[23]

[16] See Smith (2000).

[17] See Ortony et al (1990).

[18] See, among others, Algoe and Haidt (2009) (on admiration, gratitude and elevation); Keltner and Haidt (2003), Haidt and Seder (2009); Kristjánsson (2018) (on admiration and awe); and Schindler et al (2013) (on adoration and admiration).

[19] Zagzebski (2017), 37.

[20] Ibid.

[21] See Wilson (2019) (arguing that perceiving a model as unattainable may prevent people from developing a drive to emulate).

[22] See Algoe and Haidt (2009).

[23] See Zagzebski (2017), 38, and Algoe and Haidt (2009), 106. Ben Ze'ev also opposes admiration to contempt. See Ben Ze'ev (2003), 118.

In what follows, I shall be concerned with admiration for virtue (both moral and intellectual), rather than skill or talent, and I will use the term 'admiration' instead of 'elevation'. Using two different terms may overstate the differences that may obtain between admiring exceedingly competent people and exceptionally virtuous people as well as obscure the important similarities and connections that there are between both kinds of excellence. Indeed, the line between natural talent and acquired excellence (as well as that between moral excellence and non-moral excellence) is not easy to draw.[24] There are mixed excellences; natural talents may be necessary to excel at moral reasoning, and acquired excellences (like resilience or determination) are necessary to excel in non-moral domains. Thus, there does not seem to be sufficient reason to depart from common usage, which employs 'admiration' irrespective of the kind of excellence at stake. The emotion of admiration has been claimed to have consequences for the admirer, for relationships between individuals, as well as for intra and inter-group relationships.[25] In section III, I focus on the learning effects – via imitation – of admiration at the individual level; section IV examines its social effects at both the interpersonal and group level.[26]

III. Admiration and Imitation

The emotion of admiration plays a pivotal role in the process of imitation that leads to virtue development. Admiration, as argued, motivates those who experience it to emulation, thereby developing the virtuous traits of character admired in the model. How may this imitative process be characterised? And how does it result in virtue acquisition? Imitation, far from being a matter of mindless copying, is a complex cognitive task that is linked to characteristically human capacities and that plays a pivotal role in moral development and cultural evolution.[27] Some features of this process are worth highlighting.[28] First, there is an important affective dimension to imitation.[29] Emulation is not merely a matter of imitating the external behaviour of models, but also their emotional response. The emotional dispositions that are constitutive of virtue include both a disposition to experience fitting emotions as well as to express them in an appropriate way.[30]

[24] As Zagzebski acknowledges. See Zagzebski (2017), 39.

[25] For a useful survey of the literature on the consequences of admiration, see Onu, Kessler and Smith (2016).

[26] Del Mar (2020) (chapter twelve in this volume) also engages on a multi-level analysis, claiming that legal imagination plays important roles at the individual, the interactive and the collective levels.

[27] See Hurley and Chater (2005), 14. See also Gerrans (2013). See also Prinz (2005).

[28] A more detailed discussion of some of these characteristics may be found in Amaya (2018a).

[29] For a discussion of the emotional aspects of emulation, see Tan (2005), 420–23.

[30] Sherman has persuasively argued that to show the right emotions is part of the requirements of virtue. Moreover, emotional expression, argues Sherman, could bring about deeper motivational changes. See Sherman (2004).

Thus, successful imitation of models of virtue requires a full apprehension of the model's behaviours, feelings and emotional demeanour.

Second, imitation importantly involves imagination.[31] Imagination is necessary to place oneself in the model's perspective with a view to understanding her motives, actions, attitudes and feelings in the particular circumstances she was responding to. In addition to this backward-looking aspect of imagination, a related, forward-looking aspect is also central to processes of imitation. On the basis of his understanding of the model's character, the agent needs to envision how the exemplar would respond to novel situations.[32] Imagination may also contribute to the process of imitation that leads to virtue, insofar as imagining oneself as already having the admired features in the exemplar may lead to the acquisition of virtuous motivations.[33] Another way in which imagination may be useful for developing virtue through the emulation of exemplars is by prompting us to consider how these models would judge us if we were to behave in a certain way.[34]

Third, the process of imitation that eventually leads to the acquisition of virtue may be both conscious and unconscious.[35] Imitation may be mediated unconsciously by the activation of personality traits and social stereotypes that elicit the assimilation of one's behaviour to the observed behaviour.[36] For instance, novices may acquire manners, attitudes, abilities, action patterns, styles, routines and emotional responses and demeanour by unreflectively imitating the experts. They may not be, to a large extent, aware of how these imitative influences impact on their behaviour. In addition to this kind of 'covert' imitation, virtue development may be also be the product of 'overt' imitation.[37] Imitative influences may also be conscious, in that they result from a deliberate selection of models and a reflection on what makes those models admirable and worthy of emulation.

Finally, imitation results in a transformation of oneself, not in the replication of someone else's outlook.[38] The imitation of the exemplar – whether reflexive or sub-conscious – shapes one's character in important ways. It is not that by imitating (as opposed to mere copying) one assumes the exemplar's identity, ways of behaving, feeling and being. Rather, when one succeeds at imitating an exemplar, one

[31] For an argument to the effect that imagination is central for successful imitation, see Tan (2005), 417–19.

[32] Wilson suggests that knowledge about how an exemplar would act in a particular situation could be gained in advance by imagining exemplars in a variety of situations. This imaginative exercise may help us reduce the number of cases in which we are unable to work out how the exemplar would work. Such a deployment of imaginative capacities seems, however, too costly and, because of that, unlikely. See Wilson (2019).

[33] This is argued in Zagzebski (2017), 136.

[34] I thank Maksymilian Del Mar for raising this point.

[35] See Compaijen (2017), 569–70.

[36] See Dijksterhuis (2005). There is also evidence, however, of contrastive effects in automatic behaviour. See Dijksterhuis et al (1998).

[37] For the distinction between 'overt' and 'covert' imitation, see Hurley and Chater (2005), 37.

[38] On this point, see Tan (2005), 419.

develops in distinctive ways the traits of character admired in the exemplar, makes them one's own, and integrates them as stable features of one's unique personality.

Thus, the end result of this complex process of imitation, if successful, is the development of a virtuous character.[39] There are, however, several ways in which this process of emulation may go wrong. It is instructive to diagnose the sources for the potential failure of the path that goes from admiration to virtue, for such analysis helps illuminate key aspects of this process and has, as I will argue later, important educational implications.

A first problem that stands in the way of developing virtue by imitating exemplars has to do with the proper selection of the objects of imitation.[40] In cases of 'destructive mimicry', in which the model admired is not an exemplar of virtue but of vice, emulation fails to contribute to virtue development.[41] In these cases, judgments of admirability do not track moral or epistemic value, which is an important reason why the enterprise of grounding moral theory on judgments of admirability seems suspect. In destructive mimicry – of which anti-social behaviour resulting from media violence is a glaring example – a negative exemplar is recognised as a model.[42] Imitation in such cases can hardly result in virtue development, as much in law as in any other domain.[43] A student or judge in training who admires a callous judge for its purported impartiality and capacity to detach from the parties' plight, would fail to develop, via imitation, a loving gaze, a compassionate outlook, and empathetic understanding.[44] Similarly, a student clerking for a judge who is known to be stubborn, unyielding, unwilling to listen to alternative views, and reluctant to modify his own views in response to other people's arguments or novel evidence, may come to see those features as evidence of firmness and intellectual autonomy, rather than as a serious lack of open-mindedness, and may consequently recognise such a judge as a model.[45] Admiration would, in this case, lead to a corrupt rather than a virtuous intellectual character.

A second problem is posed by cases of 'misguided admiration', in which the object of admiration is properly selected, but for the wrong reasons.[46] In these cases, the agent imitates those who are arguably good exemplars of virtue, but does so for reasons unrelated to their possessing and displaying virtuous traits of

[39] Mediated by habitual performance that eventually leads to actual virtue possession. See Wilson (2019).

[40] A discussion of this problem may also be found in Wilson (2019).

[41] The term is employed in Hurley and Chater (2005), 281.

[42] See Huesmann et al (1997). For another example, see Jones (2011) (on drunken role models in sport).

[43] This is not to deny that negative exemplars have educational value, insofar as they exemplify character traits we hope to avoid (rather than emulate). See Amaya (2018a). Negative exemplars have also been shown to play important roles in professional development. Gibson (2003) has shown that middle and late-stage career individuals are more likely to see role models as sources of specific rather than general and negative rather than positive attributes. In addition, mix models (ie those who have both positive and negative attributes) have more enduring inspirational effects. See Moberg (2000), 682.

[44] Zipursky (2020)'s discussion of the attitudes of Justice Sonia Sotomayor vs Justice Clarence Thomas (chapter four in this volume) may illustrate this point.

[45] On the diversity of alternative descriptions of moral character and the possibilities of re-describing them, see van Domselaar (2020)'s Murdochian approach (chapter five in this volume).

[46] On this problem, see Irwin (2015).

character. In this case, admiration is directed at the proper object, but admiration for virtue is swamped with admiration for superiority, wealth, status and success.[47] An example that illustrates the point is a judge in training who admires a superior judge, who, as it turns out, does possess and exercise a large share of the judicial virtues and rightly deserves admiration, but the trainee is merely allured by the high status and social position that a successful career has brought for that judge. The reasons for admiration, and the motivation for emulation it triggers, are thus disconnected from the judge's virtuous character. As a result, the recognition of such a judge as an exemplar will be sterile from the point of view of virtue development.

A further way in which the admiration of a virtuous exemplar may fail to lead to virtue acquisition has to do with the attainability of the model. The effectiveness of a model is partly dependent on its attainability. If the model possesses an unusually large share of virtues (eg saints and sages) or possesses one virtue or a limited number of virtues to an exceedingly high degree (eg heroes), then admiration for the model may fail to move the agent to imitate.[48] Such models may be perceived to be so far above what we may achieve that they have a paralysing, rather than an energising effect, on us.[49] This effect may be bolstered if the exemplar's circumstances are too removed from one's own or the admirable traits are lacking in relevance for one's life, which reinforces the perception that any attempt to emulation is likely to be useless.[50] Admirable people who fall short of sainthood and perfection, and ordinary heroes, who perform worthwhile but less than glorious deeds, may be exempla with whom we may more easily identify and be moved to imitate. However, even if admiration for models that are clearly beyond reach may not result in emulation, still these exempla may be inspirational and move us to make progress and improve, to praise the values they embody, and to promote them in a variety of ways. Indeed, the imitation of an exemplar, without taking into account one's limitations, may be an utterly inappropriate response to admiration. Such imitation forces the agent to 'over-stretch' and may result in worse outcomes than those that would have been reached if one had more fitting goals in mind.[51] In the context of judging, it may be better for judges early in their career to take steps, inspired by a role model, towards professional improvement that may allow them, eventually, to successfully imitate the model, rather than straightforwardly attempt

[47] The common tendency to so doing and the risks it involves are brilliantly discussed by Adam Smith. For a lucid discussion, see Irwin (2015), 235–39.

[48] For a comparison of the effectiveness of heroes and saints as tools for character education, see Croce and Vaccarezza (2017).

[49] See Kristjánsson (2017), 179.

[50] On the importance of attainability and relevance to the effectiveness of role-models, see, among others, Croce (2019); Wilson (2019); Vos (2018), 18–19; and Han et al (2017). Attainability is also a relevant criterion for assessing the effectiveness of role-modelling in professional contexts, see Moberg (2000).

[51] On 'moral over-stretching', see Kristjánsson (2018), 179. Williams also warns against the risks of 'moral weightlifting', when failure to recognise one's own limitations compared to the moral exemplar may result in moral error. See Williams (1995), 190. For discussion, see Engelen et al (2018), 4.

to do as the model would, oblivious of the differences that there are between their own capacities and those of the exemplar.[52]

Fetishism is another case in which admiration fails to trigger a process of imitation that is conducive to the development of virtue. The problem here lies not in the object of imitation, but rather in the way in which the agent relates to the exemplar. Those who reject – much in the spirit of our time – the idea that imitation is an important tool for personal development and endorse, on the contrary, a 'be yourself' slogan,[53] refusing to acknowledge the many ways in which personal identity and one's achievements are partly the result of the influence and previous accomplishments of others, suffer not only from self-delusion but also from an excess of self-affirmation.[54] In cases of fetishism, the opposed case obtains. The agent lacks a sufficient degree of self-affirmation and, consequently, establishes a relation with the model that effaces her subjectivity.[55] In the limit, the follower aspires not to be like the model but to 'be him'. This way of relating to the model evidences a lack of autonomy and proper self-esteem, which results in a degeneration of the process of imitation into worshipping.[56] In these cases, the model is apprehended as an idol and admiration gives way to emotions of awe and adoration. Attitudes of excessive deference and uncritical devotion towards models in professional and teaching legal contexts could, arguably, partake in some of the characteristics that are distinctive of fetishism.

Finally, the process of imitation that connects up admiration to virtue may be faulty for reasons that do not have to do either with the object of admiration, or the way in which the agent relates to the admired model, but rather with the process of imitation. The object may be a genuinely virtuous exemplar, who is admired in the admirable respect, who embodies an attainable ideal, and to whom the follower relates in ways that avoid fetishism, but imitation may be so shallow and superficial as to be unproductive from the point of view of virtue development. This would be the case when the admirer does not engage imaginatively and affectively with the admired model. Imitation, as argued before, is a complex process that is distinct from mere copying. It involves an imaginative projection of the model's ways of feeling and acting into one's circumstances. This requires a full grasp of the motives, patterns of reasoning, and emotions of the exemplary model. When the agent lacks a sufficient understanding of the exemplar's character or has deficient powers of imagination, imitation may degenerate into the mere reproduction of

[52] See Stepien (2012) (arguing for the appropriateness of different models of judicial decision-making to different stages of judicial self-development).

[53] See Kaftanski, 'Becoming oneself in a world of Kardashians: Imitation, Admiration, and the Power of Role Models' http://www.abc.net.au/religion/imitation-and-the-power-of-role-models/10343072, accessed 12 October 2018.

[54] I will return to this point in section V.

[55] On self-forgetfulness as a characteristic that is inherent to admiration, but that needs to be overcome to actually recognise the other as an exemplar, see Compaijen (2017).

[56] 'Hero-worshipping' is Kristjánsson's term. See Kristjánsson (2018), 179.

external behaviour.[57] Just copying does not transform one's moral and intellectual character in ways that contribute to one's personal and professional development.

In order to avoid the foregoing pitfalls in imitative reasoning, it is necessary to cultivate among law students and legal practitioners a virtuous disposition to admire.[58] It is critical that they select role models that are fit for them and worthy of being emulated and that they imitate them for the right reasons and in the right way. I will explore the educational implications of vindicating the relevance of admiration in character formation in section V. But before this, I shall examine the social functions that admiration may be claimed to perform within the judiciary. These functions provide additional support for the claim – to be argued later – that legal education should aim to develop the emotional dispositions, traits of character, and imaginative capacities required for admiration to put in motion a process of imitation that leads to the acquisition of judicial virtue.

IV. The Social Functions of Admiration

Admiration plays, as argued, a central role in character development in that it triggers a process of emulation that results in acquisition of virtue. As such, it is an extremely useful tool for professional development, in that it helps students and professionals to acquire the traits of character that are virtues in the context of the judicial role.[59] Further, the emotion of admiration also has important social functions at the interactive and group level.[60] These beneficial social effects are consequential, as I will argue, for the role, structure, organisational cohesion and self-image of the judiciary.

A. Social Learning and Cultural Transmission

Admiration facilitates social learning from those judges who excel in the profession. Social learning occurs when people learn vicariously of the results of their own actions, not by first-hand experience but by observing others.[61] This social learning importantly leads to the cultural transmission of ways of reasoning,

[57] See Amaya (2018a). The point is also argued for in Wilson (2019).

[58] Another problem that may prevent the imitation of admirable others from delivering virtue, which I am not dealing with here, is the question of how to avoid the perverse outcomes that may result from herding, that is, from imitating others in a group. Here, I am only considering imitative relations between an agent and an admired person. For an extremely interesting study of herding, see Baddeley (2018).

[59] Interestingly, imitation remains an important tool for professional development through the whole professional career span. See Gibson (2003).

[60] On the social functions of emotions, see Keltner and Haidt (1999).

[61] See Moberg (2000), 676.

behaving, feeling and relating to others in the context of the judicial role.[62] The best expressions of legal culture – as we have currently inherited it – are passed down to next generations through the mechanisms of social learning that admiration enables. This, as Tomasello and others have argued, does not impede innovation and change; rather, the cultural matrix that is preserved through imitation provides a platform from which new ways of thinking and doing are generated.[63] Hence, the social learning and cultural transmission that admiration of exemplary judges allows is essential for both the stability of legal culture as well as its improvement and adaptation to novel challenges and new circumstances.

B. Authority Conferral

Admiration consecrates within the profession a subset of exemplary judges as worthy repositories of *auctoritas*.[64] In so doing, it helps establish a hierarchy within the judiciary based on prestige rather than dominance.[65] Within such a hierarchy, cultural reproduction is based not on fear or threat of force (in the form of disciplinary sanctions or lack of promotion opportunities), but rather on 'freely conferred deference', out of respect and esteem for a model that is worthy of admiration. The kind of judicial authority that is propelled through admiration for virtue does not sever technical expertise from moral competence, but is instead responsive to the important way in which judicial decision-making is of moral import and involves engaging in moral reasoning.[66] The associated prestige and influence of admired judges who enjoy *auctoritas* permeates through the different levels of the judiciary and, given the prominent societal place of judges, it arguably reaches beyond the confines of the judicial profession to shape legal and political culture in important ways.

C. Hierarchy Regulation

Admiration not only contributes to the formation of a prestige hierarchy within the judiciary, but it also plays an important role in regulating it.[67] There are

[62] In Onu, Kessler and Smith's model, admiration is claimed to be an emotion the central function of which is to facilitate social learning and contribute to the wider cultural transmission. See Onu, Kessler and Smith (2016).

[63] Through the so-called 'ratchet effect'. See Tomasello (1999) and Tennie, Call and Tomasello (2009).

[64] I have explored in more detail the connection between exemplarity and judicial authority in Amaya (2018b).

[65] On the distinction between prestige and dominance hierarchies and the role of admiration is establishing the former, see Henrich and Gil-White (2001).

[66] For an extremely interesting argument to the effect that current notions of expertise are oblivious to the fact that competence in a domain requires the deployment of moral capacities, see Shapin (2004). A discussion of this argument in the legal context is provided in Amaya (2018b).

[67] On the idea that emotions contribute to the maintenance, formation and change of social hierarchies, see Kelter and Haidt (1999), 307.

important behavioural consequences of admiration that help maintain social hierarchy. Most importantly, admiration is associated with a tendency to help and cooperate with those who are admired; it engenders deferential behaviour towards the admired person; and it inhibits political action aimed at dislodging the admired person's position of (legitimate) power and status.[68] Admiration for virtue in the judicial context is thus likely to have a system-maintaining effect, which is arguably essential to the stability of the institution. However, and critically, admiration also serves to challenge social hierarchy in cases in which the object of admiration is a subversive exemplar. In these cases, admiration may engender insubordination rather than deference, engender political action that challenges the status-quo, and inhibit behaviour that would maintain it.[69] Admiration for exemplary judges who subvert the accepted legal and social order – Justice Ruth Ginsburg and Justice Michael Kirby, known as the 'Great Disenter', are vivid examples – importantly contributes to bringing about radical legal and political change.

D. Social Relationships

Admiration for virtue significantly impacts the quality of social relationships. To begin with, it motivates people to behave in ways that create or strengthen their relationship with models.[70] The admirer seeks proximity with the admired person as well as her cooperation – interestingly, evolutionary pressures account for this, as greater interaction and cooperation lead to better learning environments.[71] There is also evidence that suggests that group-based admiration is associated with willingness to receive help from the admired outgroup.[72] Admiration also has beneficial effects on social relationships beyond the dyadic relation admirer-admired model, as it promotes prosocial and affiliative behaviour.[73] Thus, admiration towards exemplary judges not only contributes to establishing close bonds between these judges and those who admire them, but it also helps generate a kind and cooperative working environment as well as high levels of organisational commitment within the judiciary.

E. Identity Formation

Admiration plays an important role in identity formation.[74] Who we admire shapes who we are, both individually and collectively. Role models define in critical

[68] See Henrich and Gil-White (2001).

[69] For a defence of the claim that admiration engenders behaviour that challenges social hierarchy, see Sweetman et al (2012). For a statement of this claim in the context of the professions, see Moberg (2000), 686.

[70] See Algoe and Haidt (2009), 123.

[71] See Henrich and Gil-White (2001).

[72] See Onu, Kessler and Smith (2016).

[73] As argued in Haidt and Algoe (2009), 117, 122 and 124.

[74] See Schindler et al (2013) and Bucher (1998).

ways our self-image as well as our values and commitments as a community. Furthermore, admiration contributes to shaping who we want to be and what kind of community we want to foster. Public figures have a critical impact on younger generations' self-concept and ambitions. The visible role that admiration plays in identity formation in popular culture fully applies to legal and political culture. Erasmus wrote: 'Turn the pages of history and you will always find the morality of an age reflecting the life of its prince.'[75] Those who are the leading figures in legal and political culture signal who we are and who we aspire to be. Similarly, admiration for exemplary judges helps define how to conceive the role of a judge in current societal conditions, what sort of jurist one aims at becoming, and what are the core values that the legal community adheres to and hopes to realise and advance.[76] Admiration thus importantly contributes to developing judges' self-concept as well as to forming a collective identity within the judiciary.

V. Cultivating Admiration in Legal Education

As argued above, the emotion of admiration leads to virtue development and has a number of important social effects. Admiration for exemplary judges (or other relevant legal actors) is a critical pathway to professional development and has significant social benefits for interactive relations between members of the legal community, group dynamics in the legal profession, and legal culture. Given the learning and social effects of admiration, it is critical that legal education should aim at cultivating a virtuous disposition to admire. Those who have such a disposition will be capable of avoiding the problems concerning imitative reasoning that have been described above and will, therefore, be in a position to benefit from the ways in which the emulation of admired exemplars enriches personal and social life.[77] A virtuous disposition to admire has the following features:

(a) It is directed at a proper object of admiration, ie it leads one to pick the right models to admire and to admire them in the admirable respect.
(b) It hits the right mean, therefore avoiding the vice of obsequiousness, which results from an excessive disposition to admire, and the vice of arrogance, which results from a defective disposition to admire.[78]

[75] Erasmus (1516) (1997).
[76] On the role of admiration in shaping professional identity, see Gibson (2003) and Ibarra (1999).
[77] See Algoe and Haidt (2009), 125.
[78] Over-reaction and under-reaction would be cases of moral errors (ie defects of character). See Kristjánsson (2018), 19. In the case of admiration, Kristjánsson describes the extreme vices as resulting from 'an inferiority complex (*qua* excess) and too little will to improve (*qua* deficiency)'. See Kristjánsson (2006), 45. Rather, as I will argue below, admiration may be best understood as a mean between affirming self-debasement and self-aggrandising. In this view, the belief that there is little room for improvement would thus follow from the assertion of one's superiority, rather than it being a vice *qua* deficiency.

(c) It has the right motivation, ie displays of admiration are done for the right reason, namely, as an emotional response to excellent others, rather than, for instance, to climb the social and career ladder.
(d) It does lead to admiration when admiration is called for – therefore averting other possible emotions that might arise when witnessing other persons' excellence, such as resentment or envy.[79]
(e) It involves a reflexion about whether emulation – given one's capacities as compared to those of the model – is the appropriate response to admiration, thereby eschewing problems of moral over-stretching.
(f) When imitation is the appropriate response, it motivates the agent to imitate in ways that engage one's affective, critical and imaginative capacities thereby warding off blind copying and fetishism.

There are a number of educational strategies that could be incorporated in legal education and professional legal training with a view to cultivating a virtuous disposition to admire.

First, it is important to ensure that in both legal education and legal training law students and professionals are exposed to admirable models. There are several ways in which this could be done. Conventional educational materials include most prominently textbooks as well as case-books. It seems convenient to complement these materials with biographies of leading jurists and recover what was, until the end of the eighteenth century, a fundamental pedagogical tool, namely the book of *exempla*, the objective of which was to provide with models of virtue for students to imitate. It is important that in selecting the examples to which students and professionals are to be exposed, consideration of relevance and attainability is taken into account. Even if, as argued above, extreme models may still play an important inspirational role, exposing students and professionals to admirable models that they may easily relate to and attain is more likely to have an impact in virtue development.[80] In addition, given that, as studies in role-modelling have shown, persons from social proximity are the most frequent models,[81] it would be convenient to structure legal education and professional training so as to create ample opportunities for concrete interaction and learning from judges and other relevant legal actors who may provide models that students and early-stage professionals may admire and emulate.[82] Finally, a familiarity among students and professionals with key figures of the legal tradition may also be gained through strategies of visibility as well as by generating spaces for social

[79] On the relations between admiration, resentment and envy as possible emotions toward others' excellences, see Zagzebski (2017), 50–59; Ben Ze'ev (2003); and Smith (2000).

[80] See Croce and Vaccarezza (2017).

[81] See Bucher (1998).

[82] This may provide yet another argument to promote diversity within the judiciary and, more broadly, in the legal professions.

interaction and exchange between students, early-stage professionals and senior legal professionals.[83]

The experience of students and professionals with exemplars is likely to be an important way in which the role modelling that admiration promotes may have educational benefits. Exposure to admirable jurists is, moreover, particularly relevant if, as argued, emulation may work sometimes in less than conscious ways. Nonetheless, beyond mere exposure, reflexion on exemplary models is also an essential tool for cultivating a virtuous disposition to admire.[84] Experience with exemplars is to be combined with explicit discussion about the exposed models, why they are admirable, what their emotional reactions were, how they reasoned, the choices they made, and why they acted the way they did. Giving so-called 'meta-comments'[85] and engaging students and professionals in a critical reflexion about the admired *exempla* may enhance the positive educational effects of admiration and prevent role-modelling from degenerating into copycatting. Such explicit instruction may thus help agents to achieve a genuine self-transformation through the process of emulation.

In addition, the education of the emotions and the imagination is a substantive part of the cultivation of a virtuous disposition to admire given that, as argued above, for admiration to lead to virtue, emulation has to engage distinctive emotional and imaginative capacities. Thus, in order to benefit from admiration and the role-modelling it propels, legal education should be oriented towards the development of imaginative abilities as well as include sentimental education.[86] An important strategy for the education of the emotions as well as the imagination that aligns itself particularly well with the cultivation of a virtuous disposition to admire is the use of the arts, especially literature and film.[87] Narratives of exemplary characters (historical, fictional or contemporary) have the richness necessary to be recognised as models of admirable legal professionals that students and early-stage professionals may identify with, despite their not being from their social nearness. These narratives critically enlarge the set of admirable jurists they may hope to emulate and learn from (as well as the collection of negative examples they may strive to avoid) beyond those within their direct experience.

[83] Visibility strategies include, eg, the naming of events, chairs and spaces after outstanding jurists or the profiling of virtuous jurists in newsletter articles and webpages. On the positive effects of strategies of visibility for virtue education through role modelling in organisations, see Moberg (2000), 690.

[84] On the need to combine exposure with explicit discussion, see Sanderese (2013) and Kristjánsson (2006). For a critique, see Wilson (2019).

[85] Sanderese (2013), 38.

[86] On the education of legal imagination, see Del Mar (2018). An important tool for emotion education is the explicit instruction on the emotions. See Kristjánsson (2018) 179. Hence, explicit instruction on admiration and the ways in which it could lead us astray may also be a helpful tool for cultivating a virtuous disposition to admire.

[87] Kristjánsson lists the arts as one of the main strategies for educating the emotions (2018), 180. Although a key theme of the law and literature movement has been the importance of literature and film for emotional education, this body of scholarship has not focused on its potential for developing a virtuous disposition to admire. Indeed, there are the interesting connections between the law and literature movement and legal exemplarism, which would be worth further exploring.

Not only are emotional and imaginative capacities necessary for successful emulation, but some degree of virtue is already necessary if admiration is to lead to virtue acquisition. This is not a vicious circle; rather, it shows the way in which virtue and emotion are interlocked in character development. To begin with, some measure of virtue is required in order to be attracted by and recognise models of virtue in the first place. In addition, such models may only guide one's behaviour if one already possesses a certain degree of virtue, for only if one shares to some extent the characteristic sensibility that is distinctive of those who are worthy of admiration, is it possible to determine how the model would feel and act in the circumstances at stake and to draw the relevant analogies (and disanalogies) between the situation faced by the model and one's own experiences.[88] Thus, virtue education is pivotal in the cultivation of a virtuous disposition to admire.

The development of certain virtuous traits of character seem to be particularly needed for the process of emulation that connects up admiration with virtue to succeed. A certain degree of moral and intellectual autonomy is pivotal to engage critically in a process of emulation rather than mindlessly copycatting the exemplar. Indeed, in successful emulation, one develops the features of character that are admirable in the model, including the capacity to form one's views autonomously and act accordingly. Another virtue that is particularly important if emulation is to be a useful tool for character development is the intellectual virtue of perseverance and resilience. Witnessing the excellence of others may be inspirational, but it may also generate depressive feelings when one compares the model's achievements with one's more modest ones.[89] Negative emotions are more likely to occur when those achievements are seen as unattainable given one's career stage and capacities.[90] A drive to persist in the face of failure is central if excellent others are to help us visualise better 'possible selves'[91] and motivate us to work harder to become the sort of person and professional one aims at being.

Humility also seems to be, I would argue, a central virtue which should be possessed and exercised in order to have a virtuous disposition to admire. Self-abasement leads an agent to admire too much and to mistake models for idols. Self-aggrandising favours an attitude of reluctance to admire, or outright rejection of admiration, even when admiration is clearly called for. In fact, there is psychological evidence that supports the view that an excessive self-esteem undermines inspiration by outstanding models.[92] Humility is a trait of character that disposes those who have it to wholeheartedly adhere to a commitment to relate with

[88] Amaya (2018a).

[89] For a useful taxonomy of the emotions involved in social comparison, see Smith (2000).

[90] See Lockwood and Kunda (1997) (showing that relevant stars provoke self-deflation when their success seems unattainable in that the agent had already missed the chance of achieving a comparable success or thought that his abilities are unlikely to improve over time).

[91] 'Possible selves' are the individual's views about who they might become. See Markus and Nurius (1986) cited in Ibarra (1999), 765.

[92] See Lockwood and Kunda (1999).

others on an egalitarian basis.[93] The virtue of humility signals a mean between the extremes of excess (ie, self-aggrandisement or arrogance, in which one asserts one's superiority) and defect (ie, servility or self-abasement, in which one asserts one's inferiority).[94] Hence, humility will carry with it a disposition to properly admire and avoid the vicious extremes of excessive deference and defective recognition of admirable others.

Finally, the appreciation of the importance of admiration and role-modelling in legal education brings to light the significant pedagogical dimension of the role of a judge (and other legal professionals).[95] Judges serve important educational functions within the judiciary – as much as other senior legal professionals do for junior colleagues and law students in traineeship. In order to maximise the educational benefits of admiration, it seems critical to prepare judges (and other legal actors) for the educational aspects of their role. Legal professionals within the judiciary, as well as within other legal institutions and organisations, should be made aware of their pedagogical function and professional training should include the development of traits of character, skills and techniques that may help them be more effective pedagogical models.[96]

VI. Conclusion

In this chapter, I have argued that admiration plays an important role within a virtue-based approach to legal exemplarity. Admiration is a positive emotion that is related to, but distinct from, other positive emotions such as gratitude, awe, adoration, esteem and respect. It is variously opposed to contempt and disgust. Admiration may be felt towards diverse forms of excellence – natural and acquired. My focus has been on the kind of admiration that is felt towards models of moral and epistemic virtue. Its motivational output is complex, including inspiration, a disposition to promote the values exemplified in the object of admiration, to praise and enhance the reputation of the admired model, and critically, to imitate it. The imitation that is triggered by admiration is a central tool, I have argued, for the acquisition of judicial virtue. In addition, it has important social effects within the judiciary: it contributes to the transmission of legal culture, to attributing authority, to creating and regulating hierarchy, to generating a cooperative social environment, and to shaping the self-image of the judicial profession.

These learning and social benefits provide important reasons for making efforts towards developing a virtuous disposition to admire among law students

[93] For an egalitarian conception of humility, see Ben Ze'ev (1993) and Statman (1992).

[94] I have developed an egalitarian account of the virtue of judicial humility in Amaya (2018c).

[95] I thank Guillermo Hurtado for drawing my attention to this point.

[96] Sanderese has argued for the need to help teachers be aware of their role as models and improve their skills so as to be more effective role models in Sanderese (2013), 38.

and legal professionals, especially, judges. Those who possess a virtuous disposition to admire, I have argued, experience that emotion (rather than envy or resentment) in the face of excellent others; their admiration fits its object (ie they do not experience admiration towards negative exemplars); they admire exempla for the right reasons (out of admiration that is directed at the admirable aspects of the model); they admire in the right way (thereby avoiding the extremes of obsequiousness and arrogance); the experience of admiration motivates them to emulate in ways that properly acknowledge the distance that there is between the model and themselves (averting moral over-stretching), that engages one's critical capacities (resisting fetishism), and that is responsive to the imaginative and affective dimensions of emulation (skewing copycatting).

Finally, I have suggested some educational strategies that may help inculcate a virtuous disposition to admire in the context of the legal professions, namely, exposure to exempla, explicit discussion of exemplary models, cultivation of emotional and imaginative skills, virtue education (with a focus on moral and intellectual autonomy, perseverance and resilience, and moral and intellectual humility) and training oriented towards increasing awareness of the pedagogical dimensions of the legal professions and improving their effectiveness as role models. Thus, it would be desirable to rethink and revise legal education (and, as argued, educational materials, so as to include books of exempla and historical texts, as well as literary and filmic resources) with a view to fostering virtuous admiration among law students and professionals.

In addition to cultivating a virtuous disposition to admire through educational reform, an interesting issue – which I have not addressed in this chapter – is how the structure and organisation of the judiciary (and other legal institutions) may facilitate a productive emulation of admirable models within the profession. Nudging strategies are useful ways to bring about institutional environments that facilitate the acquisition and display of virtue.[97] Legal institutional structures have also been claimed to have a significantly impact on the emotions of individuals and groups.[98] Similarly, one could design legal institutions and legal professional organisations with a view to nurturing a virtuous disposition to admire. Nudging, in combination with education, could provide a sure-footed path to promote a virtuous disposition to admire in juridical contexts.[99] I hope that the arguments I have given in support of the relevance of admiration for the development of judicial virtue as well as its broader social effects within the judiciary have, at least, succeed in showing that its implications for legal education and institutional design may be worth further exploring.

[97] On fostering virtue through institutional design, see Anderson (2012).

[98] See Abrams and Keren (2010).

[99] On combining imitation of exemplars and nudges as two strategies for education, see Engelen et al (2018).

References

Abrams, K and Keren, H (2010) 'Who's Afraid of Law and the Emotions?' 94 *Minnesota Law Review* 1997.

Algoe, SB and Haidt, J (2009) 'Witnessing Excellence in Action: The "Other Praising" Emotions of Elevation, Gratitude, and Admiration' 4(2) *The Journal of Positive Psychology* 105.

Amaya, A (2013) 'Exemplarism and Judicial Virtue' 25(3) *Law and Literature* 428.

Amaya, A (2018a) 'Imitation and Analogy' in CE Smith et al (eds) *Analogy and Exemplary Reasoning in Legal Discourse* (Amsterdam, Amsterdam University Press) 13.

Amaya, A (2018b) 'Ejemplaridad, virtud y autoridad judicial' [Exemplarity, Virtue, and Judicial Authority], Special Issue 'Estudios Culturales del Derecho y *Making the Case*' UNA: Revista de Derecho, vol 3.

Amaya, A (2018c) 'The Virtue of Judicial Humility' 9(1) *Jurisprudence* 97.

Anderson, E (2012) 'Epistemic Justice as a Virtue of Social Institutions' 26 *Social Epistemology* 163.

Archer, A (2019) 'Admiration and Motivation' 11(2) *Emotion Review* 140.

Baddeley, M (2018) *Copycats and Contrarians: Why We Follow Others … and When We Don't* (New Haven, Yale University Press).

Ben-Ze'ew, A (1993) 'The Virtue of Modesty' 30 *American Philosophical Quarterly* 235.

Bucher, A (1998) 'The Influence of Models in Forming Moral Identity' 27(7) *International Journal of Educational Research* 619.

Compaijen, R (2017) 'Recognizing and Emulating Exemplars' 24(4) *Ethical Perspectives* 569.

Croce, M (2019) 'Exemplarism in Moral Education: Problems with Applicability and Indoctrination' *Journal of Moral Education*, DOI: 10.1080/03057240.2019.1579086.

Croce, M and Vaccarezza, MS (2017) 'Educating Through Exemplars: Alternative Paths to Virtue' 15(1) *Theory and Research in Education* 5.

Del Mar, M (2018) 'Educating the Legal Imagination' *Law and Method* 1.

Del Mar, M (2020) 'The Legal Imagination: Individual, Interactive and Communal' in A Amaya and M Del Mar (eds) *Virtue, Emotion and Imagination in Law and Legal Reasoning* (Oxford, Hart Publishing).

Dijksterhuis, A (2005) 'Why We Are Social Animals: The High Road to Imitation as Social Glue' in S Hurley and N Chater (eds) *Perspectives on Imitation* (Cambridge, MIT) 207.

Dijksterhuis, A, Spears, R, Postmes, T, Stapel, D, Koomen, W, Knippenberg, A and Scheepers, D (1998) 'Seeing One Thing and Doing Another: Contrast Effects in Automatic Behavior' 75(4) *Journal of Personality and Social Psychology* 862.

Domselaar, van, I (2020) 'All Judges on the Couch? On Iris Murdoch and Legal Decision-Making' in A Amaya and M Del Mar (eds) *Virtue, Emotion and Imagination in Law and Legal Reasoning* (Oxford, Hart Publishing).

Erasmus, D (1536) (1997) *The Education of a Christian Prince* (Cambridge, Cambridge University Press).

Engelen, B, Thomas, A, Archer, A and van de Ven, N (2018) 'Exemplars and Nudges: Combining Two Strategies for Moral Education' 47(3) *Journal of Moral Education* 346.

Gerrans, P (2013), 'Imitation, Mind Reading and Social Learning', 8 *Biological Theory* 20.

Gibson, DE (2003) 'Developing the Professional Self-Concept: Role Model Construals in Early, Middle, and Late Career Stages' 14(5) *Organization Science* 591.

Haidt, J and Seder, P (2009) 'Admiration and Awe' *Oxford Companion of Affective Science* (New York, Oxford University Press) 4.

Han, H, Kim, J, Jeong, C and Cohen, GL (2017) 'Attainable and Relevant Moral Exemplars Are More Effective than Extraordinary Exemplars in Promoting Voluntary Service Engagement,' 8 *Frontiers in Psychology* 1.

Henrich, H and Gil-White, F (2001) 'The Evolution of Prestige: Freely Conferred Deference as a Mechanism for Enhancing the Benefits of Cultural Transmission' 22 *Evolution and Human Behavior* 165.

Huesmann, LR, Moise, JF and Podolski, CL (1997), 'The Effects of Media Violence on the Development of Anti-Social Behavior' in DM Stoff, J Breiling and JD Maser (eds) *Handbook of Antisocial Behaviour* (John Wiley and Sons, Hoboken) 181.

Hurley, S and Chater, N (2005), 'Introduction: The Importance of Imitation', in S Hurley and N Chater (eds), *Perspectives on Imitation* (Cambridge, MIT) 1.

Ibarra, H (1999) 'Provisional Selves: Experimenting with Image and Identity in Professional Adaptation' 44(4) *Administrative Science Quarterly* 764.

Irwin, TH (2015) 'Nil Admirari? Uses and Abuses of Admiration' Supplementary Volume LXXXIX *Proceedings of the Aristotelian Society* 224.

Jones, C (2011) 'Drunken Role Models: Rescuing our Sporting Exemplars' 5(4) *Sport, Ethics and Philosophy* 414.

Kaftanski, W (2018) 'Becoming oneself in a world of Kardashians: Imitation, Admiration, and the Power of Role Models'. Available at http://www.abc.net.au/religion/imitation-and-the-power-of-role-models/10343072.

Keltner, D and Haidt, J (1999) 'Social Functions of Emotions at Four Levels of Analysis' 13(5) *Cognition and Emotion* 505.

Keltner, D and Haidt, J (2003) 'Approaching Awe, a Moral, Spiritual and Aesthetic Emotion' 17(2) *Cognition and Emotion* 297.

Kristjánsson, K (2006) 'Emulation and the Use of Role Models in Moral Education' 35(1) *Journal of Moral Education* 37.

Kristjánsson, K (2017) 'Emotions Targeting Moral Exemplarity: Making Sense of the Logical Geography of Admiration, Emulation and Elevation' 15(1) *Theory and Research in Education* 20.

Kristjánsson, K (2018) *Virtuous Emotions* (Oxford University Press, Oxford).

Lockwood, P and Kunda, Z (1997) 'Superstars and Me: Predicting the Impact of Role Models on the Self' 73 (1) *Journal of Personality and Social Psychology* 91.

Lockwood, P and Kunda, Z (1999) 'Increasing the Salience of One's Best Selves Can Undermine Inspiration by Outstanding Role Models' 76(2) *Journal of Personality and Social Psychology* 214.

Moberg, DJ (2000) 'Role Models and Moral Exemplars: How Do Employees Acquire Virtues by Observing Others?' 10(3) *Business Ethics Quarterly* 675.

Onu, D, Kessler, T and Smith, JR (2016) 'Admiration: A Conceptual Review' 8(3) *Emotion Review* 218.

Ortony, A, Clore, GL and Collins, A (1990), *The Cognitive Structure of Emotions* (Cambridge, Cambridge University Press).

Prinz, J (2005) 'Imitation and Moral Development' in S Hurley and N Chater (eds) *Perspectives on Imitation* (Cambridge, MIT) 267.

Sanderese, W (2013) 'The Meaning of Role Modelling in Moral and Character Education' 42(1) *Journal of Moral Education* 28.

Schindler, I, Zink, V, Windrich, J and Menninghaus, W (2013) 'Admiration and Adoration: Their Different Ways of Showing and Shaping Who We Are' 27(1) *Cognition and Emotion* 85.

Shapin, S (2004) 'The Way We Trust Now: The Authority of Science and the Character of Scientists' in P Hoodbhoy, D Glaser and S Shapin (eds) *Trust me, I am a Scientist* (London, British Council).

Smith, RH (2000) 'Assimilative and Contrastive Emotional Reactions to Upward and Downward Social Comparisons' in J Suls and L Wheeler (eds) *Handbook of Social Comparison: Theory and Research* 173.

Statman, D (1992) 'Modesty, Pride and Realistic Self-Assessment' 42 *The Philosophical Quarterly* 420.

Stepien, M (2012) 'The Three Stages of Judges' Self-Development' in A Amaya and HL Ho (eds) *Law, Virtue and Justice* (Oxford, Hart Publishing).

Sweetman, J, Spears, R, Livinsgtone, AG and Mastead, SR (2013) 49 *Journal of Experimental Social Pyschology* 534.

Tan, SH (2005) 'Imagining Confucius: Paradigmatic Characters and Virtue Ethics' 32 *Journal of Chinese Philosophy* 414.

Tennie, C, Call, J and Tomasello, M (2009) 'Ratching Up the Ratchet: On the Evolution of Cumulative Culture' 364 *Philosophical Transactions of the Royal Society Biological Sciences* 2405.

Tomasello, M (1999) *The Cultural Origins of Human Cognition* (Cambridge, Harvard University Press).

Vos, PH (2018) 'Learning from Exemplars: Emulation, Character Formation, and the Complexities of Ordinary Life' 39(1) *Journal of Beliefs and Values* 17.

Williams, B (1995) 'Replies' in JEJ Altham and R Harrison (eds) *World, Mind and Ethics: Essays on the Ethical Philosophy of Bernard Williams* (Cambridge, Cambridge University Press) 185.

Wilson, AT (2019) 'Admiration and the Development of Moral Virtue' in A Grahle and A Archer (eds) *The Moral Psychology of Admiration* (London, Rowman and Littlefield) 201.

Zagzebski, LT (2017) *Exemplarist Moral Theory* (New York: Oxford University Press).

Zipursky, B (2020) 'Austerity, Compassion and the Rule of Law' in A Amaya and M Del Mar (eds) *Virtue, Emotion and Imagination in Law and Legal Reasoning* (Oxford, Hart Publishing).

3

Impartiality and Legal Reasoning

CATHERINE Z ELGIN

I. Introduction

Philosophy of science distinguishes between the context of discovery and the context of justification.[1] The context of discovery is the actual sequence of events that led to a scientific discovery. It constitutes the circuitous chains of reasoning and investigation, replete with false starts and dead ends, that in fact led to a particular conclusion. It is the province of the history, sociology and psychology of science. The context of justification is the locus of chains of argument that justify the conclusion. It is normative, not descriptive. It is the province of the philosophy of science. A context of justification account does not purport to track the genesis of the result. Rather it supplies the arguments that demonstrate that the result is scientifically acceptable. A parallel distinction can be made in law. We see this in Zipursky's discussion of *PLIVA v Mensing*. Zipursky suggests that Justice Sotomayor and Justice Thomas arrived at diverging opinions because Justice Sotomayor reasoned compassionately while Justice Thomas reasoned dispassionately.[2] This is a context of discovery suggestion. It concerns the ways the opinions were arrived at, not what, if anything, justifies them. Zipursky, who sides with Justice Sotomayor, acknowledges that her opinion can be supported by rule-of-law considerations of consistency. In deciding against Mensing, he maintains, the court violated 'a norm of evenhandedness'.[3] No appeal to compassion is required in the context of justification to vindicate her position. The requirement that like cases be treated alike suffices. Imagination, emotion and virtue may figure in the path of reasoning by which a particular judge arrives at a particular conclusion. But, I will urge, a tenable legal finding, like a tenable scientific finding, must be supported by publicly accessible and intersubjectively acceptable reasons. This constrains the roles virtue, emotion and imagination can legitimately play in legal contexts.

[1] See Popper (2002), 7–8.
[2] Zipursky (2020) (chapter four in this volume).
[3] Ibid, p 74.

II. Requirements

Any viable legal system should respect the following principles:

> Consistency: Like cases should be treated alike.
>
> Publicity: Justice must not only be done, it must be seen to be done.

Consistency is a logical principle; it is not peculiar to the law or even to practical reason. It applies in science, journalism, athletics and ethics, as well as in law. In ethics, it emerges as a principle of fairness; to treat relevantly similar cases differently would be unfair. In law, it is a principle of justice; to treat relevantly similar cases differently would be unjust. Publicity is a principle of transparency. In a legal setting, it is not enough that like cases actually be treated alike, it should be manifest that they are treated alike. Otherwise, those who lose their cases have no grounds for confidence that the outcome was just. Publicity and Consistency constitute requirements on what might be called the public face of the law. They say nothing about how judges do or should arrive at their rulings. They do, however, set constraints on the rulings themselves.

This, of course, is hideously vague. I have said nothing about what makes two cases alike in such a way that they should be treated alike. Every two cases are alike in some respects and different in others. To render the principles capable of implementation requires specifying which similarities and differences are relevant. Thus the law specifies that being alike in being a felony, a theft, a breach of contract, or a late payment is legally relevant, while being alike in being committed by someone of a particular race, gender or sexual orientation is not. To render the liberties and constraints the law underwrites acceptable further requires showing why the similarities and differences it recognises are relevant.

III. Impersonal Judgment

The two principles seem to push in the direction of a rule-based conception of the law. They suggest that our legislative goal should be to frame articulate, satisfiable, publicly justifiable rules and articulate, satisfiable, publicly justifiable penalties for failing to abide by them. These rules might be accompanied by a list of exemptions and a list of acceptable excuses for failing to comply with them. Further refinements are apt to be wanted. We might want to recognise that for some infractions there are different degrees of failure – that going 5 miles per hour above the speed limit is not relevantly the same as going 30 miles per hour above the speed limit; that children should be subject to different penalties than adults who commit the same infraction; that first offenders should be subject to different penalties than repeat offenders. Whatever the nuances, Consistency and Publicity apply. If, for example, there is a milder penalty for a first offence, it applies to everyone convicted of a first offence, not just to likable defendants. This should be manifest to all involved. The idea of a wholly rule-based conception is that we could spell out exactly what is required or forbidden, and then apply the rules automatically.

That would make the law impersonal – indeed, practically mechanical. When we devise an impersonal system, we off-load deliberation and judgment onto rules and procedures. Under such a system, there is little if any room for discretion. To the extent that legislation can do this, it straightforwardly satisfies Consistency. It is determinate what cases count as relevantly alike and what it is to treat them as alike. This does not make things easier. For a good deal of imagination is required in framing the requisite laws. If we want a system where the application of the laws is virtually automatic, legislators need to decide in advance where various lines are to be drawn. They need to imagine circumstances where the law, as framed, would yield a decision that strikes them as unjust, unwarranted or unworkable. Suppose they frame a law with a mandatory one-year sentence for anyone found in possession of an unlicensed hand gun. Then it applies to the nun who found a gun in the park and promptly brought it to the police station. During the interval between the moment she picked it up and the moment she turned it in, she was in possession of an unlicensed gun. Clearly the legislators did not intend to jail such civic-minded people, but the law as written would apply to her. To frame a just law requires carving out the proper exceptions.

Another worry concerns how the law is applied. In eighteenth century England, farmers were required by law to pay a specific number of bushels of grain to the lord who owned the land they farmed. That seems sort of legal requirement that impersonal rules could accommodate. You owe the lord 17 bushels, you pay him 17 bushels; otherwise you are in breach of the law. But 'everybody knew that grain could be packed more densely by pouring it from a greater height'.[4] Even if poured from the same height, if one pours gently, the basket will contain less grain than if one pours with a heavier hand. Thus rules for determining whether grain had been properly poured had to be introduced as well. Further rules were needed to tell whether the pouring rules had been properly followed. And so on. Evidently we embark on a dangerous regress if we restrict our legal resources to the formulation and application of impersonal rules.

Problems of implementation can also undercut systems that seek to be wholly impersonal. Suppose the law mandates that only children who reside in a particular town are eligible to attend the local public schools. Whether homeless children living in cars currently parked on the town's streets count as residents may be uncertain. The law as written seems to deliver no verdict on this case. We can neither foresee nor regiment everything that would be required. We cannot formulate rules that are sufficiently nuanced to draw all the distinctions that a just and efficacious legal system needs. As Amaya says, 'It is the ever present possibility

[4] Porter (1995), 24.

of exceptions and the impossibility of reducing the understanding of what such exceptions would be – and what makes them exceptions – to rules or principles that renders any system of general formulations (and, more generally, any decision procedure) unfit to capture a good choice'.[5] The application of law must allow for judicial discretion. Otherwise we will have to live with unforeseen but manifestly unjust findings.

IV. Virtuous Judgments

This may make a virtue theoretic model of legal reasoning seem attractive. If judicial discretion is mandatory, then the moral/intellectual character of the judge is important. Amaya maintains that the virtuous judge, an Aristotelian phronimos, is one who sees how the particulars of the case bear on how it should be decided.[6] He detects the salient factors and assigns them appropriate weights. He uses his finely tuned perceptions and emotions to see the case aright. She suggests, following Wallace,[7] that 'virtue may be understood as a form of "connoisseurship" for the connoisseur or expert has precisely the ability to discern case-specific reasons for choice by means of perception, and can, in every case, provide a reason for her choice'.[8] She accepts McDowell's characterisation of virtuous perception[9] as 'one in which some aspect of the situation is seen as constituting a reason for acting in some way; this reason is apprehended, not as outweighing or overriding any reason for acting in other ways which would otherwise be constituted by other aspects of the situation … but as silencing them.'[10]

Amaya recognises that her account of proper legal reasoning is schematic. More needs to be done.[11] As it stands, however, her position threatens to violate both Consistency and Publicity. The threat to Publicity comes from the model of connoisseurship. Connoisseurs can often discern what ordinary observers cannot. In the arts, this is not a problem. When Roger Fry says that Cézanne's *Le Compotier* is about the construction of pictorial mass out of gradations in colour[12] and we do not understand why he thinks so, we simply conclude that he does not see the picture the way we do. We do not immediately conclude that we are wrong to see it as we do. When Clement Greenberg disagrees with

[5] Amaya (2011), 125.
[6] See Aristotle (1998).
[7] See Wallace (2006).
[8] Amaya (2011), 129.
[9] See McDowell (1998).
[10] Amaya (2011), 128.
[11] Although she elaborates her position in Amaya (2012) and Amaya (2019), she does not address the issues I raise.
[12] Fry (1952), 13.

Fry and insists that *Le Compotier* is concerned with the ineluctable flatness of the picture plane,[13] that causes no problems either. Each connoisseur can, we assume, point to features of the painting that support his reading. We may never appreciate what he is getting at. Or we may appreciate what he is saying, but disagree. We do not insist that the dispute be resolved. Although reasons can be given, disagreements in the arts may be interminable.[14] Because responses to works of art are susceptible to refinement without limit, there is no expectation that consensus can or should be reached. But if neither ordinary people nor other legal connoisseurs can see what a judge is getting at, or if having seen it, they can remain unconvinced of its legal tenability, the situation is different; the relevant parties cannot appreciate why the judge ruled as he did. The loser in a case has no reason to think that he was treated fairly. Reliance on exquisitely honed perception thus seems to cut sharply against Publicity.

Construing connoisseurship as expertise will not obviously help here. Some experts can explain why they think and act as they do. They can articulate reasons that non-experts can find creditable. But the ability to provide such explanations is not a requirement on expertise *per se*. An expert piano tuner who makes a subtle adjustment on a string or an expert auto mechanic who makes a subtle adjustment to an engine may be incapable of explaining why just that adjustment was called for. Connoisseurs and experts have exceedingly fine-tuned abilities to discern. It is unsurprising if they cannot express what they discern in words that are accessible to and assessable by those of us who lack their discernment.

Consistency is also threatened. If two seemingly similar cases result in different verdicts, there should be some available reason why. It will not do for a judge to rest on his exquisitely tuned judicial sensibility and assure us that he can detect a relevant distinction that is beyond our ken. Van Domselaar disagrees. Her Murdochian view 'allows for legal decision-making, at least to some extent, to remain obscure and unexplained'.[15] Why should the loser trust such a decision? Why shouldn't she consider it arbitrary? The idea that competing considerations can be obscure or be silenced strikes me as untenable. Rather, the judge should be able to explain why the considerations that seem to favour a different ruling are overridden or outweighed. According to Amaya, 'The perceptual capacity may be construed as a sensibility that enables the virtuous judge to appreciate the reasons which obtain in a particular case and provide the corresponding justification for her decision'.[16] But neither perception nor emotion in itself guarantees the availability of intersubjective reasons that would supply a justification.

Here the difference between individual and social epistemology is important. Many epistemologists believe that perception itself constitutes evidence for the perceiver. If you see a camel in broad daylight in the centre of your visual field,

[13] Greenberg (1961), 103.
[14] See Kant (1987).
[15] Van Domselaar (2020) (chapter five in this volume), p 92.
[16] Amaya (2011), 129.

you have strong evidence of the presence of a camel. But the fact that you see it gives no one else evidence, unless others have reason to believe that you see it and that your perception as of camels is trustworthy. When it comes to seeing camels such evidence is presumably ready to hand. But if you see something that is so subtle or fine-grained that others have no reason to believe that you see it (or even that it can be seen), and no reason to believe that your perception at that level of discernment is trustworthy, you can give no justification for your claim to see it. Similarly in the case of emotions. Some hold that emotions are perceptions of the ethical realm. If so, perhaps van Domselaar's Murdochian judge can discern subtle moral factors that are indiscernible to the rest of us. Nevertheless, that would not give us reason to think that she discerned them. Arguably she would have knowledge; but it would not be knowledge that she could convey via testimony.

Amaya's position introduces subjectivity into legal decision-making. Even if the subjectivity is the subjectivity of a phronimos, there is a problem. One reason is that we want a *system* of law that is stable across time. Even if Ruth Bader Ginsburg is a phronimos, we have no assurance that her successor will be one too. Moreover, even a virtuous judge is fallible. That being so, a judge's rulings and the reasoning that purports to justify them should be subject to review. They should be publicly available and consist of accessible and assessable reasons. We would not and should not trust her assurance that she used her exquisitely refined, virtuous sensibility, which enabled her to see aspects of the case that were imperceptible to the rest of us. Arguably, if she is a phronimos, justice would be done via her rulings. But unless she could provide reasons that others could understand and countenance, justice would not be seen to be done. In the passage I quoted above, Amaya said that in the legal case the connoisseur 'can provide, in every case, a justification for her choice' of case-specific reasons.[17] But it is not clear how the refined-perception model of discernment, particularly combined with silencing, will allow for that.

Nor is it clear that a case-by-case justification would ensure or even favour consistency across cases. Case-specificity invites bias. There are always differences between cases. If the judge is given free rein, he may treat features as salient in one case but not in another, although in fact the cases are relevantly alike. In the US it is, for example, common (but clearly unjust) that white, middle-class rapists get more lenient sentences than impoverished black rapists, even when we control for the quality of their defence attorneys. We should be very sceptical if a judge justifies the divergence by saying that she can simply see that the black defendant is more dangerous than the white one, and even more sceptical if she does so by saying that she is more afraid of the black defendant than of the white one. If reasons are narrowly case-specific, there are bound to be differences she can point to. The issue is whether they are differences that ought to matter. Amaya might reasonably respond that such a judge would not be virtuous. That may be true, but harder cases lurk nearby. She speaks of a judge with sufficient discernment to

[17] Ibid.

recognise the rights of a pregnant woman in a legal circumstance where they are not clear.[18] Perhaps it is not obvious whether the relevant disability law applies to someone whose disability is temporary. She takes such a judge to be virtuous. But suppose the judge ruled against the woman. Suppose he concluded that although the law expects businesses to make accommodations for employees who are permanently disabled, the expense of accommodating the temporarily disabled would place an undue burden on the employer. One can make up a fairly compelling case that might go either way. The idea that the virtuous judge can simply balance the competing concerns by looking at case specific details is perhaps a bit optimistic. Whichever way he rules, the loser would want to know why.

The concerns I raise here are not objections to virtue theories of judicial judgment *per se*. They pertain to theories that endorse a perceptual or connoisseurship model of what virtuous judgment consists in. Because such models emphasise subjective factors, they are in tension with the requirement that judicial decisions be justified by publicly available reasons. And because the locus of decision in such models seems to be on case-specific factors, they may be in tension with the requirement that like cases be treated alike.

V. Impartial Judgment

We seem caught in a bind. An impersonal, wholly rule-based approach to legal reasoning is too impoverished to serve. A personal, entirely virtue-based approach threatens to undermine both Consistency and Publicity. Is the situation hopeless? I suggest not. Impersonality is achieved by off-loading judgment onto rules, standards and techniques whose application is automatic. That requires setting limits on precision and on the number of dimensions and the fineness of distinctions to be considered. This means, of course, that legislators have to exercise a good deal of judgment in setting the standards, formulating the rules, and devising the techniques that produce the results. In an effort to make life easy for judges, we make it hard for legislators. Even if this sometimes works, there are areas where we are unwilling or unable to off-load judgment completely. We want or need to preserve the possibility of more complicated, fine-grained descriptions and assessments than available, or even imaginable, mechanical procedures afford. At the same time, though, we do not want to open the floodgates to idiosyncrasy, bias and chance.

We thus devise methods that are impartial but not impersonal.[19] When a method is impartial but not impersonal, people – qualified people – apply it and generate results. What makes the method impartial is that it does not matter exactly who those qualified people are. Such methods ground their findings in

[18] Ibid.

[19] See Elgin (2017), especially chapter 7.

inter-rater agreement, where the criterion for acceptability is agreement with other members of the community rather than answering to some wholly agent-independent standard.

An example of an impartial procedure is the judging of competitive diving. Each dive is to be assessed along multiple dimensions which are spelled out in advance. To that extent it is rule-based. Along each of these dimensions a dive can be done well or badly. And what it is to do well or badly in a given dimension is also spelled out in advance. These specifications remove a good deal of opportunity for idiosyncrasy and bias. The judge is required to attend to the extension of the diver's legs. He is not permitted to give or take away points for the grace with which the diver climbs the ladder. But further, more nuanced assessments need to be made within the domains marked out by the explicit standards. For example, the rules specify that entry into the water should be vertical, with the diver's body straight and toes pointed. When these conditions are not met, diving judges are instructed to deduct points. How many points is left to each judge's discretion. There, the judge is instructed to use her own judgment.[20] That discretion is needed is no surprise. Individual judges have to decide just how far from the specified ideal a given dive deviated in each of several respects. Although the rules tell them what dimensions to attend to and what standards apply, they cannot not tell them precisely how to assess or balance divergences from the ideal.

The diving judge is trained. She is not just some passer-by randomly recruited off the street. And the way she was trained involved having her initial verdicts calibrated against those of someone who was already an expert judge. The newly appointed diving judge acquires the tacit knowledge that guides more experienced judges. Even this is not the end of the story, though. A diving competition has multiple judges – typically seven or nine – and to obtain the overall rating for a dive, the highest and lowest scores are dropped, and the remaining scores are averaged. So although a diving judge's personal, finely tuned assessment has a role to play, but it is not an overriding role. If her assessment diverges significantly from the assessments of her peers, it will simply be dropped.

We do not conduct legal trials before multiple judges. But findings are subject to appeal. So each judge knows that her findings must respect the laws and precedents, and must do so in a way that is discernible and justifiable to other judges. The requirement of respect for precedents does not mean that her findings must accord with the precedents. But where they do not, an explanation is in order. She should either explain why she thinks a seemingly relevant precedent does not apply in the instant case or explain why she thinks the precedent is in error. Appellate courts issue rulings that articulate the reasons for their decisions, again grounding them in laws and precedents. Judicial discretion therefore is constrained by Consistency and Publicity.

[20] USA Diving (2013), 14.

Although agents are ineliminably involved in the assessment, in impartial proceedings, we have devised methods to control for bias and idiosyncrasy. They may take the form of rules. If so, assessors need criteria to determine how to tell whether the rules have been followed, and what margin of error there is in following the rules. They may also take the form of exemplars. Rather than an articulate or articulable rule, we may rely on instances that exemplify the features we seek to match. This is the role of precedents. They show how other judges have applied the law in the past, thereby exemplifying the features that previous judges thought should be salient. The novice diving judge who knows the rules is well served by being shown clear cases. He would see what a perfect dive is supposed to look like. He might be presented with foils that show what should count as a definite mismatch. This would enable him to figure out how far an instance can deviate from the exemplar without being defective. There will, no doubt, be border-line cases. But with suitable exemplars and foils, the range of uncertainty is narrowed. Similarly in the legal case. A precedent shows what counts as a clear case of tax evasion and how it compares with a clear case of mere tax avoidance. The precedents give direction to judicial attunement. The greater number of relevant precedents she is aware of, the more accurately fine-tuned her capacity to discern the difference gets. This guides the judge in making further rulings. The suggestion then is that the articulate laws, procedural rules and precedents constitute an impartial system that satisfy Consistency and Publicity.

VI. Virtue, Emotion and Imagination

What room does this leave for virtue, emotion and imagination in legal reasoning? No one would deny that judges should be virtuous. The thinking of such a judge may be informed by emotion and enhanced by imagination. A good judge may use her imagination to reconfigure the facts of the case – to see a new pattern in them, or to imagine different motivational structures underlying the events. It may enable her to see how the residency law for public school attendance can be extrapolated to apply to the unanticipated case of children living in a car. She may use her imagination to broaden her conception of what qualifies as someone's home. Her emotions may be in play, guiding her to discern features she would otherwise miss. She may thereby bring aspects of the situation to the fore and appreciate their significance in ways that she otherwise would not.

Imagination and empathy can, however, be two-edged swords, as the 2015 case *California v Brock Allen Turner* shows.[21] Brock Turner, a wealthy, white, Stanford University swim team member was convicted of sexually assaulting an inebriated, unconscious young woman. Judge Aaron Persky, himself a

[21] I am grateful to Mfundo Radebe for this example.

well-to-do, white, former Stanford swimmer, sentenced Turner to a mere six-month term in the county jail, followed by three years' probation. He noted that Turner had ruined his once promising future, and seemed to think that, given that fact, a longer sentence would be unduly punitive. Judge Persky evidently strongly empathised with the perpetrator, with whom he identified, but seemed to have little empathy for the victim. Turner's sentence was widely seen as a miscarriage of justice.

Is it possible to recruit the emotions in judicial deliberation without inviting such partiality? Nussbaum holds that it is.[22] She suggests that the emotional dexterity of readers of novels provides a good model for judicial flexibility. She recognises that what one might call egocentric emotions could be problematic. If an agent has an investment in the outcome, her emotions might be swayed. This is one reason why a judge ought not be a judge in his own case. But, Nussbaum notes, the emotions of fiction readers are detached. Readers have no personal investment in the situations they react to. They display the profile that Adam Smith characterises as that of a judicious spectator.[23] A reader of fiction is adept at shifting stance, taking up the perspectives of the different characters and experiencing (in a detached way) the emotions proper to each perspective.[24] Thus, Nussbaum's judiciously spectatorial judge would not so strongly identify emotionally with one party that he blinded himself to the claims of the other.

Still, one might wonder what good recruiting the emotions of the judicious spectator does. If the judge's empathy for the victim counterbalances his empathy for the perpetrator, doesn't that leave him in the same state as the mechanical, unfeeling judge? It would, if the function of emotion in judicial reasoning was to tip the scales. Then balancing the scales would give the emotions nothing to do. But this is not the function of emotions in deliberation. Nor should it be. How much sympathy the judge feels for the victim and how much outrage he feels toward the perpetrator should not weigh in his decision. What role can emotions legitimately play?

Elsewhere I have argued that emotions are sources of salience.[25] They highlight features we might otherwise minimise or overlook. Thus, for example, a frightened pedestrian, walking down a dark, lonely street, may become sensitised not just to how dangerous her situation is, but also to the presence or absence of opportunities for, and obstacles to, fight or flight. Those opportunities and obstacles were there all along, but at midday, when the sun was shining, the shops were open, and other pedestrians were strolling about, she never noticed them. The same shifts in salience occur through emotions evoked by fiction. When we take up a protagonist's perspective, we become emotionally engaged with her predicament and sensitised to the opportunities and obstacles available to her. We then

[22] See Nussbaum (1995).
[23] See Smith (1976).
[24] Nussbaum (1995), 74–75.
[25] See Elgin (1996, 2007).

shift our gaze and do the same for another protagonist. Nussbaum's point is that when we do this in response to a novel, we do it in a detached, non-partisan way.[26]

Emotions disclose; they do not typically confabulate. The features and patterns they disclose are there to be seen, even if we ordinarily overlook them. So if a judge recruits her emotions in deliberating about a case before her, she can discern patterns and features she might otherwise miss. If she is a judicious spectator, she can dexterously shift her stance, so that by empathising with different parties, she can discern features available from multiple points of view. Empathy, moreover, enables her to access other emotions and their deliverances – the fear, rage, greed, indifference, or whatever, that the subjects feel – and access the patterns and features of the situation that these emotions afford.

In some cases, she will discern fine-grained features that are ordinarily invisible – how offensive what passes for sexual banter might be to someone relentlessly subjected to it in the workplace.[27] In other cases, insight might come from moving to a coarser grain – noticing that if we ignore sexual orientation, there is no relevant difference between heterosexual and homosexual couples who seek to marry. In yet others, it may be a matter of restructuring the realm; being able to see, for example, how a long-term victim of domestic violence might construe killing her sleeping husband as self-defence, even though he was not, at that very moment, beating her.

Imagination, emotion and virtue can be valuable traits in a judge because they enable her to reconfigure the facts of a case, highlighting aspects that may otherwise be occluded. But her ruling should satisfy Consistency and Publicity, so her thinking should be constrained by the bounds that they set. If she wants to point to fine-grained considerations that others have failed to notice, she needs to make them epistemically accessible to others, and show why they are relevant and why they should be salient. In her ruling, she cannot simply silence seemingly salient and relevant considerations, so she is ill-advised to do so in her thinking. She should be able to explain why they are irrelevant, overridden or outweighed, if they are. She should be able to show why the considerations she relies on are consonant with relevant laws and precedents. Her ruling is subject to judicial review, so it must consist of considerations that are susceptible of review – considerations that are accessible to others.[28] Even a wise judge is fallible, so she should reason and articulate her reasons in such a way that if mistakes

[26] See Nussbaum (1995).

[27] Ibid, 104–11.

[28] There may be cases where the demands of justice per se diverge from the demands of Publicity, so Publicity is not a necessary condition on a just ruling. But divergences from Publicity should be rare, since unless Publicity is generally respected the people will lack reason to trust the judicial system. And even if legally valid considerations preclude full Publicity (as, eg, might be the case if state secrets had to be admitted as evidence in an espionage trial), there should be a range of competent assessors to whom the considerations on which the decision is based are made public (eg other jurists with appropriate security clearances). I thank Benjamin Zipursky for noting this limitation on Publicity.

are made they can be discovered and corrected. This may mean that she has to sacrifice some measure of the exquisite, fine-grained sensibility of the connoisseur, recognise her fallibility, and orient her thinking to the public domain.

References

Amaya, A (2011) 'Virtue and Reason in Law' in M Del Mar (ed) *New Waves in Philosophy of Law* (New York, Palgrave) 123.

Amaya, A (2012) 'The Role of Virtue in Legal Justification' in A Amaya and HL Ho (eds) *Law, Virtue and Justice* (Oxford, Hart Publishing) 51.

Amaya, A (2019) 'Virtuous Adjudication; or the Relevance of Judicial Character to Legal Interpretation' 40(1) *Statute Law Review* 87.

Aristotle (1998) *Nicomachean Ethics* (Oxford, Oxford University Press).

Domselaar, van, I (2020) 'All Judges on the Couch? On Iris Murdoch and Legal Decision-Making' in A Amaya and M Del Mar (eds) *Virtue, Emotion and Imagination in Law and Legal Reasoning* (Oxford, Hart Publishing).

Elgin, C (1996) *Considered Judgment* (Princeton, Princeton University Press).

Elgin, C (2007) 'Emotion and Understanding' in G Brun, U Dogouglu and D Kunzle (eds) *Epistemology and Emotions* (London, Ashgate) 33.

Elgin, C (2017) *True Enough* (Cambridge MA, MIT Press).

Fry, R (1952) *Cézanne* (London, Hogarth).

Greenberg, C (1961) *Art and Culture* (Boston, Beacon).

Kant, I (1987) *Critique of Judgment* (Indianapolis, Hackett).

McDowell, J (1998) *Mind, Value, and Reality* (Cambridge MA, Harvard University Press).

Nussbaum, M (1995) *Poetic Justice* (Boston, Beacon Press).

Popper, K (2002) *The Logic of Discovery* (New York, Routledge).

Porter, T (1995) *Trust in Numbers: The Pursuit of Objectivity in Science and Public Life* (Princeton, Princeton University Press).

Smith, A (1976) *Theory of Moral Sentiments* (Indianapolis, Liberty Press).

USA Diving (2013) *Official Technical Rules 2015–2017* <usadiving.org>.

Wallace, R (2006) *Normativity and the Will* (New York, Oxford University Press).

Zipursky, B (2020) 'Austerity, Compassion and the Rule of Law' in A Amaya and M Del Mar (eds) *Virtue, Emotion and Imagination in Law and Legal Reasoning* (Oxford, Hart Publishing).

4

Austerity, Compassion and the Rule of Law

BENJAMIN C ZIPURSKY*

I. Introduction: Compassion and Respect for the Rule of Law

Saying of a judge that he or she consistently displays 'respect for the rule of law' is paying a compliment to the judge, much as calling a political system genuinely 'democratic' is praising it. In each case, as Joseph Raz has pointed out,[1] there is a tendency to overuse the phrase or term and, by so doing, to dilute its meaning. That is, to some extent, because it is typically uncontroversial that one is commending a decision insofar as one is expressly recognising its compliance with 'the rule of law' and criticising it, at least in part, when indicating a shortfall from the rule of law.

References to judicial 'compassion' are both similar and dissimilar to references to 'respect for the rule of law'. They are similar because there is no uncontested account of what constitutes being 'compassionate' in adjudication or showing 'respect for the rule of law'. They are dissimilar because references to respectfulness for the rule of law, when made, are *invariably* used to praise a judge, while references to a judge's compassion are *sometimes* used in praise, but not invariably so; sometimes, those describing a judge as compassionate mean to intimate a lack of judicial rigor or impartiality.

Compassion and respect for the rule of law are also sometimes said to clash. It is illuminating to see, again, an asymmetry in how they are treated. Many scholars urge that the impulse to exercise compassion in adjudication must occasionally be clipped, on the ground that exercising compassion would conflict with the rule of

* I am grateful to Clare Huntington, Jill Anderson and Maksymilian Del Mar for helpful comments on an earlier draft, to Brinkley Rowe, Auran Buckles and Zahra Takhshid for research assistance, and to workshops at the University of Connecticut School of Law, Fordham Law School, and the XXVII International Congress for the Philosophy of Law and Social Philosophy at Georgetown Law School.

[1] Raz (1985) 139.

law. Those who disagree – those who do not favour the narrowing of the exercise of compassion – *do not*, however, typically argue that *the impulse to adhere to the rule of law must be clipped*, because doing so would stand in the way of exercising compassion. Rather, they tend to reject the idea that there is a conflict, and they tend to point to a misunderstanding of what the rule of law actually requires. They do not challenge the supremacy of the rule of law, only the implications of such supremacy.

My ultimate goal is to examine the relationship between these two attributes of judges – *compassionateness* and *respectfulness for the rule of law* – and to do so in a way that can illuminate the normative theory of adjudication. I want to offer first-cut analyses of the concepts that will enable us to discuss this apparent asymmetry more effectively. Preliminarily, note that my topic here is not so much compassion as an emotion; I am using the word 'compassion', in this chapter, largely to refer to the personal attribute of 'being a compassionate person' or 'compassionateness'. Let us suppose that some judges are more inclined than others to find in favour of a litigant because they have a strong affectively laden apprehension of the litigant's need for a remedy. More specifically, let us suppose that some judges do have strong affectively laden apprehensions of the potential healing impact of a win or the potential injurious impact of a loss for some litigant, and have a disposition to act in ways that will heal others or spare others from excessive suffering, and that such judges are consequently more disposed to decide for a litigant or at least to persevere in finding possible justifications for such litigants to prevail.[2] The degree of compassionateness of the judge might then be understood as the degree to which the judge is so disposed. And let us suppose that the degree of respectfulness for the rule of law is the degree to which a judge is less inclined to decide the case in a manner that deviates from a sound model of the allocation of power to the judicial institution as compared to other legal institutions (or branches).

On this model, it is unsurprising that respect for the rule of law is always praised, but we can also see why there is such uncertainty as to what qualifies. The virtue of respectfulness for the rule of law draws upon some prior conception of the domain of judicial authority and power. Conversely, it remains controversial whether affective perception of need ever counts as a reason to decide one way rather than another, and it certainly seems right that such an affective perception

[2] The decision to define 'compassion' in this way for this chapter is complicated. It certainly does not stem from a belief on my part that compassion is solely affective (and not in any way cognitive), or from a belief that compassion is non-rational or epistemically inert, or from a belief that compassion and sympathy are identical. Indeed, I argued at length 29 years ago against all three of these claims. See Zipursky (1990). Nonetheless, I think there is value in analysing the relationship between compassion and the rule of law in a manner that is consistent with a conception of compassion that is not, so to speak, epistemically loaded. Note also that the definition stipulated in the text refers only to how a judge is initially inclined, not to how that judge would ultimately rule. On the connection between compassion and suffering, see Del Mar (2017).

should not always be decisive.[3] Whether right or wrong, ultimately, it is certainly clear enough why someone would say that such an affective perception would not warrant reaching a result if it lies outside of the independently demarcated authority of the judiciary to reach such a result. And it is also understandable why advocates of compassion in adjudication would not choose to attack the proposition that judges should stay within their constitutionally and institutionally allocated judicial role. Rather, they would challenge the narrowness of the conception of judicial role.

In a prior publication,[4] I expressed the concern that some judges may have begun to overinflate their uneasiness with compassion in adjudication. My worry is that a contrasting attribute – dispassionateness or cold-bloodedness or toughness – is sometimes praised as a virtue when it should not be. In essence, the worry is that some results' actual divergence from what an affective perception of need might generate makes the judge reaching that result seem to have a virtue of dispassionateness, and that itself may be taken as a reason for thinking the result to be superior.

Being dispassionate is arguably a virtue when it means allowing a sound and independently determined demarcation of judicial authority to trump a decision motivated principally by a desire to use judicial authority to serve a perceived need. However, the cultivation of a dispassionate attitude is virtually identical to the embrace of toughness, unfeelingness, or what I shall call 'austerity' in responding to the human problems one encounters.[5] Being tough or austere, however, ought not be deemed an adjudicative virtue in and of itself. Such austerity is not a virtue where the boundary of judicial power is not independently demarcated in a manner that excludes or at least tends to push against the result towards which the compassionate adjudicator is pulled. A fortiori, austerity is certainly not a virtue when it actually pushes against the answer that would be dictated by the proper allocation of judicial authority. Judicial austerity, I shall argue, can threaten the rule of law.

Some of the jurisprudential critics of compassion in adjudication will be more irritated than impressed by my efforts to depict certain kinds of dispassionateness as the enemy of the rule of law. They will suspect that too much has been built into the equation of the rule of law with the proper allocation of authority to various legal actors. And they will turn to a harder conception of the rule

[3] Elgin's brief discussion of the Brock Turner Stanford rape case is a striking illustration of this concern; a judge, who had himself been a Stanford swimmer, imposed a shockingly light sentence on Turner, apparently influenced by his empathy for Turner. See Elgin (2019).

[4] Zipursky (2012).

[5] The term 'austerity' – especially given its association with EU politics over the past decade – is certainly not optimal. However, no other term so clearly contains the connotation of 'strictness' and 'severity', suggests a kind of resistance to influence (in a manner that might seem to approach impartiality), and conjures up the putative virtue of keeping a stiff upper lip.

of law – one that Justice Scalia sometimes described as 'the rule of law as a law of rules'.[6] Principle-of-legality virtues such as consistency, evenhandedness and transparency may seem to be the core of the rule of law. Compassion, because it responds to differences of individuals, still appears as a threat to advocates of rule-like qualities in the legal system and thus to the advocates of the rule of law. By contrast, cultivated dispassionateness – practiced resilience to gripping individual circumstances – appears a deeply valuable attribute, at least in appellate judges.

While there are a number of serious difficulties with a conception of the rule of law as a law of rules, I do not wish to explore those difficulties in this chapter. On the contrary, I wish to assume for the purposes of argument that at least two different types of adjudicative attributes that might be called 'respect for the rule of law' are properly treated as judicial virtues. The first is respect for boundaries of judicial authority that our constitutional system demarcates. A second is respect for principle-of-legality virtues in the law itself and in the place of the judiciary in implementing and interpreting the law.

My principal claim in this chapter is that the attribute of austerity in adjudication sometimes conflicts with the attribute of respect for the rule of law, under either of the prior conceptions. Because this is what logicians would call an existential claim, it is a very modest one; one case is enough to establish it. Of course, I am hoping to suggest a far broader theme: that the putative tension between compassionateness and respect for the rule of law does not yield an easy practical inference that judges should cultivate the attribute of austerity, because austerity is sometimes in tension with the respect for the rule of law. In other words, a judge who is too cold-blooded might, for that very reason, fail to live up to the demands of the rule of law. That is what I claim occurred in the 2011 Supreme Court case, *PLIVA v Mensing*.[7] In a broader sense, this chapter aims to illustrate and render plausible the contention – elegantly set forth in one sense by van Domselaar in this volume, that a certain kind of emotional openness is not just a virtue in adjudication, it is an epistemic virtue that can enable better compliance with juristic desiderata.[8]

Let me concede in advance that, in addition to the suspicious fact that I am featuring only one case, I am – in a way that may appear more cartoonish than scholarly – featuring just one judge as the exemplar of cultivated austerity and one judge as the exemplar of self-confident compassionateness. Even worse, the austere judge – Justice Clarence Thomas – is a conservative Republican man proclaiming that a corporation should win against an injured victim, and the compassionate

[6] Scalia (1989).

[7] *PLIVA, Inc. v Mensing* (2011).

[8] This is of course not van Domselaar's point, but it is related: she describes a Murdoch-designated kind of virtue (including emotional openness) which is said to enhance moral epistemic capacity, and contends that similar attributes may be crucial to legal-epistemic capacity. See van Domselaar (2020) (chapter five in this volume).

judge – Justice Sonia Sotomayor – is a liberal Democratic woman standing up for the injured woman. In my own defence, however, the subtlety of the legal issue we shall explore – traversing constitutional law, state products liability law, drug regulation law, and federal preemption doctrine – will make readers grateful for the oversimplified parts of the argument. Moreover, there is plenty of evidence to suggest that, as to both Justice Thomas and Justice Sotomayor, the *PLIVA* case is representative of their own proclivities towards austerity and compassionateness, respectively.

II. Overview of *PLIVA*

Before it was manufactured and sold as a generic drug, metoclopramide was sold by Wyeth under the brand name 'Reglan'.[9] First approved in 1980, Reglan was used to treat gastrointestinal disorders such as diabetic gastroparesis and esophageal reflux disorder ('reflux').[10] In 1985, generic manufacturers began selling metoclopramide.[11]

Mensing suffered from diabetic gastroparesis and her physician therefore prescribed metoclopramide in 2001.[12] It helped to relieve her symptoms and she therefore continued on the drug for several years.[13] As a result of taking metoclopramide, she developed a serious side effect, tardive dyskinesia.[14] Tardive dyskinesia is a neurologic disorder. Those who suffer from it have persistent involuntary facial movements, particularly in the lower part of the face. It is typically irreversible.

Mensing's principal tort claim – brought in federal court under Minnesota law[15] – was that PLIVA was aware that metoclopramide carried a serious risk of causing tardive dyskinesia, but failed to provide adequate warnings of this risk to doctors and patients.[16] Her factual case on the inadequacy of the warning was quite powerful. PLIVA's informational label indicated that there was, potentially, a 0.2 per cent chance that those who took the drug for more than six weeks could develop some symptoms of tardive dyskinesia; in fact the rate of developing the disorder may have been as high as 29 per cent[17] – more than 100 times greater than that which had actually been indicated.[18] While it is not clear that PLIVA knew

[9] Ibid, at 609.
[10] Ibid.
[11] Ibid.
[12] *PLIVA, Inc. v Mensing* (2011), 610.
[13] Ibid.
[14] Ibid.
[15] Ibid.
[16] Ibid.
[17] *PLIVA, Inc. v Mensing* (2011), 610.
[18] Brief for Respondents Gladys Mensing and Julie Demahy, *PLIVA, Inc. v Mensing* (2011).

that its figure was off by so many orders of magnitude, there is substantial evidence that PLIVA was aware of a far greater risk than it indicated, and simply failed to warn of it.[19] In light of the seriousness of tardive dyskinesia, there is every reason to believe that Mensing's physician would not have continued to prescribe it had he been made aware of these data.

In response to Mensing's claim, PLIVA argued that it had followed the FDA's instructions about how metoclopramide was to be labelled, and that such compliance precluded imposing tort liability under state products liability law.[20] PLIVA's argument, in short, was that federal regulatory law preempted state tort law. The United States Court of Appeals for the Eighth Circuit rejected PLIVA's argument,[21] for a similar preemption argument had just been rejected by the Supreme Court in *Wyeth v Levine*.[22] Like PLIVA, Wyeth had argued that its compliance with federal regulatory law preempted a failure-to-warn products liability claim against a pharmaceutical manufacturer under state law.[23] The Supreme Court had rejected that argument, deciding 6-3 that the injured patient's failure-to-warn claim was not preempted.[24]

PLIVA argued in the Eighth Circuit that, while Wyeth was a brand name manufacturer, PLIVA was a generic manufacturer, governed by a different statute and different regulations.[25] Because generic manufacturers – unlike brand name manufacturers – are not permitted to make unilateral changes to their labels without prior FDA approval, Mensing's case was distinguishable and the opposite result was warranted.[26] The Eighth Circuit rejected the relevance of the distinction, held there was no preemption, and ruled that Mensing's claim should proceed.[27] PLIVA petitioned the Supreme Court to hear its case, pushing the Court to treat plaintiffs suing generic manufacturers in a different manner than those suing manufacturers of brand name drugs.[28] Actavis, another pharmaceutical company that manufactured metoclopramide, simultaneously asked the Court to hear *Demahy v Actavis, Inc.*,[29] a directly parallel Fifth Circuit case by a Louisiana woman who had also developed tardive dyskinesia taking metoclopramide (for reflux disorder).[30] The Fifth Circuit, like the Eighth Circuit, had rejected

[19] Ibid, 9.

[20] *PLIVA, Inc. v Mensing* (2011), 610.

[21] *Mensing v Wyeth, Inc.*, 613–14 (2009) *rev'd sub nom PLIVA, Inc. v Mensing* (2011) and opinion vacated in part, reinstated in part, 658 F.3d 867 (8th Cir. 2011).

[22] *Wyeth v Levine* (2013).

[23] Ibid, 562.

[24] Ibid, 576–77.

[25] *Mensing v Wyeth, Inc.* (2009), 605.

[26] Ibid, 608–09.

[27] Ibid, 614.

[28] *PLIVA, Inc. v Mensing* (2011), 610–14.

[29] *Demahy v Actavis, Inc.* (2010), *rev'd sub nom PLIVA, Inc. v Mensing* (2011).

[30] Ibid, 430.

the manufacturer's 'generics are different' argument and ruled that Demahy's case should go to trial.[31]

The Supreme Court reversed and ruled that Mensing and Demahy were not entitled to go to trial because their claims were preempted.[32] Writing for a five-person majority,[33] Justice Thomas accepted PLIVA's 'generics are different'[34] argument and distinguished *Wyeth v Levine*.[35] The Court's *PLIVA* decision reached the broad and important holding that, so long as a generic manufacturer has complied with FDA warning requirements, no person injured by such a drug is entitled to sue the company for failure-to-warn in any state of the nation. Given that generics constitute about 75 per cent of the market, Justice Thomas's opinion instantly wiped out about three-fourths of failure-to-warn claims against pharmaceutical companies.[36]

Justice Sotomayor wrote an impassioned dissenting opinion, in which Justices Ginsburg, Breyer and Kagan concurred. Generics are *not* really so different, she argued.[37] PLIVA's argument that it had no way out of liability was both untrue and disingenuous, she suggested.[38] And although generics are indeed governed by a different statute, there was no reason to think that Congress wanted preemption for generics but not for brand name pharmaceuticals.[39] To the contrary, there was every reason to suppose just the opposite; the whole point of the Hatch Waxman Amendments was that generics should be just the same.[40] Creating two different worlds for persons injured by brand names and persons injured by generics in this way cut directly against Congressional intent.[41] In the end, the majority was abandoning the entire world of persons injured by defective generic drugs.

III. *PLIVA* and the Rule of Law

A. The First-Blush Interpretation of the Thomas and Sotomayor Opinions

On first blush, the majority opinion in *PLIVA* appears to be the product of a judge – Justice Thomas – who does not allow his respect for the rule of law to

[31] Ibid, 449.
[32] *PLIVA, Inc. v Mensing* (2011), 624.
[33] Justice Kennedy concurred in the judgment and concurred in all of Justice Thomas's opinion except for Part III-B-2, which related to reading the Supremacy Clause as a *non obstante* provision. Ibid, 646, n.*. As to that Part, Justice Thomas' opinion for the Court is a plurality.
[34] Ibid, 626.
[35] See *Wyeth v Levine* (2009).
[36] *PLIVA, Inc. v Mensing* (2011), 627 (Sotomayor, J, dissenting).
[37] Ibid, 630–32.
[38] Ibid, 635.
[39] Ibid, 643, 645.
[40] Ibid, 644–45.
[41] Ibid.

be compromised or outweighed by compassion for an injured and sympathetic plaintiff suing a large corporation. Indeed, Justice Thomas seems to say as much, when he writes 'We acknowledge the unfortunate hand that federal drug regulation has dealt Mensing, Demahy, and others similarly situated'[42] and he goes on to say why – even if the case seems unfair from the plaintiffs' perspective – the Supreme Court's business is only to apply the law, not to decide whether the law is as it should be.[43]

It is possible to deepen the interpretation of Justice Thomas's opinion as a *rule-of-law* decision by utilising both of the conceptions of the rule-of-law virtues indicated in section I: respect for boundaries of judicial authority that our constitutional system demarcates, and respect for principle-of-legality virtues, such as evenhandedness, consistency, generality and notice. In continuing his response to the argument from the plaintiffs' 'unfortunateness' perspective, he writes:

> '[I]t is not this Court's task to decide whether the statutory scheme established by Congress is unusual or even bizarre.' *Cuomo v Clearing House Ass'n., L.L.C.*, 557 U.S. 519, 556 (2009) (THOMAS, J., concurring in part and dissenting in part) (internal quotation marks and brackets omitted). It is beyond dispute that the federal statutes and regulations that apply to brand-name drug manufacturers are meaningfully different than those that apply to generic drug manufacturers. Indeed, it is the special, and different, regulation of generic drugs that allowed the generic drug market to expand, bringing more drugs more quickly and cheaply to the public. But different federal statutes and regulations may, as here, lead to different pre-emption results. We will not distort the Supremacy Clause in order to create similar pre-emption across a dissimilar statutory scheme. As always, Congress and the FDA retain the authority to change the law and regulations if they so desire.[44]

In noting that it is the job of Congress and the FDA to design the law and that too much judicial improvisation would interfere with their work, Justice Thomas is displaying his allegiance to the separation-of-powers/institutional role side of the conception of the rule of law. Moreover, in insisting that it is wrong to treat cases as similarly situated, under the law, when they are in fact governed by different legal standards, he purports to be taking seriously the norms of evenhandedness built into a conception of the rule of law as a law of rules. And so, it seems, Justice Thomas is essentially refusing to exercise judicial discretion to tweak the law so that the outcome will serve plaintiffs who understandably see themselves as facing an inequitable denial of rights. This would seem to be the essence of ignoring compassion in order to respect the rule of law.

Conversely, Justice Sotomayor was famously described by President Obama and others as a compassionate and empathetic judge.[45] It might seem quite

[42] *PLIVA, Inc. v Mensing* (2011), 625 (Thomas, J).

[43] Ibid, 625–26.

[44] Ibid.

[45] In announcing his nomination of then-Judge Sotomayor, President Obama stated: 'It is experience that can give a person a common touch and a sense of compassion; an understanding of how the world

straightforward to suppose that compassion – or at least empathy or sympathy – tipped the balance in this case. Perhaps Justice Sotomayor (herself a diabetic, like Mensing)[46] found it quite easy to package her empathy for Mensing in the wrapping of the Court's recent *Wyeth v Levine*[47] decision. Compassion, the argument goes, is perhaps what drew her to this reading of *Wyeth*, even if doing so was not in fact the most rigorous and justifiable application of the preemption doctrine, given that generics fell under a different statute. On this view, a compassionate judge relaxed her respect for the rule of law in order to provide compensation to a person or persons in need.

B. A More Careful Reading of *PLIVA*: Institutional Role

A more careful reading of *PLIVA* leads to the conclusion that it is Justice Thomas's decision in *PLIVA* that fails to display appropriate respect for the rule of law, and it is Justice Sotomayor's that succeeds in doing so. As shown below, this conclusion is reached whether one understands respect for rule of law in terms of a well-defined conception of the judicial role and the separation of powers, or one understands the rule of law in principle-of-legality terms. To make this argument, I will essentially run my own critique of the majority opinion in *PLIVA*, drawing in several places from Justice Sotomayor's opinion. I will then connect the concerns driving my critique with questions about the rule of law, showing that Justice Thomas's opinion is actually very weak on rule of law grounds, whatever its other strengths might be.

First, a brief overview of the federal preemption doctrine. The touchstone of preemption is legislative purpose.[48] The Court is not supposed to say which liability rule would be equitable or fair. The question is whether the statute does in fact preempt state products liability claims.[49] Of course, answering this question is not always easy, especially where a defendant has claimed that there was 'implied preemption' of plaintiff's claim by the FDA. *Express preemption* – where a statute actually states that state laws that are inconsistent are preempted – is the gold standard.[50] *Field preemption* – in which the Constitution is deemed to have reserved an entire field to federal law[51] – is also deeply entrenched in our system and quite powerful. Implied preemption is more controversial than either.[52]

works and how ordinary people live. And that is why it is a necessary ingredient in the kind of justice we need on the Supreme Court.' Text: 'Obama's Remarks on His Choice of Sotomayor' (26 May 2009) *New York Times*.

[46] Stolberg (2009).

[47] See *PLIVA, Inc. v Mensing* (2011), 636–37.

[48] *Medtronic, Inc. v Lohr* (1996); *English v Gen. Elec. Co.* (1990) ('Preemption fundamentally is a question of congressional intent').

[49] See *Wyeth v Levine* (2013), 583.

[50] See Nelson (2000).

[51] See ibid.

[52] See eg Kenneth Starr et al (1991) (criticising implied preemption, though not advocating its complete abandonment).

Implied preemption – sometimes called 'conflict preemption' – is usually understood to have two related but somewhat different forms: impossibility and frustration. Impossibility preemption applies when 'compliance with both federal and state [law] is a physical impossibility'.[53] Frustration preemption can exist even where it is not literally impossible for a person to comply with both the federal and the state law, as Justice Breyer's decision in *Geier v American Honda Motor Co.*[54] nicely illustrates.

Justice Thomas's *Wyeth* concurrence[55] was expressly antagonistic to the very idea of frustration preemption because of its link to purposivism in statutory interpretation and its tendency to cut into federalist values. In this sense, he appeared to be hostile to the theoretical framework used by the other eight justices in *Wyeth*, especially (but not only) those in dissent.[56] While he did not wish to be associated with the purposivism of Justice Stevens' majority opinion, he ruled against Wyeth because he essentially agreed with the majority that Wyeth's impossibility-preemption argument, while in principle of a kind that could succeed, did not in fact succeed.[57] Justice Thomas was persuaded that Wyeth could have changed its label to include stronger warnings without running afoul of federal law.[58] In other words, it was not true that it was impossible to comply with both federal and state law. Under a federal regulation promulgated by the FDA, Wyeth could have utilised what is called a CBE or 'change-being-effected' procedure.[59] The manufacturer proactively stiffens its warning, and asks the FDA for post hoc approval of its more vigilant warning.[60] Wyeth could have done this, Levine argued, so it was not impossible to comply with both state and federal law.[61] Justice Thomas agreed.

The key question in *PLIVA*, as Justice Thomas saw it, was thus whether impossibility preemption applied.[62] Each side had quite an impressive argument; PLIVA argued that it did apply, and Mensing argued that it did not. PLIVA drew an important distinction between its own position, under the Hatch-Waxman Amendments governing manufacturers of generics, and Wyeth's position in *Wyeth*. CBE procedures do not apply to generic manufacturers, and thus PLIVA (unlike Wyeth) did not have the right unilaterally and prospectively to change its label.[63]

[53] *Florida Lime & Avocado Growers, Inc. v Paul* (1963).

[54] *Geier v American Honda Motor Co.* (2000).

[55] See *Mensing v Wyeth, Inc.* (2009), 582.

[56] Ibid.

[57] See ibid.

[58] Ibid, 590–91.

[59] Ibid, 569.

[60] 'The CBE process permits drug manufacturers to "add or strengthen a contraindication, warning, [or] precaution," 21 CFR §314.70(c)(6)(iii)(A) (2006), or to "add or strengthen an instruction about dosage and administration that is intended to increase the safe use of the drug product," §314.70(c)(6)(iii)(C).' *PLIVA, Inc. v Mensing* (2011), 614.

[61] *Wyeth v Levine* (2013), 581.

[62] *PLIVA, Inc. v Mensing* (2011), 613.

[63] Ibid, 615.

PLIVA thus did face a strict dilemma (according to Justice Thomas): follow federal law and be liable under Minnesota state law for failure to warn, or follow state law and be liable under federal law for violating the labelling requirements applicable under the Hatch Waxman Act.[64] Therefore, impossibility preemption applied.

Mensing had several comebacks, but one stood out: *PLIVA's impossibility argument stems from artificially narrowing the time line to exclude its own realistic and plainly appropriate options*.[65] PLIVA, the plaintiff argued, had allowed decades to go by knowing that its warning of tardive dyskinesia was inadequate but feeling fortunate that both Wyeth and generic manufacturers were not being forced by the FDA to strengthen these warnings.[66] If, instead of abiding by a policy of calculated taciturnity during those decades, PLIVA had at any point actually communicated to the FDA that data on metoclopramide warranted a much stronger warning, the FDA might have changed the required warning.[67] Given that PLIVA (and all of the other metoclopramide manufacturers) had indulged themselves in silence on this risk, the FDA, with its limited resources, never knew that it should change its warning requirement, and never did so.[68] But there is no reason to utilise the defence lawyers' timeline to frame the question of whether PLIVA could have lived up to state law and federal law simultaneously. 'Impossibility' is simply an artefact of a self-serving corporate strategy of silence.

PLIVA replied that Mensing was assuming too much; it was assuming that the FDA would have exercised its discretion to demand warning label changes had PLIVA been proactive.[69] If it is possible for PLIVA to comply with both state and federal law, it should be something PLIVA could accomplish *unilaterally*, the reply went. So impossibility preemption should apply after all.

Each of the nine justices on the Court faced the question of which side of this nuanced argument over the meaning of 'impossibility' to embrace. Preemption scholars will know that federal doctrine is actually quite well designed to help the justices finesse this question, if they perceive it as a close one. It is well established that there is a *presumption against preemption* – that in a close case, where the legal materials could be read either way, the Supreme Court should presume there is no preemption.[70] The doctrine exists for federalist reasons, and also in order to incentivise Congress to make preemption consequences explicit. Hence, it could easily be argued – and was argued by Mensing – that *Wyeth* along with the presumption against preemption should decide this case. The Eighth Circuit in *Mensing* and the Fifth Circuit in *Demahy* both utilised the well-established presumption against preemption to resolve what might have been regarded as a

[64] Ibid, 616.
[65] *PLIVA Inc. v Mensing* (2011), 637 (Sotomayor, J, dissenting).
[66] Ibid.
[67] Ibid.
[68] Ibid.
[69] Ibid, 621–32.
[70] See ibid, 637–38.

close issue on 'impossibility'. Indeed, as Del Mar suggested in this volume,[71] judges are often searching for devices that will allow them to acknowledge the limited access to knowledge in their situation, and to recognise that humility through use of certain legal devices. The presumption against preemption is one of those devices.

Eschewing the easy finesse, Justice Thomas advocated a wholesale rejection of the presumption against preemption – a position I will discuss below. For the moment, it is worth noting that even without the presumption against preemption, there are other arguments that should play into the consideration of the impossibility argument. One is that preemption is ultimately about whether a federal statute should be interpreted to supplant state tort law. On this point, Justice Stevens' *Wyeth* argument was well developed and powerful: there is no evidence in the text of the statute (the FDCA) or in its history that Congress intended to supplant state tort law.[72] Indeed, whenever drug manufacturers have lobbied Congress to insert a regulatory compliance defence, they have failed. The very same is true of the Hatch-Waxman Amendments. For textualists like Justice Thomas and Justice Scalia, *implied* preemption should be something of an embarrassment. *All of implied preemption* – not simply frustration preemption – should be rejected from within a truly strict textualist mindset. It is hard to know where a textualist should turn if text does not provide a hint of the desired argument. It is striking that there is no evidence whatsoever of Congressional intent to displace state products liability law in the FDCA, as Justice Stevens concluded in his majority opinion in *Wyeth*.[73] And there is certainly nothing in the text of the Hatch-Waxman Amendments that suggests it was intended to have preemptive force as to tort claims.

Justice Thomas entirely overlooked these normal guideposts of statutory interpretation and wrote as if the whole issue were about the presumption against preemption, mistakenly supposing that without a presumption against preemption, the plaintiff had no argument. He then rejected the presumption, citing a law review article by Professor Caleb Nelson of the University of Virginia, which offered a novel reading of the Supremacy Clause.[74] On Nelson's reading, the Supremacy Clause was what eighteenth century lawyers called a *non obstante* provision.[75] According to Justice Thomas (quoting Nelson), a *non obstante* 'provision "in a new statute acknowledged that the statute might contradict prior law and instructed courts not to apply the general presumption against preemption."'[76] And so Justice Thomas inferred that the Supremacy Clause should not lead to

[71] Del Mar (2020) (chapter thirteen in this volume).
[72] *Wyeth v Levine* (2009).
[73] Ibid.
[74] Nelson (2000).
[75] Ibid, 238–240, nn 43–45.
[76] *PLIVA, Inc. v Mensing* (2011), 2581.

an application of the presumption against preemption, brushing to one side a powerful history for the presumption.[77] Notwithstanding Nelson's high quality as a scholar, it bears mention that his view is idiosyncratic and cuts against the grain of dominant scholarship. The larger point, however, is that Justice Thomas was happy to reject the presumption against preemption, which is well-established federal preemption doctrine and has been for the better part of a century.

Justice Thomas thus arrived at a preemption conclusion in *PLIVA* in spite of the relevant authorities, not because of them. He ignored statutory text, paid little attention to statutory purpose, and displayed a complete lack of interest in what Congress intended. He casually tossed out centrally important precedent in the preemption area – the presumption against preemption. And he rejected the arguments put forward by the FDA itself, which had advocated against preemption in *PLIVA*. For all of these reasons, it simply will not work to see Justice Thomas's decision as stemming from a devotion to the rule of law as exacting respect for the bounds of institutional authority. To the contrary, Justice Thomas seemed to be bending over backwards to reject Mensing's claim, allowing the sources of law and the positions of other branches to be pushed around so as to find preemption.

When we see just how far Justice Thomas was from applying the text and purpose of the statute and sticking with well-established precedent, his almost apologetic words take on a different cast. 'We acknowledge the unfortunate hand that federal drug regulation has dealt Mensing, Demahy, and others similarly situated. … But "it is not this Court's task to decide whether the statutory scheme established by Congress is unusual or even bizarre."'[78] This mindset – *sorry but the law is the law; I am not playing games to permit the sympathetic plaintiff to win* – implicitly suggests that the other Justices are inappropriately being influenced by emotions – by sympathy or compassion – to rule for the plaintiff, while he (Justice Thomas) and four other Justices have the strength of judicial character to hold the line. My suggestion is that this is a decision by a judge who is deeply suspicious of compassion and more confident that an austere approach will capture the law. If I am right, however, the attraction to austerity and dispassionateness may have allowed Justice Thomas to place far greater credence in PLIVA's argument than it deserved.

IV. *PLIVA* and the Principle-of-Legality Version of the Rule of Law

In the Introduction, I mentioned that the ideal of 'the rule of law' is notorious for its plasticity and indefiniteness, and I suggested that we try on two versions

[77] See *Cipollone v Liggett Grp., Inc.* (1992) (citing *Rice v Santa Fe Elevator Corp.*, 331 U.S. 218, 230 (1947)).

[78] *PLIVA, Inc. v Mensing* (2011), 637–38.

of it.[79] The discussion above attended to an 'institutional role' conception, and interpreted the judicial virtue of respect for the rule of law as a kind of acquiescence to the decisions the legislature had actually made and placed in the statute, combined with respect for well-established precedent and a restrained judicial role. By this standard, Justice Thomas' opinion fell short dramatically.

Another way to think about the rule of law pertains to what is sometimes called 'the principle of legality'.[80] On this view, there are abstract, structural features of a legal system in light of which a community governed by that system can claim to enjoy the rule of law. Thus, for example, laws must be general and announced prospectively; potential liability must be provided explicitly; the legal system must be reasonably clear and consistent. As Lon Fuller made famous in his classic book *The Morality of Law*,[81] a putative legal system beset by too little predictability, too much inconsistency, too much retroactivity, and too much capriciousness might even fail to qualify as a legal system at all. Conversely, under the spirit of (procedural) due process and the basic idea of a constitutional order, we treasure our legal system and our rule of law. Notice, clarity, generality and consistency are some of the earmarks of the rule of law; vagueness, inconsistency, retroactivity and unpredictability are examples of its absence.

An argument can be made that the doctrine of impossibility preemption itself stems from a judicial commitment, supported by a respect for due process principles in the Constitution, to preserve principle-of-legality features in our legal system as a whole. The Supreme Court that first ruled on impossibility preemption did not engage in statutory interpretation of federal law to discover that Congress was dictating that some piece of state law be vacated. The reality is that both the state and the federal law were real and valid under their own respective standards of validity, and neither purported to displace the other. The need for judicial intervention under preemption doctrine, if there was such a need, arose because of a certain kind of fairness argument by the defendant: *the legal system is putting me between a rock and a hard place, and you should use the Supremacy Clause to help me out of this untenable position*. The Supremacy Clause, when used in such a case, is not being used to bolster Congress's assertion that its statute trumps state law, because Congress has not made such an assertion. It is being used in conjunction with an implicit Constitutional protection for individuals that the legal system as a whole will not put them in an impossible situation. Like a vagueness or retroactivity claim, this is an argument rooted in part in procedural due process norms going back to the Magna Carta.

On this reading, what Justice Thomas is saying amounts to the following: *Mensing, we see that you need compensation and want compensation and find it unfair that you are not getting it, but our job as judges is to back up and to see the*

[79] See section I.
[80] See eg Lim (2013); Meagher (2014).
[81] Fuller (1964).

larger view of our legal system. From this more comprehensive perspective, we see that to allow Minnesota to force PLIVA to give you compensation is, in effect, to overlook the untenable spot manufacturers occupy with respect to the combination of federal and state law: they are damned if they do and damned if they don't. Sad as it may be to force you to go uncompensated, it is part of a system of law that we respect and uphold that a legal actor like PLIVA is not sanctioned for failing to live up to state law when its reason for that failure was that federal law did not permit it to do so.

My concern about *PLIVA* is that this is exactly what Justice Thomas and the other four Justices in the majority thought, and that part of the attraction of this view is that one places oneself on the side of austerity rather than the side of compassion: one *feels* the attraction of letting Mensing win, but one *cognitively recognises* that, at a more fundamental level, PLIVA really has a Supremacy-Clause-based argument to be shielded from liability. The reason this concerns me is that the appearance of rationality, comprehensiveness and 'sober truth' surrounding this perspective are actually just a façade.

Here is why. Unless the Roberts Court's concern with federalism is disingenuous, it is critical to understand the state law in question before moving to the preemption inquiry. Several mutually reinforcing observations emerge from a closer analysis of state products liability law. First, state strict products liability law is not a law of sanctioning defendants because they have violated a rule of conduct. It is not a law of sanctions at all, but a law of liability for injuries.[82] Second, it has long been the case that tort law, in various scenarios (although perhaps not at its core), is willing to impose liability on a defendant who has acted reasonably and, according to the court, has not engaged in behaviour that the court considers faulty. *Vincent v Lake Erie Transportation Co.*,[83] *Rylands v Fletcher*,[84] and *Escola v Coca-Cola Bottling Co. of Fresno*[85] are classic first-year torts examples of strict liability in this sense. Third, strict products liability law was developed in the second half of the twentieth century with a particular goal of compensating injured consumers even apart from whether a manufacturer had engaged in wrongdoing, so it is especially misguided to read the imposition of liability under state law as predicated on manufacturer wrongdoing. State strict products liability law (in its failure-to-warn branch) insulates manufacturers from liability for the injuries their products cause if their warning was adequate, but not otherwise. It is quite different to treat an adequate warning as providing a kind of safe harbour for a cost-shifting form of strict liability, than it is to treat the failure to

[82] Of course, state tort law as a whole is not simply a cost-shifting mechanism; my co-author John Goldberg and I have indeed been at the forefront of combating the pure-liability rule analysis of tort law. Nonetheless, just because tort law holds defendants responsible for injuries, it does not mean that it is sanction-based. See Goldberg and Zipursky (2006).

[83] *Vincent v Lake Erie Transportation Co.* (1910).

[84] *Rylands v Fletcher* (1898).

[85] *Escola v Coca-Cola Bottling Co. of Fresno* (1944).

warn as a kind of fault that needs to be sanctioned. It is not *impossible* to comply with the FDA labelling requirements *and* pay patients compensation when your drug injures them through a risk you had inadequately warned against. Perhaps it is *unfair* or poor public policy, but it is not impossible. Fourth, even if we were to suppose that juries in state products liability cases are ascertaining whether the defendant acted wrongfully, after-the-fact jury determinations of defendant conduct in individual cases does not count as state law prohibiting a defendant's future conduct. And, lastly, all of the nuanced issues raised in this paragraph will typically differ in nuance and meaning, state by state.

Once we see that PLIVA's 'impossibility' argument is less of a sharp inconsistency problem than a plea for corporate protection, a number of parts of the historical picture come into focus. Manufacturers have argued to state courts and state legislatures for decades that it is unfair to hold them liable for products liability when they have complied with regulations, and – although they have sometimes prevailed at state legislatures – states have generally made a substantive decision to leave things as they are. And manufactures have made this 'fairness' argument to Congress with respect to pharmaceuticals in particular, and Congress has declined to enact legislation shielding them from this conflict. Finally, Congress has long legislated against a background where it understood that, in our system, strict products liability is both strict and loss-shifting, not fault based and sanction-imposing. To suppose there is 'implied preemption' under the Hatch-Waxman Amendments, under such circumstances, is fantasy.

'Fantasy' is the wrong word, for the conclusion that should be drawn from the above description of what other parts of government have thought about strict products liability and federal regulation is *not* that drug company litigators are imagining things. The conclusion to be drawn is not one about fabrication but politics and advocacy: manufacturers had tried state courts, state legislatures, Congress and the FDA, but had still come up empty-handed in their 'fairness'-based principle-of-legality concerns, so they decided to try their luck with the federal courts. And they have had some success. But the Supreme Court should be especially loath to enter the fray under these circumstances. Were preemption in fact written into the text of the Hatch-Waxman Amendments, that would be one thing. But in fact the opposite is true; this is entirely a matter of judicial improvisation; improvisation designed to move the Supreme Court to shield pharmaceutical manufacturers from juries in products liability cases.

Ironically, there are, indeed, at least two serious principle-of-legality issues at stake in *PLIVA*, but they cut in favour of Mensing, not against her. As Justice Sotomayor recognised, there is a bizarre asymmetry in the legal treatment of those whose pharmacists provide them with generics compared with those who are given brand name drugs.[86] The violation of a norm of evenhandedness is especially dramatic given that there is, by definition, no relevant difference between the drugs. Beyond this, consumers are routinely placed on one side of this

[86] *PLIVA, Inc. v Mensing* (2011) at 645 (Sotomayor, J, dissenting).

immunity line or the other without any knowledge or voluntary act themselves; their legal rights to a remedy – turning as they often do on the happenstance of a pharmacy's supply-room shelves – are typically outside of their control or choice. The arbitrariness of *the rights/non-rights distinction* and *the denuding of patient choice over the rights regime* are both paradigmatic of rule-of-law failures.

V. Conclusion

In one respect, Justice Sotomayor's capacity to get to the right answer in *PLIVA* had nothing to do with compassion; her decision was principally based in a down-to-earth and compelling interpretation of statutes against the backdrop of all of the relevant precedent. My suggestion, however, is that Justice Thomas's failure to get to the right answer in *PLIVA* had much to do with his anti-compassionate stance – his proclivity to embrace interpretations that resonate with the spirit of austerity – a judicial attribute seemingly constituted by the disposition to turn away sympathetic plaintiffs when larger system issues seem to point in the direction of doing so.

Being a judge is difficult business; it is, of course, easy for law professors to stand back and criticise judges and justices for coming out in the wrong place. But the difficulty of being a judge is one of the reasons compassion is important. The capacity to turn away sympathetic litigants when they do not have a legal right to win under an impartial interpretation of the relevant legal materials *is* undoubtedly an important attribute in judges. As with any attribute, however, it is a matter of degree. Justices of the United States Supreme Court have plenty of reason to develop thick skins, to be able to stand back, to be somewhat austere or dispassionate in a range of cases where the emotional draw of the litigants is actually quite independent of the merit of their claims. Any number of decisions display that Justice Sotomayor herself has this attribute.

And yet unbridled austerity in adjudication creates risks, just as unbridled compassion does. This chapter aimed to point out that, even on one of the dimensions for which dispassionateness might seem most important – respect for the rule of law – an overcharged sense of austerity and unyieldingness can subvert the rule of law. In this context, a judge who can hit the right balance between dispassionateness and compassion is best suited to act in accordance with respect for the rule of law.

References

Cases

Cipollone v Liggett Grp., Inc., 505 U.S. 504, 516 (1992).
Demahy v Actavis, Inc. 593 F.3d 428 (5th Cir. 2010).

English v Gen. Elec. Co. 496 U.S. 72, 78–79 (1990).
Escola v Coca-Cola Bottling Co. of Fresno 24 Cal. 2d 453 (1944).
Florida Lime & Avocado Growers, Inc. v Paul 373 U.S. 132, 142–43 (1963).
Geier v American Honda Motor Co. 529 U.S. 861 (2000).
Medtronic, Inc. v Lohr 518 U.S. 470, 485 (1996).
Mensing v Wyeth, Inc. 588 F.3d 603, 613–14 (8th Cir. 2009).
PLIVA, Inc. v Mensing 564 U.S. 604 (2011).
Rylands v Fletcher 52 P. 274 (1898 Nev.).
Vincent v Lake Erie Transportation Co. 109 Minn. 456 (1910).
Wyeth v Levine 550 U.S. 555 (2013).

Articles and Books

Del Mar, M (2017) 'Imagining by Feeling: A Case for Compassion in Legal Reasoning' 13(2) *International Journal of Law in Context* 143.

Del Mar, M (2020) 'The Legal Imagination: Individual, Interactive and Communal' in A Amaya and M Del Mar (eds) *Virtue, Emotion and Imagination in Law and Legal Reasoning* (Oxford, Hart Publishing).

Domselaar, van, I (2020) 'All Judges on the Couch? On Iris Murdoch and Legal Decision-Making' in A Amaya and M Del Mar (eds) *Virtue, Emotion and Imagination in Law and Legal Reasoning* (Oxford, Hart Publishing).

Elgin, CZ (2020), 'Impartiality and Legal Reasoning' in A Amaya and M Del Mar (eds) *Virtue, Emotion and Imagination in Law and Legal Reasoning* (Oxford, Hart Publishing).

Fuller, LL (1964) *The Morality of Law* (Yale University Press).

Goldberg, J and Zipursky, CB (2006) 'Seeing Tort Law from the Internal Point of View: Holmes and Hart on Legal Duties' 75 *Fordham Law Review* 1563.

Lim, B (2013) 'The Normativity of the Principle of Legality' 37 *Melbourne University Law Review* 372.

Meagher, D (2014) 'The Principle of Legality As Clear Statement Rule: Significance and Problems' 36 *Sydney Law Review* 413.

Nelson, C (2000) 'Preemption' 86 *Virginia Law Review* 225.

Obama's Remarks on His Choice of Sotomayor (2009) *New York Times* (26 May).

Raz, J (1985) 'The Obligation to Obey: Revision and Tradition' 1 *Notre Dame Journal of Law, Ethics & Public Policy* 139.

Scalia, A (1989) 'The Rule of Law as a Law of Rules' 56 *University of Chicago Law Review* 1175.

Starr, K et al (1991) *The Law of Preemption: A Report of the Appellate Judges Conference* 34.

Stolberg, SG (2009) 'Court Nominee Manages Diabetes With Discipline' *New York Times* (9 July).

Zipursky, BC (1990) '*DeShaney* and the Jurisprudence of Compassion' 65 *New York University Law Review* 1101.

Zipursky, BC (2012) 'Anti-Empathy and Dispassionateness in Adjudication' in J Flemming (ed) *Nomos LV: Passions and Emotions* (NYU Press).

5

All Judges on the Couch? On Iris Murdoch and Legal Decision-Making

IRIS VAN DOMSELAAR*

'It is a *task* to come to see the world as it is.'[1]

I. Introduction

Largely ignored during her own professional lifetime, over the last three decades Iris Murdoch's vision-based moral philosophy has received increasing attention from those who sympathise with the idea that the concept of moral perception should have a more prominent place in moral philosophy.[2] However, as Murdoch herself was largely evasive on matters of public morality,[3] thus far the potential relevance of Murdoch's moral philosophy for the law – a public institution par excellence – has hardly been addressed.

In this chapter, I flesh out the relevance of Murdoch's moral philosophy for the law – in particular, legal decision-making. The main motivation for this endeavour is that legal decision-making is a public institutional practice that, if anything, deals with particulars: with concrete, unique (constellations of) facts and persons. These particulars do not jump into the judge's sight of their own accord, but require a particular capacity on the part of the judge: the capability to

* A draft version of this article was first presented at the colloquium 'Virtue, Emotion and Imagination in Legal Reasoning', which was organised by the Universidad Nacional Autónoma de México and Queen Mary University of London. The author is grateful to the participants for their comments. An earlier version of this text was presented at the research colloquium of the Paul Scholten Centre for Jurisprudence at the University of Amsterdam. The author would like to thank the participants – Wouter de Been, in particular – for their valuable comments. Also, the author is grateful to the editors of this book for their careful reading of the manuscript and their insightful comments and suggestions. Of course, any mistakes, imprecisions or inaccuracies remain mine.

[1] Murdoch (1999), 375.

[2] See eg Blum (1991), Antonaccio and Schweiker (1996), Antonaccio (2000), Broackes (2012) and Browning (2018).

[3] Nussbaum (2001) provides an articulate and outspoken critique of this apolitical aspect of Murdoch's work. I will come back to this point later.

adequately discern the particulars and to respond accordingly. Arguably, Murdoch's vision-based moral philosophy, with its prominent role for moral perception, can help us account for this capacity.

To begin, I offer an outline of Murdoch's vision-based moral philosophy. Subsequently, I expound the contours of a Murdochian approach to legal decision-making (MAL). Finally, I will discuss three objections that can be raised against MAL from the perspective of (the ideals underlying) a liberal rule of law.

II. Murdoch's Moral Philosophy: An Introduction

Highly influenced by the work of Heidegger and Wittgenstein, Murdoch takes a phenomenological approach to morality in that she tries to go back 'to the things themselves',[4] to make sense of the first-person experience, of the lived experience of moral life.[5] It is on the basis of this perspective that she claims, both in an empirical and a normative sense, that 'vision' plays a key role in our moral lives.[6]

She juxtaposes her vision-based account of the moral life with those accounts that envisage morality as a 'series of overt choices which take place in a series of specifiable situations', such as utilitarianism and Kantianism.[7] These theories falsely ignore that it is one's vision, rather than a 'free-floating' detached reason, that largely determines the choices that one makes. Murdoch: 'Man is not a combination of an impersonal rational thinker and a personal will. He is a unified being who sees and who desires in accordance with what he sees.'[8] In support of this claim, Murdoch uses the image of a magnetic field to describe the way the world imposes itself compellingly on the will of an agent.[9]

For Murdoch, however, vision is not merely a crucial explanatory factor for the actual choices that people make; it is also a vital and prominent moral capacity independent of these choices. As she puts it: 'The moral life … is something that goes on continually, not something that is switched off in between the occurrences of explicit moral choices.'[10]

In addition to these claims based on her philosophy of mind, Murdoch's account of vision also has a highly normative dimension. For this morally-implicated

[4] Iris Murdoch (2012).

[5] By 'phenomenological approach to morality', I have in mind an approach that is committed to what Hegel, Husserl and Heidegger meant by getting back 'to the things themselves'. For Murdoch's discussion of Heidegger see Murdoch (2012), 93–114. See for this point also Bagnoli (2012).

[6] For a critical and illuminating discussion of Murdoch's use of different visual metaphors, see Blum (2012).

[7] Murdoch (1997), 77.

[8] Ibid, 332.

[9] Ibid, 200–01.

[10] Ibid, 329. See also Murdoch (1992), 297, 303.

account of vision[11] – which I will here call *moral perception* – Murdoch drew inspiration from Simone Weil's concept of *attention*.[12] In Weil she found, inter alia, the idea that to perceive *adequately* is not directly under one's control, or a matter of simply opening one's eyes, or directing one's attention. Rather, as Murdoch puts it: '[I]t is a *task* to come to see the world as it is.'[13]

Murdoch's idea, that perceiving adequately in the moral domain is a matter of hard work and discipline, hinges on her pessimistic conception of the moral ability of average human beings. Influenced by Weil, but also by Plato's moral psychology, and to some extent by the work of Freud,[14] she holds that most people find themselves in a state of illusion due to the influence of the 'fat relentless ego'.[15] Due to their childish, egocentric need for security, stability and reassurance, they have difficulty seeing moral reality for what it is: contingent, ambiguous and largely obscure. As Murdoch states: 'We are anxiety ridden animals. Our minds are continually active, fabricating an anxious, usually self-preoccupied, often falsifying veil which partially conceals the world.'[16]

Indeed, Murdoch's account of moral perception is largely a negative one in that it entails, if anything, that people must try to 'break the barriers of egoism'.[17] In so doing, they become emotionally mature and thereby able to genuinely face the complex nature of the real – in particular the unique reality of other people. However, in addition to this negative requirement, moral perception also requires the possession of a loving attitude, an empathic bearing towards other people that allows one to see them as unique individuals with their own needs.[18]

As moral perception is concerned with grasping *external* reality, Murdoch emphasises the vital role of the imagination in moral life.[19] Moral imagination is 'the ability to picture what is quite other, especially to picture and realise, make real to oneself, the existence and being of other people'.[20] For instance, it allows one to get a sense of what it means to be 'unemployed, persecuted, or very poor'.[21] Whereas fantasy is a mechanical, deluded, egoistic and predominantly

[11] For illuminating discussions of the specific terminology that Murdoch uses to distinguish between what Lawrence Blum has dubbed 'a morally-implicated visual term' and a 'non-morally-implicated one', see Holland (1998) and Blum (2012).

[12] Murdoch reviewed the Notebooks of Simone Weil and, as Broackes observes, 'more or less every part of it was adopted by Murdoch into her own philosophy'. See Broackes (2012), 20.

[13] Murdoch (1999), 375.

[14] Murdoch emphasises that she is not a 'Freudian', yet she does endorse both his 'realistic and detailed picture of the fallen man' and the idea that 'much of human conduct is moved by mechanical energy of an egocentric kind'. See ibid, 341–42. Several similar passages can be found in Murdoch's oeuvre: eg Murdoch (1992), 296, 322 and 331.

[15] Murdoch (1999), 342.

[16] Ibid, 369.

[17] Murdoch (1992), 297.

[18] See ibid 301, 317, 354 and 374.

[19] Murdoch (1999), 11, 255 and 292–94.

[20] Murdoch (1992), 322.

[21] Ibid.

self-enclosing activity, creative imagination according to Murdoch is 'truthful and free'.[22]

Notably, in this context Murdoch stresses the resemblance between (good) art and morality. Acknowledging that living a good life might in the end be more difficult than making good art, she claims that a good novel and the moral life are both the outcome of imagination as opposed to (selfish) fantasy.[23] 'We are all artists', she states:[24] both the artist and the good man have the ability 'to see the other thing, what one might call, nature, reality, the world'.[25] Good art and a good person share that they both seek 'not to escape the world but to join it'.[26]

Murdoch, in addition, warns us that using one's moral imagination can be a form of 'playing with fire' as it may be difficult to distinguish this activity from mere fantasy.[27] Moral imagination includes *counter*factual thinking, ways of freely expanding and broadening one's 'ordinary' take on situations or persons and as such always risks to escape the 'here and now'.[28]

We can now see why, according to Murdoch, moral life with its prominent role for moral perception consists of a complex interplay between activity and passivity. Passivity, because at important moments of choice the world is, to a large degree, already 'fabricated' when we come to look at it and we will be likely to respond in a particular way.[29] In these situations, we cannot change our perception simply by an act of 'pure' will, in the same way that one cannot stop being in love or feeling resentment merely by choosing to do so.[30] Hence, for Murdoch at important moments of choice, whether we act rightly is often not under one's *direct* control.[31]

The active dimension of moral life according to Murdoch predominantly lies in the attempt to gradually gain control over the 'forces' within us. As she puts it: '[W]e can change what we are, but not quickly or easily …'[32] Moral perception is a form of moral freedom in that it is the outcome of this long, slow and difficult process of personal transformation, of liberating oneself from a deluded,

[22] Ibid, 321.

[23] Murdoch (1992), 333. Murdoch has been highly influential on scholarship that examines the (close) relationship between morality and literature. Martha Nussbaum, for instance, draws on Murdoch when developing the claim that the good novel is a paradigm of moral activity. See eg Nussbaum (1990).

[24] Murdoch (1992), 322.

[25] Ibid, 255.

[26] Ibid, 374. See also Liao and Gendler (2019).

[27] Murdoch (1999), 11.

[28] 'The difficulty is to keep the attention fixed upon the real situation and to prevent it from returning surreptitiously to the self with consolations of self-pity, resentment, fantasy and despair.' Ibid, 375.

[29] Murdoch (1999), 200.

[30] Ibid, 345.

[31] Eg Murdoch (1999), 375. 'We act rightly "when the time comes" not out of strength of will but out of the quality of our usual attachments and with the kind of energy and discernment which we have available.'

[32] Murdoch (1992), 325.

infantile perspective.[33] As such, for Murdoch moral perception is emphatically also an expression of virtue – of excellence of character that allows one to have access to reality, to truth.[34]

Murdoch famously substantiates her understanding of moral perception and, relatedly, of moral progress by the fictive example of M. M is a mother who bears hostility toward D, her daughter-in-law. M considers D to be 'unpolished', 'lacking in dignity and refinement', and 'tiresomely juvenile, and brusque'.[35] Yet, because M is an intelligent and well-intentioned woman, she decides to 'look again' and give D 'careful and just attention'.[36]

Murdoch's discussion of M. bears a resemblance to a phenomenon that Wittgenstein calls 'aspect-seeing', the activity of 'seeing something as something', an activity that sometimes leads to 'aspect-change' (*Aspektwechseln*) – a different way of seeing an object or person.[37] There has been no change in M.'s external world, and she has not been the victim of a visual illusion. Yet, as a result of her changing attitude – of her adoption of a more 'loving' attitude – M comes to see other aspects of D's behaviour.[38] That is, 'D. is discovered to be not vulgar but refreshingly simple, not undignified but spontaneous, not noisy but gay, not tiresomely juvenile but delightfully youthful, and so on'.[39] M takes up the task that, according to Murdoch, any morally responsible agent should be committed to: '[T]o try to see justly, to overcome prejudice, to avoid temptation, to control and curb imagination, to direct reflection.'[40]

Importantly, for Murdoch M's inner activity is in itself a moral achievement regardless of the outcome. For this reason, she stipulates that D is either absent or dead.[41] It illustrates that much of what characterises one's moral life and a moral person does not happen at important moments of choice, but somewhere in between.[42]

Yet, at the same time, this kind of 'inner activity' ('the task of attention goes on all the time') is precisely the kind of moral work that according to Murdoch will be

[33] Murdoch (1999), 331.

[34] Ibid, 284. For this reason, Murdoch's moral philosophy can be characterised as a vision-based account of virtue (see eg Murdoch 1999, 375), but also as a virtue-based account of moral vision. As to the latter, Murdoch for instance stresses the importance of compassion, courage and humility for perceiving well. See eg Murdoch (1992), 324.

[35] Murdoch (1992), 313.

[36] Ibid.

[37] Wittgenstein (2009) [1953] para 129. Wittgenstein describes Jastrow's famous rabbit–duck illusion in which a rabbit or a duck can be seen. For a discussion of the relevance of Wittgenstein's idea of aspect-seeing for moral thought, see Agam-Segal (2018). For Murdoch's critical discussion of these passages in Wittgenstein, see Murdoch (1992), 277–83.

[38] Murdoch (1999), 317.

[39] Ibid, 313.

[40] Ibid.

[41] Ibid.

[42] Ibid, 80–81.

likely to improve the quality of one's responses in the outer world.[43] This is what is implied when stating that 'true vision occasions right conduct.'[44]

The example of M brings us to another defining element of Murdoch's moral philosophy: the intimate connection between moral perception and (using) language. As she puts it: 'How we see our situation is itself, already, a moral activity, and one which is, for better as well as worse, "made" by linguistic processes.'[45] More specifically, her account of moral perception is inextricably linked to the vital role she assigns to thick ethical values (or what she calls normative-descriptive, specialised or secondary value words), concepts such as those we came across in M's description of D: '[V]ulgar', 'spontaneous', 'noisy'.[46] Murdoch emphatically demarcates the practical importance of thick value concepts from the limited practical use of thinner concepts such as 'right' or 'good'.[47] Due to their abstract and allegedly a priori character, these concepts are less helpful for grasping the moral bearing of the persons and situations one is confronted with.

Thick value concepts, by contrast, do give substance to moral perception because, characteristically, they contain a descriptive as well as a normative element.[48] They are, as Murdoch puts it, 'patently tied on to the world', thereby enabling agents, in a more or less pre-reflective way, to perceive an evaluative landscape and to respond accordingly.[49] It is for this very reason that Murdoch stresses that we should 'protect the precision of these secondary moral words, exercise them and keep them fit'.[50]

Indeed, following the later Wittgenstein, Murdoch stresses that the meaning of these thick ethical values largely depends on the way they are commonly used

[43] Murdoch (1999), 334, stating that 'those little peering efforts of imagination have such cumulative results'. See for this point also: ibid, 375.

[44] Murdoch (1999), 353.

[45] Murdoch (1992), 315. As Bagnoli (2012, 221) puts it: 'According to Murdoch, what is distinctive of live individuals is that they perpetually engage in the activity of reassessing, redefining, and redescribing reality.'

[46] Murdoch (1999), 324 and 333. The introduction of 'thick ethical concepts' is generally accredited to Bernard Williams. However, Williams was, in this regard, greatly inspired by a seminar organised by Iris Murdoch and Philippa Foot in the 1950s. See Williams (1985), 218 n 7 and Broackes (2012), 15. For an illuminating discussion of the role of thick ethical concepts in Murdoch's work, see Diamond (1996).

[47] Murdoch (1999), 82, 333.

[48] Williams (1985), 129 describes this point as follows: Thick concepts 'seem to express a union of fact and value. The way these notions are applied is determined by what the world is like (for instance, by how someone has behaved), and yet, at the same time, their application usually involves a certain valuation of the situation.'

[49] Again, this is one of the reasons for Murdoch's scepticism of Kantian and utilitarian normative theories of morality: They largely rely on the normative role of thin concepts. For instance, she states: 'We were too impressed by words when we assumed that the word "good" covered a single concept which was the centre of morality. We were not impressed enough when we neglected less general moral words such as "true", "brave", "free", "sincere", which are the bearers of very important ideas.' Murdoch (1999), 73.

[50] Murdoch (1992), 327.

in everyday life, embedded as they are in 'forms of life' – that is, socio-material contexts in which these concepts make sense.[51] Hence, for moral life and moral perception to flourish, such social-cultural contexts, too, must be kept in place. According to Murdoch, '[u]ses of words by persons grouped round a common object is a central and vital human activity'.[52]

Besides this conventional dimension, the use of thick value concepts has a highly individual and personal component. Their application is always intimately linked with one's personal history and background.[53] Indeed, as the example of M illustrates: Murdoch sees the ability to adequately use thick value concepts as a function of the moral progress one has made during one's life.[54] At the same time, the practice of reflectively using these concepts is also indispensable for making moral progress. '"Becoming better" is a process involving an exercise and refinement of moral vocabulary and sensibility', Murdoch states.[55]

Importantly, this claim is far from an assertion that the meaning of thick value concepts is inherently arbitrary or exclusively subjective.[56] It does, however, suggest that striving towards objectivity, for Murdoch, is not tantamount to taking up an *im*personal point of view. The conceptual content of a notion such as 'courage' or 'cruelty' is formed by (partaking in) social practices and by means of a situated and thus inherently personal process of applying them.[57] This is what Murdoch means when she states that moral terms 'must be treated as concrete universals'.[58] The way they are used reveals something of the person applying them.[59] In this context, Murdoch also emphasises that the learning process required for grasping 'reality' must be understood as endless. That is, thick concepts are 'infinitely to be learned' in the sense that the process of applying them has no 'point of arrival'.[60] As one interpreter of Murdoch has put it: '[C]orrectness

[51] Murdoch (1999), 97. Note that Wittgenstein himself never explicitly defined this notion of 'forms of life'. Pitkin (1973, 132) describes its general significance as follows: '[H]uman life as we live and observe it is not just a random, continuous flow, but displays recurrent patterns, regularities, characteristic ways of doing and being, of feeling and acting, of speaking and interacting. Because they are patterns, regularities, configurations, Wittgenstein calls them *forms*; and because they are patterns in the fabric of human existence and activity on earth, he calls them forms of *life*.'

[52] Murdoch (1999), 325.

[53] Ibid., 322.

[54] See eg ibid, 324 and 352.

[55] Ibid, 324.

[56] For this point, see also Clarke (2018).

[57] See Bagnoli (2012).

[58] Murdoch (1999), 322–23.

[59] See Clarke (2018, 46) who neatly illustrates the plausibility of this idea by using the example of an accomplished musician. A jazz player 'puts a personal stamp on the tunes he covers and *thereby* illuminates those tunes. [T]his is a way – in jazz, *the* way – of realizing the music itself. Coltrane's inimitable rendition of "My Favorite Things" taught us about the song, extended our sense of its possibilities and emotional reach. He lit up the song precisely by making it his own … To see moral concepts as concrete universals, in the relevant sense, is to see them as akin to established tunes that we must realize in our own special way if we are to successfully realize them at all.'

[60] Ibid.

in practical matters admits of infinite gradations; even the agent who acted well can ask how she might have acted better.'[61]

For Murdoch, thick value concepts also play a vital role in justifying to others why one sees what one sees and, on that account, also in convincing them of the rightness of one's response. One way of explaining one's negative evaluation of a particular behaviour would be, for instance, to say that it is crude. Thick value concepts are useful tools for giving a truthful account of reality to others, one that moral agents should use skilfully. Here again Murdoch sees an important resemblance with the artist, in particular with the novelist who tries to communicate the real in a highly skilful and creative way.[62] For it will necessarily depend on the context in what way one can best describe what one holds to be true.[63]

However – also in a way similar to artists – during this communicative and creative endeavour moral agents will also experience (discursive) limitations on what they can explain to others.[64] Murdoch emphasises that one's choices and vision can never be exhaustively explained, articulated or justified.[65] Due to the 'inexhaustible richness' of the practical world, but also to our own obscurity, our choices and vision are always more than any explanation can cover.[66] Hence, for Murdoch, being morally mature means that one can cope with the fact that sometimes, as she puts it, 'we are moved in a manner which we are at a loss to explain'.[67]

Both moral philosophy and moral agents should also take this into account in cases of moral disagreement.[68] Not surprisingly, Murdoch does not conceive of such disagreements – for instance, over the question of whether an interaction between two children amounts to 'bullying' – as controversies over the application of publicly accessible concepts to a well-defined, value free constellation of facts. Rather, she understands such disagreements as often the result of the fact that we 'see different worlds'.[69] For Murdoch, in view of the embodied and situated nature of one's vision, such disagreements require, if anything, creative and skilful form-free *persuasion* that takes into account the specific features of one's opponent

[61] Clarke (2010), 288.

[62] Murdoch (1992), 315.

[63] Murdoch (1999), 53. ('It is the context which decides what is the specific utterance of an experience.')

[64] Ibid.

[65] Murdoch (1999, 74) states: 'There may be no deep structure. This is the lesson of Wittgenstein and one which, incidentally, has not been taken enough to heart by those who want to reduce morality to a single formula.'

[66] Ibid, 53, 90.

[67] Ibid, 58.

[68] Ibid, 91.

[69] Ibid, 82. Clarke (2010, 287), thereby drawing on McDowell, has phrased this point as follows: 'In the absence of knock-down arguments, phrases such as "You have to see it" mark the point at which discursive justifications have *run out* … This point may never be reached in a given exchange, or it may take a long time to reach it.'

and the concrete context in which the disagreement takes place. How one can best try to convince others of one's own take on the situation is a matter of situational appreciation, and may even lead to one remaining silent.[70]

III. A Murdochian Approach to Legal Decision-Making: A Tentative Sketch

In the section below I explore what a Murdochian approach to legal decision-making (MAL) amounts to. Again, this is a tentative sketch: Murdoch herself has hardly written about the implications of her moral philosophy for the public domain; and, within legal theory, the concept of 'vision' has so far rarely been explored.[71]

It goes without saying that MAL is strongly at odds with the idea, widely embraced in legal theory, that the moral core of legal decision-making essentially boils down to legal judgments. These judgements are then understood as the application of (morally defensible) legal rules and principles to a well-defined, value-free constellation of facts.[72] MAL, by contrast, holds that the judge's vision plays a key role in coming to grips with the moral nature of legal decision-making.[73] This is based on the premise that judges, like other human beings, do not see a value-neutral world when confronted with a legal case; rather, they face an evaluative landscape that 'invites' them to respond, for instance, by addressing certain comments to a litigating party during a court session or when writing a judgment.

In addition, MAL holds that this evaluative landscape is largely influenced by a judge's prior 'beings and doings'. Hence, to know why a legal decision is as it is, or why a judge uses a certain rule in a particular way, requires knowledge of his entire life history. In this respect, MAL shows a strong resemblance to legal realism, most notably to the work of Jerome Frank – the enfant terrible of legal realism, who emphasised that the person of the judge is the 'pivotal factor' in the

[70] In this regard, see also McDowell (1998, 85) who – I think fully in line with Murdoch – states: 'One exploits contrivances similar to those one exploits in other areas where the task is to back up the injunction "See it like this": helpful juxtapositions of cases, descriptions with carefully chosen terms and carefully placed emphasis, and the like. (Compare, for instance, what one might do and say to someone who says "Jazz sounds to me like a mess, a mere welter of uncoordinated noise".' For this citation, see also Clarke (2010), 287.

[71] For exceptions, see eg Solum (2003), Amaya (2011), Michelon (2018) and Van Domselaar (2018). For discussions of (elements of) Murdoch's moral philosophy in relation to law see Del Mar (2016) and White (2020) (chapter six in this volume).

[72] For a discussion of this 'fact-evasiveness' within legal theory, see Van Domselaar (2018).

[73] It is important to note that MAL does emphatically not defend the claim that judicial perception is the *only* dimension of judicial agency that merits attention in an account of legal decision-making. It does claim that it is a central dimension of judicial agency.

administration of law.[74] Indeed, in view of its empirically loaded assumptions, MAL can be said to be naturalistic. That is, its understanding of the workings of a judge's mind is corroborated by contemporary legal–psychological findings that put in perspective the role of explicit legal principles and rules in actual judgements, stressing the influence of pre-reflective thought on the act of judging.[75]

As to its normative dimension, MAL holds that the crucial difference between a good and a bad judge is that the former possesses a capacity for *judicial perception*. Judicial perception is a species of moral perception that allows a judge, because of his excellence of character, to have access to 'legal reality'. This in any case includes the ability to perceive the 'otherness' of the parties involved and the complex, ambiguous and unique nature of the case while at the same time making adequate use of the available legal resources.[76]

A judge who possesses this capacity is a virtuous judge who has, if anything, freed himself of egoistic, escapist fantasies and projections, such as all kinds of 'scripts' or frameworks that impede him from facing the complexity and ambiguity of a legal case. For instance, from the perspective of MAL, a bad judge is arguably one who 'portray[s] the chosen decision as certain, singularly correct, and as determined inevitably by the legal materials'.[77] Such a decision would likely be an affront, to use Murdoch's words, to the 'inexhaustible detail of the world, the endlessness of the task of understanding, the importance of not assuming that one has got individuals and situations "taped"'.[78]

MAL characterises a good judge as someone who maintains an attitude of loving kindness and empathy towards the parties involved, even, and perhaps in particular, if the litigants or defendants are very different from himself. Such a judge does not restrict empathic responses to the private domain; rather, he integrates these into his professional viewpoint, allowing them to 'push' in a certain direction or toward a certain outcome.[79] Importantly, these outcomes may – but do not necessarily – consist of an alleviation of the suffering of the parties involved.[80]

[74] See Frank (2009) [1931]. Interestingly, (the philosophical claims underlying) Frank's legal realism reveal(s), on more points, resemblances with MAL. This is an important topic in itself which, for reasons of scope, will not be fully addressed in this chapter, but will merely be touched upon incidentally.

[75] Eg Simon (1998); Guthrie, Rachlinski and Wistrich (2001); Maroney (2011). These empirical findings, but also the views of the legal realists, are highly relevant for assessing the merits of the criticism that is sometimes raised against virtue-based accounts of law and legal decision-making for allegedly allowing for subjectivity and biases to play a central role in legal-decision making. I think that a realistic empirically informed view on the nature of legal decision-making leads to the conclusion that rule-based approaches to legal-decision-making are (even) more vulnerable to allowing for caprice, arbitrariness and biases on the part of the judge to influence legal decision-making.

[76] So conceived, it could be stated that MAL defends a vision-based account of judicial virtue.

[77] Simon and Scurich (2013). For a discussion of the (many) ways in which a (constitutional) judge can fail to live up to this Murdochian ideal, see White (2020) (chapter six in this volume).

[78] Murdoch (1999), 87.

[79] See also Henderson (1987); Bandes (2009); Maroney (2014); Van Domselaar (2015), Del Mar (2017) and, in this volume, White (2020) and Zipursky (2020) who argue that empathy should play a constitutive role in our understanding of law and legality (chapters six and four). For an outspoken critique of empathetic judging in law, see Massaro (2015).

[80] Henderson (1987) and Bandes (2009). See for this point also Kind (2020) (chapter ten in this volume).

Empathy is constitutive of the judicial viewpoint, and judicial perception requires a certain level of emotional maturity on the part of the individual judge. Because of this, the personal and the professional are intimately linked in MAL. Accordingly, the scope of evaluation of legal decision-making is not limited to actual legal judgments and the reasons offered to support them. It includes all the data that can sensibly be understood to express the judge's vision. On the basis of MAL, we have, for instance, reason to criticise a judge who during informal gatherings – be it in a professional or a personal setting – regularly expresses a cold-hearted attitude towards the fate of immigrants, or who makes sexist jokes, or who is keen to stress that he has never been troubled by any of his decisions. These spontaneous utterances are all relevant 'data' – expressions of the judge's vision. In this case, they indicate that the evaluative landscape the judge sees when confronted with a legal case may be distorted due to a failure of vision.

This point brings us to the difference between a judge's *judicial* perception as opposed to the *moral* perception of a private person, and in particular to the role that legal discourse plays in understanding the difference. In this regard, it is important to note that, although Murdoch pays relatively little attention to the public realm, she does emphasise the importance of demarcating private and public life: '[W]e do not live the world of politics in the way we live our private lives.'[81] According to Murdoch, public life differs from private life most notably because it is characterised by certain firmly ensconced 'axioms', such as the ideas of equality, dignity and inviolable rights.[82] In addition, Murdoch acknowledges the importance of conformity to generally accepted rules and principles in a liberal democratic society.[83] Yet, this 'morality of axioms', she states, 'needs the intuitive control of a more widely reflective and general morality. In a good society these ways of thinking, while always in tension, know their roles and places, and when they have rights against each other.'[84]

Within MAL codified legal rules, legal principles and the aforementioned axioms do have an important role to play in its account of a legal order. At the same time, it takes Murdoch's naturalistic view on (moral) agency and the inherent role of perception therein seriously. As a vision-based account of legal decision-making it rejects the idea that legal norms, principles and rules are to be understood as context-independent norms that can directly guide the judge's decisions. Legal resources do have a practical role to play in constituting and forming the judge's perception, that is, to the extent that they have a 'contour' – a culturally, socially and historically mediated meaning that more or less spontaneously arises in confrontation with a constellation of facts. A judge may, for instance, have to decide whether

[81] Murdoch (1992), 386.

[82] According to Murdoch (ibid, 365), these axioms are 'isolated unsystematic moral insights which arise out of and refer to a general conception of human nature such as civilized societies have gradually generated'.

[83] See eg ibid, 362.

[84] Murdoch (1999), 362.

a social interaction in the workplace is an instance of 'sexual intimidation' or just a 'friendly tap on the back', or whether certain utterances defaming a minority group amount to 'hate speech'. Insofar as these thick legal value concepts have been instilled in the judge by means of social, institutional and professional 'practices of attention', they spontaneously arise, possibly leading to a legal inclination regarding the adequate response.[85]

The way these legal concepts are used will – in addition to their conventional meaning – also reveal and manifest something highly personal, mediated as they are through the consciousness of the individual judge. Again, MAL understands legal thought as at least partly also reflecting the life history of a judge, but without this necessarily amounting to mere caprice or biases. Legal objectivity does emphatically not require that a judge takes up an *im*personal point of view. As Edlin has put it: 'the recognition that the subject who authors a judgment must draw upon her experiences and values in articulating the judgement does not defeat the object of producing a judgement that can be evaluated and validated as an abiding contribution to our community's law'.[86]

By implication, within MAL legal disagreements between judges (eg between lower and higher courts) are seen as possible indications that the judges in question have conflicting (value-laden) 'visions' of the legal case, which may have their roots in the respective personal backgrounds of the judges involved. Such disagreements cannot then be solved by merely making a reference to an alleged publicly accessible legal rule, principle or precedent that is to be applied to the 'naked' facts of the case. Instead, they require that judges possess the ability to use the available discursive materials creatively so as to persuade those who are involved, including the judicial community itself.

Indeed, MAL also assigns an important role to legal rules, norms and precedents as discursive resources that judges can use to motivate their decision. This practice of reason-giving is (ideally) also an expression of the judge's perceptive sensitivity and skilfulness as to how to use the available discursive materials in the most effective and truthful way.[87] For a judge to 'truthfully' express himself when dealing with a legal case requires a situational appreciation. He may, for instance, express himself with regard to tone and style in one way during a court-session when facing the concrete parties involved, and in another way in the written sentence.

In this regard, a good judge might also qualify as a poet-judge who, like a poet, possesses the knowledge and ability to imaginatively and skilfully work with and within the constraints posed by (legal) language.[88] Such an emotionally mature

[85] I owe the term 'legal inclination' to Crowe (2011). For discussions of (the role of) thick concepts in law, see eg Wang and Solum (2013), Enoch and Toh (2013) and Van Domselaar (2018).

[86] Edlin (2016), 122.

[87] Below, in section IV, I will further discuss the extent to which MAL can accommodate for this reason-giving dimension of legal decision-making.

[88] For this idea of the poet-judge, see also Nussbaum (1995).

judge would in any case also instinctively honour the fact that not all the factors that play a role in forming his response to a legal case can be exhaustively articulated and that, as Jerome Frank puts it, '[the] decisional process, like the artistic process, involves feelings that words cannot ensnare'.[89]

In Murdochian vein, I will now further expound the contours of MAL by giving an example of how an individual judge could make progress and sharpen his vision.[90] A judge (J) presided over a case involving a young woman (W). W was nineteen years old and worked at the only supermarket in a small, predominantly orthodox Christian village. W had been prosecuted for killing her newborn baby. As she was well known in the village, the case upset the local community tremendously. In court, W gave a detailed account of how she had attempted to conceal her pregnancy from her boyfriend, parents, colleagues and fellow villagers and how she had managed to hide the corpse in her parents' attic for two years.

On the basis of W's declaration during the police interrogation and the court hearing, J found her to be rather 'cold-hearted'. W had given birth to the baby in seclusion and killed it with her bare hands. Therefore, J saw W as a woman who had operated in a 'callous' and 'calculating' manner; after all, she seemed to possess an almost 'super-human degree of self-control', because she had hardly made any noise while giving birth to avoid attracting attention from her family. J also saw her as 'irresponsible' for not having used contraceptives or for not opting for abortion. During the court's deliberations, J convinced the other judges on the panel to find W guilty of murder and to impose the maximum penalty.

As a highly professional, self-critical and well-intentioned judge, J continued to ponder the case long after handing down the decision. She tried to think of W empathically and lovingly and as part of this 'aspect-seeing' reflected upon the quality of her earlier, perceptive judicial deliverances. Perhaps she then felt that her vision of W and her deeds had been largely influenced by her own projections: That is, that she had projected too much agency on W, keeping her at a remove because, unconsciously, she did not wish to confront her own ambivalent feelings about vulnerability and about being a mother.

If she were to become fully aware of the extent to which her own emotional state had blocked her from grasping W's reality, J might very well start to see W and her deed differently. She might, for instance, as part of an 'aspect-change' arrive at the conclusion that W had not killed the baby and hidden the corpse in her parents' house out of 'calculation', but had only done so out of 'utter despair'. W's deeds would then not be 'cold-hearted', 'calculated' or 'callous' but rather a sign of 'helplessness' and 'loneliness'. After all, she expected that her pregnancy would lead to severe criticism on the part of her Christian family and fellow villagers.

[89] Frank (2009) [1931], 73.

[90] This example is based on a real legal case in which the trial court and appellate court arrived at completely different interpretations of the facts.

From the perspective of MAL, it would be through this kind of (sometimes painful) pondering and self-scrutiny that J could make progress, both as a person and as a judge.[91] Like Murdoch's example of M, the example of J illustrates that we have reason to praise J for her change of perception as a way of making moral progress – independently of the impact this has in the outside world. This change is in itself an expression of judicial goodness.

But, in addition, MAL holds that the moral progress made by J is also likely to have a positive effect on J's future legal decisions. Her increased ability to not let her own experiences with vulnerability and with motherhood cloud her vision, will possibly improve her 'responsiveness to normative significance'[92] and, as such, will better enable her to spontaneously 'hit' the right response in future cases.

The example also shows that MAL does not endorse an account of legal decision-making that justifies a practice in which '[j]udges too often rely on their intuitive, emotional reactions without subjecting them to "the light of intense study" that is supposed to produce rational choices'.[93] MAL indeed denies that reflection – understood as an activity of detached, disembodied, free-floating 'legal reason' – could be of direct action-guiding value to a judge when facing a legal case.[94] But at the same time it does assign an important role to a more engaged form of reflection, which does not occur 'in detachment from [the judge's] deepest sense of self'.[95] J tried to think lovingly and imaginatively of W, reflecting upon the quality of her earlier perceptive judicial utterances. Indeed, MAL assumes not only an appropriate degree but also *different* degrees of reflection and, relatedly, self-consciousness during all kinds of judicial activity in which judicial perception plays a role.[96] Think for instance of a judge's communications at trial with litigating parties and their lawyers, or his ponderings about how to legally qualify certain facts.[97]

Certainly, in order for MAL to be feasible further thoughts must be spent on how judicial perception could flourish within the context of the judiciary and more specifically that of legal proceedings. For instance, during these proceedings,

[91] For the importance of an engaged, post facto way of acknowledging loss for making moral progress see Van Domselaar (2017) and Van Domselaar (2018).

[92] Rietveld (2010), 183, 87, 202.

[93] Guthrie, Rachlinski and Wistrich (2001). For the view that perception-based accounts of judicial virtue indeed advocate immediate apprehension at the expense of reflection see eg Amaya (2019).

[94] Indeed, Murdoch's account of moral agency has been criticised by Blum for being 'over-enamoured of situations in which the agent can *immediately* see both the need for her to act and what act she should perform'. Blum (2012), 323.

[95] Clarke (2012). Brackets are my addition. MAL is thus strongly at odds with accounts of law founded on the dichotomy between emotion and reason, or 'the heart versus the head'. The legal viewpoint, at least when it is the result of judicial perception, is not at odds with 'having' emotions, but rather comprises emotions that are carefully thought through. See for this point Maroney (2015).

[96] As already hinted at above, MAL indeed shows some resemblance to a 'law-as-craft' approach in the way it is able to make sense of the idea of unreflective judicial action. For this point, I am indebted to Del Mar (2011) fn 20.

[97] A strong fictive example of such an engaged kind of reflective judicial activity that lies at the heart of what MAL understands as judicial perception can be found in McEwan's *The Children Act*. See Van Domselaar (2018).

the interaction between the judge and litigating parties is typically – and to a large degree – 'off-line' or indirect. As regards the actual, real-time court sessions, they are a one-off encounter. This is, ceteris paribus, in strong contrast to a family relationship, such as Murdoch's example of the relationship between a mother and her daughter-in-law.

Moreover, in the context of court proceedings, there is often more than one person involved. Can we expect judges – of whom MAL demands an attitude of loving kindness – to 'apply their hearts and minds to every litigant in any deep empathic sense'?[98]

At pains of projecting too much moral activity onto encounters between judges and citizens involved in legal proceedings, MAL must hold that in this specific setting the conditions for a meaningful 'context of attention' sufficiently apply.[99] Thereto it must further develop the concept of a 'context of attention' for the judicial domain so that it can offer guidance in (critically) assessing current developments within the judiciary, such as digitalisation, increasing time-constraints, and the rise of other efficiency arrangements such as the division of labour between judges and law clerks. It may well be that these are impediments for the judge to actually be able to perceive well in an individual case.

The idea of a legal proceeding as a 'context of attention' would ideally also be functional for identifying 'best practices' within the judiciary. In this regard, an interesting question would be whether MAL would welcome the range of initiatives that seek to bring judges closer to citizens, for instance by making legal proceedings more informal and by securing that courts are firmly embedded in local communities and neighbourhoods.

Finally, it may not come as a surprise that one of the central questions within MAL is *how* to foster judges to become more unselfish, emotionally mature, humble and just. Or, to phrase it in Murdoch's terms, which techniques are most suitable 'for the purification and reorientation of an energy which is naturally selfish, in such a way that when moments of choice arrive we shall be sure of acting rightly'?[100] For instance, should all judges as part of the process of 'unselfing' undergo psychoanalysis as judge Jerome Frank suggested and himself did?[101] Or should they, in addition, enhance their imagination by contemplating great art? For according to Murdoch it is great art that 'teaches us how real things can be looked at and loved without being seized and used, without being appropriated into the greedy organism of the self'.[102]

Drawing on Murdoch's pessimistic account of the moral abilities of the average human being, MAL emphasises that to become a good or a better judge is a difficult, slow, piecemeal process that, if anything, starts long before one enters the

[98] Massaro (2015), fn 99.
[99] Murdoch (1999), 326.
[100] Murdoch (1999), 344.
[101] Cp Posner (2006), 1066. Posner himself finds this a 'ridiculous suggestion'.
[102] Murdoch (1999), 353.

profession. For this process the (aspirant) judge is largely dependent on the extent to which social practices are available as ways to transcend one's narcissism, such as family life and other, in the words of psychoanalyst Winnicott, 'potential space' such as play, culture and art, in which 'roles and options can be tried out without real life stress'.[103]

How to decide which techniques and social practices will be conducive to this ideal is, of course, itself a complex task.[104] But, regardless of the outcome, the implications of MAL for the education and training of (aspirant) judges are quite radical. In any case, MAL is at odds with dominant accounts of professional morality, which embrace a marked distinction between the role and the person inhabiting that role.[105] MAL will, to some extent, promote *personal* transformation as a goal of one's professional training.

IV. Illiberal?

Now that we have a sense of the contours of MAL, this section discusses three objections that can be raised against MAL from the perspective of (the ideals underlying) a liberal rule of law.

It is widely held that in a liberal rule of law respect for individual citizens requires that legal judgments, as an exercise of state-power, are based upon publicly accessible reasons.[106] From this viewpoint a genuinely moral danger arises if one allows for legal decision-making, at least to some extent, to remain obscure and unexplained. Why should self-respecting and free citizens accept such decisions?[107] On this count, MAL must plead guilty as charged, at least insofar as it demands from both judges and citizens that they are able to live without the 'fantasy' of a final, justificatory, transparent scheme that 'goes all the way down'. In the end, judges can never *conclusively* argue why they perceive and legally qualify a constellation of facts as 'X' rather than as 'Y'. As Solum has put it: 'explanations must come to an end somewhere'.[108]

At the same time, MAL can take the liberal idea of respect for the rule of law to heart by trying to strike a balance between the need for public justification in

[103] As cited in Nussbaum (2013), 181.

[104] Note that these can be both legal and non-legal practices and techniques. For instance, the claim has been defended that the central value of doctrinal reasoning is that it entails a practice 'through which a decision maker turns away from her usual subjective point of view'. See Allen (2018).

[105] For influential critiques on this distinction, see Postema (1983) and Wolgast (1992).

[106] See eg Lyons (1984), Tamanaha (2004) and Waldron (2016).

[107] This point has been famously developed in Fuller's classic *The Morality of Law* by the allegory of king Rex. See Fuller (1969).

[108] Solum (2003), 201. For this reason, I do not think that MAL is sensitive to the critique that, for instance, Dare (1998) and also Elgin (2020) have voiced against virtue-ethical approaches to law as not being able to acknowledge the reason-giving dimension of legal practice. For a more general account of how a virtue-based approach to legal decision-making can account for the reason-giving dimension of adjudication see eg Amaya (2012) and Amaya (2019).

a liberal pluriform society on the one hand, and honouring the highly particular and thus inherently obscure and messy nature of decision-making on the other. In striking the right balance, Bernard Williams' idea of society as an *ethical federation* will prove instructive and consistent with Murdoch's thought.[109] In such a federation a state agency '[does] not try to justify what it is doing to everybody, or every possible person'.[110] According to Williams the more regulatory the activity of a state agency is and the larger the group that is affected, the more need there is for public justifications in general and abstract terms, at least in a pluriform society.

By contrast, public decision-making at a more 'local' or concrete level, in which primarily unique particulars are to be addressed, will be allowed more leniency to draw upon untheorised 'thicker' considerations and narratives as ways to also be meaningful and hence respectful for the concrete, affected citizen(s). Thus, as stated above, within MAL a good judge will know how to use appropriate styles of justification, depending among others on the (societal impact of the) actual decision, the parties who are involved and the composition of the relevant audience(s).[111]

Next, and closely related: it is a general requirement of a liberal rule of law that it 'allow[s] people to plan their activities with advance knowledge of its potential legal implications'.[112] Thus, or so is the idea, legal decisions must at least to a sufficient degree be foreseeable. However, within MAL the outcomes of legal proceedings will largely depend on how a particular judge perceives and qualifies the particularities of the concrete case and weighs the considerations that are pertinent for that case. What is more, within MAL it may well be that in similar cases two 'opposite' decisions can be right. For this reason this element of foreseeability might also be in jeopardy.

Indeed, MAL cannot account for the requirement of foreseeability, at least where the actual outcomes of legal decisions are concerned. However, it can honour this requirement regarding the kind of considerations that judges bring to bear upon the cases they are confronted with. Drawing upon thick legal value concepts judges are likely to use concepts with which citizens are familiar. Ideally, citizens can thus make 'sense' of the decisions of judges relatively easily, and as such they are able to relate to these decisions, also in terms of their own views on the matter. This shared social context that the judge brings to bear on his decisions adds to the predictability of legal decisions as regards the kinds of considerations that a judge will use and address.

[109] Williams (2005), 49–50 and Williams (1981).

[110] Williams (2005), 49.

[111] In distinguishing different types of justifications in legal sentences Cass Sunstein's conceptual framework may prove instructive. In Sunstein's typology the concept 'narrow' as opposed to 'wide' refers to the fact that a particular motivation is exclusively meant for the case at hand, whereas 'wide(r)' motivations have a broad(er) scope of application. In addition, 'shallow' in contrast with 'deep' means that the motivation remains largely untheorised, it does not refer to some underlying principle or rule. See Sunstein (2001), 3–23.

[112] Tamanaha (2004), 94.

Finally, from a liberal perspective it may also be questioned whether the value of equality is sufficiently protected within MAL. That is, it remains to be seen whether MAL, by the important role it assigns to moral *self*-scrutiny and 'unselfing' on the part of the individual judges, pays sufficient attention to the importance of dismantling *socially* or *conventionally* constructed biases, such as racism and sexism, that may influence the judge's perception.[113] Will the equal rights of citizens be sufficiently protected by judges who are well aware of how their personal idiosyncratic biography might influence their take on a situation, yet at the same time naively reproduce prevailing *social* 'illusions'. This concern resonates the criticism that Martha Nussbaum voiced: Murdoch's moral philosophy seems to 'lack interest in the political and social determinants of a moral vision, and in the larger social criticism that ought, one feels, to be a major element in the struggle against one's own defective tendencies'.[114]

This concern is particularly pertinent for MAL because of the central role it assigns to thick value concepts that, precisely because of their social embeddedness, are vulnerable to corruption and corrosion. Think, for instance, of the aforementioned judge who has to decide whether a particular social interaction in the workplace amounted to 'sexual harassment' as opposed to a 'friendly tap on the back'. It could well be that the conventional use of these concepts – as well as the relevant adjacent non-legal concepts that define a judge's vision – are permeated with sexist biases.

It is of course highly difficult for an individual judge to dismantle at will socially constructed 'fantasies' when confronted with a legal case, if these have already been inculcated during one's upbringing and social formation. For MAL to be able to meet this concern it, again, largely relies on the quality of formative background practices such as family life and educational practices being in place. These practices may form an antidote for the corruption or corrosion of thick value concepts. Indeed, for judicial perception to flourish, it would require that society at large, or at least its most important formative social practices, merit being labelled what Nussbaum felicitously dubbed a 'society of perceivers'.[115] MAL cannot but be intimately linked to a vision-based account of justice, an account that provides an answer to the question of what it means, in concrete terms, to – as Murdoch puts it – 'feel socially responsible about what in our society people always or never see'.[116]

[113] In response to the criticism – as for instance voiced by Nussbaum – that Murdoch pays insufficient attention to the social and political forces that may lead to immorality, Blum (2012), Clarke (2012), Lovibond (2011), Antonaccio (2012) and Hämäläinen (2015) have tried to interpret Murdoch's moral philosophy in a way that incorporates social criticism into the process of moral self-scrutiny.

[114] Nussbaum (2001).

[115] Nussbaum (1990), 101.

[116] Murdoch (1992), 329.

V. Conclusion

In the foregoing, I have expounded an approach to legal decision-making that is based on Murdoch's vision-based moral philosophy. Furthermore, I have confronted this approach with three concerns stemming from the perspective of (the ideals underlying) a liberal rule of law.

Admittedly, in this contribution, I have simply assumed rather than argued that there is no strict divide between moral life and legal life – indeed, that a bad person can never be a good judge. From the perspective of MAL, this is not the end of the story. It is simply where our inquiry must begin.

References

Agam-Segal, R (2018) 'Moral Thought in Wittgenstein: Clarity and Changes in Attitude' in R Agam-Segal and E Dain (eds) *Wittgenstein's Moral Thought* (New York and London, Routledge) 67.

Allen, J (2018) 'Doctrinal Reasoning as a Disruptive Practice' 6(2) *Journal of Law and Courts* 215.

Amaya, A (2011) 'Virtue and Reason in Law' in M Del Mar (ed) *New Waves in Philosophy of Law* (Hampshire, Palgrave Macmillan) 123.

Amaya, A (2012) 'The Role of Virtue in Legal Justification' in A Amaya and HL Ho (eds) *Law, Virtue and Justice* (Oxford, Hart Publishing) 51.

Amaya, A (2019) 'Virtuous Adjudication; or the Relevance of Judicial Character to Legal Interpretation' 40(1) *Statute Law Review* 87.

Antonaccio, M (2000) *Picturing the Human: The Moral Thought of Iris Murdoch* (New York/ Oxford, Oxford University Press).

Antonaccio, M (2012) *A Philosophy to Live By: Engaging* Iris Murdoch (New York/Oxford, Oxford University Press).

Antonaccio, M and Schweiker, W (eds) (1996) *Iris Murdoch and the Search for Human Goodness* (Chicago, University of Chicago Press).

Bagnoli, C (2012) 'The Exploration of Moral Life' in J Broackes (ed) *Iris Murdoch, Philosopher: A Collection of Essays* (Oxford, Oxford University Press) 197.

Bandes, S (2009) 'Empathetic Judging and the Rule of Law' *Cardozo Law Review. De Novo* 133.

Blum, L (1991) 'Moral Perception and Particularity' 101(4) *Ethics* 701.

Blum, L (2012) 'Visual Metaphors in Murdoch's Moral Philosophy' in J Broackes (ed) *Iris Murdoch, Philosopher A Collection of Essays* (Oxford, Oxford University Press) 307.

Broackes, J (ed) (2012) *Iris Murdoch, Philosopher: A Collection of Essays* (Oxford, Oxford University Press).

Browning, G (2018) *Why Iris Murdoch Matters: Making Sense of Experience in Modern Times* (London, Bloomsbury Publishing).

Clarke, B (2010) 'Virtue and Disagreement' 13(3) *Ethical Theory and Moral Practice* 273.

Clarke, B (2012) 'Iris Murdoch and the Prospects for Critical Moral Perception' in J Broackes (ed) *Iris Murdoch, Philosopher: A Collection of Essays* (Oxford, Oxford University Press) 227.

Clarke, B (2018) 'Virtue as Sensitivity' in NE Snow (ed) *The Oxford Handbook of Virtue* (Oxford, Oxford University Press) 35.

Crowe, J (2011) 'Pre-Reflective Law' in M Del Mar (ed) *New Waves in Philosophy of Law* (Basingstoke/New York, Palgrave MacMillan) 103.

Dare, T (1998) 'Virtue Ethics and Legal Ethics' 28 *Victoria University Wellington Law Review* 141.

Del Mar, M (2011) 'Introduction' in M Del Mar (*New Waves in Philosophy of Law* (Basingstoke/New York, Palgrave MacMillan) 1.

Del Mar, M (2016) 'The Education of Attention and Encounter in the Legal Academy' in Z Bankowski and M Del Mar (eds) *The Moral Imagination and the Legal Life: Beyond Text in Legal Education* (New York, Routledge) 33.

Del Mar, M (2017) 'Imagining by Feeling: a Case for Compassion in Legal Reasoning' 13(2) *International Journal of Law in Context* 143.

Diamond, C (1996) '"We Are Perpetually Moralists": Iris Murdoch, Fact, and Value' in M Antonaccio and W Schweiker (eds) *Iris Murdoch and the Search for Human Goodness* (Chicago, University of Chicago Press) 79.

Domselaar, van, I (2015) 'Moral Quality in Adjudication: On Judicial Virtues and Civic Friendship' 1 *Netherlands Journal of Legal Philosophy* 24.

Domselaar, van, I (2017) 'On Tragic Legal Choices' 11(2) *Law and Humanities* 184.

Domselaar, van, I (2018) 'The Perceptive Judge' 9(1) *Jurisprudence: An International Journal of Legal and Political Thought* 71.

Edlin, DE (2016) *Common Law Judging: Subjectivity, Impartiality and the Making of Law* (Ann Arbor, University of Michigan Press).

Elgin, CZ (2020) 'Impartiality and Legal Reasoning' in A Amaya and M Del Mar (eds) *Imagination, Virtue and Emotion in Law and Legal Reasoning* (Oxford, Hart Publishing).

Enoch, D and Toh, K (2013) 'Legal as a Thick Concept' in W Waluchow and S Sciaraffa (eds) *Philosophical Foundations of the Nature of Law* (Oxford, Oxford University Press) 257.

Frank, J (2009) [1931] *Law and the Modern Mind* (New Brunswick, Transaction Publishers).

Fuller, LL (1969) *The Morality of Law*. Revised Edition (New Haven, Yale University Press).

Guthrie, C, Rachlinski, JJ and Wistrich, AJ (2001) 'Inside the Judicial Mind' 86 *Cornell Law Review* 777.

Hämäläinen, N (2015) 'Reduce Ourselves to Zero? Sabina Lovibond, Iris Murdoch, and Feminism' 30(4) *Hypathia* 743.

Henderson, LN (1987) 'Legality and Empathy' (1987) 85 *Michigan Law Review* 1574.

Holland, MG (1998) 'Touching the Weights: Moral Perception and Attention' 38 *International Philosophical Quarterly* 299.

Kind, A (2020) 'Empathy, Imagination, and the Law' in A Amaya and M Del Mar (ed) *Virtue, Emotion and Imagination in Law and Legal Reasoning* (Oxford, Hart Publishing).

Liao, SY, and Gendler, T (2019) 'Imagination' in *The Stanford Encyclopedia of Philosophy* (last visited April 2019).

Lovibond, S (2011) *Iris Murdoch, Gender and Philosophy* (London and New York, Routledge).

Lyons, S (1984) 'Justification and Judicial Responsibility' 72(2) *California Law Review* 178.

Maroney, TA (2011) 'Emotional Regulation and Judicial Behavior' 99 *California Law Review* 1485.

Maroney, TA (2014) 'As a Father Shows Compassion for His Children: Ancient and Contemporary Perspectives on Judicial Empathy' 93(3) *Journal of Law, Religion and State* 239.

Maroney, TA (2015) 'Why Choose? A Response to Rachlinski, Wistrich, & Guthrie's "Heart versus Head: Do Judges Follow the Law or Follow Their Feelings?"' 93 *Texas Law Review* 855.

Massaro, TM (2015) 'Empathy, Legal Storytelling, and the Rule of Law: New Words, Old Wounds?' 87 *Michigan Law Review* 2099.

McDowell, J (1998) *Mind, Value & Reality* (Cambridge US, Harvard University Press).

Michelon, C (2018) 'Lawfulness and the Perception of Legal Salience' 9(1) *Jurisprudence: An International Journal of Legal and Political Thought* 47.
Murdoch, I (1992) *Metaphysics as a Guide to Morals* (London, Vintage Classics).
Murdoch, I (1999) [1997] *Existentialists and Mystics: Writings on Philosophy and Literature* (Harmondsworth, Penguin Books).
Murdoch, I (2012) 'Sein und Zeit: Pursuit of Being' in J Broackes (ed) *Iris Murdoch, Philosopher: A Collection of Essays* (Oxford, Oxford University Press) 93.
Nussbaum, MC (1990) 'The Discernment of Perception: An Aristotelian Conception of Private and Public Rationality' in *Love's Knowledge: Essays on Philosophy and Literature* (Oxford, Oxford University Press) 54.
Nussbaum, MC (1995) *Poetic Justice. The Literary Imagination and Public Life* (Boston, Beacon Press).
Nussbaum, MC (2001) 'When She Was Good' *The New Republic* 28.
Nussbaum, MC (2013) *Political Emotions: Why Love Matters for Justice* (Cambridge US, Harvard University Press).
Pitkin, HF (1973) *Wittgenstein and Justice: On the Significance of Ludwig Wittgenstein for Social and Political Thought* (Berkeley, University of California Press).
Posner, R (2006) 'The Role of the Judge in the Twenty-First Century' 86 *Boston University Law Review* 1049.
Postema, G (1983) 'Self-Image, Integrity, and Professional Responsibility' in D Luban (ed) *The Good Lawyer* (New Jersey, Rowman and Allanheld) 286.
Rietveld, E (2010) 'McDowell and Dreyfus on Unreflective Action' 53(2) *Inquiry* 183.
Simon, D (1998) 'A Psychological Model of Judicial Decision Making' 30 *Rutgers Law Journal* 1.
Simon, D and Scurich, N (2013) 'Judicial Overstating' 88 *Chicago-Kent Law Review* 411.
Solum, LB (2003) 'Virtue Jurisprudence: a Virtue-Centered Theory of Judging' 34(1/2) *Metaphilosophy* 178.
Sunstein, CR (2001) *One Case at a Time. Judicial Review on the Supreme Court* (Cambridge US, Harvard University Press).
Tamanaha, BZ (2004) *On the Rule of Law: History, Politics, Theory* (Cambridge, Cambridge University Press).
Waldron, J (2016) 'The Rule of Law' *The Stanford Encyclopedia of Philosophy*, EN Zalta (ed) https://plato.stanford.edu/archives/fall2016/entries/rule-of-law/ (last visited March 2019).
Wang, L and Solum, LB (2013) 'Confucian Virtue Jurisprudence' in A Amaya and HL Ho (eds) *Law, Virtue and Justice* (Oxford, Hart Publishing) 105.
White, EK (2020) 'On Emotions and the Politics of Attention in Judicial Reasoning' in A Amaya and M Del Mar (eds) *Virtue, Emotion and Imagination in Law and Legal Reasoning* (Oxford, Hart Publishing).
Williams, B (1981) 'Conflicts of Values' in B Williams *Moral Luck: Philosophical Papers 1973–1980* (Cambridge, Cambridge University Press).
Williams, B (1985) *Ethics and the Limits of Philosophy* (London, Fontana Press).
Williams, B (2005) *Bernard Williams: In the Beginning was the Deed. Realism and Moralism in Political Argument* (G Hawthorn ed, Princeton, Princeton University Press).
Wittgenstein, L (1953) [2009] *Philosophical Investigations* (GEM Anscombe, PMS Hacker and J Schulte, trans, Oxford, Wiley-Blackwell).
Wolgast, E (1992) *Ethics of an Artificial Person: Lost Responsibility in Professions and Organizations* (Stanford, Stanford University Press).
Zipursky, BC (2020) 'Austerity, Compassion and the Rule of Law' in A Amaya and M Del Mar (eds) *Virtue, Emotion and Imagination in Law and Legal Reasoning* (Oxford, Hart Publishing).

PART II

Emotion – and Virtue, Imagination

6

On Emotions and the Politics of Attention in Judicial Reasoning

EMILY KIDD WHITE*

I. Introduction

> . . .
> If you catch him,
> Hold up a flashlight to his eye. It's all dark pupil,
> an entire night itself, whose haired horizon tightens
> as he stares back, and closes up the eye. Then from the lids
> one tear, his only possession, like the bee's sting, slips.
> Slyly he palms it, and if you're not paying attention
> he'll swallow it. However, if you watch, he'll hand it over,
> cool as from underground springs and pure enough to drink.
>
> 'Man-Moth', Elizabeth Bishop, *The Complete Poems 1926–1979*

Legal doctrine regularly requires judges to both understand and use emotions in different ways.[1] This chapter explores the role of emotions in fixing and sustaining judicial attention on the impact of a law on the constitutional rights of an individual or group.[2] That certain forms of wrong or harm, including forms of political

* This chapter was presented at the 'Virtue, Emotion and Imagination in Legal Reasoning' colloquium, convened by Amalia Amaya and Maksymilian Del Mar at the Universidad Nacional Autónoma de México. The author was grateful for the invitation and also to the participants and conveners, for their deep and incisive comments. An early draft was presented at New York University School of Law with Samuel Scheffler offering a series of pressing questions as the forum commentator, at the *PULSE* lecture series convened by Gerry Simpson at the London School of Economics, and at a panel at the Law and Society Association annual meeting in Toronto, convened by the head of the *Law and Emotion Collaborative Research Network*, Susan Bandes. The chapter benefitted a great deal from these interactions, and also from discussions with Jeremy Waldron.

[1] See White (forthcoming).

[2] This analysis is relevant to those constitutional law regimes where a law or government action can violate a constitutional right not only in purpose, but in effect. Judicial considerations of the impact or effects of the impugned law or government act can occur at the stage of the analysis where it is determined whether a right has been violated, and/or at the stage of the analysis where the judge must determine whether a violation is justified via a proportionality analysis. See eg White (2014), and Huscroft, Miller and Webber (2014).

and social exclusion, are difficult to detect in the absence of focused attention is, I think, what Elizabeth Bishop's poem 'Man-Moth', excerpted here in epigraph, intends to express. This chapter explores the role of emotions in setting up the serious, sustained inquiry into the impact of a law on the constitutionally guaranteed rights of an individual or group that is required under various legal regimes. When named, this emotional aspect of legal reasoning is often relayed as a call for judicial empathy,[3] but, as this chapter aims to show, this is neither a sufficient nor apt description of the emotionally-laden, political practice of fixing one's attention on a subject.[4] Drawing on the philosophy of emotion,[5] we can sketch, for example, various ways in which judicial attempts to pay attention to the claimant might go awry such that they prove anathema to core legal values,[6] or fail to comport with the professional demands on the practicing judge in the adjudication of a constitutional rights case. This chapter aims to bring this aspect of legal reasoning more clearly into focus by delineating a series of ill versions of judicial attention, and so too by recognising some persistent problems with the related concept of judicial empathy, which can be roughly defined as the attempt to enter either the mind or situation of the person before the court.[7]

Iris Murdoch called the process of imagining a 'moral discipline of the mind', an effort comparable to that 'of "composing" and "holding" a difficult work of art in one's attention'.[8] The focus of this chapter is on precisely these kinds of *efforts of attention* that are involved in legal reasoning, and its principal task is to explore how emotions motivate and facilitate the kind of attention necessary to ascertain whether a legal commitment to a right has been violated. Emotions play an integral role in the form of attention that judges must, as a matter of law, pay to the claimant in a rights case.[9] For, as the chapter concludes, certain forms of constitutional reasoning require from judges a certain politics of attention (meaning here the conscientious and effortful attempt to both pay attention and effectuate a principled distribution of attention) in which emotions play indispensable roles.

[3] See eg Breyer (2013) and Leben (2011).

[4] Kind's chapter in this volume (chapter ten) offers an invaluable discussion on the complex difficulty of defining empathy in the context of judicial reasoning (Kind, 2020).

[5] See eg Goldie (2010), Blum (1980), De Sousa (1987), Leighton (1985), Leighton (2003), Abrams and Keren (2010), Solomon (1988), Solomon (1977), Nussbaum (1996) and Nussbaum (2001).

[6] As Jeremy Waldron writes, 'A legal system is a normative order, both explicitly and implicitly. Explicitly it commits itself publicly to certain rules and standards. Some of these it upholds and enforces, but for others, in certain regards, it fails to do so. The explicit content of the norms recognised by the legal system provides us with a pretty straightforward basis for saying, on these occasions, that the legal systems has fallen short of its own standards, without necessarily licensing the cynical conclusion that these were not its standards'. Waldron (2012a), 65–66.

[7] For a deeper discussion on this, see Kind (2020) (chapter ten in this volume).

[8] Murdoch (1993), 322. For a rich application of the philosophy of Iris Murdoch to the practice of judicial reasoning, see van Domselaar (2020) (chapter five in this volume).

[9] This chapter aims only to set to light on the overlooked emotional aspects of the judicial reasoning prescribed under some constitutional regimes (questions that set aside how this all bears out in practice). An inquiry which leaves open the possibility of distinct, even potentially competing, sets of moral or political reasons to use emotions to interact with rights claimants in other ways.

II. Two Legal Reasons for Paying Attention

There are different sorts of ethical and political reasons for fixing one's attention on a subject, which may or may not comport with the legal reasons that judges have for doing so.[10] Parsing out the legal reasons for judges to pay attention to claimants opens space for asking whether a legal system can deliver on the standards to which it has been publicly committed. Wholesale prescriptions of emotions to the judicial role pay insufficient attention to the normative situation of the law (altered necessarily by its public, institutional and coercive aspects),[11] and fail to heed to both the political quality, and the structure of specific legal regimes (eg judicial empathy might be required at certain stages of a constitutional rights analysis, but unsuitable to judicial reasoning at certain stages of criminal law sentencing).[12] This chapter focuses only on the emotional aspects of judicial reasoning that are required under a particular set of constitutional regimes, where judges work to determine whether the impact of a law on an individual or group amounts to a rights violation, and/or whether this violation might be justified under a form of proportionality reasoning.[13] The constitutional systems in mind have two general features. First, a normative or political conception of the human person that serves as a foundational constitutional value (for the last fifty years or so, we have seen the concept of human dignity frequently take this place in a number of constitutional law regimes).[14] Second, the concern here is with those legal systems that consider the impact, or effect, of a law or government action when determining whether the constitutional rights of an individual or group have been violated.[15] Together, these two features offer distinct sets of role-based reasons for judges to pay a specific sort of attention – one that evidences respect and concern – to the person in the well of the court bringing forth a rights claim. The assumption that the legal values underpinning the constitutional system demand that respect be shown to the claimant, is related but distinct from the need to ascertain a technical and/or strictly cognitive understanding of the law's impact on the claimant's constitutional rights. This is because judges have role-based reasons to see human

[10] On legal reasoning as a distinct form of reasoning, see MacCormick (1978), and, in particular, chapter IX 'Legal Reasoning and Legal Theory'.

[11] The point here is simply that an emotion that facilitates perception, right action, and/or virtuous activity in daily life won't necessarily have the same effect in the context of adjudication. The social, political, and coercive aspects of law alter the ethical landscape.

[12] A recurring theme in the emerging law and emotions scholarship is the concern with breaking down overly general claims about both emotion and law, highlighting the need to study specific emotions within the context of specific legal regimes. See eg White (2014), Maroney (2006) and Bandes (1999).

[13] Eg Huscroft, Webber and Miller (2014).

[14] See eg Waldron (2012a), McCrudden (2008), and Kretzmer and Klein (2002).

[15] 'It is perfectly proper, he writes, for judges to disagree about what the Constitution requires. But it is disgraceful for an interpretation of the Constitution to be premised upon unfounded assumptions about how people live.' *United States v Kras*, 409 U.S. 434, 460 (1973) (Marshall, J, dissenting), cited by Corso (2014), 95.

persons as bearers of a deep sort of value,[16] in addition to having reasons to see them as holding valuable information concerning the impact of the legal regime under constitutional scrutiny. This latter set of reasons concern the capture of relevant information in a constitutional rights case, and, as such, are epistemic in nature.[17] The former gives the judge a set of value-based reasons to pay attention to the claimant that are sourced from the value (and standing) that the law deems the claimant to possess.[18]

The picture, thus far, looks relatively uncomplicated. At certain stages of reasoning through a constitutional rights case, judges must make efforts to understand the experiences of the claimant under the impugned law or legal regime, and for this, something like attention, or empathy (here posited as a facet of attention), appear necessary. This prescription, however, is tricky and prone to misuse, and this chapter raises several complications with respect to the judge's ability to pay the required attention to the claimant in a rights case. This is not to say that constitutional systems would be better served were judges required to altogether abandon such efforts of attention, or related empathetic stances.[19] Were this even possible,[20] this would amount to an abdication of the role and responsibility assigned to the judge in the constitutional systems outlined above.[21] Nevertheless, it is only after getting down into the reeds with the question that the possibility of mapping out this form of judicial reasoning emerges (and later, the possibility of holding judges accountable for errors, or, more broadly, holding a legal system accountable for laying claim to a normative or political good that it isn't set up to deliver).

III. Errors of Attention

Some emotions precipitate or compound an inability to pay quality attention to other persons, while other emotions play indispensable roles in fixing and holding attention on a subject.[22] Simone Weil wrote of the difficulty of witnessing the suffering of another without either moving to obscure the other's pain (often by way of erasing their subjectivity, and/or lowering their status), or by entertaining some

[16] 'The Athenians adopted a legal principle of treating one another as equals, not because of any moral conviction about real equality between them, but because such a principle made possible a form of political community they could not otherwise have' Waldron (2012a), 20. Thus, for our purposes here, we can raise the question as to whether this political commitment mirrors a pre-existing moral commitment.

[17] See Elgin (2007) for a rich discussion on epistemology and understanding. See also Elgin (2020) on emotions and salience (chapter three in this volume).

[18] Ibid.

[19] See White (forthcoming). See also Zipursky (2020) (chapter four in this volume).

[20] On the subject of this not being possible, see Gardner (2008).

[21] See eg White (2014). None of this precludes the possibility of a set of political or ethical reasons for judges to either abdicate from their position and/or engage in civil disobedience or resistance.

[22] Ibid.

measure of self-satisfaction or voyeuristic pleasure.[23] For Weil, the efforts of holding one's attention on a subject, while actively and conscientiously resisting the slide into more pleasurable (or simply less agitating) emotional states, constituted an ethic.[24] A disciplined resistance was therefore necessary to contend with those habits of thought that worked to obstruct the practice of paying attention to the other (or which facilitated only a selective sort of attention to certain others). This section broadly outlines two different ways in which judicial efforts at paying attention to the claimant might go awry such that the practice would amount to something akin to a false or *anti*-attention. More perniciously, it suggests that some judicial efforts might result in a publicly announced, and self-satisfied, claim to attention, where the situation and perspective of the other had been wholly obscured, colonised, misread or glossed over. The forms of false or *anti*-attention highlighted in the second case flow from the failure to recognise empathy's structural selectivity, and vulnerability to bias and stereotype. In both cases, a disciplined resistance to a known tendency to err requires judges to practice a politics of attention that puts emotions to work in their reasoning through a constitutional case.

A. The Error of Taking Up Too Much Space

> Sometimes I turn, there's someone there,
> other times it's only me.
>
> Bob Dylan, 'Every Grain of Sand' (1981)

Robert Solomon describes some emotions as having an intersubjective focus, meaning that they aim at an understanding that sits, in a sense, somewhere between the person experiencing the emotion and its subject.[25] Solomon offers pity as an example of such an emotion, and uses this criteria of intersubjectivity to illustrate how ill-versions of the emotion might arise. If the focus of pity, for example, moves too close to the self and away from its subject, it risks becoming narcissistic and/or self-indulgent.[26] If it moves too far away from the self, the suffering of another might fail to register as it should or might have, causing one, at times, to be obtuse, heedless, hard-hearted or cruel.[27] This view echoes in John Berger's 'Photographs of Agony', where Berger emphasises the politics of an attention that tends to slide back to the self.[28] Berger writes how the mind can move inwards to wrestle with questions of moral inadequacy after witnessing a

[23] Weil (1956).
[24] Ibid. See, also, Murdoch (1993).
[25] Solomon (2003), 223.
[26] Ibid.
[27] Where the affective component of pain and concern is traded for pleasure, the suffering of others could be met with a form of gawking or titillation. See White (forthcoming).
[28] Berger (1980).

photograph depicting anguish or horror, in a process that effectively transmutes the reality of the other into a private, general and abstract, existential question that remains far removed from the concrete political realities that precipitated the war, the attack, the mass drowning, the famine, etc. Where, for Berger, angst felt by the witness does result in action, it is invariably token if it is aimed at relieving an internal emotional or psychic discomfort as opposed to work aiming at political recognition, confrontation or resistance.[29]

In each of these instances, the commitment to seeing the other as a distinct other that is situated in time and place and worthy of attention, gets obscured by self-serving mental processes that result in a form of inward-focused, false or *anti*-attention. Solomon's criteria of intersubjectivity helps elucidate this error as the error of the self taking up too much space. Here we see clearly how this error of attention is bound up with an error of recognition. Peter Goldie's work on the ironies and inconsistencies embedded in various conceptions of empathy offers further contour. Empathy is not our practice of interest, and much has been written querying whether empathy is better cast as an emotion, as opposed to a cognitive skill.[30] Nothing turns here on the conclusion, though a form of empathy motivated by respect and concern, interest or awe, might satisfy a definition of emotion that required an affective component, and would present as a facet of this idea of attention that we've been working towards as it concerns an affectively charged political desire to recognise and learn something about the other.[31]

Goldie distinguishes between a conception of empathy that involves a form of perspective-shifting, from one that aims at an 'in his shoes' position-taking.[32] While Goldie's work does not address judicial reasoning, we can extrapolate from his analysis to note several ways in which judicial attempts at empathy might backfire. A perspective-shifting empathy would see a judge attempting to enter the head of the individual alleging a rights violation, ('what is it like to be this other person'), whereas an 'in his shoes' form of empathy would have judges attempting to place themselves in the same position as the claimant ('what would I have done in this situation').[33] Goldie argues that the first category of 'empathetic

[29] Ibid.

[30] See Kind (2020) (chapter ten in this volume). See also White (forthcoming).

[31] Peggy Cooper Davis writes: '… how easy it is, even for people with the most egalitarian intentions, to slip into imagining a political institution or community in terms of its more affluent and powerful sectors … Assumption of a superordinate perspective is, of course, not only easy but also deeply consequential. It is important, but not often difficult, to avoid fallacious reasoning in public discourse. The difficult and often more consequential moves are made in the construction of premises rather than in reasoning from them. And a great deal turns on whether those premises are chosen from a subordinate or a superordinate perspective'. Cooper Davis (2009), 1378–79.

[32] Goldie (2011), 302.

[33] Goldie later introduces a third conception that involves an 'imagining how it is' for another person, which would have the judge maintain their position while aiming to pay dedicated attention to the features of another's situation. As Goldie stresses, however, this form of imaginative thinking requires an intimate knowledge of the other person (knowledge of them as a unique, almost idiosyncatic other), an intimacy that seems wholly out of reach in the context of ajudication. Ibid.

perspective-shifting' is unworkable beyond simple cases[34] given that it is a category that is 'conceptually unable to operate with the appropriately full-blooded notion of first-personal agency that is involved in deliberation.'[35] This suggests a further normative problem concerning the assumption that one might easily take over the thinking of the other, presuming an ease of access to their mind, reservoir of experiences, and ways of seeing. The idea that one might help oneself so easily to the perspective of another suggests a lack of humility, and/or curiosity about the other, which are ways of thinking that appear anathema to a genuine inquiry into the impact of a law on the rights claimant. For, if the person in the well of the court is so easily understood, and their processes of thinking so replicable, they wouldn't need to be listened to as the source of information about the effects of a law – and this seems contrary to the respect that is meant to be attributed to the claimant under our constitutional systems of interest. This also stands in explicit tension with the emerging jurisprudence in discrimination law that stresses both that laws can have disparate impacts on individuals and groups, and that facially neutral laws can violate equality rights where they serve to exacerbate existing vulnerabilities for historically marginalised persons and communities.[36]

Perspective-shifting empathy as a model for judicial reasoning seems to offer an insufficiently complex picture of the person for it assumes that there are no deep or difficult-to-access differences among the experiences of persons or groups under an impugned law. A related objection exists for the category of the 'in his shoes' form of empathising, which risks minimising the politics and privilege of imagining it possible to catapult one's self into the situation of another person or group under law, while claiming a steadfast ability to read the relevant context. Prescriptions for judicial empathy must attend to the structural features of the judicial role, including the social, political and economic power of judges, their standing, immunities and hindsight privilege. Otherwise, such prescriptions serve only to encourage impervious-to-stakes, flippant and fantasy-rich, imagined excursions into the lives of others under law. For example, it was not long ago that the Canadian Judicial Council recommended the unseating of a judge who, during the course of a rape trial, attempted to put himself in the position of the victim, offering her a number of offensive stereotypes and comments about what he might have done in the same situation to resist sexual violence (ignoring, amongst other things, her physical vulnerability vis-à-vis her attacker).[37] This example

[34] Goldie uses the term, 'base cases' to refer to those 'where the empathizer has the same psychological dispositions (including character and personality) as the target; where there are no non-rational influences on the target's thinking; where the target is not confused about his state of mind; and where the target is not psychologically conflicted in his deliberations'. Ibid.

[35] Ibid.

[36] See eg Moreau (2010) and Moreau (2007).

[37] In the Matter of an Inquiry Pursuant to s. 63(1) of the *Judges Act* Regarding the Honourable Justice Robin Camp Report and Recommendation of the Inquiry Committee to the Canadian Judicial Council.

highlights some of the pernicious consequences of an unserious form of 'in his shoes' empathising.[38]

Under either of the forms of empathy outlined above, the legal demand to confront the claimant as a distinct 'other' worthy of respect and attention is both diluted and obscured. What is needed as antidote is a practised politics of attention which includes the use of emotions to paint the other as worthy of a certain inviolability, and/or gravity. This entails the conscientious wielding of emotions like respect and awe to give adequate heed to the other, instead of basing one's legal findings on what one thinks they might have thought, felt or done under the same circumstances.

There is a related error that results in the claimant not only being obscured in the process of judicial reasoning, but having selective excerpts of her experiences co-opted into the service of a pre-conceived narrative schema. In the mid-1950s, the poet and literary critic Randall Jarrell found himself lamenting the late poetry of Wallace Stevens. A short piece in Jarrell's collection of essays, *Poetry and the Age*,[39] found Jarrell at last able to characterise the error he felt emerging in Stevens' late work. Jarrell charged Stevens with moving towards a form of 'philosophical poetry' – Jarrell's (derogative) term for using descriptions of things or persons in the world in the service of positing a general truth. The error for Jarrell consisted in the failure to be open and responsive to specificity, which had the effect of rendering the self immune from being called up, or changed via a confrontation with a particular person, event, object, or place. Jarrell thought this was a difficult to error to spot, for it consisted in well-crafted descriptions of things (persons, events, object or place) that weren't, in the end, about them being real or seen or confronted in the world, but, rather, about their being co-opted and fashioned into a broader narrative account. The objective of the description was to select and use particular facets of the subject in the service of positing a general theoretical understanding. Jarrell offered the following description:

> But Stevens has this weakness – a terrible one for a poet, a steadily increasing one in Stevens – of thinking of particulars as primarily illustrations of general truths, or else as aesthetic, abstracted objects, simply there to be contemplated; he often treats things or lives so that they seem no more than generalizations of an unprecedentedly low order. But surely a poet has to treat the concrete as primary, as something far more than an instance, a hue to be sense, a member of a laudable category – for him it is always the generalization whose life is derived, whose authority is delegated. …[40]

Jarrell's characterisation of this move is useful for delineating a difficult-to-pinpoint ill-version of attention in judicial reasoning. For Jarrell, a 'philosophical

[38] For further critiques of our ability to read the emotions of others. See eg Bandes (2016); Feldman Barrett (2017). On the difficulty of reading emotions over time and place, see Williams, *Shame and Necessity* (2008); Cotter (2017).

[39] Jarrell (1955).

[40] Ibid, 124–25.

poetry' sees the poet no longer paying the sort of attention required by the practice at hand. The insistence on using a specific instance to draw out a general theory entails a failure to remain open and attentive to the actual subject. Reasoning of this sort is dismissive of the independent existence and status of the subject. It also, for Jarrell, constitutes a betrayal of craft. In legal reasoning, a corollary of this error would consist in a judge selectively employing some of the claimant's own evidence to confirm a previously held general understanding of a purview of a right, for example, without ever having been open to a serious reconsideration of the legal matters before the court. We might think here of a judge dutifully displaying in the reasons for judgment some of the claimant's evidentiary record, or even drawing upon some of the claimant's own language – knowing on a pragmatic level that this could render a judgment less prone to appeal, bolster its legitimacy, or offer the impression of understanding, rigour and/or compassion. Even more mundanely, judges might also include this sort of mimicking language in their reasons because they understood it to be part of their own technical practice of judgment writing. Jarrell's identification of this error of attention isn't dependent on a malicious will but is, in fact, generally committed in the service of one's own (distorted) sense of craft. It is imperative to notice here how language use masks the error, making it particularly challenging, if not nearly impossible, to discern. As such, judicial reasoning requires a politics of attention to counteract this well-hidden but nevertheless pernicious form of a false attention. In the absence of a politics of attention – that is, a form of attention concerned with its own principled distribution – there is only a rhetoric, a claim, and an illusion of attention.

A form of judicial attention that actively cultivated a sense of respect, or even awe towards the claimant as a legal subject might work to resist this pull to obscure, erase or co-opt their perspective into a pre-conceived narrative. Cynical judges who say to themselves, 'I've seen this before. I've seen you (as a type of person) before', betray core legal value commitments, and they do so by failing to pay attention to the subject in their legal reasoning practices. In his Dewey Lecture at Harvard Law School, Thomas Nagel came close to describing the phenomenology of this politics of attention that we are piecing together here, when he said that 'Each person with whom I interact presents me with the same stubborn and impenetrable moral surface that I present to him …'[41] This points to the need to develop practices of legal reasoning that actively reinforce the standing, respect and/or dignity that the law has attributed to the claimant. The two legal rationales for judicial attention are important here. Were empathy only required for epistemic reasons relating to how the individual or group was impacted by the impugned law then the judge could be permitted to sidestep any real attempt to take the claimant seriously where information about the law's impact was thought to be otherwise available.

[41] Nagel (2015).

B. Errors of Application

The preceding section analysed the need to course correct against a series of errors that judges might make in their attempts to pay the required form of attention to the claimant in the hearing of a constitutional law case. Empathy can be cast as a facet of attention and this section considers the tendency to empathise unevenly, and selectively, and how this poses deep challenges for legal reasoning in a constitutional system committed to recognising something akin to the equal dignity of persons.[42] Most working definitions suggest that empathy involves the attempt to enter the mind of another, or to move closer to another's experience of the world.[43] Empathy can be defined as a facet of attention when it is motivated by an affective respect or concern for the other. It is this form of empathy that can be said to facilitate the required practices of legal reasoning in the constitutional systems outlined above[44] as it reinforces the respect owed to the claimant, and cultivates a serious interest in lived experiences under the impugned law.[45]

While this form of judicial empathy is required to adjudicate rights,[46] it is a practice of legal reasoning that is prone to errors of application.[47] A politics of attention is needed to remedy the structural selectivity of empathy. This requires the work of a series of emotions (respect, curiosity, concern) to animate, motivate and sustain the legal value-based commitments to seeing all claimants as deserving of attention, and capable of possessing valuable information about the impact of the impugned law.

How empathy is triggered is an old question. Over 2500 years ago, in Book VII of his *Problemata*, Aristotle set down a puzzle for empathy and imagination when he queried:

> Why is it that when we see anyone cut or burned or tortured or undergoing any other painful suffering, we share mentally in his pain? Is it because nature is common to us all, and it is this which shares in the sufferer's pain, when we see any of these things happening to him, through kinship with him? Or is it because, just as the nose and hearing

[42] For a powerful examination of a failure to accord equal dignity to all persons under law, see Blum (2020) (chapter seven in this volume).

[43] Ibid.

[44] If empathy is defined solely as the ability to know or predict the minds of others, then there is no definitional component that rules out calling the sociopath, or the skilled emotional manipulator, empathetic. For deeper discussion on this, see Hansberg (2020) (chapter nine in this volume). Some philosophers of emotion reject the categorisation of empathy as an emotion for this reason. The posited working conception above contains an affective dimension, as well as a constitutive desire (to learn about the other out of respect and concern) and, as such, could be plausibly categorised as an emotion (see Solomon, 1977; Solomon, 2003), though nothing in the overall argument turns on this.

[45] Whether this bears out as a matter of empirics is a separate question. The aim of this chapter is to clarify the emotional elements of the prescribed legal reasoning.

[46] Forwarding a related claim, see Zipursky's wonderful chapter on compassion and austerity in judicial reasoning (2020) (chapter four in this volume).

[47] Nevertheless, empathy remains a regular aspect in judicial reasoning. See Kind's excellent chapter (2020) (chapter ten in this volume).

> according to their faculties receive certain emanations, so also the sight does the same as the result of things pleasant and painful?"[48]

This line of questions raises a series of others. Must a recognition of kinship or equality always precede the 'sharing of another's pain,' or might the witnessing of another's pain instigate or facilitate this recognition of kinship or equality. This is a critical sequencing question. Lynn Hunt has argued for the latter position, suggesting that, over time, literary depictions of pain and suffering have worked to generate more inclusive conceptions of justice through empathy.[49] Hans Joas resists this view by using historical examples to illustrate how the pain of 'the other' remained unseen and un-affecting prior to the recognition that they were sacred or equal.[50] While these views needn't be mutually exclusive, the productive potential of empathy in the law rests on the sequencing of pain and recognition that the emotion is presumed to entail. A judge who empathised only with those claimants whom they – consciously or unconsciously – understood to be part of their in-group would be in serious error.[51] As Martha Nussbaum writes,

> Humanity does not automatically reveal itself to strangers. No placard hung on the front of a fellow citizen announces that this one is a full-fledged human being (and not a vile bug or piece of refuse). Seeing the shape of a human being before us, we always have a choice to make: will we impute full equal humanity to that shape, or something less? Only by imagining how the world looks through that person's eyes does one get to the point of seeing the other person as a someone and not a something.[52]

Critics have pointed to features of empathy that make it unsuitable for use in political decision-making, and from these critiques we can extrapolate several concerns with the use of empathy in judicial reasoning.[53] Empathy may be too intimate[54] an emotion to expect in such a formal setting, or where there are such clear power dynamics at play. Paul Bloom has argued that the structure of empathy makes it a poor guide for social policy, given that it operates most easily when the other is thought to be like us or is found attractive (ie criteria that would clearly be anathema to legal commitments to equality). Judges would undermine legal commitments to equality were they to feel only pity, compassion or moral outrage over the unjust treatment of the claimant because the judge felt a kinship towards them.[55] It is

[48] Aristotle in Barnes (1984), 1371.

[49] Hunt (2007).

[50] Joas (2013).

[51] This echoes the concern with deep-seated prejudice, which is generally accompanied by emotions of contempt or enmity. Beliefs and extraneous emotions that contradict core legal values must be excluded, to the extent possible, from judicial reasoning that is committed to equal concern and respect. Whether this is, in fact, achievable is a pressing question. On unconscious bias, see Lane, Kang and Banaji (2007).

[52] Nussbaum (2004), xvii.

[53] See eg Bloom (2014).

[54] See Leighton (2007).

[55] Recall the outrage over the sentencing of Stanford swimmer Brock Turner: see Koren (2016). The sentencing judge in that case found himself empathising with the accused (Justice Aaron Persky of the Santa Clara Superior Court was also a Stanford alumnus and gave Turner a markedly reduced sentence,

often a concern over the partiality of empathy, and other emotions, that underlies calls to remove their influence from judicial reasoning. Such concerns are valid but the prescription is misleading. We would not, for example, want a judge to feel nothing when confronted with evidence of a rights violation.[56] Rather, the aim is to establish a boundary that excludes those emotions that do not easily extend to all persons, and to cultivate political practices that work against certain habits of thought and feeling that undermine commitments to equal protection under the law. Despite its structural flaws, the right version of empathy plays an indispensable role in judicial reasoning because it cultivates and reinforces a serious interest in the lived experiences of others under the law.[57] What is needed, then, is an affectively-charged, serious attempt at understanding that aims at recognition to actively resist the errors of co-option, obstruction and selectivity outlined above. This requires judges to summon, construct and/or revive an emotional state necessary for reasoning through constitutional rights case before the court. Given the pull of these errors, a neutral emotional state will result in legal reasoning that is prone to error, and which violates its own legal-value based commitments to showing equal respect and dignity to persons. Margalit stresses the problem of indifference in moral life, and its evil. He writes: 'There is not so much banality of evil as banality of indifference.'[58] Martha Nussbaum voices a related concern. In her book *Poetic Justice*, she argues that we need to work to cultivate the necessary empathy to practise justice in a world full of division, hatred and violence.[59] Both views highlight the need for the presiding judge to exercise empathy politically, that is, conscious of distribution and conscientiously, in the judicial assessment of the harms caused by a government act or legislative scheme.

Evidence of humiliation, exclusion, pain and degradation should alert the judge and call up her attention. A cool cynicism, apathy or numbness would clearly betray the respect owed to the claimant and the severity of the alleged rights violation. In a distinct but related vein, a judge who never felt anger, pity, compassion, respect or indignation in response to evidence of a rights violation could not be said to be reasoning in line with legal values that emphasised equal concern and

which seemed inconsonant with the crime of rape and representative of the privilege of confronting the criminal justice system as a white, elite male). As such, empathy stood in strong contrast to the commitment to equal treatment before the law. This case highlighted some of the pernicious features of empathy that are well documented in Paul Bloom's book (that we empathise most easily with those who we consider most like us, etc). See Bloom (2016). This case is also discussed in Elgin (2020) (chapter three in this volume).

[56] Neutrality can signal a lack of respect or understanding. See, famously, Aristotle, 'Nicomachean Ethics', in Barnes (1984), 1104b 15-30. See White (2014) and Zipursky (2020) (chapter four in this volume).

[57] One of Bloom's central criticisms of the use of empathy in the construction of social policy is that it 'is narrow; it connects us to particular individuals, real or imagined, but is insensitive to numerical differences and statistical data'. Note that this concern is somewhat neutralised in the judicial setting, where the focus is properly placed on an individual's experience under the law. See Bloom (2014).

[58] Margalit (1996).

[59] Nussbaum (1997).

respect. The same is true for judges who never experience these emotions with respect to certain groups of persons, delineated perhaps by race, socio-economic class, ethnicity, gender, sexuality, citizenship, age, physical ability, etc. The failure to respond emotionally to a legal wrong suffered by a certain group demarcated as the 'other' has long been attributed to judgments about differential status.[60] One of the harms of diminishing the humanity of a group is that this works to block feelings of sympathy, solidarity, empathy or compassion with the victims, and so too feelings of indignation or moral outrage at the law over its unjust treatment of that group.[61] A judge's failure to recognise and respond to the pain and suffering of others either in general or with respect to a particular group is evidence that their reasoning betrays legal commitments to attribute a full and equal humanity to all persons.[62]

IV. Addressing an Objection to a Judicial Politics of Attention

We have thus far outlined a series of errors that judges might make when they seek to pay attention to a claimant in a constitutional law case. While prone to error, there are nevertheless legal reasons for judges to pay a particular form of attention to the claimant. An objection follows from this prescription – what are the implications for the rule of law where if the judge succeeds in paying attention to the claimant?[63] Won't the proscribed judicial politics of attention render the claimant's subjective experience of the law determinative on the question of a potential rights violation, thereby undermining rule of law type commitments (that the law be general, knowable in advance, prospective, etc). This charge oversimplifies the role of judicial attention in judicial reasoning. In a constitutional rights case, the objective of judicial reasoning is to determine whether the impugned law violates the claimant's constitutionally guaranteed rights. An affectively rich practice of judicial attention facilitates this inquiry, and while it pays heed to the emotions and the subjective experience of the claimant, it renders neither determinative of the constitutional question at hand.[64]

Emotions can play positive epistemic roles in judicial reasoning[65] by gripping and focusing the attention[66] of the presiding judge or judicial panel, thereby

[60] See eg Garland (1993).

[61] See eg Waldron (2012b). See also, the Supreme Court of Canada's reasoning on hate speech in *Saskatchewan (Human Rights Commission) v Whatcott*, 2013 SCC 11.

[62] For an in-depth discussion on this, see White (2014).

[63] See Elgin (2020) (chapter three in this volume) for a rich discussion on impartiality and impersonality in legal judgement vis-à-vis the rule of law criteria of generality.

[64] White (2014). See also Zipursky's authoritative work on compassion in judicial reasoning (1990).

[65] I am grateful to Thomas Nagel for pressing for this clarification.

[66] Brady (2013), 5.

prompting a re-evaluation of the impugned law or government action. While it is not the case that a claimant's subjective experience of a rights violation will ever be constitutive of a legal rights violation, a claimant's evidence and testimony can work to capture the attention of the judge or judicial panel and prompt them to reappraise their understanding of the situations on the ground that should engage existing rights protections. A claimant's emotions can, at times, work to initiate a related emotional response in the judge, which 'can motivate the search for reasons that bear on the accuracy of their own initial assessment of some object or event, and thus motivate the rational reappraisal or reassessment of that object or event'.[67] An emotion, for example, might begin with a strong physiological response – such as the quickening heartbeat that is characteristic of fear – that works to focus critical attention on the object of that emotion, inviting a process of cognitive reflection[68] that can work to diffuse, intensify or change the emotion (we can think of fear moving to indignation, or laugher upon further reflection, for example). A person who has been taken to a secondary screening room at an airport Customs and Immigration office and subjected to an arduous and demeaning round of questioning might shake, perspire and feel nervous or fearful at the time. Afterwards, however, this same person might come to have a different set of emotional reactions, such as anger or indignation, while thinking about this episode, its particular features and politics, and perhaps even the emotions that she experienced while undergoing it.[69] As Peter Goldie suggests, we can think both internally and externally about the emotional import of a past event.[70] As in our example, moving across these categories (from an internal to an external reference point) can cause the emotional response to shift. This reflection and processing is motivated by the very structure of the emotion. Emotions aid thinking in this way by setting up internal and external viewpoints. Similarly, we can have different emotional responses to an event depending on whether we take a broad or narrow view of it.[71] An occurrence might be more painful (or irritating, or pleasing), for example, when we recognise it to form part of a pattern of interactions. Robert Solomon has likened this reflective feature of emotion to a camera lens that is capable of different resolutions. Looking at law, then, through a historical lens, we can see how a claimant's depiction of humiliation and/or degradation under law may claim a history, rationality and validity that another instance does not.[72]

We might also think of the ways in which the emotions experienced by the judge (or by individual judges sitting on a panel) hearing a case might be mediated

[67] Ibid.

[68] See eg Robinson (2005).

[69] I do not wish to give the impression that there won't be variations – wide ones, even – in how this example might affect different groups in a society. The interaction might rationally present as a threat to a group that has been historically marginalised and/or victimised by public officials, while not experienced directly as such by others.

[70] Goldie (2009).

[71] Ibid.

[72] 'Debo justificar lo que me hiere' (Trans. by Rocio Lorca: I have to justify what wounds me). This is the first line on Jorge Luis Borges's headstone. Cited in Berger (2006). See also Cooper Davis (2009).

or unmediated.[73] That is, the emotion's object might be either the factual features of the claimant's situation under the impugned law (unmediated) or the claimant's own subjective experience of that same situation, including the claimant's emotional experiences (mediated). With respect to the latter, the judge will be concerned with the subjective experience of the claimant, and may focus, for example, on the 'testimony' documenting the humiliation and pain that flowed from the legal wrong of the alleged rights violation.[74] This does not mean that the emotions of the claimant are in any way determinative of a rights violation.[75] The version of empathy outlined in this chapter serves as an evidence-gathering skill, that supports the construction of the relevant factual matrix before the court, and assists in interpreting the constitutional right in question (as well as justified limits to that right).

Consider the form of a trenchant dissent, written against a court majority who, in the opinion of the dissenting judges, failed to see something imperative in the determination of a rights case. As Terry Maroney writes, dissenting opinions written in this register are legion.[76] While a dissenting judge or judicial panel might feel moved to indignation for a variety of reasons, it is nevertheless useful to explore some distinctions. We could, for example, distinguish between instances where the dissenter was indignant over (1) the belief that the majority failed to altogether grasp the harm or wrong experienced by the claimant in a rights case (set off, perhaps, by the majority's cold appraisal of certain facts), from those with their roots in (2) the belief that the majority, while grasping the harm or wrong experienced by the claimant, nevertheless failed to find that a right had been violated.[77] In both cases, the absence of certain emotional reactions in the judicial reasoning reveals, in the view of the dissenters, an absent or poorly applied legal value. In the first instance, the failure to react with certain emotions to the evidence in the case calls into question the majority's understanding of the relevant factual matrix, as interpreted through the lens of the governing legal values (this brackets questions of relevance and admissibility).[78] The reference to *legal* values here is intended to set aside those instances in which a dissent appears to abandon the idiom of law altogether, writing in indignation in a purely ethical register, for example, to

[73] I am here using Del Mar's useful distinction between mediated and unmediated emotions. Del Mar (2017), 145–46. For a deep enquiry into the role of artefacts and imagination in legal reasoning, see Del Mar (2020) (chapter thirteen in this volume).

[74] Some have argued that it is better to describe empathy, not as an emotion (where it does not involve a 'feeling with'), but as a cognitive process of understanding the emotional states of others. See eg Coplan and Goldie (2011) and Goldie (2011).

[75] See also Elgin (2020) (chapter three in this volume).

[76] See Maroney (2011), 629.

[77] A third scenario would occur where a dissenting judge feels moved to indignation believing that the majority was improperly swayed by the evidence to find a rights violation where one did not exist.

[78] Here the assumption is that the emotion-inducing evidence is relevant to the legal determination at hand.

admonish the majority's reasoning. What remains is the charge that the majority would have apprehended the relevant evidence differently had it properly applied the governing legal values. Another sort of epistemic function that emotional reactions serve is more pronounced in the second scenario, where we imagine the dissent's indignation flowing from the majority's failure to interpret the right at issue in light of the evidence. This does not ground the interpretation of the right in the emotional reaction; rather, it highlights precisely how the experience of the emotion pushes the judge or judicial panel to interpret the purview of the right in question in line with the guiding legal value.[79] The strong emotional reaction of the judge prompts a searching and sustained inquiry into whether the law or government act violates the right in question as interpreted through the lens of the guiding value. Judicial attention fulfils an epistemic function here by pressing the judge to see if the impugned law or government act violates a constitutional right, motivating the re-examination of the purview of the right. This is the second epistemic function that emotions fulfil in judicial reasoning – the flagging, attention-capturing function.

V. Conclusion

Legal commitments to equality and respect require judicial reasoning practices that reflect a politics of attention that reinforces a broad and deep, curious and concerned understanding of how the impugned law has impacted an individual or group. This judicial politics of attention works to critically engage with and press upon the boundaries of the category of what constitutes a rights violation. An affectively charged judicial politics of attention draws on emotions to animate and reinforce legal commitments to equality and dignity, and works to attribute a gravity[80] and inviolability to the claimant. In Nagel's terms, they work to cloak the claimant with an 'impenetrable moral surface' such that judicial efforts to understand a case don't obscure, or run roughshod over, a claimant's rightful legal standing. An unaffected, banal, or cynical read of the claimant will be insufficient to guard against the habits of thought and feeling outlined above that would lead judges to obscure, dismiss or selectively empathise with the claimant.

A political attention concerns itself with a principled distribution of attention, and draws on emotions to generate and hold steady the respect owed to the claimant under the strictures of the constitutional order. Where a judge fails to consciously cultivate a political attention, they risk offering only a firm of false or *anti*-attention that undermines legal values and legal commitments. Calling up the right emotional frames for reasoning through a case is difficult and careful work.[81] Emotional motivation cannot be

[79] See Zipursky's seminal work on this (1990).
[80] See eg Halbertal (2015).
[81] See White (forthcoming).

abandoned simply because it is difficult to get right, nor in the face of political contestation over what laws or government acts constitute a rights violation. Iris Murdoch held that curiosity was a matter of morality, agitating us away from certainty toward truths previously unseen. Recognising, through adjudication, instances of humiliation, exclusion and degradation made possible under law is an urgent and critical matter. The normative foundations of our constitutional systems of interest set this objective for legal reasoning. In light of this, we cobble together pieces for a judicial politics of attention, and take seriously our task of setting to light the work of emotions (like respect, curiosity and humility) in resisting the pervasive forms of *anti*-attention that would prevent a judge from seeing what the law has asked them to look for.

References

Cases

Saskatchewan (Human Rights Commission) v Whatcott, 2013 SCC 11
United States v Kras, 409 U.S. 434, 460 (1973)

Articles and Books

Abrams, K and Keren, H (2010) 'Who's Afraid of Law and the Emotions?' *Minnesota Law Review* 94.

Aristotle (1984) 'Nicomachean Ethics' in J Barnes (ed), *The Complete Works of Aristotle* (Bollingen series, II; Princeton, Princeton University Press), 1729.

Bandes, S (2016) 'Remorse and Criminal Justice' *Emotion Review* 8(1).

Bandes, S (1999) *The Passions of Law* (New York, New York University Press).

Barrett, L (2017) 'The Law's Emotion Problem' *New York Times Sunday Review* (March 11).

Berger, J (2006) *Here Is Where We Meet: A Story of Crossing Paths* (Vintage).

Berger, J (1980) *About Looking* (New York, Pantheon Books).

Bloom, P (2016) *Against Empathy: The Case for Rational Compassion* (New York, Ecco Press).

Bloom, P (2014) 'Against Empathy' *Boston Review: A Political and Literary Forum*. Available at http://bostonreview.net/forum/paul-bloom-against-empathy.

Blum, L (1980) 'Compassion', in AO Rorty (ed), *Explaining Emotions* (Los Angeles, University of California Press).

Blum, L (2020) '"Black Lives Matter": Moral Frames for Understanding the Police Killings of Black Males' in A Amaya and M Del Mar (eds) *Virtue, Emotion and Imagination in Law and Legal Reasoning* (Oxford, Hart Publishing).

Brady, M (2013) *Emotional Insight: The Epistemic Role of Emotional Experience* (New York, Oxford University Press).

Breyer, S (2013) 'On Reading Proust', *New York Review of Books* available at https://www.nybooks.com/articles/2013/11/07/reading-proust.

Cooper Davis, P (2009) 'Responsive Constitutionalism and the Idea of Dignity', *University of Pennsylvania Journal of Constitutional Law* 1373.

Coplan, A and Goldie, P (eds) (2011) *Empathy: Philosophical and Psychological Perspectives* (Oxford, Oxford University Press).

Corso, L (2014) 'Should Empathy Play any Role in the Interpretation of Constitutional Rights?' 27(1) *Ratio Juris* 94.

Cotter, H (2017) '"A World of Emotions" in Greek Art Unmasks the Stony Faces' *New York Times* (23 March).

Del Mar, M (2017) 'Imagining by Feeling: A Case for Compassion in Legal Reasoning', 13(2) *International Journal of Law in Context* 143.

Del Mar, M (2020) 'The Legal Imagination: Individual, Interactive and Communal' in A Amaya and M Del Mar (eds) *Virtue, Emotion and Imagination in Law and Legal Reasoning* (Oxford, Hart).

De Sousa, R (1987) *The Rationality of Emotion* (Cambridge, The MIT Press).

Domselaar, van, I (2020) 'All Judges on the Couch? On Iris Murdoch and Legal Decision-Making' in A Amaya and M Del Mar (eds) *Virtue, Emotion and Imagination in Law and Legal Reasoning* (Oxford, Hart Publishing).

Elgin, C (2007) 'Understanding the Facts' 132 *Philosophical Studies* 33.

Elgin, C (2020) 'Impartiality and Legal Reasoning' in A Amaya and M Del Mar (eds) *Virtue, Emotion and Imagination in Law and Legal Reasoning* (Oxford, Hart Publishing).

Gardner, J (2008) 'The Logic of Excuses and the Rationality of Emotions' (35) *Oxford Legal Studies Research Paper.*

Garland, D (1993) *Punishment and Modern Society: A Study in Social Theory* (Chicago, University of Chicago Press).

Goldie, P (2009) 'Narrative Thinking, Emotion, and Planning' 67(1) *The Journal of Aesthetics and Art Criticism* 97.

Goldie, P (2010) *The Oxford Handbook of Philosophy of Emotion* (Oxford, Oxford University Press).

Goldie, P (2011) 'Anti-Empathy' in A Coplan and P Goldie (eds) *Empathy: Philosophical and Psychological Perspectives* (Oxford, Oxford University Press) 302.

Halbertal, M (2015) 'Three Concepts of Human Dignity' *The Dewey Lecture at the University of Chicago Law School.*

Hansberg, O (2020) 'Emotional Intimacy' in A Amaya and M Del Mar (eds) *Virtue, Emotion and Imagination in Law and Legal Reasoning* (Oxford, Hart Publishing).

Hunt, L (2007) *Inventing Human Rights: A History* (New York, WW Norton & Co).

Huscroft, G, Miller, BW and Webber, G (2014), *Proportionality and the Rule of Law: Rights, Justification, Reasoning* (New York, Cambridge University Press).

Jarrell, R (1955) *Poetry and the Age* (London, Faber).

Joas, H (2013) *The Sacredness of the Person: A New Genealogy of Human Rights* (Washington, Georgetown University Press).

Lane, KA, Kang, J and Banaji, MR (2007) 'Implicit Social Cognition and the Law' (3) *Annual Review of Law and Social Science* 427.

Kind, A (2020) 'Empathy, Imagination, and the Law' in A Amaya and M Del Mar (eds) *Virtue, Emotion and Imagination in Law and Legal Reasoning* (Oxford, Hart Publishing).

Koren, M (2016) 'Why the Stanford Judge Gave Brock Turner Six Months' *The Atlantic* (17 June).

Kretzmer, D and Klein, E (2002), *The Concept of Human Dignity in Human Rights Discourse* (The Hague, Kluwer Law International).

Leben, S (2011) 'An Expectation of Empathy' 51(1) *Washburn Law Journal* 49.

Leighton, S (1985) 'A New View of Emotion' 22(2) *American Philosophical Quarterly* 133.

Leighton, S (2003) *Philosophy and the Emotions: A Reader* (New York, Broadview Press).
Leighton, S (2007) 'On Pity and Its Appropriateness' *Religion in Philosophy and Theology*.
MacCormick, N (1978) *Legal Reasoning and Legal Theory* (Oxford, Clarendon Press).
Margalit, A (1996) *The Decent Society* (Cambridge, Harvard University Press).
Maroney, T (2006) 'Law and Emotion: A Proposed Taxonomy of an Emerging Field' 30 *Law and Human Behavior* 119.
Maroney, T (2011) 'The Persistent Cultural Script of Judicial Dispassion' 99(2) *California Law Review* 629.
Moreau, S (2007) 'The Promise of Law v. Canada' 57(2) *The University of Toronto Law Journal* 415.
Moreau, S (2010) 'What is Discrimination?' 38(2) *Philosophy and Public Affairs* 143.
Murdoch, I (1993) *Metaphysics as a Guide to Morals* (New York, Penguin Press).
Nagel, T (2015) *The Dewey Lecture at Harvard Law School.*
Nussbaum, M (1996) *The Therapy of Desire: Theory and Practice in Hellenistic Ethics* (Princeton, Princeton University Press).
Nussbaum, M (1997) *Poetic Justice: The Literary Imagination and Public Life* (Boston, Beacon Press).
Nussbaum, M (2001) *Upheavals of Thought. The Intelligence of Emotions* (Cambridge, Cambridge University Press).
Nussbaum, M (2004) *Hiding from Humanity: Disgust, Shame, and the Law* (Princeton, Princeton University Press).
Robinson, J (2005) *Deeper than Reason: Emotion and its Role in Literature, Music, and Art* (Oxford, Oxford University Press).
Schoolman, M (2001) *Reason and Horror: Critical Theory, Democracy and Aesthetic Individuality* (New York, Routledge).
Solomon, R (1988) 'On Emotions as Judgments' 25(2) *American Philosophical Quarterly* 183.
Solomon, R (1977) *The Passions: Emotions and the Meaning of Life* (New York, Anchor Books).
Solomon, R (2003) *Not Passion's Slave: Emotions and Choice* (New York, Oxford University Press).
Waldron, J (2012a) *Dignity, Rank, and Rights*, M Dan-Cohen (ed) (New York, Oxford University Press).
Waldron, J (2012b) *The Harm in Hate Speech* (Cambridge, Harvard University Press).
Weil, S (1956) 'The Iliad, or The Poem of Force' 18(2) *Chicago Review* 5.
White, EK (2014) 'Till Human Voices Wake Us: The Role of Emotion in the Adjudication of Dignity Claims' 3 *Journal of Law, Religion and State* 201.
White, EK (forthcoming) *Emotions in Legal Reasoning* (Oxford, Oxford University Press).
Williams, B (2008) *Shame and Necessity* (Berkeley, University of California Press).
Zipursky, B (1990) 'DeShaney and the Jurisprudence of Compassion' 65 *New York University Law Review* 1101.
Zipursky, B (2020) 'Austerity, Compassion and the Rule of Law' in A Amaya and M Del Mar (eds) *Virtue, Emotion and Imagination in Law and Legal Reasoning* (Oxford, Hart Publishing).

7

'Black Lives Matter': Moral Frames for Understanding the Police Killings of Black Males

LAWRENCE BLUM

I. Introduction

In the past few years, police killings of black people in the United States, especially but not only black men, have garnered wide public attention. Some of the killings or aspects of the events surrounding the killing have been recorded by video cameras, often wielded by random passersby, and sometimes by videocams worn by police officers; and the greater public visibility of these killings has certainly contributed to the widespread public concern. The US government does not keep national statistics on police killings, and the prominence of the killings mentioned have led some news media – the *Washington Post*, a prominent American newspaper, and, strikingly, the British newspaper, the *Guardian* – to try to keep informal if unofficial track of the killings. In several of the cases, the outcry over the killings has triggered a (US) Department of Justice inquiry into police practices in the jurisdictions in question, not necessarily, though sometimes, focused on the specific killing itself.

These killings have sparked widespread public protest and outrage, and a movement known as Black Lives Matter has arisen, often organising the protests and calling attention to the injustice involved. But the name of the movement also means to express a moral concern implicated in many or most of the killings. The idea is that so many killings reveal a deficiency in society or white people's regard for black people – a failure to appreciate that black lives matter. The attitude that is being charged as missing or inadequate here is an emotion-based attitude, what Angela Smith calls an emotional attitude.[1] That is, recognising and appreciating that someone's, or a group's, life matters involves an attitude that necessarily involves emotion; caring about someone's life, caring that that life has been snuffed out, is part of that emotional attitude.

[1] See Smith (2005).

The Black Lives Matter movement charges, at least by implication, various parties with a failure to possess this attitude – the particular police officers involved in the killings in question, police more generally, white people, or American society in some general way. I focus primarily on the specific police officers in question.

I will concentrate on four killings from 2014 (Michael Brown, Eric Garner, Akai Gurley and Tamir Rice) and one from 2015 (Freddie Gray), all of which attracted a great deal of public attention and concern. I will argue that 'black lives matter' helps supply a necessary moral resource for thinking about these killings. I will do so in part by contrasting this black lives matter framework with three other views or frameworks often used in thinking about racial victimisation – stereotypes, implicit bias and Naomi Zack's rights-based approach. Having advocated for the significance of a black lives matter emotional attitude framework as distinct from (though not incompatible with) these others, I will then go on to consider four objections to that framework.

II. Five Black Men Killed by Police

Let me begin with a brief account of the cases in question. Michael Brown, 18 years old, was shot by Officer Darren Wilson. Brown was not armed and Wilson knew he was not armed; nor was Brown within striking distance of Wilson. But by plausible accounts Brown was heading toward Wilson, and a few minutes earlier, the two had scuffled, with Brown plausibly claimed to have reached for Wilson's gun.

Eric Garner was a 43-year-old father of six, apparently illegally selling untaxed single cigarettes on the street, as he had done in the past. He had just broken up a fight when officers approached him. After resisting arrest by several officers he was placed in what is called a 'chokehold' by Officer Daniel Pantaleo, taken down by several officers, and kept in that chokehold as he said 'I can't breathe' several times – a series of events captured on a bystander's video. Garner died soon after.

Akai Gurley was a 28-year-old man shot by accident by a rookie police officer, Peter Liang, who fired his gun in a darkened stairwell in a housing project where Gurley was visiting his girlfriend.

Tamir Rice was a 12-year-old boy playing with a toy gun in a playground with no one around. He was killed by Officer Timothy Loehmann who was responding to a citizen call. Loehmann killed Rice within two seconds of driving right up to him. The events were recorded on a surveillance video.

Freddie Gray was a 25-year-old man arrested for allegedly possessing an illegal switchblade knife. He was placed inside a police van but was not secured, and fell into a coma as a result of injuries sustained in his time in the van, dying a week later. The medical examiner's office concluded that Gray's death was a homicide, rather than an accident, because officers failed to follow safety procedures 'through acts of omission'.

Of these five cases, only the officers in the accidental killing of Gurley, and the Freddie Gray case, were indicted for committing a crime.[2] The families of Garner, Gurley and Rice were given several million dollars by the cities in which they resided.

I have provided here only the bare bones of these five cases, omitting many details of interest, some of which I will provide in the subsequent discussion. But I provide these brief details in part because knowing someone's name and some individuating information about them better enables people who do not know them, like my readers, to be able to appreciate that their lives mattered.

III. Stereotypes and Stereotyping

In many popular discussions and accounts of police killings, and the more general perceived mistreatment of black persons and communities by police, one encounters references to stereotypes and stereotyping. I will define 'stereotype', for our purposes, as an evidence-resistant association, broadly though not generally universally shared among members of a society, between a group and a particular characteristic – an association in which the stereotype holder has some cognitive investment that need not be as robust as an actual belief (and so need not be conscious).[3] It is said that many especially white police officers hold stereotypes of black people as criminals, as dangerous, as aggressive.

What exactly is wrong with stereotyping? Basically the harms or wrongs of stereotyping fall into two general categories – harms of all stereotyping as such, and harms attaching to particular stereotypes. In the first category, someone can object to being stereotyped, independent of any particular stereotype held of that person, for several different reasons: (1) false attribution – the stereotype does not apply to the particular person (he [a black male] is not dangerous, she [an Asian American] is not a good maths student); (2) stereotypes mask the internal diversity within the group stereotyped (some young black males are dangerous, most are not; some Asian Americans are good at maths, many are not); (3) stereotypes mask the individuality of a given member of the stereotyped group; that is, the stereotype holder is not seeing the particular person as an individual ('I'm a young black male/an Asian American student, and you are not seeing me as an individual but only as a stereotype.') All these are forms of epistemic injustice toward the individual or group.

In addition, there are other less personalised cognitive and moral distortions involved in all stereotyping, independent of content: exaggerating differences

[2] Three of the officers in the Gray case were found not guilty at trial; prosecution of another resulted in a mistrial. In the wake of these verdicts, the district attorney dropped charges against the other officers. Liang was found guilty of manslaughter and misconduct in the Gurley case, but was not ordered to serve any prison time.

[3] This account of stereotyping drawn from Blum (2004), which also clarifies the distinction between a stereotype and a valid generalisation. On the latter see also Blum (2016).

between groups; leading the stereotype holder to forget that members of other groups also possess the characteristic attributed to the stereotyped group; encouraging 'moral distance' between one's own and the stereotyped group.[4]

Thus all stereotyping is harmful to or commits a wrong against individuals within a group, and to the group itself. But such harms obviously do not fully capture what is harmful about *particular* stereotypes. The real-world consequences of being stereotyped as threatening and dangerous are much more harmful and full of risk than being stereotyped as good at maths. The mayor of New York, Bill de Blasio, captured this harm in his reported words to his black son, 'Don't move suddenly, don't reach for your cell phone', and his later explanation of these remarks: 'There's that fear that there could be that one moment of misunderstanding with a young man of color and that young man may never come back. It's different for a white child. That's just the reality in this country.'[5]

This second category of harms is the aspect of stereotyping many people believe has been operating in the police killings I am concerned with, as well as many others over the years. Officer Darren Wilson said he saw Michael Brown as a 'demon' and he presumably brought that stereotype of the dangerous young black man to his encounter with Brown. Perhaps officer Tim Loehmann perceived the tall 12-year-old Tamir Rice through a 'dangerous black kid' stereotype, and so did not recognise Tamir's youth, nor appropriately assess the danger he posed.[6] (Loehmann's initial story that he asked Rice three times to drop his gun and Rice refused is not credible within the two-second time frame revealed in the video.) In these two cases, it is plausible to postulate that the 'dangerous black male' stereotype is part of the motivational mix that produced the homicides.[7]

These stereotypic associations generally operate below the level of explicit awareness.[8] So, when Darren Wilson was interviewed on television and asked whether he would have acted in any way differently if Michael Brown had been white, he answered without a mini-second's hesitation, 'No'. But there is no reason to take Wilson's conscious belief (or his expressed claim, whether he believed it or not) as the truth about his racial stereotypes or biases.

[4] On harms of stereotyping in general, and their contrast with harms connected with particular stereotypes, see Blum (2004).

[5] Greenberg (2015).

[6] Studies suggest that white adults frequently overestimate the age of black young people (American Psychological Association, 2014).

[7] The Gurley situation differs from the other three in that Officer Peter Liang did not see Gurley before he shot his gun. But it is plausible to suppose that Liang would make the assumption that an individual he encountered in this largely black housing project was black, and so anti-black stereotypes could well have been operating in his mind also.

[8] Banaji and Greenwald (2013). In fact the level of violent crime in general and in black communities in particular has continued to decrease over the past 25 years or so. In New York city, the homicide rate has dipped from 2245 in 1990 to 328 in 2014 (Eckholm, 2015). See also Sharkey (2018). Yet the stereotype of dangerous black males persists largely unchanged, suggesting its weak responsiveness to actual evidence.

The point I wish to make is that this 'stereotype' framework, encompassing both the general harms of all stereotyping, and the particular harms of the 'dangerous black male' stereotype, does not, I think, fully capture the moral wrongfulness of the states of mind that prompted these killings. It provides only part of the picture. I think the idea of 'black lives matter', which has come to be the main label under which the movement protesting these killings operated, provides a moral framework that we need to add to stereotype for a more complete moral picture of the situation. I think 'black lives matter' opens us to a deeper moral understanding.

By 'black lives matter' I refer to the elemental point that it matters if a black person is alive rather than dead, and it matters as much and in the same way as this matters for human beings in general, of any racial group. I will leave aside a richer notion of lives mattering that can refer to flourishing. An individual can manifest an appreciation, or a failure to appreciate, that black lives matter in a number of ways. Many people thought that the police officers in these and other cases of black people being killed evinced a lack of concern for black lives, a lack of recognition that black lives matter; that grand juries and prosecutors did so by failing to indict or try the perpetrators; and that the larger society also did so by allowing so many black people to be killed by police officers without the officers suffering any legal punishment. (There are instances of police officers being found guilty of malfeasance in these sorts of cases, but they have been very rare.)

IV. Police Behaviour after Killing – Failures to Care

I am very much in sympathy with the view that the emotional attitude constituting a failure to appreciate that blacks lives matter has played a role in the killings discussed above, and have joined in the protests that have followed in the wake of these cases. But I am not going to try to defend that view here. Instead I want to look at a different aspect of the five cases mentioned – not the original taking of life, but the way the police officers in all of the cases comported themselves once the black men or boys were either dead or subdued. I bypass the killings themselves because killing in self-defence seems permissible, and police officers' lives are indeed often threatened. In at least some of the police killings, some have claimed that the officers plausibly believed that their lives, or those of others in the vicinity, were threatened and that deadly force was necessary to stop this threat. I do not think this claim is at all plausible in any of the five cases in question, but I wish to put this issue aside. I focus on the post-encounter behaviour simply to attend to a different feature of these situations, one not given much attention, and one that raises somewhat different issues of appropriate moral and emotional response, of vice and virtue.

The video of Eric Garner's last moments is particularly revealing in this regard. The video shows several officers standing around while Garner protests their trying to arrest him. He is not cooperative, indeed, but nor does he pose any physical threat (it is also evident that he is unarmed[9]), especially given the five or six police officers in his immediate vicinity. We see Officer Pantaleo put Garner in a chokehold and take him down to the pavement. We hear Garner say 'I can't breathe' over and over, then go quiet. Pantaleo does not respond; he does not loosen his hold or show any recognition that he might be risking Garner's life, not merely subduing him. He isn't deliberately trying to kill Garner. But he shows an appalling indifference to the possibility that he might nevertheless be doing so. The indifference is not only Pantaleo's. None of the other officers gathered around Garner try to physically stop Pantaleo, though one sergeant is heard to say 'Let up, you got him already'. The officers stand around, try to clear the crowd of passers-by, and provide the arriving emergency medical technicians (EMTs) access – but not showing any sense of urgency about a life being snuffed out before their eyes. Garner was dead within an hour.

The apparent indifference to Garner's life continues with the arrival of the EMTs. They look at Garner, but don't do anything to help him. They do not administer cardio-pulmonary resuscitation (CPR) to him. The president of the EMT union commented afterwards, with an implied criticism of their behaviour: 'There was a lack of initial intervention. They were not aggressive. If they're not breathing [that is, if the suspect is not breathing], assist with their ventilation. This is something that is ingrained in your training.'[10] It did not seem to have actually been 'ingrained' in their training in the sense implied by the union leader, that is, internalised as a requirement. The union president's collapsing of the 'is/ought' distinction here may reflect blindness to the actual effect of the trainings to which he refers (or it may just be a form of damage control).

Did any of these many parties to the Garner encounter (with the possible partial exception of the sergeant suggesting that Pantaleo ease up) evince a recognition that Garner's life mattered? Is there any evidence of human concern toward or with regard to Garner? We don't see it.

The aftermath of the killings of Akai Gurley and Tamir Rice reveal similar apparent unconcern or indifference. After firing their guns, and in the process (accidently) hitting Gurley, Officer Liang and his partner Officer Landau did not immediately try to determine whether anyone had been hit. When they did discover that Gurley had been shot, they did not immediately phone this in, calling for help. Rather, during the six and a half minutes before doing so, Liang texted his union representative, presumably to check on what kind of trouble he was in, or could avoid, for the shooting.[11] He did so while the two officers'

[9] See the excellent discussion of the Garner events, including an assessment of the chokehold, in Kleinig (2014).

[10] Duncan (2014). There were two different videos, one of the officers taking Garner down, and a second (by a different individual) of the medical response. It took twelve minutes for EMTs to upgrade the seriousness of the situation to 'Segment 1', the highest priority; and an article on the case reports the taker of the second video telling how the prosecutor at the grand jury hearing tried to pressure her to refrain from testifying the officers had Garner in a chokehold. Baker et al (2015).

[11] Parascandola and Yaniv (2014).

commanding officer and an emergency operator, responding to a neighbour's 911 call, tried unsuccessfully to contact Liang and Landau.

Tamir Rice suffered the same apparent unconcern for his life and harm suffered. After Officer Loehmann shot Rice, neither he nor his partner, Officer Frank Garmback, checked his vital signs or offered any sort of first aid to Rice.[12] He was alive and they did nothing to help him. Rice died several hours later. Only almost four minutes after Rice was shot did a police detective and an FBI agent in the area try to help him.[13] The point is that once Rice was shot and on the ground, Loehmann could no longer believe he was a threat; nor is Loehmann reported as continuing to believe Rice was a threat to anyone. Even if someone was once a threat, or perceived (wrongly or not) to be one, an entirely different moral framework – a way of morally perceiving the situation – should kick in once the individual can no longer plausibly be regarded as a threat. An injured and unthreatening individual requires help, especially from the person who caused the injury and also especially from police officers, whose role obligation is to 'protect and serve'. It shouldn't matter morally whether the person had been a threat (or even committed a crime) one minute before. Officer Pantaleo, flanked by several other officers, knew that once Garner was chokeholded to the ground he was no longer a threat to them. Garner's poignant cries for them to enable him to breathe, then going limp and no longer speaking should shift their framework of experiencing Garner from 'threatening' (again, not to say that this perception was justified) to 'a human being who needs help and is possibly in danger'. Part of the shift should be emotional in character. That is, whatever feelings of anger or fear attend a threatening situation should give way to emotions of care and concern once the threat is removed and the suspect is both demobilised and in pain, suffering, or in a health- or life-threatening situation himself.

With respect to the Michael Brown encounter, let us leave aside whether Wilson was justified in shooting Brown once Brown was known by Wilson to be unarmed and was no longer within striking distance of Wilson.[14] After Wilson did shoot him, Brown lay face down in the street. Wilson did not check to see if Brown was breathing or if he had a pulse; he did not render aid in any form. A neighbour also reported that two white police officers on the scene (one of them likely to have been Wilson) prevented a nurse (also a neighbour) from administering CPR to Brown, which she was begging them to do.[15] Wilson evinced the same lack of human concern and care as the officers in the Garner and Rice cases.

[12] Dawan and Oppel (2015).

[13] Accounts of Rice, Garner and Gurley incidents also from King (2014a).

[14] King (2014b). On 5 March, the Department of Justice issued a report clearing Wilson of civil rights violations in regard to the shooting of Brown. The *New York Times* account of the report said that the preponderance of evidence is that Brown was moving toward Wilson when Wilson shot him (again) (Healy et al, 2015). It does not explicitly address the distance between the two men nor whether it was necessary to use deadly force to stop Brown. Perhaps there is more evidence on this matter in the full report, which I have not read.

[15] Hemingway (2014).

This failure of care, and to provide aid, is over and above a different matter that drew much attention at the time: that Brown's body was left for four hours in the middle of the street. Certainly that fact shows a deep disregard for Brown as a human being; how we treat the dead is governed by moral norms that draw on the fact that a dead person is still a human being. But in addition, leaving Brown's body in that way also shows disrespect for the (African American) neighbourhood, the community, of which Brown was a part and in which Brown lived. Leaving the dead body of a community member in that way constitutes a distinctive form of civic demeaning and devaluing – of a piece with the general failure to indict, convict and punish police through the justice system.[16]

Considerations relevant to the excusability or justifiability of using lethal force in the original encounter no longer apply once the victim is 'down' and obviously injured and disabled. The attitude underlying the officers' failure of concern, perhaps compassion, and aid to a badly injured party is precisely what the 'Black Lives Matter' slogan is meant to call attention to and challenge. (Other police officers arriving later sometimes did help, further highlighting the actions the original officers should have taken.) As the civil rights leader, Ella Baker, said in the 1960s: 'We can't rest until the killings of black mother's sons is just as important as the killings of white mother's sons.'[17]

Perhaps adherence to the proposition 'black lives matter' is not simply equivalent to feeling and having concern or compassion for a particular black human being in a state of suffering or need whom the agent encounters, as in the situations discussed. The former is a more general and somewhat more abstract form of regard for the lives of a particular group. Nevertheless, the belief requires an emotional disposition to have some form of emotional response like compassion or concern when a member of that group is encountered.[18]

V. Stereotyping and Black Lives Matter as Moral Frameworks

To summarise, then, I am suggesting that stereotyping as a morally problematic cognition is plausibly thought to have played some part in the motivational set

[16] The police have acknowledged that leaving the body was wrong but have not, as far as I am aware, acknowledged the full scope of the communal insult and human indifference manifested.

[17] 'Interview with Crystal Feimster on Ferguson, Police Brutality, and Activism', 2014.

[18] I do not think that *empathy* is required in the situations at hand, nor do I regard empathy as necessarily entailed by a sincere belief that 'black lives matter'. This is partly because, as White (2020) and Hansberg (2020) argue (chapters five and eight in this volume), there are too many different conceptions of 'empathy' on offer in the current literature to give it this sort of definitional centrality. But it is also because, even if we confine empathy to one common understanding of it involving an acute awareness of what someone else is feeling, the emotional attitude we require of the police in these situations seems to me less robust than this. Concern does not require this acute awareness, but only that one be moved in some way by the other's plight, involving some degree of motivation to assist.

that led to the officers killing Michael Brown, Tamir Rice and Eric Garner. Stereotyping is morally problematic for two different kinds of reasons: one concerning stereotyping in general, the other concerning specific stereotypes (such as seeing young black men as dangerous or threatening). But these moral wrongs do not fully express the devaluing of black life that seems to have been manifested in these encounters, considered in their totality. Seeing someone's life as not mattering, or not mattering very much, or not mattering as much as the lives of people in other groups, is not the same as stereotyping the person; it is not a question of attributing a definite characteristic to that person, like being dangerous or violent, as stereotypes do. It is less cognitive than stereotyping, involving an emotionally infused perceiving or experiencing of someone in a defective way – a way that withholds appropriate concern or care for them as a fellow human being. Care and concern, as emotional attitudes, are expressions of valuing life, for example when that life is threatened.

Of course, some stereotypes can *contribute* to the devaluing of life. If I see someone as inherently criminal and violent, I am more likely to demonise or dehumanise that person, and thus to care less about their life, as seems to have been illustrated by Officer Wilson saying, as mentioned earlier, that he saw Michael Brown as a 'demon'.[19] Also, the stereotype of black males as dangerous is not pertinent to the situation with which we are primarily concerned, when the black male in question is subdued and clearly no longer posing a threat.

VI. Implicit Bias and Zack's Rights-Based Approach

The notion of 'implicit bias' has garnered a good deal of attention in relation to race and racial discrimination recently. Implicit bias is a complex issue and I will be able to deal with it only briefly. Implicit bias is generally understood as an unconscious favouring or disfavouring of a group, or a negative or positive association with a group. It differs from what I am defining as 'stereotyping' because it does not attribute a definite characteristic to the group in question. However, like stereotyping it seems to me plausible to see implicit bias as operating in many of these police killing incidents, and thus as part of the moral repertoire we have for assessing them from a moral point of view. There is indeed dispute in the literature over whether an agent can be blameworthy if the agent's action or inaction stems from implicit bias, since implicit bias is regarded by many as entirely unconscious and outside of the agent's control; but the presence of implicit bias can be diminished by indirect methods, leading to a possibility of blameworthiness for not engaging in such methods.[20]

[19] Wilson's full statement: 'He looked up at me and had the most intense aggressive face. The only way I can describe it, it looks like a demon, that's how angry he looked' (Blow, 2014).

[20] For a representative source of this literature, see Brownstein and Saul (2016).

But I wish to make a different point about implicit bias, and that is that the idea of 'bias' does not capture a lack of concern for someone's life. It is a lesser moral deficiency or vice – very important certainly (eg possibly leading to job discrimination), but not at the level of the failure of human response in 'subdued subject' situations. No doubt someone who does not recognise that black lives matter would also be likely to have biases against black people, and it may be plausible to attribute implicit bias to many of the officers involved in these and similar cases. But bias itself does not entail failure to believe that black lives matter.

In her recent book, *White Privilege and Black Rights*, Naomi Zack is leery of the slogan 'black lives matter'.[21] She thinks it diverts from what in her mind should be the central focus in the police killings, which is the violation of the rights of black people involved in taking their lives wrongfully, not the caring issue highlighted in the 'black lives matter' approach. Zack says that black lives can matter to a politician who wants their votes, and that a life matters to the person whose life it is. She implies that purely instrumental mattering and self-mattering exhaust the options. But these are not the only ways that lives matter. They also matter in a way that is analogous to the way Zack thinks rights matter – that is, they matter in themselves, and in that respect are something that everyone has reason to care about. We have reason to care about someone else's life and someone else's rights, because those things matter in themselves and ground a claim on our concern. The slogan 'Black Lives Matter' aims to capture that type of mattering, specifically in relation to black people, that is, reminding us that black people are a group whose lives are more at risk of not being regarded as mattering than are other groups, especially whites. But Zack is right that violation of the rights of black people is involved in these cases and, like stereotyping and implicit bias, provides appropriate moral criticism of the actions of the police officers in these cases.

This last point leads to a criticism sometimes made of the Black Lives Matter movement, that its slogan appears to single out black people as a distinctive group whose lives matter, when everyone's life matters, and, it is suggested, we should be saying 'All Lives Matter'. This criticism is misplaced. The focus on black lives is not meant to say that only they matter but that they are a group particularly vulnerable to people not recognising that their lives matter. This is why it is important to highlight that black lives matter.

VII. Objections

I will now consider four objections to the idea that the cases I have discussed evidence a failure to care or to recognise that black lives matter.

[21] Zack (2015).

A. Aggressive Mindset

The first, suggested to me in an interview with a chief of police of a medium-sized city, who has a PhD in police ethics, is that it is a fact of human nature that someone who has had a prolonged and violent or potentially violent encounter with a second party, for example, after a chase (a common precursor to police killings), cannot immediately switch over to a mindset in which they become concerned for that person's well-being or even life. My interviewee told me that police officers are indeed required to call medical assistance in such situations but are not required to administer assistance themselves, in recognition of this switchover problem. Let us call this the 'aggressive mindset' objection.

One thing to note is that some of the cases I have discussed do not seem to present situations to which the aggressive mindset objection applies. Regarding Akai Gurley, Officer Liang had no prior contact with Gurley before shooting his gun and killing him, so Liang was not in an aggressive mindset. Regarding Tamir Rice, Officer Loehmann had only just pulled up alongside Rice when he shot him; even if, as Loehmann claimed, Rice had reached for what Loehmann had reason to think was a real gun, Loehmann killed him within two seconds, presumably not enough time to take on the aggressive mindset the objection requires.

Nor does the case of Eric Garner seem to fit the objection, though this case is arguably closer to it than the others. Officer Pantaleo, with the assistance of four other officers, wrestled Garner to the ground. Prior to that, while Garner protested and said he was tired of being harassed by police and hadn't done anything wrong, the officers themselves just warily stood around, presumably trying to figure out what they should do, or perhaps just waiting for the right moment to disable Garner. There was no aggressive interchange which would have emotionally pumped up the officers in the way the objection requires.[22]

The Michael Brown case presents the best-case scenario for the aggressive mindset objection. If Officer Wilson had had a prior physical encounter with Brown, had chased him down the street, then felt that Brown was charging at him, perhaps he was indeed in an emotional state not easily converted to one in which he would check on the fallen Michael Brown to see if he was alive and in need of attention.

However, and again repeating that I am operating from a somewhat insufficient knowledge base here, I am simply not prepared to accept the idea that it is impossible for a police officer who has had an extended, violent and even life-threatening encounter with a suspect to then shift, once he sees that the suspect poses no danger to him, is clearly subdued, and may be in need of assistance, to a mindset involving a different set of emotions (including concern), which prompts the officer to approach the suspect in order to ascertain whether that assistance is needed.

[22] I do not mean to suggest that my interviewee claimed that the specific cases did fit his objection. He was making an observation about police killings in general.

Indeed, in a sense my interviewee agrees with this. In his own police department, he requires his officers to carry tourniquets, bandages and latex gloves, precisely in order to be able to offer minimal medical assistance until the more knowledgeable EMTs arrive on the scene, and he expects his officers to use these medical materials in situations in which they themselves have harmed the suspect. He reported to me two cases in which white officers offered CPR to black drug-dealers whom they had shot moments before. In light of these observations, I think my interviewee's objection is best understood as claiming that there is a natural tendency to disengage from or to not be readily able to access a caring or concerned emotional state with regard to someone whom you have just harmed in a violent confrontation; but that this tendency is not incapable of being overcome, and that having policies, trainings and sanctions in place in a police department can help that process of overcoming.[23]

B. Focus on Behaviour Not Emotions

This last point bleeds into the second objection from my police commissioner interviewee. That is that we should not focus on the police officers' emotional responses but on their behaviour. And we do this through changing policies governing police practice, both at local department level and also at broader levels, such as the recommendations of President Obama's 2015 Task Force on Policing.[24] Even if a white police officer is definitively racist and is indifferent to the lives of black perpetrators of crimes, or persons he believes to be perpetrators, if he is bound by a rule in his department that he must offer aid to someone whom he has harmed, that rule and the sanction attached to it can lead him to offer that aid even if he lacks the appropriate emotions that would prompt him to do so.

Reform of police practices, as this line of thought calls for, is indeed a central goal of the Black Lives Matter movement, and is also in line with Zack's call for a focus on rights to certain treatment (see section VI). There is no contradiction between calling for 'behavioural reform' as well as appealing to the moral sentiments of Americans and police officials to fully recognise and respond to black humanity. Furthermore, legal and behavioural change often leads to at least some change in sentiments of the heart. The concept of 'community policing' relies on the idea that if police officers are mandated to get to know members of communities they serve as persons, citizens and individual human beings, they will come to care about them, and also to be sensitive to individual qualities that will be relevant in encounters of a law enforcement nature.

[23] In addition, this analysis is perfectly consistent with another implication of my interviewee's view – that officers should defer to the superior medical expertise of EMTs when the situation is not so dire that emergency measures must be taken before the EMTs arrive.

[24] President's Task Force on 21st Century Policing, 2015.

Sentiments cannot be directly mandated, and the mandated helping behaviour is of greater moral importance than sentiments. Nevertheless, when the police officer engages in helping, feelings of care or concern may be prompted by the human encounter involved.

I am trying to locate a particular kind of moral vice of a partly emotional nature that we seem to be seeing in many police officers' response to black people, especially in their behaviour toward them after they have been harmed and subdued. By saying this vice is of an emotional nature, I do not mean that it necessarily involves distinct vicious emotions such as hatred, antipathy or contempt (though it may on particular occasions). Rather the vice consists in part in the absence of emotions appropriate to the situation at hand, such as concern. In his classic virtuist account of racism, Jorge Garcia proposes that ill-will on the basis of race is at the heart of the vice of racism; but he extends ill-will to include indifference.[25] So on his account a lack of (appropriate) emotion, when based on race, would constitute a vice in the situations discussed here.

My suggestion complements Garcia's account. I think that indifference, thus lack of emotion of the appropriate sort, can be vicious. What makes the indifference vicious is the police officers' professional role, to 'protect and serve', which arguably involves care and concern for citizens in need especially (but not only) when the officer in question has been the agent of their plight.[26] This vice is not racial in character. But when that indifference is toward a particular racial group as such – a failure to appreciate that black lives matter – that is a racial form of the vice just mentioned. And I agree with Garcia that the racial form has a distinctive moral valence not fully present in the more general form.

C. Police Kill White People Too

A third objection, or at least concern, with my view is that American police often kill white people. According to the *Guardian's* 'The Counted' project, 53 per cent of the people killed by American police in 2016 were white. I don't have figures on the killing of *unarmed* people specifically, nor on the post-killing behaviour I have been foregrounding in this chapter, and it is not possible to say anything very definitive without that information.[27] But let us assume that police officers

[25] Garcia (1996).

[26] Thus, I am not here taking up the question of whether a random passerby exemplifies vice if they fail to have concern for a needy stranger.

[27] One incident caught on video shows a white policewoman chasing and screaming at a 58-year-old white man who was stopped at a traffic light for a minor automobile infraction. He falls to the ground, in the snow, as she continues to tell him to get down on the ground, she tases him, and she, and the viewer, cannot always see where his hand is with respect to his coat; the officer ultimately shoots and kills him, saying she was afraid he was going for a gun (which he did not have). (Note that although I can't find a citation for this, I have viewed the video.)

sometimes fail to offer aid to white persons they have harmed. If so, this might seem to suggest that if there is some kind of indifference to or failure to appreciate the value of life, it is not as racialised as I have been claiming.

This racial observation is an important point. American police kill more people, and a higher percentage of the population, than many other comparable countries.[28] The Obama administration took some steps to reduce the use of deadly force, as recommended by the 2015 Task Force, partly in recognition that American police resort to it too often.[29] Something problematic in their attitudes (probably partly emotional in character) toward suspects too easily leads to the use of deadly force, no matter the race of the suspect. My superintendent interviewee's perspective is important here. If we change the rules of engagement, for example, training police officers in de-escalating confrontations, standing away from the suspect, calling in back-up before resorting to violence, and other proposed reforms, fewer officers would kill people than they now do. And, indeed, the rate of killing of unarmed people dropped significantly from 2015 to 2016 and the total deaths were also reduced, perhaps as a result of such reforms. (The overall crime rate in the US has been falling fairly significantly for about 20 years [though it increased between 2015 and 2016], and that could also be having some effect on the police killing rate.[30])

Activists in the Black Lives Matter movement do not think that blacks are the only victims of unwarranted violence; but the public protests, and the public discussions, do not always recognise the broader group of victims. Such recognition would have to affect our way of thinking about the black victims. It will mean recognising that in cases of black victims, sentiments other than purely anti-black animus or race-based failure to appreciate the value of black lives might also be operating. One might speculate on what some of those other contributing factors might be – dehumanisation of suspects, belief in the likelihood that one will not be punished for violent misbehaviour, or a diminishing of moral constraints attendant upon having power over another. These factors are of differing moral significance and character, but they all involve environmental, psychological or cultural factors that feed into morally bad behaviour toward suspects.

But I do want to emphasise that the existence of these other contributors to bad behaviour and sentiment that can come into play with white victims, does not preclude specifically black-focused sentiments – involved in failing to appreciate that specifically black lives matter – from being present, and being part of the mix in the black case that is not present in the white case. After all, the rate of killing of blacks remains substantially higher than that of whites. The *Guardian* calculates that blacks are killed at four times the rate of whites.[31]

[28] Vox (2018) (comparing to, and higher than, Italy, Canada, Sweden, France, UK and Germany).
[29] Final Report of the President's Task Force on 21st Century Policing, May 2015.
[30] Sharkey (2018).
[31] All references to the *Guardian*'s 'The Counted' are from Swaine and McCarthy (2017).

Race analysis in the US is often framed in an all-or-nothing way: either race is the sole and total explanation of some phenomenon that affects racial minorities or a particular such group, or race has nothing to do with it at all. This approach should be resisted. In the case of police killings, it is entirely plausible that various non-racial factors having to do with police attitudes, practice, culture and rules in the US *coexist* with biases against and stereotypes of blacks and with a failure to appreciate the worth of black lives, and that the specific mix differs among individual incidents, officers, locales, times and departments.

D. Some Police Officers Who Victimise Blacks are Themselves Black

A fourth objection to a 'devaluing black lives' analysis is that some of the victimisation of black people has been perpetuated by black police officers. One might think that black officers cannot devalue black lives unless they devalue their own life, and that that is very unlikely. Yet it is an entirely common human phenomenon that members of a group may look down on sub-groups of that group, and not value those people's humanity as much as that of their own sub-group of the larger group. Rich white people often demean poor white people. Middle class blacks sometimes look down on poor blacks. Why would it be surprising if black police officers did the same with black men, especially younger ones who live in largely black or Hispanic poor urban neighbourhoods?

In addition, black police officers are members of police departments, often white dominated, and which almost always contain a higher percentage of whites than the surrounding community.[32] There is strong evidence that the cultures of many such departments involve disrespect toward black people and black communities. This disrespect is implicit and explicit in official reports on those departments, such as recent ones on Cleveland (Ohio) and Ferguson (Missouri), the sites of two of the killings (Rice and Brown), as well as the aforementioned President's Task Force on 21st Century Policing document.[33] Especially given the

[32] 'Minorities are underrepresented in nearly every large law enforcement agency in America' (Maciag, 2015).

[33] 'The public confers legitimacy only on those whom they believe are acting in procedurally just ways. Procedurally just behaviour is based on four central principles: 1. Treating people with dignity and respect 2. Giving individuals "voice" during encounters 3. Being neutral and transparent in decision-making 4. Conveying trustworthy motives' (Final Report of the President's Task Force on 21st Century Policing, May 2015, p 7). The Report makes it clear that these principles are frequently not honoured by police departments. See also US Department of Justice, 'Report on the Ferguson Police Department', March 2015. See https://www.justice.gov/sites/default/files/opa/press-releases/attachments/2015/03/04/ferguson_police_department_report.pdf, and Department of Justice, Investigation of the Cleveland Division of Police, December 2014 (good summary in https://www.washingtonpost.com/news/the-watch/wp/2014/12/05/the-dojs-jaw-dropping-report-about-the-cleveland-police-department/?utm_term=.5ed25bf94bac).

powerful in-group culture of police departments, it would be extremely surprising if black police officers were entirely unaffected by this disrespect toward young black men in poor, urban communities.

Finally, it is also an entirely familiar phenomenon that if a group is stigmatised in the wider society, some members of that group will internalise that stigma, against members of their own group or even toward themselves. This is often called 'internalised racism'. Thus, for all these reasons, the presence of anti-black sentiment among blacks, and bad behaviour toward blacks, provides no reason for doubting that racially problematic sentiments are operating among white officers who victimise blacks.

VIII. Conclusion

I have identified a particular moral failing, a vice, of a partially emotional character, consisting in a failure to recognise that black lives matter, which is closely related to but not exactly the same as failure of appropriate concern for those warranting that concern from the agent in question. These related failings are both related to but distinct from three other moral failings: stereotyping, implicit (racial) bias, and failure to recognise the rights of black people. I have argued that it is plausible to see many police officers involved in the shootings and subsequent behaviour toward black men in the US as exemplifying all these failings. I have suggested that the behaviour of some of these officers after the black subjects had been subdued or wounded provides particularly striking evidence of the failure to value black lives, apart from the actual killings themselves.

The focus on individual moral failings should not, however, mislead us about the more fundamental source of the failure to recognise that black lives matter. It lies in a stigmatising of black people, the roots of which are deep in American, and indeed Western, history and society.[34] Perhaps this stigmatising also at least partly underlies some of the other, including structural, factors contributing to such a high rate of killing of black people in the US: the relative leniency of the legal system for sanctioning such behaviour, public deference to police accounts of their behaviour in trials, and the pervasive disparities between blacks and whites by virtually every measure of social well-being. In any case, taking seriously how one might root out these attitudes requires recognising this history, and recognising that the attitudes in question are more than merely individual failures. Moral philosophy should not remain focused on the purely individual level in dealing with socially and culturally embedded vicious sentiments.

[34] Christopher Lebron argues that the moral approach underlying 'black lives matter' has a long and influential history in African American protest thought. Lebron (2017).

References

'Interview with Crystal Feimster on Ferguson, Police Brutality, and Activism' (2014) *Broad Recognition: A Feminist Magazine at Yale* (21 December). Available at http://broadrecognition.com/uncategorized/interview-with-crystal-feimster.

American Psychological Association (2014) 'Black Boys Viewed as Older, Less Innocent Than Whites, Research Finds' [newsletter report of article by PA Goff] (6 March).

Baker, A, Goodman, JD and Mueller, B (2015) 'Beyond the Chokehold: The Path to Eric Garner's Death' *New York Times* (6 June). Available at http://www.nytimes.com/2015/06/14/nyregion/eric-garner-police-chokehold-staten-island.html?_r=0.

Banaji, M and Greenwald, A (2013) *Blindspot: Hidden Biases of Good People* (New York, Bantam Books).

Blow, C (2014) 'This is Your Moment' *New York Times* (10 December).

Blum, L (2004) 'Stereotypes and Stereotyping: A Moral Analysis' 33(3) *Philosophical Papers* 251.

Blum, L (2016) 'The Too Minimal Political, Moral, and Civic Dimension of Claude Steele's "Stereotype Threat" Paradigm' in M Brownstein and J Saul (eds) *Implicit Bias and Philosophy, volume 2: Moral Responsibility, Structural Injustice, and Ethics* (New York, Oxford University Press, 2016) 147.

Brownstein, M and Saul, J (eds) *Implicit Bias and Philosophy, Volumes 1 and 2* (New York, Oxford University Press, 2016).

Dawan, S and Oppel, R (2015) 'Many Errors by Cleveland Police, Then a Fatal One *New York Times*, 1/25, A14. Available at http://www.nytimes.com/2015/01/23/us/in-tamir-rice-shooting-in-cleveland-many-errors-by-police-then-a-fatal-one.html?_r=0.

Duncan, J (2014) 'Eric Garner's Case: Video of chokehold's aftermath raises new questions' CBS News (6 December). Available at http://www.cbsnews.com/news/second-tape-of-nypd-chokehold-raises-new-questions-in-eric-garner-case/.

Eckholm, E (2015) 'In a Safer Age, U.S. Rethinks its "Tough on Crime" System' *New York Times* (14 January).

Garcia, JLA (1996) 'The Heart of Racism' 27(2) *Journal of Social Philosophy* 5.

Greenberg, M (2015) 'The NY Police vs. the Mayor' *New York Review of Books* (5 February) 39.

Hansberg, O (2020) 'Empathy and Negative Intimacy' in A Amaya and M Del Mar (eds) *Virtue, Emotion and Imagination in Law and Legal Reasoning* (Oxford, Hart Publishing).

Healy, J, Stolberg, S and Lee, V (2015) 'Ferguson Report Puts "Hands Up" to Reality Test' *New York Times* (4 March). Available at https://www.nytimes.com/2015/03/06/us/in-ferguson-both-sides-see-vindication-in-justice-department-reports.html.

Hemingway, S (2014) 'Ferguson Police's *Other* Sin: Why Grand Jury Must Probe Brown Shooting's Aftermath' *Salon* (10 November).

King, S (2014a) 'About the strange behavior of officers after they killed Akai Gurley, Tamir Rice, and Eric Garner' *DailyKos* (8 December). Available at http://www.dailykos.com/story/2014/12/05/1349673/-About-the-strange-behavior.

King, S (2014b) 'Video: Police Lied. Mike Brown was Killed 148 Feet Away from Darren Wilson's SUV' *DailyKos* (20 November). Available at www.dailykos.com/story/2014/11/20/1346374/-BREAK.

Kleinig, J (2014) 'Chokeholds, Eric Garner, and Police Ethics' *The Critique* (22 August). Previously available at http://www.thecritique.com/author/johnKleinig/ [site no longer exists].

Lebron, C (2017) *The Making of Black Lives Matter: A Brief History of an Idea* (New York: Oxford).

Maciag, M (2015), 'Where Police Don't Mirror Communities and Why It Matters' (28 August) *Governing the states and localities.* Available at https://www.governing.com/topics/public-justice-safety/gov-police-department-diversity.html.

Parascandola, R and Yaniv, O (2014), 'Rookie NYPD officer who shot Akai Gurley in Brooklyn stairwell was texting union rep as victim lay dying' *New York Daily News* (5 December). Available http://www.nydailynews.com/new-york/brooklyn/exclusive-texted-union-rep-akai-gurley-lay-dying-article-1.2034219.

President's Task Force President's Task Force on 21st Century Policing, *Final Report of the President's Task Force on 21st Century Policing,* Washington, DC: Office of Community Oriented Policing Services, May 2015.

Sharkey, P (2018) *Uneasy Peace: The Great Crime Decline, the Renewal of City Life, and the Next War on Violence* (New York: WW Norton & Co).

Smith, A (2005) 'Responsibility for Attitudes: Activity and Passivity in Mental Life' 115(2) *Ethics* 236.

Swaine, J and McCarthy, C (2017) 'Young Black Men Again Faced Highest Rate of US Police Killings in 2016' *The Guardian* (8 January).

Vox (2018) 'American Police Shoot and Kill Far More People Than Their Peers in Other Countries'. Available at https://www.vox.com/cards/police-brutality-shootings-us/us-police-shootings-statistics.

White, EK (2020) 'On Emotions and the Politics of Attention in Judicial Reasoning' in A Amaya and M Del Mar (eds) *Virtue, Emotion and Imagination in Law and Legal Reasoning* (Oxford, Hart Publishing).

Zack, N (2015) *White Privilege and Black Rights: The Injustice of U.S. Police Racial Profiling and Homicide* (Lanham, MD: Rowman and Littlefield).

8

Suffering and Punishment

MICHAEL S BRADY*

I. Introduction

Suppose one thinks that judicial punishment is sometimes appropriate. Suppose one also thinks that appropriate punishment necessarily imposes burdens or hard treatment on the criminal. Suppose, finally, one thinks that in order to be genuinely burdensome, the wrongdoer needs to *suffer*. The resulting account of just punishment raises a host of interesting and important questions concerning the relation between the negative emotions that constitute suffering, punishment, the rights of offenders, and sentencing. Perhaps the most important concerns the final supposition, and asks: Why must hard treatment take the form of imposing suffering? A plausible answer to this question, according to those who support the *Communicative Theory of Punishment*, will appeal to the communicative value that such imposition has. On this view, the imposition of suffering constitutes a legitimate form of censure for wrongdoing, wherein the state communicates to the offender the seriousness of his or her wrongdoing. At the same time, hard treatment, in the form of suffering, provides the opportunity for and enabling conditions in which wrongdoers can come to recognise the nature of their wrongdoing, repent, make reparations, and reform themselves. Suffering thus provides the means by which wrongdoers can make amends to those they have wronged – who are owed repentance and reparations – and also restore their own moral balance and character. Of course, the theory does not hold that suffering *necessarily* brings about these goods, or any others. Clearly, the suffering imposed by the judiciary can have no positive effect, and indeed can (and often does) make things considerably worse, for the offender and for society as a whole. Nevertheless, the communicative

* A version of this chapter was presented at the Virtue, Emotion and Imagination in Legal Reasoning conference at the Institute for Philosophical Research, UNAM, in March 2017. I would like to thank the speakers and delegates at this conference for their helpful feedback. I would like to especially thank the organisers of the conference – Maksymilian Del Mar and Amalia Amaya – for inviting me to this event, and for their very helpful comments on an earlier draft. Some of the ideas about the importance of suffering for justice here are developed from Chapter 5 of my *Suffering and Virtue* (Brady, 2018). This itself was the result of the Value of Suffering Project, funded by the John Templeton Foundation, which ran in Glasgow from September 2013–May 2016 (Grant ID 44167).

theorist argues that suffering is extremely important for the provision of these goods, in the sense that they would not be achieved in its absence.

This account faces a number of objections concerning the necessity of hard treatment, in the form of suffering, for the achievement of the stated goods. In this chapter I will examine two of the most pressing worries, raised in a recent paper by Matt Matravers. These are (i) that suffering is not needed for censure and (ii) that the imposition of suffering can lead to unfair sentencing. After outlining the objections, I will suggest how the communicative theorist can respond, by invoking the idea that censure requires the expression of appropriate emotions, and the actions that are part and parcel of these. Hard treatment is thus warranted as an expression of appropriate emotion.

II. Suffering as Ensuring Just Punishment

It is something of a platitude in moral philosophy that pain and suffering are bad; indeed, it would be difficult to find a more obvious candidate for intrinsic disvalues than these. Hedonists are surely right about this, even if we can doubt that pain and suffering are the *only* things that are intrinsically bad. However, pain and suffering also have great (extrinsic) value: those who are pain insensitive don't live very long; we might say something similar about those who are unable to feel fear. Feelings of shame and guilt would seem to be essential to co-operative living with others; feelings of disappointment have great motivational force in getting us to do better next time. And so on.

We might think that suffering is valuable from the social perspective in another important way: namely, suffering is an appropriate form of payment for wrongdoing. Here suffering has value as *coin*. This claim is most straightforwardly understood in religious traditions as the idea that suffering is just punishment for sin. But the claim has obvious secular counterparts when we look at judicial punishment. Here many people think that pain and suffering are valuable because they are an essential part of punishment, and so an essential element in the proper functioning of society itself. To see this idea in more detail, let us look more closely at the nature of punishment, and make the case for a particular account of the justification of the imposition of suffering in punishment, namely the *Communicative Theory*.

What is punishment? In *Leviathan*, Thomas Hobbes wrote that 'punishment is an evil inflicted by public authority on him that hath done or omitted that which is judged by the same authority to be a transgression of the law, to the end that the will of men may thereby the better be disposed to obedience'.[1] In 1968, HLA Hart defined punishment as involving five necessary conditions:

(1) it must involve pain or other consequences normally considered unpleasant;
(2) it must be for an offence against legal rules;

[1] Hobbes (1651/2008).

(3) it must be of an actual or supposed offender for his offence;
(4) it must be intentionally administered by human beings other than the offender;
(5) it must be imposed and administered by an authority constituted by a legal system against which the offence is committed.[2]

A more contemporary definition yet is due to Hugo Bedau and Erin Kelly in the *Stanford Encyclopedia of Philosophy*: judicial or criminal punishment is 'the authorized imposition of deprivations – of freedom or privacy or other goods to which the person otherwise has a right, or the imposition of special burdens – because the person has been found guilty of some criminal violation, typically (though not invariably) involving harm to the innocent'.[3]

There are a number of important common elements in these definitions, which I assume go to the heart of our thinking about what punishment is. But for our purposes, the most significant one is that punishment for wrongdoing, in the form of illegal or criminal acts, involves the imposition of pain or unpleasantness, deprivation or burdens. (Sometimes this is referred to as 'hard treatment', and includes, as Antony Duff puts it in his 2018 *Stanford Encyclopedia* article, 'material impositions or exactions that are in themselves typically unwelcome: they deprive people of things that they value (liberty, money, time); they require people to do things that they would not normally want to do or do voluntarily (to spend time on unpaid community labour, to report to a probation officer regularly, to undertake demanding programmes of various kinds)'.[4])

It is thus tempting to think that the legal/secular model of punishment is defined as necessarily involving the imposition of *suffering* onto the guilty, in the sense of some negative affective state of a suitable intensity. Now it might be objected here that negative affect need not be involved; the deprivations that Bedau and Kelly and Duff cite – of freedom and privacy and similar goods – are not themselves instances of negative affect or experienced suffering. Nevertheless, I take it that such losses only count as losses and as genuine deprivations *for the subject* insofar as they are experienced *as* burdens by the subject: that is, in a way that essentially involves negative affect. This explains our intuitions about the injustice of punishing the very rich with fines or other financial penalties. Such things will only count as losses or as burdensome insofar as the rich care about what is lost, and in the case of fines they typically don't. As a result, whilst punishment ought not to involve the imposition of *physical* pain on criminals, punishment is of its essence meant to be burdensome, and it is difficult to see how something can be a burden unless it is experienced as such by the wrongdoer. So legal punishment involves the intentional imposition, by the appropriate authority, of suffering on the wrongdoer.

[2] Hart (1968) 4–5.
[3] Bedau and Kelly (2015).
[4] Duff and Hoskins (2018).

This is what punishment *is*. It's another question whether the imposition of suffering by legal authorities is ever *justified* or *appropriate*. This is something which traditional retributivist accounts of punishment have had great difficulty in explaining, and a central reason why this approach to punishment fell out of favour in the twentieth century. As Matt Matravers writes, the reason for the theory's 'moribund state was that retributivism seemed to be plagued by a blank space where an argument was needed. Specifically, the retributive claim that "past wrongdoing (by an offender) justifies present suffering (inflicted on that offender for that wrongdoing)" appears to be either deeply mysterious or meaninglessly circular.'[5] However, a recent development of a retributivist theory – the *Communicative Theory of Punishment* – fares much better on this account. In what follows I will outline how the communicative theory explains the appropriateness of punishment, in a way that highlights the importance of suffering in achieving punishment's legitimate aims.

At the heart of the communicative theory is the idea – as the name suggests – that punishment is essentially a communicative enterprise, and that the ultimate justification for the imposition of suffering is that it serves a communicative purpose. This view accommodates both retributivist and reformist thinking, since (i) what is communicated in punishment is something merited or deserved by the criminal, and (ii) an internal goal of such communication is that the criminal recognise and acknowledge their wrongdoing, repent, make reparations, and reform themselves. To see the theory in more detail, let us turn to the work of perhaps the best-known communicative theorist, Antony Duff; in what follows I focus in the main on his monograph *Punishment, Communication, and Community*.[6]

Duff is concerned to argue against both consequentialist and 'pure' retributivist accounts of punishment. The former, he proposes, are ultimately inconsistent with acknowledging the rights of the innocent *and* the guilty, and as such will not ensure justice. The latter, on the other hand, fail to provide a plausible answer to the questions of *why* the guilty deserve to suffer. We can reject the retributivist line that wrongdoers deserve to suffer because this is a way of ensuring the social value of *fairness*. This, Duff argues, is implausible, because it 'offers a distorted picture of the punishment-deserving character of crime'.[7] The wrongs of physical assault or arson, for instance, clearly don't consist in taking unfair advantage of the law-abiding or in being a free-rider. By the same token, the idea that punishment is a matter of paying back what one owes is problematic: murder victims are unable to be recompensed for their loss, and a murderer doesn't (arguably) owe *the state* recompense. Moreover, there are many criminal activities that are not characterised as a form of profit-making, and punishment for these is again poorly understood as a kind of paying back. Think again of physical assault or arson. So standard retributivist attempts at explaining why the wrongdoer deserves to suffer fail.

[5] Matravers (2011), 69.
[6] Duff (2001).
[7] Ibid, 22.

Duff maintains that punishment has a different function to that of deterring crime or ensuring fairness. Instead, he thinks that legal punishment serves to communicate 'the condemnation or censure that criminals deserve' for their crimes.[8] Such condemnation is *required* by the state's concern for the rights and values that its laws are set up to protect, since failure to condemn implies that the state does not mean what it says when it prohibits certain activities. It is in this sense that punishment, as a form of condemnation and censure, is merited or deserved: it follows from the state's commitment to the rights and values that the legal and judicial system are set up to protect and preserve, and the criminal's violation of these rights and undermining of these values. In addition, by condemning and censuring criminal activity, the state also communicates concern for and solidarity with the victims of crime, and a willingness to punish others who break the law. These too would seem to be implications of a genuine commitment to the values at stake.[9]

Consider, in this light, the sentencing remarks made by Lady Rae in the High Court in Glasgow, upon sentencing Tanveer Ahmed for the murder of Assad Shah:

> It is clear from the agreed facts presented to me that this was a barbaric, premeditated and wholly unjustified killing of a much loved man who was a pillar of the local community … Let me be clear, no one in any civilised country including Scotland has the right to take the life of another, whatever offence that individual perceives that he or she has suffered. It is vitally important in modern society that respect and tolerance for others of every race, creed, colour, ethnic origin or religious belief is maintained and protected by the law of the land … I shall have regard to the various factors put forward as mitigation but none of them can truly mitigate, to any great extent, the brutality of your actions; the premeditation and motive behind those actions; your lack of remorse and your pride in what you did. For all of these reasons I intend to impose an exemplary sentence.[10]

Lady Rae's words here clearly condemn the offender for his offence, in a way that expresses censure in the strongest terms, respect for the values that the offender violated, and a clear willingness to punish as a result. (As we'll see later, it is plausible to think that the words also express strong emotions on Lady Rae's part, and at the same time generate, through imaginative engagement, emotions in those who hear or read them. It is not implausible to therefore view Lady's Rae's sentencing as a part of a pattern of emotional expression for the values that have been violated by this crime.)

Insofar as punishment communicates the censure that criminals deserve, it captures the retributivist intuition that punishment should be 'backward-looking', and address itself to the fact and nature of what a criminal did. But the retributivist element is only a part of the communicative theory, since the

[8] Ibid, 27.

[9] The issues of care and concern, and their relation to valuing lives, is the focus of Blum (2020) (chapter seven in this volume).

[10] At http://www.scotland-judiciary.org.uk/8/1639/HMA-v-Tanveer-Ahmed.

theory also wishes to accommodate the intuition that punishment should also be 'forward-looking' and thus aim at reforming offenders. Duff explains this element by noting that the communication of censure treats the offender as a rational agent, and in doing so aims to promote a particular kind of response. (It is part of the *nature* of communication to regard the other person in this way.) In particular, the offender 'is expected (but not compelled) to understand and accept the censure as justified: to understand and accept that he committed a wrong for which the community now properly censures him. His trial and conviction thus address him and seek a response from him as a member of the political community who is both bound and protected by its laws.'[11] By communicating censure and condemnation in this way, the state hopes that the offender will come to understand and recognise his wrongdoing and to repent for his offences; moreover, the state hopes that the offender will, as a result of such recognition, be moved to make reparations to the victim, and to commit to reforming himself so that he does not behave that way in the future. Just as the state's concern for particular values commits it to condemn acts that violate such values, so too does the criminal's acknowledgement and understanding of his wrongdoing commit him to repentance, the making of reparations, and reformation. For without the latter commitments, we can doubt that the offender really does acknowledge and recognise that he did something wrong, or really does understand what he did.

Legitimate or justified punishment therefore aims at giving criminals what they deserve, and at persuading them to recognise and acknowledge their wrongdoing, to repent, and reform. Still, we have yet to see exactly why censure, in the form of *suffering*, is essential for communication. What, in other words, is the justification for imposing hard treatment on criminals? Why must we communicate and motivate reform by making offenders suffer losses and deprivations?

There are two strands to the communicative theorist's answer to these questions. One focuses on the suffering necessarily involved in acknowledging and accepting one's wrongdoing. For Duff, 'an authentic recognition that I did wrong must bring with it repentance of that wrong. I recognize and own it as mine – I do not deny it or seek to justify or excuse it. But I also disown it, as something that I should not have done and now wish I had not done. *Repentance is necessarily painful*, since it must pain me to recognize and admit (to myself and others) the wrong I have done. In aiming to induce repentance, punishment thus aims to bring offenders to suffer what they deserve to suffer – the pains of repentance and remorse.'[12] On this view, suffering, in the form of feelings of remorse, is an essential part of the recognition and reform that punishment aims to bring about. In a paper from 2003 called 'Probation, Punishment and Restorative Justice', Duff continues this idea, stating that 'censure must aim to produce pain, in that if the person is not pained by it, it has failed to achieve its aim. That aim is not, of course, simply to cause or induce pain: it is to induce the appropriate

[11] Duff (2001), 80.
[12] Ibid, 107. (My emphasis.)

kind of pain – the pain that is intrinsic to accepting criticism from one's fellows and, even more importantly, the pain that is intrinsic to the recognition that one has wronged someone.'[13]

The other focuses on a different kind of burden and deprivation that the state intentionally imposes, namely community service, or probation, or some other burdensome reparative work.[14] Here the communicative theorist appeals to different but related ideas about the nature and function of communication involved in censure and condemnation. One idea is that censure and condemnation that is expressed *verbally* – for instance, by a guilty verdict and judge's summing up of the offender's wrong in a court of law – fails to constitute the kind of censure or condemnation that we need. Duff writes:

> With more serious wrongs, mere words cannot suffice: they cannot suffice to express, or to assure others of, the offender's repentant recognition of what she has done, any more than they can suffice to communicate to the offender the censure that she deserves. Punishment can then constitute a more forceful communication both of censure to the offender, and of apology to those whom she has wronged.[15]

The thought here would seem to be that the imposition of hard treatment is indeed necessary for the communication of censure; for communication has to be suitably forceful, and only hard treatment can supply the requisite force.

The second idea is that hard treatment in the form of suffering has important effects on attention, and this can play a significant role in bringing about repentance and the other goods in question.[16] This is because suffering focuses and captures attention, and in so doing makes it both difficult to ignore some important or significant object or event, and motivates reflection about that object or event. The suffering of hard treatment helps to ensure that the criminal cannot (so easily) ignore his criminal activity and his wrongdoing. As Duff points out:

> When I have done wrong, it is often tempting and all too easy to distract myself from the fact. I might say, to myself or to others, 'Yes, I did wrong and am sorry for it.' I might think that I have now repented the wrong. But all too often I have not seriously repented, because I have not thought seriously enough about, that wrong … Repentance, at least with serious wrongs … must go deep with the wrongdoer and must therefore occupy his attention, his thoughts, his emotions, for some considerable time.[17]

So another function of the imposition of burdens on the offender is 'to focus his attention on his crime', and ensure that repentance is suitably deep. Here suffering plays a similar attention-directing role to that played by physical pain or forms of

[13] Duff (2003), 186.

[14] Duff is resistant to the idea that imprisonment and fines are appropriate forms of censure, and he thinks that we need to think of more humane and effective forms of condemnation. See Matravers (2011), 76.

[15] Duff (2003), 189.

[16] For a discussion of the role of emotion in motivating attention to legal questions, and in particular the attention of judges to matters of law, see White (2020) (chapter six in this volume).

[17] (2001), 108.

emotional suffering: just as physical pain rules out the option of easily ignoring putative sources of physical damage, so too does the suffering in legitimate forms of judicial punishment keep the offender's criminal wrongdoing in mind. So, at the very least, hard treatment makes it difficult for the criminal to ignore his wrongdoing, and ignore how seriously this kind of wrongdoing is regarded by the state and his fellow citizens.[18]

There is another connection between suffering and attention that is important here. For suffering not only directs attention, but captures attention, and this helps to facilitate – at least in the right circumstances – an imaginative engagement with, and an understanding of, emotional objects and events.[19] By making the criminal suffer, therefore, the state puts in place conditions for the criminal to reflect and deliberate on what he did, in part through imaginatively engaging with the harm his wrongdoing caused to his victim, with what his victim felt, with the kind of reparations that might be appropriate, and with a future existence where his wrongdoing has been addressed and his moral character repaired. In this way the wrongdoer will hopefully come to recognise and understand the *nature* of his wrongdoing, understand the effect it had on his victim, understand what he needs to do, and understand the shape his life from hereon has to take. As Duff puts it, penal hard treatment 'provides a structure within which, we hope, [the criminal] will be able to think about the nature and implications of his crime, face up to it more adequately than he might otherwise (being human) do, and so arrive at a more authentic repentance. As fallible moral agents, we need such penances to assist and deepen repentance.'[20]

That suffering provides the opportunity for focused attention and imaginative engagement does not, of course, mean that it will bring about recognition, repentance, reform and reparations. Sometimes – perhaps often – wrongdoers will seek to shift the blame elsewhere. The wrongdoer might believe, therefore, that he suffers because *he* is the victim of the judicial system, or his upbringing, or the police, or society in general. Such rationalising explanations of why he is being so deprived are doubtless common amongst those who suffer judicial punishment. But this need not be the outcome of suffering's imposition. Instead, sometimes a criminal will come, through having his attention fixed on his wrongdoing and on how seriously the state takes this violation of these laws, to a recognition and an understanding of his wrongdoing, and of the steps he needs to take to rectify it. So in some instances at least, suffering imposed will motivate acknowledgement and

[18] In his *Stanford Encyclopedia* entry on 'Legal Punishment', Duff writes: 'Punishment … should aim not merely to communicate censure to the offender, but to persuade the offender to recognise and repent the wrong he has done, and so to recognise the need to reform himself and his future conduct, and to make apologetic reparation to those whom he wronged. His punishment then constitutes a kind of secular penance that he is required to undergo for his crime: its hard treatment aspects, the burden it imposes on him, should serve both to assist the process of repentance and reform, by focusing his attention on his crime and its implications, and as a way of making the apologetic reparation that he owes.'

[19] For more on this, see Brady (2013).

[20] Duff (2001), 108.

understanding, and the repentance and remorse that are a part of these. The point here, then, isn't that suffering will *necessarily* bring about a valuable end. Nevertheless, the understanding that is central to repentance and reform will be, for fallible agents like us, highly unlikely without the focused attention and imaginative engagement that suffering brings. If the state wants to achieve these valuable social goods, therefore, it will have to make criminals suffer.

So, at least, the communicative theory maintains. But there are worries about this approach to the justification of hard treatment. In the following section I will examine two such worries, and show how the communicative theorist can appeal to the connections between censure and emotion in order to respond.

III. Are Words Sometimes Enough?

In a recent paper, Matt Matravers has raised worries about the need for suffering in legitimate punishment, and in particular about Duff's explanations of its importance. Matravers makes two related criticisms.[21] The first is that suffering is not necessary for censure – on the grounds that sometimes words *are* enough – and so the censure at the heart of the communicative theory, and the imposition of suffering, can diverge. If this is the case, then a second criticism becomes germane: in many cases, the imposition of suffering will then be unfair, since those who come to acknowledge their wrongdoing, repent, reform themselves, and make reparations as a result of verbal censure alone will be unfairly punished by further impositions such as probation or community service. Let us take these criticisms in turn.

(i) Matravers begins by noting that on Duff's view, punishment is an intrinsically appropriate response to crime. This is because wrongdoing deserves moral criticism or censure, and wrongdoing of a certain kind is serious enough that it merits or deserves censure by the state. But Matravers notes that 'the common or garden way in which one communicates censure or gratitude is by using certain words or phrases'.[22] And it is at least *possible*, he thinks, that communication of this sort can succeed in bringing about the suffering at which punishment aims: namely the pain and suffering that is intrinsic to accepting the criticism and condemnation of others, and recognising the wrongs that one has done. Matravers writes:

> The claim is that sometimes words cannot suffice to communicate to the offender the censure that she deserves. But, why? It cannot be that we genuinely cannot think of words that will do the job … a combination of the richness of language and the fact that (as Duff emphasizes) this is a two-way *communication* in the context of a wrong done, makes me skeptical about applying the everyday thought that sometimes "words are not enough" too quickly to these cases.[23]

[21] Matravers (2011).
[22] Ibid, 75.
[23] Ibid, 78.

Now even if it is the case that *some* people might come to fully accept the criticism and come to fully recognise and understand their wrongdoing, this is surely not true for most people. In these cases, Matravers notes that 'it takes more than just verbal expression to focus one's mind on what one has done. A repeat wife-beater may need not merely to hear censure, but to feel it, and he may need time over which to think through what he has done.'[24] This is where the second dimension of Duff's approach to the imposition of suffering comes in: for many or most offenders suffering 'provides a structure within which, we hope, [the offender] will be able to think about the nature and implications of his crime, face up to it more adequately than he might otherwise (being human) do'. But Matravers thinks that this is also problematic. For 'in cases such as these, it is much harder to see that censure is simply being expressed in hard treatment and the latter is thus intrinsically appropriate. Rather, it seems more natural to say that the offender has failed, or will fail, to appreciate the appropriate censure and so hard treatment is deployed to focus his mind on the censure that would otherwise be appropriately only verbal.'[25] So hard treatment – in the form of community service, probation, etc – is not itself part of or intrinsic to the censure or condemnation. Instead, it is best regarded as a valuable way in which the offender's mind can be focused on the state's censure or condemnation, in the hopes that he will take it to heart and come to recognise and acknowledge his wrongful behaviour. If words can be enough for censure, therefore, then coerced punishments such as probation and community service are not the vehicles through which censure is expressed.

(ii) This gives rise to the second worry – one that has been raised before against accounts of punishment that appeal to a 'subjective' component like suffering.[26] The worry is that the communicative theory – indeed, any account that appeals to the necessity of suffering for punishment – will lead to unfair and hence unjust punishments, and differential treatment for the same crimes. Matravers puts the argument as follows:

> Once censure and the hard treatment needed to ensure the censure is heard are decoupled, then differential punishments will result. Some offenders will grasp immediately the full force of the wrong that they have done. For reasons to do with the need to reassert the values of the community and to express the appropriate censure, the state must of course nevertheless censure them. However, why should that censure take a non-verbal form? One answer is that it is proportionate to the censure expressed in other cases where hard treatment was needed. But this looks as if the level of hard treatment appropriate as censure will be dictated by the offender who is least able to respond to verbal signals and that surely cannot be right. Duff, I think, would say that the mistake here is to think of censure and hard treatment as two things and not one. The appropriate censure for a given offence just is what it is, and if that means words are not enough then words are not enough. However, as noted above, it is hard to grant that claim.

[24] Ibid, 79.
[25] Ibid.
[26] See, for instance, David Gray (2010).

> Words are enough to express censure of all kinds, but sometimes they are not enough to be heard. That, though, returns us to the baseline of the most thick-skinned offender.[27]

The thought is, therefore, that it is possible that some offenders will, when facing censure from the state, quickly recognise the wrongness of their behaviour, repent, commit to reforming themselves, and make appropriate reparations. Other offenders will not. Since the state needs to ensure parity of sentencing, and assure the community that we treat like cases alike, the state must impose the same hard treatment, in the form of coercive punishments, on those who accept the censure and repent, and on those who do not. But this seems both unfair to those who have 'heard' the censure and accepted it, and contrary to the aims and spirit of the communicative theory. For in the former case, communication of censure has *worked* and the aims of the theory have been achieved. Any further imposition of hard treatment would therefore only be warranted on other – possibly consequentialist – grounds. (This is Matravers's suggestion on p 80, where he is worried that such imposition is a matter of using that person 'as a means to other ends'.) If so, then the communicative theory is both unfair, and inconsistent with its own requirements.

In the following section I will argue that the communicative theorist can respond to both of these worries, by focusing on the importance of emotion for sincere and forceful communication.

IV. The Role of Emotion in Censure and Condemnation

Matravers thinks that words can be enough to express censure and condemnation, and that as a result censure and hard treatment can be decoupled. I think that he is wrong on the first count and (therefore) wrong on the second as well. For a condition on the successful expression of censure and condemnation is the presence of appropriate emotions, and the suite of evaluations, feelings, facial and bodily expressions, and actions that are their *constituents*. 'Saying the words' is only part of this suite, only part of what is really called for by the wrongdoing or offence. As a result, words are not enough to express censure: other elements, including actions that constitute hard treatment, need to be in place. Since this is all rather abstract, let me explain by appeal to a non-judicial case of wrongdoing and censure, the kind of thing that can happen in a loving relationship.[28]

Imagine that Alice and Ted are in a long-term relationship; indeed, they are thinking of getting married, raising a family, and are looking forward to

[27] Matravers (2011), 79.

[28] The importance of emotions, and in particular of empathy, for intimate relationships is examined in Hansberg (2020) (chapter nine in this volume). My example focuses on the role that negative emotions have in such relationships, when it comes to expressing condemnation and motivating appropriate behaviour.

spending the rest of their lives together. Six months before the wedding, at a Christmas party, Alice catches Ted kissing one of their friends, Carol, and experiences a range of emotions: anger, hurt and contempt are prominent here. Confronting Ted later that evening, Alice expresses these emotions in a variety of ways. She condemns Ted's appalling behaviour, tells him how let down she feels, and how shocked that he would do this. There are tears, curses, insults. Ted, mortified, apologises profusely, and genuinely feels terrible. He reiterates his commitment to Alice, promises never to do anything like this again, and begs Alice to forgive him. Alice, though still deeply hurt, believes Ted. Nevertheless, the next few weeks are marked by temporary changes in their relationship: Alice gives Ted the 'cold shoulder', refuses physical contact, is often abrupt and cutting in her remarks to him, and insists that he spends time away from the flat that they share together. She insists that they go to couples counselling if the wedding is to go ahead, in order that Ted comes to think about and understand himself and his wrongdoing more clearly. Ted is, for his part, motivated to be a better person: to be kinder, more considerate, more committed, more loving, to Alice. After a sufficient amount of time, their relationship takes on something like the shape it did before Ted acted so badly. Indeed, in some ways the relationship is stronger and deeper, although in other ways it has been damaged by the affair.

Suppose we now ask: what is needed for Alice to express her censure and condemnation to Ted? In this instance, would words be enough? Clearly, Alice's simply *saying* the relevant words – 'How could you do this to me? You heartless bastard', and so forth – isn't enough to express censure. Alice might after all say the words in a flat, bored manner, in a tone that expresses her lack of concern about the values that Ted's behaviour has damaged. At the very least, Alice will have to say the words in way that expresses or reflects her anger, hurt and disappointment. Her words will, in other words, have to express her *emotions* if they are to genuinely express censure and condemnation.[29] This isn't merely an epistemic point – that Ted won't *believe* that Alice thinks he behaved wrongly, in the absence of an exhibition of her emotions on her part – although that is surely true. It's the substantive point: that Alice's words won't express censure *at all* unless they are the vehicle for the emotions generated by and themselves warranted by Ted's wrongdoing. For it is not just censure, in the form of words, that Ted's wrongdoing merits. It also merits the whole range of Alice's emotions – her anger, hurt, disappointment, sadness, and the like. Such emotions are not merely *expected* in response to Ted's betrayal. Instead, they are normatively *called for*: they are warranted, fitting, justified, appropriate, rational responses, so that someone who didn't feel as Alice feels in the relevant circumstances would violate the relevant norms, and might well be criticisable for this reason.

[29] This point will be familiar to, and readily accepted by, *internalists* about moral judgements, who maintain that sincere moral judgement is essentially linked with *motivation*. On that account, those who 'say the words' but lack any motivation to act accordingly don't really make moral judgements. See Smith (1995), for this line. Here I'm making a similar point, but focusing on the necessity of emotional responses for sincere or legitimate censure and condemnation.

How can Alice's words be the vehicle for her warranted emotional response? It seems to me that this can only be the case if her verbal expression also expresses other emotional elements or aspects. Emotions typically involve facial and bodily expressions, and Alice's words need to be accompanied by the relevant facial and bodily movements associated with anger and hurt, therefore. By the same token, Alice's words will need to express her affective state – how she *feels* – and so will have to have a particular tone or force. Again, these are not merely epistemic points – that Ted won't believe that Alice thinks he behaved wrongly, in the absence of the relevant facial expressions and feelings on her part – although this is also surely true. It's the substantive point: that Alice's words won't express censure *at all* unless her expression of them embodies the facial and bodily and affective elements that are characteristic of anger, hurt, and the like. To be sure, some of these might be subtle: a slight change in the tone of voice, a stiffening of the posture, a downturn of the mouth, a narrowing of the eyes – these can all convey or express anger, and so bodily and facial expressions don't have to be as overt as they would be in the case of someone who is 'pure ragin', to use the excellent Scottish phrase. Still, it would be difficult to understand how Alice's words can express censure in the absence of any facial and bodily changes, and in the absence of any feelings on her part. It is certainly difficult to see how any verbal expressions could be *forceful*, in the absence of these emotional components.

This paves the way for a response to Matravers. For it is plausible to claim that expression of censure equally requires the appropriate behaviour on Alice's part. Could Alice express censure and condemnation to Ted *without* giving him the cold shoulder, without breaking off physical contact, and the like? Consider how anomalous her angry words, and angry facial and bodily postures, would be if Alice immediately welcomed his apologies with warm embraces, if their loving intimacy resumed without pause, if there were no period *at all* where Ted was shunned, left alone to think and reflect on what he'd done, to stew in his misery. This suggests not simply that Alice's behavioural responses are normal or typical responses to infidelity; instead, they are what is to be expected in the normative sense, where the absence of such responses would again be anomalous and indeed *criticisable*. (Imagine how Alice's friends would react if Alice failed to give Ted the cold shoulder, at least for a while. Wouldn't they – and we – be inclined to think that Alice isn't acting as she ought, that she is perhaps lacking in self-esteem to some degree, or too dependent upon or reliant on Ted for her own good?) If so, then we might claim that certain patterns of behaviour are required if Alice is to appropriately express censure and condemnation of Ted's actions. It isn't enough for her to say the words, to say them with emotion, and to look as though she means them; she has to *act* as though she means them as well, and so her behaviour will have to follow suit for her expression to be genuine. If so, then (forceful) expression of censure and condemnation requires the appropriate words, said with feeling, expressed by the appropriate facial and bodily expressions, and accompanied by particular and fitting patterns of behaviour. The relevant actions, in other words, are not mere focusing devices whereby

Ted is given the opportunity to reflect and repent. Instead, they are part of what (forceful) censure and condemnation *is*.

The application to the judicial case should, I hope, be reasonably clear. The state's censure and condemnation of an offender cannot consist in merely 'saying the words', no matter how rich the language involved, if we think that the words must also express the appropriate emotions. Here, too, I assume that the appropriate emotions are (legitimate) anger, with a wide range of other emotional possibilities: perhaps contempt; perhaps moralised disgust in the case of particularly reprehensible crimes. Judicial condemnation must reflect and express the (legitimate) feelings of the state: feelings that are fitting when its laws are violated and its values undermined. As with the case of a loving relationship, this isn't merely an epistemic point – that the offender won't believe that the state thinks he acted wrongly, in the absence of the underlying emotions and their expression in the courtroom – although this is also surely true. It is the more substantive point: that the court's words won't express censure *at all* unless they are accompanied by the emotions, and emotional expressions, that are characteristic of moralised anger and hurt. At the very least, it is difficult to see how any verbal expression of censure could be suitably forceful in the absence of emotions and their elements.

Given all this, we can claim that the state's (forceful) expression of censure *requires* appropriate action on the state's part. Indeed, we might think that appropriate action is the most obvious and most effective way in which the state can express emotion, and so express what the offender deserves. (It is less easy to see how the state could convey particular facial expressions or other emotional components.) Just as Alice's expression of censure and condemnation of Ted's actions required a certain pattern of behaviour that is meant to be burdensome for Ted – that is intended to make Ted suffer in addition to his pains of remorse and regret – the state's expression of censure and condemnation of criminal offences likewise require the imposition of hard treatment on the offender. Anything less than this makes the state itself liable to criticism, in much the same way that Alice is liable to criticism should she fail to impose burdens on Ted as a result of his actions. The imposition of hard treatment on to criminals is not a mere focusing device; it is, on this view, intrinsic to the censure that the offender deserves.

Now there are, of course, clear differences between the case of Alice and Ted, and the case of the state's imposition of hard treatment on someone who commits a criminal offence. It might be claimed, for instance, that the state is not the kind of thing that can *have* emotions, and hence not the kind of entity that can express them in words or actions. It doesn't make sense, therefore, to talk as if the state's censure is only legitimate insofar as it expresses the state's anger etc. However, claims like this about the possibility or otherwise of group emotions are clearly controversial, and so provide questionable grounds for detaching state censure and hard treatment. After all, we often *talk* as if groups, indeed states and nations, have emotions: we naturally say things like the following: that the country is ashamed of its wartime conduct, the citizenry are anxious about the state of the economy, the nation is overjoyed at winning the World Cup, the populace is in mourning over the death of the princess. And whilst it might be plausible to deny that states or collectives can have genuinely shared *feelings* or *affective experience*, it is much less plausible to deny that states can have collective beliefs, collective values, and engage in collective action. Indeed, the claim that the state takes seriously violations of its laws, that it respects all of its citizens, and so forth, only makes sense if we think that the state is the kind of thing to which we can attribute values, cares and concerns. It is hardly a stretch, therefore, to think that states can express things like anger when its laws are violated.[30]

A second worry is more serious, and might nudge us towards a weaker response on behalf of the communicative theorist. The worry is that arguably only *some* emotional elements need to be in place for censure to be expressed, rather than all, and so censure need not require action. There are, after all, emotions without particular behavioural expressions – some aesthetic emotions, for instance wonder, might be like this – and so it is not true that all emotions require expression in action as well as words. Might it not be possible, therefore, for Alice to express censure of Ted's behaviour by verbal means alone? If so, then censure and the imposition of hard treatment can come apart. By analogy, the state can succeed in censuring an offender by saying the relevant words in a court of law in a way that expresses the state's seriousness and anger, without imposing hard treatment in the form of probation, community service, and the like. Hard treatment is not, on this view, intrinsic to censure.

As we saw, Matravers thinks that this leads to problems for the communicative theorist. Matravers asks: 'why should … censure take a non-verbal form? One answer is that it is proportionate to the censure expressed in other cases where hard treatment was needed. But this looks as if the level of hard treatment appropriate as censure will be dictated by the offender who is least able to respond to verbal signals and that surely cannot be right.' The worry, recall, is that imposing hard treatment on someone who has recognised their offence and is genuinely remorseful and repentant, on the grounds that this imposition is appropriate for offenders who do not and are not, is both unfair, and can only be justified on extrinsic grounds, such as the need for proportionality in sentencing. But it seems inappropriate to punish someone who is genuinely remorseful on the grounds that another offender is not.

[30] There are, of course, significant differences between groups, collectives and states. Groups and collectives suggest a level of informality, whereas states are institutional structures. Nevertheless, institutional structures can arguably have beliefs, values and other attitudes: for instance, the University of Glasgow values educational opportunities for all, the pursuit of knowledge and understanding, and so on. In the UK Parliament, it is often said that 'this House believes', etc. Small-scale groups can also be institutional: think of the golf club, with its rules and regulations. So the differences of scale between groups and states don't, I think, undermine the central point that I'm making here. Thanks to the editors of this volume for pushing me to say more on this issue.

There are two responses we might make to this objection. The first acknowledges that certain emotions – such as aesthetic emotions – lack an 'actional' element, but insists that the emotions involved in expressing censure are not of this category. Instead, they are precisely the kinds of emotions that have a behavioural response at their heart: emotions such as anger, a sense of justice, compassion for the victims of crime, and so on. Not all emotions require behavioural expression, therefore, but arguably those involved in censure and condemnation do. If so, then censure and the imposition of hard treatment do not come apart.

A second response admits (for the sake of argument) that censure and actional elements can diverge, but maintains that this does not entail that the imposition of hard treatment is unfair. For if censure expresses appropriate emotion, and if hard treatment is an appropriate behavioural expression of this emotion, then the imposition of hard treatment would seem to be warranted, even if it is not required. The fact that censure *need not* involve the imposition of hard treatment – the fact that in some circumstances words and facial and bodily expression might be enough to express censure – does nothing to undermine the appropriateness of hard treatment when it *is* imposed. For since such an imposition is a perfectly appropriate way for emotion to be expressed, then the offender can have no grounds for complaint about its imposition, and so the imposition cannot be in some way unfair or unjust. Consider again the case of Alice and Ted. Perhaps it is possible for Alice to express censure verbally, provided that enough of the other components of emotion are in place; perhaps, then, she doesn't need to give Ted the cold shoulder, ask him to leave the flat for a period of time, and so on. Nevertheless, since such behaviour is an entirely appropriate way for Alice to express her anger, Ted could hardly have any complaints if Alice *did* behave in this way. He might count himself fortunate in a situation where Alice does not do so, but is in no position to object to treatment that is merited by his bad behaviour. This remains true *even if* Ted fully recognises his wrongful behaviour, and is fully remorseful and apologetic, as a result of verbal censure. Even in this instance, Ted will have no grounds to complain if Alice also gives him the cold shoulder.

Something similar can be said about the judicial case. Even if censure need not involve the imposition of hard treatment, the offender is in no position to object should the state impose such treatment – given that the state's anger is merited by the wrongdoing, and the imposition of hard treatment is an appropriate behavioural expression of that anger. Such treatment is an intrinsically appropriate response to wrongdoing, therefore. This remains true *even if* the offender fully recognises his offence, and is fully remorseful and apologetic. Moreover, given the *extrinsic* benefits of hard treatment – both in terms of increasing the likelihood of recognition and apologetic reparations in most cases of offence, and in terms of the deterrent effect on others – there are additional reasons for the state to impose hard treatment that go beyond its intrinsic appropriateness.

So even if the imposition of hard treatment is not strictly necessary for the expression of censure, there might nevertheless be good intrinsic and extrinsic reasons to do so.

V. Conclusion

The communicative theory of punishment, especially as that theory is formulated by Antony Duff, maintains that hard treatment is an intrinsically appropriate response to criminal wrongdoing. Matt Matravers questions this account, and maintains that the imposition of suffering is at best a focusing device to enable offenders to 'hear' the censure that can be fully expressed by words alone. But I think that Matravers is wrong on this point. Words alone will not express censure, unless they are also expressive of the emotional responses that are themselves merited by wrongdoing. Since emotional responses involve appropriate behaviour, then such behaviour is itself merited or warranted by wrongdoing. On a strong version of this response, this means that censure and hard treatment do not come apart. On a weaker version, then it is possible for censure and hard treatment to diverge, but the offender is in no position to complain about its imposition. Either way, Duff is right in thinking that hard treatment is an intrinsically appropriate response to wrongdoing. The communicative theory can therefore explain why it is legitimate for the state to make offenders suffer through the intentional imposition of hard treatment.

References

Bedau, H and Kelly, E (2015) 'Punishment' in *The Stanford Encyclopedia of Philosophy* (Winter 2017 Edition), Edward N Zalta (ed). Available at https://plato.stanford.edu/archives/win2017/entries/punishment/.

Blum, L (2020) '"Black Lives Matter": Moral Frames for Understanding the Police Killings of Black Males' in A Amaya and M Del Mar (eds) *Virtue, Emotion and Imagination in Law and Legal Reasoning* (Oxford, Hart Publishing).

Brady, MS (2013) *Emotional Insight* (Oxford: Oxford University Press).

Brady, MS (2018) *Suffering and Virtue* (Oxford: Oxford University Press).

Duff, RA (2001) *Punishment, Communication, and Community* (Oxford: Oxford University Press).

Duff, RA (2003) 'Probation, Punishment and Restorative Justice: Should Altruism be Engaged in Punishment?' 42(2) *The Howard Journal of Criminal* Justice 181.

Duff, A and Hoskins, Z (2018) 'Legal Punishment' *The Stanford Encyclopedia of Philosophy*, Edward N Zalta (ed). Available at https://plato.stanford.edu/archives/fall2018/entries/legal-punishment.

Gray, D (2010) 'Punishment as Suffering' 63(6) *Vanderbilt Law Review* 1619.
Hansberg, O (2020) 'Empathy and Negative Intimacy' in A Amaya and M Del Mar (eds) *Virtue, Emotion and Imagination in Law and Legal Reasoning* (Oxford, Hart Publishing).
Hart, HLA (1968) *Punishment and Responsibility: Essays in the Philosophy of Law* (New York: Oxford University Press).
Hobbes, T (1651/2008) *Leviathan* (Oxford: Oxford University Press).
Matravers, M (2011) 'Duff on Hard Treatment' in R Cruft, M Kramer and M Reiff (eds) *Crime, Punishment, and Responsibility: The Jurisprudence of Antony Duff* (Oxford: Oxford: Oxford University Press) 68.
Smith, M (1995) *The Moral Problem* (Oxford: Blackwell Publishers).
White, EK (2020) 'On Emotions and the Politics of Attention in Judicial Reasoning' in A Amaya and M Del Mar (eds) *Virtue, Emotion and Imagination in Law and Legal Reasoning* (Oxford, Hart Publishing).

9

Empathy and Negative Intimacy

OLBETH HANSBERG

I. Introduction

In most human relationships, emotions and affectivity in general, play a more or less central part. Our life in society depends in some measure on them. Many social structures – legal, political, medical, commercial, among others – and kinds of relationships – like those of citizen, judge, lawyer, doctor, commercial and service exchanges, and other function-based relationships between individuals – can have an affective aspect. This feature is more obvious in more personal relations, like those between colleagues, or acquaintances, and especially in those which are more intimate, like between family members, friends, lovers, and so on.

In this chapter I shall examine some ways in which emotions and other affective states intervene in interpersonal relationships of two or more individuals, which we call 'intimate'. Affectivity is, to a certain degree, part of any interpersonal relationship, and emotions that take part in these relationships are what Strawson called 'reactive' emotions.[1]

I shall not try to elucidate the nature of emotions here,[2] but shall only highlight that, in one way or another, we have to take into account the cognitive, evaluative and motivational features of many human emotions. That is, the emotions human beings acquire along with their cognitive development in a linguistic and socio-cultural context. Although humans also have primitive emotions linked to automatic, unreflective and non-cognitive behaviour, they are also able to establish a *distance* between how things are experimented immediately and how they can be described and experimented after applying certain concepts.[3] With the term 'emotions' I shall refer to emotional episodes or occurrent emotions, to disposition to have emotions and to emotional attitudes, or traits, which are a special

[1] Strawson (1962), 15, talks about attitudes and feelings, but his examples include what we understand as emotions.

[2] There are many theories of emotion: feeling, cognitive, perceptual, enactive theories, are a few and there are also many combinations. A good recent introduction is Deonna and Teroni (2012).

[3] See eg Deigh (2004; 2009) and Hansberg (1996; 2008).

kind of disposition that are characteristic of long or stable relationships.[4] I shall assume that people involved in these long-term relationships have an evaluative or emotional profile that will show in their actions and other attitudes.[5] I shall go into some of these features in more detail later.

Assuming that close relationships are a subset of personal relationships and that intimate relationships are a subset of close relationships, my aim is to examine some aspects of intimate relationships. According to Giddens 'Intimacy is above all a matter of emotional communication, with others and with the self, in a context of interpersonal equality'.[6] I don't think that intimacy only takes place in a context of interpersonal equality, as I shall argue later, but I shall take the feature mentioned by Giddens of 'emotional communication' as essential for characterising intimacy.[7]

Intimacy is sometimes described as a combination of the following components: self-revelation, mutual support, trust, physical exchanges, being affected by the other, and sharing activities and experiences, among others.[8] Of these possible features which may be characteristic of intimacy in general, and also of different particular cases, I shall limit myself to the feature of 'emotional communication' mentioned before. I shall assume, then, that 'emotional communication' is a defining feature of intimacy, that is, that all intimacies are, so to say, 'emotionally charged'.[9]

Examples of a variety of intimacies are: intimacy between partners, lovers, friends, family, between mother and child, and also, on *special* occasions, between doctor and patient, teacher and student, lawyer and client, etc. As these examples show, one can make at least two distinctions among relationships that are intimate.

[4] The classifications of emotional states vary depending on the area of study and the authors. I distinguish emotional episodes as those with a relatively short duration and which have physiological aspects, observable gestures, especially facial, and a phenomenology: they are felt or experienced in certain ways. For example: he was proud when he received the award; he was mad with joy, the fear paralysed him. Examples of dispositions are: every time he sees her, he gets mad; he is outraged when he sees a starving child. Attitudes or traits are dispositional features characteristic of long-term emotions or narratives (Goldie) that can include emotional episodes, but that are attributed to explain the motives, behaviour, preferences and habits of others. For example: he has hated his mother since he was a kid; he has loved her all his life. Love and hate can be also characterised as dispositions to have different emotions. Deonna and Teroni call them 'sentiments'. Emotions and other affective features can be part of the characterisation of personality and character traits: eg, affable, pessimistic, kind, shy, egoistic, cruel, trustworthy, among many others.

[5] Thus, when, eg, a person admires or is afraid of somebody or something, we keep attributing admiration or fear as a long-term attitude to that person. It is part of her emotional and evaluative profile or make up; part of the characterisation of what kind of person she is.

[6] Giddens (1992), 130.

[7] For the relevance of emotional communication in expressing censure in judicial proceedings and the reasons for imposing suffering on offenders, see Brady (2020) (chapter eight in this volume). Brady also uses a case of an intimate personal relationship to illustrate the importance of the emotions for understanding the experiences of the people involved.

[8] See eg Gaia (2002), 157–59.

[9] I have no general characterisation of all the aspects that make a relationship intimate. But I hope that examples will offer an intuitive understanding. See Hansberg (2017).

The first distinction is between intimacy among *equals*, as (ideally) in romantic or friendly relationships, and intimacies that are essentially *asymmetric* as between a child and its caretaker, or sometimes between a doctor and patient, especially in the cases of mental illnesses, or between lawyer and client. In asymmetric relationships, one side of the intimacy is dependent on the other person, who has the power to influence, affect, shape or even destroy the life of the less powerful participant.[10]

Then there is the *positive-negative* division of intimate relationships. The intimate relationship which exists is not necessarily a positive relationship, which rests on good affective communication and understanding and results in the benefit of the participants. There can also be intimacy between people who hate or despise each other, between people who have developed a psychological dependency such as fear, humiliation and lack of self-esteem on one hand, and of wrath, violence and domination on the other. There can *even* be intimacy between a torturer and the victim. There are of course many cases in which there is no intimacy between torturer and victim, but there are a variety of such examples – cases of psychological dependence between prisoners and jailers, or guards and hostages in kidnappings; cases of sexual abuse, often by family or family friends; or even more extreme cases, such as a father who keeps his daughter as a prisoner and abuses her. What I want to stress is the idea that intimacy can be a feature of many different kinds of close relationships, of which many develop over time in special circumstances.

When talking of positive or negative intimacies we are not referring to precise notions; whether the intimacy is positive or negative will depend on the emotional components and how they are related, the emotional quality and assessment of these components, and on how they benefit or damage the participants in the relationship. In real life, most intimate relations are neither clearly positive, nor clearly negative: in most cases it is a question of degree and of finding the adequate balance. Even in intimacies one would mostly describe as positive there are moments when one hurts or manipulates the other.

The usual elements mentioned when talking about positive intimacy are empathy, trust, mutual attachment, respect for each other, mutual acceptance, and concern for their wellbeing. These features appear in a variety of degrees and ways in different types of intimate relationships: romantic love, say, is different from love of one's children or family. Other emotions such as affection, fondness, worry and admiration can also be present, even though the relevant aspect will change according to the specificity of particular intimate relationships.[11]

[10] Although I shall not dwell on this distinction, it is worth noting that asymmetric intimate relationships pose distinctive problems worth examining. Here I address only relationships which are positive or negative, be they between equals or asymmetric.

[11] In this context one could ask questions like the following: are there emotions that are necessary for intimacy or that promote (positive) intimacy? Which emotional states hinder or obstruct intimacy? Some of these questions can be answered only by analysing particular instances, real or fictional, and others answered only in conformity with empirical findings.

Using the previous rough framework, and taking into account the emphasis on 'emotional communication' mentioned above, my aim in this chapter is to try to make sense of empathy as an element present in many human interactions, and which seems necessary at least for close relationships and especially for different kinds of intimacy. I shall argue that empathy is necessary for intimacy in general, but the main purpose of my chapter is to explore the role of 'empathy' and its connection to positive, but especially to negative, intimacy.

II. Empathy

So many things are now attributed to empathy that it is difficult to keep track of them. Empathy is seen as the key to happiness, as essential for good interpersonal connections, as essential for understanding and explaining the behaviour of others, for developing the capacity to attribute mental states (thoughts, beliefs, desires and emotions) to others, and often also considered necessary for morality. Here I shall only raise the question of empathy as necessary for personal relations and especially for intimacy. The reason for this is because my purpose here is to make sense of the relation between empathy and negative intimacy.

Empathy is a concept that lacks clarity and precision, which is used in diverse contexts and with different meanings that can refer to different psychological processes that vary in function, phenomenology, mechanisms and effects attributed to them. In order to try to understand 'empathy' better, I shall mention some distinctions that may be useful for characterising empathy and avoiding confusion as much as possible.[12]

According to Coplan, some of the most popular conceptions of empathy are:

(A) Feeling what someone else feels.
(B) Caring about someone else.
(C) Being emotionally affected by someone else's emotions and experiences, though not necessarily experiencing the same emotions.
(D) Imagining oneself in another's situation.
(E) Imagining being another in that other's situation.
(F) Making inferences about another's mental states.
(G) Some combination of the processes described in (A)–(F).[13]

Taking most of the items in this list into account,[14] I shall try to describe some of the emotional responses that have been considered as empathic. These are

[12] Many of the following distinctions are not new but can be found in the philosophical and psychological literature. For the characterisation of empathy, I rely mainly on Coplan (2011), Goldie (2011) and Maibom (2014).

[13] Coplan (2011), 4.

[14] In this chapter, I don't discuss (F) in the list, because my aim is to stress the emotional element in empathy, accepting of course that, apart from the early forms or precursors of empathy that can be non-conceptual and automatic, empathy is also cognitive so that in most cases we can hardly separate these two elements. Some prefer to take empathy as a purely cognitive understanding of the experiences of

interpersonal emotional reactions produced by the awareness of the subject who has them, of what is happening to someone else. I start with the most simple and primitive emotional reactions in order to get to the more complex ones as far as it concerns psychological (emotional, cognitive, imaginative …) interpretative and factual resources that are needed to have them. They have been considered as steps in the development of full-fledged empathy. These are:

A. Emotional Contagion

It consists in automatically imitating and synchronising expressions, vocalisations, postures and movements with those of others. It is uncontrollable, unintentional, automatic, and in most cases, it is transmitted as a disease is, that is, the origin and the object of the emotion are often unknown. Examples are the emotional contagion of babies, the contagion of fear in a crowd that flees, or the wrath of an angry mob.[15]

B. Affective Matching

It happens when one has qualitatively the same affective states as another person, although they may vary in intensity. In these cases, we can distinguish different degrees that can range from an almost automatic coincidence to something that requires imagination and cognitive processing. For example, the semi-automatic response that animals share in front of a predator would be a primitive case, and it is possible to distinguish several levels up to, for instance, the desperation shared by several people looking at a screen showing China's stock market fall. In contrast with emotional contagion, in these cases, those who share the emotion are aware of what triggered it. The similar reaction is produced by the object of the emotion, for example, when an audience is moved by an eloquent speech, or when parents experience the same type of fear when they hear their child screaming, even though they are not together and do not communicate with each other.[16]

C. Affective Imitation

Even though there is much more to be said about imitation, I would like to briefly mention affective imitation,[17] since affective imitation has been considered as a

others. See Del Mar (2017), 144, but I doubt that one can speak of understanding the experiences of others without taking into account any affective element.

[15] For more on (1) see Hatfield, Cacioppo and Rapson (1993), 96–99. And for an overview of the empirical work on emotional contagion, see Hatfield, Cacioppo and Rapson (1994).

[16] See eg Hartfield, Cacioppo and Rapson (1992), 153–54 and (1994), 96–100.

[17] The study of child development and the place imitation (particularly affective imitation) takes, is an exciting and complex topic that is beyond the limits of this chapter. There has been much discussion

requirement for the development of adult empathy.[18] Imitation consists, first in copying or mimicking behaviour one sees in others. Early affective imitation is rudimentary, it is based above all on copying gestures, especially facial, and other simple actions and it is pre-linguistic. But imitation goes also back and forth between caretaker and baby. Mothers often imitate the behaviour of their infants, and infants imitate actions of their mothers. It is a mechanism for social learning that can be considered as an early form of interpersonal communication which is essential for developing the capacity to attribute mental states to others, that is, to learn that other people have their own mental states and forms of interacting with each other and with the environment. In contrast to emotional contagion, in early imitation it is fundamental to understand, even if rudimentarily, the purposes and intentions of others. Later imitation of the actions of others can be independent of the presence of the role models and applies to a much larger spectrum of instances.

The point of including imitation here is because it is a crucial factor, in combination with others, ie cognitive and motor, of the process of learning that other people can have different mental states and ways of interacting with each other and with the environment. And of learning also that one can share emotions and other psychological states with others. It is often thought that affective sharing is essential to empathy.[19]

III. Sympathy (Compassion) vs Empathy

After describing some of the steps towards developing mature empathy and before entering the discussion of full-fledged empathy and how it can be understood as an element of intimacy, it is important to distinguish empathy from sympathy and/or compassion, because they are often confused or used interchangeably. Distinguishing between sympathy and empathy is critical in law and relevant to some of the chapters in this volume.[20]

A. Sympathy

Sympathy is being worried or interested in someone else's wellbeing when they suffer, or when they are in a difficult or painful situation. But the emotion a

about the exact role of imitation and whether it is innate or not. But my point is that the development of empathy has roots in early human development and that it depends to a great extent on interpersonal and especially intimate relationships.

[18] See eg Decety and Meltzoff (2011).

[19] See eg '... empathy is an interaction between two individuals, with one experiencing and sharing the feeling of the other' (Decety and Meltzoff 2011), 67 and many others.

[20] For another more detailed version of the development of empathy see Hoffman (2011) 'Empathy, Justice and the Law' in Coplan and Goldie (2011). He has a different conception of the connection of empathy with sympathy. For him empathy has a sympathetic component that makes empathetic

sympathetic person feels does not need to match the emotion of the person with whom they sympathise. One can be emotionally affected by people, individuals or groups, who are in distress, who live in dreary circumstances, who are starving, or who are subjected to discrimination or injustice, without having had such an experience. The target could also be an animal, a plant, an object, or a person. It is not even necessary that the object of one's sympathy feels something, although in most cases what produces sympathy or compassion is the suffering one detects in others. One may feel sympathy for a mother who lost her child, for children who starve, or for someone wounded in an accident, without having any idea about how it feels to starve, or to lose someone close. What is important here is to feel sympathy or compassion for someone who is in a difficult situation and to have a *motivation* to console or do something to alleviate the situation, even when one cannot in fact do anything, or for any other reason do not actually act on their behalf. This emotion is different from empathy, because it is not about sharing emotions or understanding the experiences of others, but rather about having a motivation to help, to show solidarity, or to care about something or someone. Sympathy has a different phenomenology than empathy. Of course, one may suffer because others suffer, but what is essential is that the suffering is 'for the other' and not for oneself.[21]

B. Empathy

Empathy has different features, and without going into much detail, I would like to point out its essential characteristics.[22] I shall consider empathy as a complex state (affective, cognitive and imaginative), whose essential attributes are:

(a) Feeling what the other feels. This involves having an emotion of the same kind as the other, although it can be with less intensity, because it depends on the imaginative powers of the empathiser.[23]
(b) Assuming a perspective oriented towards the other. This is 'an imaginative process through which one constructs another person's subjective experience

distress pro-social and motivating. By contrast, see Del Mar (2017) who claims that empathy is cognitive and not emotional. I don't discuss here the distinction between sympathy and compassion, because my interest is in the distinction between empathy and other motivating emotions like sympathy and compassion. See also White (2020) on the problems of empathy and the complex emotional state required for judicial empathy, and Kind (2020), who criticises empathy and argues in favour of a sophisticated capacity for imagination (chapters six and ten in this volume).

[21] See Goldie (1999; 2000) and Maibom (2014), 4.

[22] This is of course only one way of understanding empathy, but even if one has a different conception one has to take into account these elements despite disagreeing with them.

[23] One of the problems with this condition is to fix the meaning of an emotion 'of the same kind' because the person who feels empathy is experiencing the emotion by imagining the experience of somebody else. Some think that this condition is not necessary for empathy. In this chapter I don't want to discuss all the different ways of understanding empathy, my purpose here is to argue that empathy as here characterised, is not only necessary for *positive* intimacy, but is also necessary for *negative* intimacy. There are difficulties here that will be discussed later.

by simulating the experience of being in the other's situation'.[24] Goldie and Coplan mention two ways of doing this:[25]

(i) Projecting oneself in the situation of others, that is, imagining how I would feel if I were in another's situation. If I put myself in *their shoes*. Say, if I were to lose a loved one, or become paralysed, or win the lottery, etc.[26]

(ii) Representing the other's situation from their point of view,[27] given their preferences, values and particular circumstances. To do this, it is essential to consider (c).

(c) Making a distinction between oneself and others, that is, to clearly separate the identities of each.

Inasmuch as it is possible to distinguish (a), (b) and (c) in empathy, we will, to some extent, avoid confusion and get a better understanding of the thoughts and feelings of other persons, and to some extent predict their behaviour. Of course, this sophisticated form of empathy and comprehension is not always achieved, it seldom is. In most cases, there would be a mixture of different elements, most of which one does not have to be aware of or make explicit. To make the above-mentioned division is to highlight some of the steps and a way of analysing this process. It is also a starting point to highlight its problems.

Each of the features of empathy mentioned before can give rise to distortions and problems. Just as seeing another as akin in many respects is one way of understanding them, it can also lead to a false consensus that may produce *pseudo-empathy*. For instance, when somebody tells another 'I know how you feel' when he comes back from war wounded, although the speaker has never experienced a war or been wounded.[28] One of the difficulties is that we make many mistakes when trying to *emotionally* understand the viewpoint and situation of other people or groups who have had very different experiences in different circumstances from our own.[29]

[24] Coplan (2011), 9.

[25] This distinction is crucial to understand some of the reactions to these ways of assuming perspectives. See Goldie (1999, 2000), and Goldie and Coplan (2011). See also Kind (2020) (chapter ten in this volume).

[26] This is a way we have of understanding, and to a certain degree predicting, another's mental state, and it can sometimes also be a way to self-knowledge. See also n 29 below.

[27] This requires, amongst other things, an imaginative ability and a greater mental flexibility that involves a capacity to regulate one's own emotion and knowing much of the other's circumstances, and also their cognitive and emotional profile. A very basic example is: He was extremely close to his daughter, so he must be feeling very sad now that she has left home.

[28] In these cases, one may have a merely cognitive knowledge of what a war is and about the damage it can bring about. This would be only descriptive knowledge and not an affective experience of empathy. Imagination could bring one closer to the experience, and using imagination one may feel sympathy or compassion for someone in that condition. For some of the drawbacks of empathy in legal reasoning, see Kind (2020) (chapter ten in this volume).

[29] See eg Blum (2020) or the analysis in Zipursky (2020) of the PLIVA ruling in 'Austerity, Compassion and the Rule of Law' (chapters seven and four in this volume). Elgin (2020) (chapter three in this volume),

Another problem of imagining oneself in the other's situation is that this may cause *personal distress*. This is an affective state that invades the empathic subject and hinders him, to use Goldie's phrase, from 'feeling towards', the other. In this case the subject himself becomes the object and it is no longer about the one who suffers, but about how much he is suffering by seeing the other's situation. The distress is about one's own affliction and about trying to deal with one's own stress – and that is what one wants to alleviate (by escaping the situation, or by avoiding seeing others in distress).[30]

This is why it is important to emotionally represent the other's situation as closely as feasible from the other person's point of view – what one imagines or senses that the other experiences. Assuming this perspective requires a much greater mental flexibility, a capacity for emotional regulation, and for taking a distance from one's own mental state, preferences and personality. To represent in a correct way the suffering of others from their own point of view, one needs to have a clear awareness of the limits of both.[31]

A possible way of defining empathy, that takes into account what has been said so far, is the one Coplan suggests: 'empathy is a complex imaginative process in which an observer simulates another person's situated psychological states while maintaining clear self-other differentiation. To say that empathy is "complex" is to say that it is simultaneously a cognitive and affective process'.[32]

IV. Empathy and Intimacy

After hopefully getting a better, or maybe only a less confused, picture of empathy, I would like to go back to the starting point, namely, to the connections between intimacy and empathy. Empathy, or a more elemental form of it, is not only important for psychological development, but also essential for interpersonal

also recognises the importance of emotions as 'sources of salience' and how they can enable us to discern features not obviously visible, and the use of imagination to emotionally understand different experiences and people. She also mentions how empathy can enable judges to access the emotions of subjects and share their emotions 'in a detached way' and 'access the patterns and features of a situation that these emotions afford'. In judicial cases there are of course other important constraints that must be in place.

[30] See Goldie (1999, 2000, 2011). Personal distress is often an excuse for not getting involved, or one may help only to get rid of one's guilt. But sometimes personal distress can be a defence or a protection – a way to deal with being overwhelmed by the suffering of others. Health and other social workers are often subject to this kind of distress. I thank Ute Frevert for pointing this out in discussion.

[31] Mistaking one's situation, experience and personality for the other's, or confusing one's thoughts, desires and feelings with those of the other person, may lead to a wrong perception of oneself and, in extreme cases, to the loss of one's own identity.

[32] Coplan (201), 5–6. Goldie claims that empathy is (a) itself an experience, (b) a representation of the experience of the target of empathy and (c) implies first-person representations. We try to share the experience of the other or understand him 'from within'.

communication and for positive intimate relationships. Empathy is one element among other features mentioned before: either general, like the quality of the emotional communication between participants, the sharing of experiences, and trust, or specific characteristics of each particular case.[33] An intimate relationship can be called positive as long as there is empathic and sympathetic understanding from each participant towards the other or others, and when each member can rely on them and fully trust them, so that we can describe the relationship as beneficial for the people involved. The difference between positive and negative intimacy depends on whether it benefits or harms the participants in the relationship. But there would also be a difference in the way the intimacy is cognitively, conatively and emotionally apprehended. In negative intimacy the relationship is apprehended as a target for victimising and an occasion for producing suffering, pain and harm, and the reactions of the other participants in the relationship can be of fear, dependence, distrust, resentment among others, depending on the particular case.[34]

In this chapter I am not raising questions about positive intimacy, but my aim is to explore what happens with empathy when intimacies are negative. In such cases there is a difficulty I would like to address in this chapter: the question is how to think about the connection of empathy with forms of intimacy I have characterised as negative, that is, when there is violence, cruelty, contempt and psychological torture, among many other elements. I mean the kind of situation in which the person who inflicts pain on other(s), has a strongly developed and subtle capacity for feeling something similar to empathy, in the sense that he can put himself in other's shoes, but this 'empathic' skill to understand the other's feelings and susceptibility leads him to produce harm, to rejoice in their suffering (*Schadenfreude*), or to take advantage of his own sensibility to the feelings of others in order to make them suffer more intensely, more accurately, and in a more cruelly refined way.

How to understand these cases? There is emotional communication, because it is an intimate relationship, and these relationships involve emotional communication of some kind. We can also distinguish some of the characteristics of empathy: If *A* and *B* are individuals; *A* has the ability to put himself in the shoes of *B*. She imagines what it is for *B* to be in that situation, that is, she can assume the perspective of *B* from *B*'s point of view, and she can clearly distinguish between herself and *B*. But we *cannot* say that, when she is inflicting pain or behaving cruelly to *B*, she feels an emotion of the same kind as *B*. She is not

[33] Here I have given only a quick overview of empathy, but although there is massive literature on empathy, I think we still need to better understand the components and precursors of empathy in infant development and in the different stages of emotional, cognitive and linguistic development. See eg Dunn (2000); Eisenberg, Spinrad and Knafo-Noam (2015); Hamlin, Ullman, Tenenbaum, Goodman and Baker (2013); and Kochanska (2002).

[34] The difference in the way the participants in the relationship see each other can be due to many other things, including attitudes to values, beliefs, desires, other emotions, personality, character traits, and circumstances. I shall come back to this later.

sharing emotions with the victim – she is not suffering with the sufferer – but feels *different* emotions, say, joy if it is *Schadenfreude*, or some other form of pleasure in hurting or causing suffering to *B*. Or, depending on how we characterise the particular case and its circumstances, that she feels anger towards *B*, or a feeling of revenge, or contempt, or a different affective combination, among many other possibilities.

But regardless of the emotion of *A* in a particular occasion, we can attribute to her emotional understanding of *B*, in the sense that she knows what hurts more, and how to produce the most damage. She is deeply aware of *B*'s weaknesses and deficiencies. *A*'s cruelty is especially and effectively directed to the person or persons with whom she has a specific intimate relationship. You could say that she sees her intimate counterpart as a target to hurt. It is important to point out that in a relationship, it is not the case that one is always a victim and another the victimiser, but the roles can change, or both can hurt each other. Nor does it have to be an intimate relationship between two; there may be more people involved, for example, in family violence, or among gang members, or prisoners in a cell, when members of those groups live intimately.

A mere cognitive understanding or knowledge, for instance a description of who *B* is and how to harm him, would not be enough for my case. A psychopath – say, a serial killer who kills people who respond to a particular description, for instance prostitutes, homosexuals, or street kids – is, in most cases, someone with a deficient emotional intelligence, or incapable of having certain emotions, and even unable to imagine or understand what others feel.[35] Such a person could not be part of an intimate relationship in the sense of a personal relationship in which, among other things, emotional understanding and communication is necessary.

I want to suggest that the person who is part of a relationship we call 'intimate' is, to a certain degree, able to understand and emotionally comprehend the other person with whom he stands in such a relationship. And this includes the ability to put oneself in the other's shoes, to see from the other's perspective, and to distinguish between oneself and others. If this is right, we can find some of the features of what we have characterised as empathy. There is, however, a feature that seems necessary for empathy, namely, to have an emotion of the same kind as the person with whom one empathises. But we said that *A*'s emotion is different from *B*'s on a given occasion. So, to return to the questions posed before, is that empathy?

One possibility is to suppose that *A* has suffered once, or perhaps repeatedly been hurt or tortured, in some similar way as she now wants *B* to submit to. That is, that at some other moment in her life, she participated in intimate relationships similar to the present one: for instance, if she experienced abuse or cruelty towards her or if she participated in a toxic relationship with intimate others.

[35] Of course, it is possible that they have physical deficiencies or that they experienced mistreatment or abuse by people who respond to a certain description, and so developed a tendency to harm such persons. But the point is that they don't have an intimate relationship with their victims. See Farrington (2006) and Ostrosky-Solis (2008).

We could say that she knows what it feels like to be in the other's place when she tortures another and makes him suffer. This would explain, at least in part, her current sensibility and affective understanding of how to make the person with whom she has an intimate relationship suffer.[36] I do not know if it is necessary for *A* to have experienced something similar to the present situation, that is, for her to have been treated cruelly or participated in negative relationships and experienced similar emotions to those *A* wants *B* to feel by her mistreatment of *B*. But regardless of how she acquired this emotional awareness, it allows her to hurt *B* more effectively.

Empathy is often thought of as *positive* because it can help us to understand what is happening to others and how they feel about it, and this imaginative understanding can motivate us to do something for the sufferer. But taking into account the distinctions made before, I would like to suggest that we need a different understanding of empathy, where empathy is not always positive, but can also be used as an instrument to inflict more personalised suffering. Compassion or sympathy can be described more obviously as positive, because to sympathise with someone who is suffering is to have a motivation to do something to alleviate their suffering. If there is no such motivation, one would not say of someone that he sympathises or has compassion for them. To have a motivation to do something is, of course, not always followed by actually acting, that is, by helping or caring behaviour, but often the motivation only causes some other mental states, like wishes, mental images or other affective states. Sometimes this is due to the actual impossibility of doing something in particular, or to other personal or contextual features characteristic of a given situation.

With respect to empathy on the other hand, I would like to suggest that empathy is different from compassion or sympathy, in that it does not always involve a motivation to do something that benefits the other. It sometimes does, but that is not a necessary feature of empathy as it is of sympathy. My proposal is that empathy and its developmental antecedents are necessary for intimacy in general, because they are necessary, among other things, for seeing the other as *minded*, for understanding the experiences of others and for establishing interpersonal relationships, and especially when these relationships are intimate. And this is independent of the kind of intimacy and whether it is positive or negative.

If this is a possible interpretation, namely that there is empathy in positive *and* negative intimacies, there is still the problem of explaining that in negative intimacy the victimiser does not experience the same kind of emotion as the victim in a given episode, and also that he has the disposition to see intimate situations of a certain kind as opportunities to enjoy acts of cruelty and violence towards others. But, although *A* has emotions that she doesn't share with the victim, we

[36] I am interested here in pointing out the emotional communication that is characteristic of such intimacies, but I do not want to suggest that one can clearly distinguish between cognitive and emotional understanding, or that both are not required.

can attribute some of the other features of empathy that make it possible for her to torture, hurt or manipulate the target more perceptively and effectively. She needs to have some kind of empathy, or something like it, to know exactly where and how to produce the greatest suffering. The problem here is how to interpret this very developed ability some people have to produce targeted suffering in others, especially intimate others, because, in intimacy, positive or negative, emotional communication is essential.[37] So the question remains: is this empathy?

I don't have a clear answer to this question, but I would like to make some suggestions[38] for further discussion, and to better understand negative intimacy as I have described it.

First, there is the possibility of claiming that there is something similar to empathy in negative intimacies, but which is not really empathy because it lacks one of the crucial elements of empathy, namely the sharing of emotions. This suggestion would have to explain what goes on in the development of an empathic ability or skill which is so important for establishing interpersonal relations, and which depends in part on the sharing of affective and other psychological states. That is, sharing is needed for the development of an empathic ability that is important for understanding the feelings, emotions, thoughts and attitudes of another, and crucial for intimacy. This does not mean that, in each particular case, the participants have to share the same affective states. In negative intimacy the attention is on the victim: the victimiser has the sensibility to understand what the other is feeling – what the other is going through – but he does not suffer 'for them'.[39]

Second, there is the possibility of revising the conception of empathy and holding that the sharing of emotions is *not* a necessary feature of empathy, but that only points (b) and (c) above are, that is, assuming a perspective oriented towards the other, and differentiating between oneself and others, that is, to clearly separate the identities of each. This would introduce a different conception of empathy, one that is not clearly distinguished from sympathy or compassion, where there is no need of affective sharing, but only of detecting that others are suffering. If one wants to help others, sympathy or compassion would be much more effective and psychologically less demanding in cognitive, imaginative and affective resources, because one can detect in various ways that another is suffering without much imagination, and without any profound understanding of what another person is experiencing. As we said before, sympathy and compassion are motivating, and empathy need not be.

[37] I would like to reiterate that I am not speaking of social institutions like marriage, family and other kinds of legally accepted social relationships. Couples, partners and family members can of course be distant and uncomprehending. I would say that such relationships are not intimate; intimate relationships of whichever kind, must have an affective quality.

[38] I would like to thank the editors for pointing out problems which I tried to clarify, but of course much more needs to be said.

[39] They can of course share other psychological states like the attention directed to each other, beliefs, desires, and some other emotions, for instance, resentment.

The question here is that without (a), the sharing of affective states, one would need to explain *why* someone would go through this complicated imaginative process of perspective taking from the other's point of view, unless they had a very special affective and personal interest in the other person. Another question that needs an answer is *how* one could do it without imagining what the other is experiencing, and such an imagination involves some kind of affective sharing. Besides, if successful, empathy could be a better instrument for understanding the experiences[40] of other people, but it is difficult to see how this can be done without imaginatively sharing some affective states and points of view with them.[41] And in intimate relationships, affective communication and understanding is much more important than in other interpersonal relations.

Finally, I shall explore how to understand positive and negative intimacy by putting it as part of a larger framework, in this case by appealing to character traits.[42]

V. Intimacy and Character Traits

Although this is a complex matter that cannot be dealt with here appropriately, the attribution of personality and character traits is a useful and common means for interpreting actions, intentions and other psychological states, for anticipating the reactions of other people in particular circumstances, and for planning how to respond in accordance. It works by assigning patterns of thought, emotional and behavioural tendencies in determinate circumstances.

To get a better idea of how this works, it is important to say more about the distinction made before between, on the one hand, episodes and dispositions that are or can be actualised in particular situations or in a variety of circumstances, and that have relevant common features. For instance, experiencing or *feeling empathy* at a given moment is an emotional episode of empathy. A *disposition* to feel empathy in various circumstances, is having the disposition to put oneself in another's shoes, *feeling with* them, but maintaining the self/other distinction.

[40] Empathy is such an umbrella term that it has become almost useless. Coplan's definition is so strict that one can hardly attribute it to anyone. It is very difficult to find people who, in a specific situation, have the background knowledge, the variety of experience, and imaginative requirements needed for full-fledged empathy. It is worth thinking about what kind of understanding, cognitive but also affective, is needed to understand the experiences of other people. We know that some people are better at it than others, and that some of them use this ability in order to produce more suffering and enjoy the results.

[41] The question here is if one can have such a rich and varied imagination without affective sharing.

[42] This is important because it rests on the general idea that one cannot explain and understand the mental states and actions of other individuals without putting them in context, that is, that such mental states or actions cannot be attributed to others and explained in isolation, but only by considering them in relation to other mental states, actions, and in specific circumstances. And this is also the case with traits, or so I shall argue.

Traits on the other hand are a special kind of disposition. They are dispositions that have developed into more stable traits. A trait can be considered as a feature of the characteristic way a person thinks, imagines, feels and acts in different kind of circumstances. It is part of the affective, cognitive and evaluative set up of an individual. Another way of putting this is to say that people differ in personality, or that they have different character traits. Examples of personality traits are elegant, dignified, charming and pessimistic, among many others; character traits are ways of valuing and acting in accordance with those values like being honest, kind, generous, cruel, egoistic, mean, dishonest and jealous.[43] When we consider the ability to emotionally understand others, and the way it is manifested in specific circumstances and towards certain persons, in our case intimate ones, can be regarded as an element of the affective, evaluative and cognitive constitution of different individuals. Say, for example, a kind person has the disposition to be kind towards others in different circumstances, but this disposition is *not* manifested in some circumstances or towards certain persons. In such cases we describe that person as acting 'out of character'.

In intimacy, a *kind* person is more prone to feel empathy in a particular situation and care about the other's welfare, while a *cruel* person, although he can have the same general ability to emotionally understand other participants in an intimate relationship, will make them suffer and will react to their suffering with emotions such as pleasure or excitement. He will regard the situation as an opportunity for hurting and maybe also enjoying the suffering of his victim. Attributing contrasting emotions in particular instances is not enough to explain the difference between *A* and *B*, and the quality of their intimacy as positive or negative. Attributing different traits, like kind, gentle or generous on the one hand, and cruel, selfish or ruthless on the other, takes us a bit further. But one has also to take into account that traits are not isolated either, which means that each person has different traits, and a special combination of traits.

In negative intimacy the perpetrator enjoys the episode or has some other motivation or disposition to hurt or inflict harm on his intimate counterpart. But he has developed an empathetic capacity or sensibility as a more stable trait of his personality, which allows him to be aware of the feelings of other people and to *emotionally* understand them. And this general 'empathic' sensibility can be used, in particular cases, to produce pain, abuse and harm.

Deonna and Teroni distinguish two kinds of multi-track dispositions: one is a multi-track affective disposition, like love and hatred, which consists, among other things, in feeling several emotions in different circumstances. The second sort of multi-track dispositions focuses on any object 'apprehended in some particular evaluative light'. Character-traits have this structure, that is, they are

[43] There is an enormous literature in philosophy, and psychology, on character traits, personality, virtues and vices. Here I barely touch the subject, but I raise the issue only as a way to approach the problem of empathy, especially in negative intimacies. For more on character traits see Miller (2018).

multi-track dispositions that 'focus on values rather than on particular objects'.[44] Character-traits are manifested in emotional tendencies of a particular sort and expressed also in 'one's actions and habits of thought'. Virtues and vices are a subset of these traits that have to do with 'our moral or intellectual life'.[45] Rossi and Tappolet also mention that 'virtues should be understood as character traits that consist in multi-track dispositions to act, think and feel in a certain way'.[46]

This kind of explanation of the way different people react, feel and behave towards, in this case, the suffering of others, by attributing to them different personality traits, has, of course, only a *weak* predictive power, as many personal or contextual features of particular situations could alter the motivational, affective, intentional and behavioural conduct that one would expect of particular individuals characterised as possessing character traits such as courageous, cruel, kind and generous. One can have a trait without acting in accordance with it on a specific occasion or type of situation, or towards certain persons, or one may act, for instance, cruelly on a specific occasion, despite being in general a kind person. But although in particular cases the attribution of traits can fail, it is also a common and useful means of relating to other people and knowing generally what to expect from them.

In intimate relationships things can get a bit more complicated, because in intimate relationships one needs to attribute traits to all the participants in the relationship. These traits can conflict with each other, for instance when somebody considers the other person to be so annoying that she reacts with impatience, anger and uncharacteristic rudeness. One could say that sometimes the mechanics of a particular relationship can change the habitual forms of relating to other people. In these cases, one needs to take a more complex view of how people influence and react specifically to each other. This is, I suppose, more obvious in negative intimacies. As said before, one can act out of character in certain contexts. For instance, *A* and *B* are in a negative intimate relationship, but *A* can be kind in some contexts, although in general she is a cruel person. But what if *A* is in general a kind person but cruel specifically in interactions with *B*? Here one has to take into account not only the personality traits of each, but also how they can conflict with each other and how the intimate relationship can develop into a toxic relationship. Personality traits alone are, of course, not enough to explain some negative intimate relationships. Traits are only indicative of what one can expect of other people. One has to examine in each case how the dynamics of the relationship evolves.

To characterise participants in an intimate relationship as possessing different personalities is one way, among others, to better understand the different attitudes and behaviour towards others with whom they interact. To put it simply and in

[44] Deonna and Teroni (2012), 8.

[45] Ibid, 9.

[46] Rossi and Tappolet (2016), 116. I mention virtues and vices only in passing, because we could also characterise one as virtuous and the other as vicious, if we were to take a moral stand on this issue. For more on virtues see Snow (2015), Snow (2018), Miller (2018) and Thompson (2014).

black and white, if *A* is empathetic, selfish and cruel, and *B* is empathetic, kind and generous, this difference in personality will be reflected in a different perspective towards the suffering of others.

VI. Conclusions

In this chapter I tried to highlight some connections between emotions and intimacy and concentrated on one of its central characteristics: 'emotional communication'. I distinguished between positive and negative intimacy, and also intimacy between peers and asymmetrical intimacies. Among the different issues that arise in these kinds of relationship, I focused on the question of empathy and its role in intimacy. I gave a characterisation of empathy, which has to be understood in a certain way so that it can be considered as a necessary aspect of intimacy. First, I described the components and precursors of empathy in the development of infants (emotional contagion, affective matching, and imitation) and, second, the features of mature empathy (sharing psychological states, assuming a perspective, and clearly differentiating between the self and others). My claim is that empathy is essential for understanding interpersonal relations in general, and especially when there is intimacy. And that empathy should be distinguished from sympathy and compassion.

The problem I addressed in this chapter was to understand what I called negative intimacy and its connection to empathy and emotional communication in general. I asked if there was empathy, or something similar to empathy in negative intimacy: when someone takes advantage of their affective understanding of the feelings of others to produce pain or suffering in a highly effective manner. I made some suggestions and discussed the possibility and limits of understanding the difference between positive and negative intimacy by attributing contrasting character traits.

References

Blum, L (2020) '"Black Lives Matter": Moral Frames for Understanding the Police Killings of Black Males' in A Amaya and M Del Mar (eds) *Virtue, Emotion and Imagination in Law and Legal Reasoning* (Oxford, Hart Publishing).

Brady, M (2020) 'Suffering and Punishment' in A Amaya and M Del Mar (eds) *Virtue, Emotion and Imagination in Law and Legal Reasoning* (Oxford, Hart Publishing).

Coplan, A (2011) 'Understanding Empathy' in A Coplan and P Goldie (eds) *Empathy: Philosophical and Psychological Perspectives* (New York, Oxford University Press) 3.

Coplan, A and Goldie, P (2011) *Empathy: Philosophical and Psychological Perspectives* (New York, Oxford University Press).

Decety, J and Meltzoff, AN (2011) 'Empathy, Imitation and the Social Brain' in A Coplan and P Goldie (eds) *Empathy: Philosophical and psychological perspectives* (New York, Oxford University Press) 58.

Deigh, J (2009) 'Concepts of Emotion in Modern Philosophy and Psychology' in P Goldie (ed) *The Oxford Handbook of Philosophy of Emotion* (Oxford University Press) 17.

Deigh, J (2004) 'Primitive Emotions' in RC Solomon (ed) *Thinking About Feeling: Contemporary Philosophers on Emotions* (Oxford University Press) 9.

Del Mar, M (2017) 'Imagining by Feeling: A Case for Compassion in Legal Reasoning' 13(2) *International Journal of Law in Context* 143.

Deonna, J and Teroni, F (2012) *The Emotions: A Philosophical Introduction* (New York: Routledge).

Dunn, J (2000) 'Mind-Reading, Emotion Understanding, and Relationships' 24(2) *International Journal of Behavioral Development* 142.

Eisenberg, N, Spinrad, T and Knafo-Noam, A (2015) 'Prosocial Development' in W Damon (ed) *Handbook of Child Psychology and Developmental Science* (Hoboken, Wiley) 610.

Elgin, E (2020) 'Impartiality and Legal Reasoning' in A Amaya and M Del Mar (eds) *Virtue, Emotion and Imagination in Law and Legal Reasoning* (Oxford, Hart Publishing).

Farrington, DP (2006) 'Family Background and Psychopathy' in CJ Patrick (ed), *Handbook of Psychopathy* (New York, Guilford) 229.

Gaia, AC (2002) 'Understanding Emotional Intimacy: A Review of Conceptualization, Assessment and the Role of Gender' 77(3/4) *International Social Science Review* 151.

Giddens, A (1992) *The Transformation of Intimacy: Sexuality, Love and Eroticism in Modern Societies* (Stanford: Stanford University Press).

Goldie, P (1999) 'How We Think of Others' Emotions' 14(4) *Mind & Language* 394.

Goldie, P (2000) *The Emotions: A Philosophical Exploration* (New York, Oxford University Press).

Goldie, P (2011) 'Anti-Empathy' in P Goldie and A Coplan (eds) *Empathy* (New York, Oxford University Press) 302.

Goldie, P and Coplan, A (eds) (2011) *Empathy* (New York, Oxford University Press).

Hamlin, JK, Ullman, T, Tenenbaum, JB, Goodman, N and Baker, C (2013) 'The Mentalistic Basis of Core Social Cognition: Experiments in Preverbal Infants and a Computational Model' 16(2) *Developmental Science* 209.

Hansberg, O (1996) *La diversidad de las emociones* (México, Fondo de Cultura Económica).

Hansberg, O (2008) 'Aspectos cognitivos de las emociones' in E Kronmüller and C Cornejo (eds) *Ciencias de la mente: Aproximaciones desde Latinoamérica* (Santiago, Chile, JC Saez) 27.

Hansberg, O (2017) 'Emociones, intimidad y confianza' in O Hansberg and R Esteinou (eds) *Acercamientos multidisciplinarios a las emociones* (México, Universidad Nacional Autónoma de México) 17.

Hatfield, E, Cacioppo, JT and Rapson, RL (1992) 'Primitive Emotional Contagion' in M Clark (ed) *Review of Personality and Social Psychology: Emotion and Social Behavior* (Thousand Oaks, Sage) 151.

Hatfield, E, Cacioppo, JT and Rapson, RL (1993) 'Emotional Contagion' 2(3) *Current Directions in Psychological Science* 96.

Hatfield, E, Cacioppo, JT and Rapson, RL (1994) *Emotional Contagion* (Cambridge, Cambridge University Press).

Hoffman, ML (2011) 'Empathy, justice and the law' in A Coplan and P Goldie (eds) *Empathy: Philosophical and psychological perspectives.* (New York, Oxford University Press) 230.

Kind, A (2020) 'Empathy, Imagination, and the Law' in A Amaya and M Del Mar (eds) *Virtue, Emotion and Imagination in Law and Legal Reasoning* (Oxford, Hart Publishing).

Kochanska, G (2002) 'Mutually Responsive Orientation Between Mothers and Young Children: A Context for Early Development of Conscience' 11 *Current Directions in Psychological Science* 191.

Maibom, HL (2014) 'Everything You Wanted to Know About Empathy' in HL Maibom (ed) *Empathy and Morality* (Oxford, Oxford University Press) 12.

Miller, C (2018) 'Virtue as a Trait' in N Snow (ed) *The Oxford Handbook of Virtue* (New York, Oxford University Press) 9.

Ostrosky-Solis, F (2008) *Mentes asesinas. La violencia en tu cerebro* (México, Quo Libros).

Thompson, AR (2014) 'The Development of Virtue: A Perspective from Developmental Psychology' in N Snow (ed) *The Oxford Handbook of Virtue* (New York, Oxford University Press) 279.

Rossi, M and Tappolet, C (2016) 'Virtue, Happiness, and Wellbeing' 99(1) *The Monist* 112.

Snow, N (2015) 'Models of Virtue' in L Besser-Jones and M Slote (eds) *The Routledge Companion to Virtue Ethics* (New York, Taylor and Francis).

Snow, N (ed) (2018) *The Oxford Handbook of Virtue* (New York, Oxford University Press).

Strawson, PF (1962) 'Freedom and Resentment' in G Watson (ed) (2003) *Free Will* (New York, Oxford University Press).

White, EK (2020) 'On Emotions and the Politics of Attention in Judicial Reasoning' in A Amaya and M Del Mar (eds) *Virtue, Emotion and Imagination in Law and Legal Reasoning* (Oxford, Hart Publishing).

Zipursky, BC (2020) 'Austerity, Compassion, and the Rule of Law' in A Amaya and M Del Mar (eds) *Virtue, Emotion and Imagination in Law and Legal Reasoning* (Oxford, Hart Publishing).

PART III

Imagination – and Emotion, Virtue

10

Empathy, Imagination and the Law

AMY KIND*

I. Introduction

At his Supreme Court confirmation hearings in 2005, John Roberts famously employed an analogy comparing judges to umpires: 'Judges and justices are servants of the law, not the other way around. Judges are like umpires. Umpires don't make the rules, they apply them.'[1] In line with this comparison, he swore that as a justice he would 'remember that it's my job to call balls and strikes'.[2]

While the judge-as-umpire analogy did not originate with Justice Roberts, his use of it thrust the analogy into the public and political limelight.[3] The analogy again took centre stage when, in 2009, the retirement of Justice David Souter left a new vacancy on the Supreme Court for President Barack Obama to fill. As ranking member of the Senate Judiciary Committee, then-Senator (and subsequently Attorney General) Jeff Sessions noted in a conversation with the *National Journal* that 'The core strength of American law is that a judge puts on that robe and he says, "I am unbiased; I'm going to call the balls and strikes based on where the pitch is placed, not on whose side I'm on. I don't take sides in the game."'

Sessions' invocation of the umpire model was explicitly meant to contrast with another way we might characterise the ideal judge. On this alternative, rather than

* Thanks to the participants at the conference on Virtue, Imagination and Emotion in Legal Reasoning (Mexico City, March 2017) for their helpful feedback on this chapter, and especially to Maksymilian Del Mar and Amalia Amaya for comments on a previous draft. Thanks also to my two undergraduate research assistants, Patrick Hennessey and Seoyoon Choi, for background research at an early stage of this project.

[1] United States Senate Committee on the Judiciary (2005), 55.

[2] Ibid, 56.

[3] See Zelinsky (2010) for a helpful discussion of the history of the judge-as-umpire analogy. Interestingly, Zelinsky notes that when comparisons between judges and umpires were first made in the late 1800s, such comparisons were rejected, ie the conclusion drawn was that judges should not act simply as umpires. It was not until the middle of the twentieth century that the comparison of judges to umpires came to be seen as a positive one. Zelinsky credits this change to a 1951 speech by Justice Jackson: '[T]he test of an independent judiciary is a simple one – the one you would apply in choosing an umpire for a baseball game. What do you ask of him? You do not ask that he shall never make a mistake or always agree with you, or always support the home team. You want an umpire who calls them as he sees them' (Zelinsky, 2010, 116).

putting primary focus on a judge's ability to be neutral, we instead focus on a judge's ability to be empathetic. Barack Obama has been perhaps the most prominent advocate of this latter picture, at least in the public sphere. In his own remarks on Souter's retirement, Obama forcefully described the qualities for which he would be looking in a judicial nominee:

> I will seek someone who understands that justice isn't about some abstract legal theory or footnote in a case book. It is also about how our laws affect the daily realities of people's lives – whether they can make a living and care for their families; whether they feel safe in their homes and welcome in their own nation. I view that quality of empathy, of understanding and identifying with people's hopes and struggles as an essential ingredient for arriving as [sic] just decisions and outcomes.[4]

Such remarks were not the first time that Obama extolled the virtues of empathy. In outlining his vision of America in *The Audacity of Hope*, he noted that we all have a moral obligation to try to understand our opponent's views, even in the face of very serious disagreement. In his view, it's empathy that enables us to discharge this obligation. We can achieve greater understanding of differing perspectives when we see the world through another's eyes: 'That's what empathy does – it calls us all to task, the conservative and the liberal, the powerful and the powerless, the oppressed and the oppressor. We are all shaken out of our complacency. We are all forced beyond our limited vision.'[5]

These two pictures of a judge's role – the umpire model and the empathy model – have recently received increasing attention in both the popular press and the legal scholarship. But while this attention has helped us to begin to refine our sense of the two different pictures, I don't think we have yet achieved an adequate understanding of either of these models or how they relate to one another. This chapter aims to achieve greater clarity by consideration of six different lessons on these issues. I start with three lessons that seem to me to have already been fairly well learned. Then I turn to three lessons that I think still need to be learned. Ultimately, we will see not only that these two models are not as starkly opposed as might initially appear but also that we would do best to move past this debate and instead look to moral imagination as a key component in allowing judges to satisfy many of the concerns that motivate both the umpire conception and the empathy conception.

II. Some Preliminary Remarks About Empathy

Attending even to our first three lessons requires us to have before us at least a basic conception of what empathy is. Amidst the relevant legal scholarship, it is common for authors to claim that empathy is not a particularly well understood notion.

[4] Obama (2009).
[5] Obama (2006), 89.

Bandes suggests that, when it comes to empathy, the 'definitional difficulties are daunting', and that the term 'has multiple meanings across and even within disciplines'.[6] Similarly, Franks notes that empathy is not 'an intuitive concept or one with clearly defined contours'[7] and Henderson claims that empathy is 'never defined or described'.[8]

But while there are various issues about empathy that continue to be the subject of scholarly debate, and while there are also some vagaries at the borderlines of the concept, it does seem possible to get at least a rough handle on the notion of empathy, and there are some basic facts around which there seem to be widespread agreement. As Karsten Stueber notes in a survey article on empathy: 'In ordinary parlance, empathy refers to our ability to feel with and be concerned about another person and her states of mind.'[9] Likewise, in a different survey article, Adam Morton offers a 'broad and basic definition' of empathy in terms of 'the sharing of states'.[10] On both of these construals, then, empathy can be seen as a *resonance* phenomenon, ie as a phenomenon in which the emotional states of one individual are replicated in some way in the mind of another.[11] There is much more that could be said about this process of replication. One important issue concerns how much the replicated emotion must match the original emotion. If the process of replication occurs by simulation, for example, it might be of a lesser degree of intensity. Another important issue arises from the issue of perspective: does the replication come from projecting oneself into the situation of the other or from representing the situation from the other's point of view? Settling these issues is crucial for developing a complete analysis of the notion of empathy, but however this turns out, the basic understanding of empathy-as-resonance-phenomenon will still remain.[12]

Empathy is thus importantly different from sympathy. When I am feeling sympathetic towards you, I orient myself towards you and your feelings and I am concerned about your well being. But when I am feeling empathetic towards you, I do more than simply orient myself towards your feelings. Rather, I come actually to share them in some way.[13]

[6] Bandes (2011), 5.

[7] Franks (2011), 62. Likewise, in chapter nine in this volume, Hansberg (2020) claims that 'empathy is a concept that lacks clarity and precision, that is used in diverse contexts and with different meanings that can refer to different psychological processes that vary in function, phenomenology, mechanisms and effects attributed to them'.

[8] Henderson (1987), 1578.

[9] Stueber (2016), 368.

[10] Morton (2017), 181.

[11] After describing empathy as a resonance phenomenon, Bloom notes that this 'is how most psychologists and philosophers use the term' (Bloom, 2016, 3–4).

[12] Though the notion of empathy-as-resonance-phenomenon is common in the literature, it is not universally accepted. See eg Del Mar (2017) for a conception of empathy as cognitive rather than affective.

[13] Hansberg (2020) draws a similar distinction between sympathy and empathy in chapter eight in this volume. As she puts it, 'the emotion a sympathetic person feels does not need to match the emotion of the person with whom they sympathise'; in contrast, one of the 'essential attributes' of empathy is that one feels what the other feels.

Though Stueber and Morton's definitions of empathy both treat empathy as a resonance phenomenon, they differ in one further respect. For Morton, *any* resonance phenomenon will count as empathy. On his view, empathy includes instances of emotional contagion – cases where someone catches the emotions of someone else, as when someone starts to feel anxious simply as a result of being in a roomful of anxious people. In contrast, since Stueber understands empathy to require not just resonance with another person but also concern for that person, his conception of empathy excludes cases of emotional contagion.

I suspect that neither the proponents nor the opponents of the empathy model picture have cases of emotional contagion in mind when they are respectively promoting or denigrating the importance of empathy. Given the way that empathy has been invoked in discussions of judicial decision-making, there seems to be a focus not just on resonance but also on concern.[14] In what follows, then, I will use Stueber's definition as a rough guide for how we should understand empathy.

III. Three Easy Lessons

With this preliminary understanding of empathy in place, I now turn to our six lessons. We will start with the three easy – or perhaps I should say 'easier' – lessons, several of which have already been discussed in the literature. As we will see, each of these lessons involves disconnecting empathy from some problematic association to which it has been mistakenly tied.

A. Lesson One: Empathy Does Not Entail Activism

Insofar as the umpire/empathy debate has often played out against the background of Supreme Court confirmation battles, it's perhaps not surprising that it has become politicised. Moreover, as so often happens in politicised debates, nuance is sacrificed at the expense of partisan posturing. As described by Mary Franks in her 'Lies, Damned Lies, and Judicial Empathy', the national conversation following the announcement of Justice David Souter's retirement in 2009 was essentially a 'pitched battle between two caricatures: the activist judge who decides cases based on his feelings and political agenda and the impartial judge who dispassionately applies the rules of law'.[15]

The battle was fought largely on two fronts: first, on network news programs and, second, after Sonia Sotomayor was announced as the nominee, during her

[14] Note that even if there were disagreement on this particular definitional matter, such disagreement is unlikely to be playing much of a role in the debate about whether we should aspire to have judges who are empathetic.

[15] Franks (2011), 61.

confirmation hearings themselves. Appearing on *This Week*, Senator Orrin Hatch claimed outright that Obama's use of the word 'empathy' was really just code for judicial activism.[16] Activist judges are typically seen as making law rather than interpreting and applying it; as such, critics of judicial activism see it as an inappropriate overreaching beyond the proper duties of the judiciary. That said, it's not clear that the notion of judicial activism is itself very well understood; as argued by Theodore McKee, it is ultimately a meaningless notion that 'offers little more than reflexive criticism and convenient sound bites'.[17]

A similar dialectic played out the following year during the confirmation hearings for Elena Kagan. As Senator Charles Grassley claimed, a reliance on empathy 'encourages judges to usurp the functions held by the executive and legislative branches of Government'.[18] In a similar vein, Senator Jon Kyl associated a reliance on empathy with 'results-oriented judging' and an improper use of the bench towards the advancement of 'progressive goals that have been stalled in the political process.'[19]

But there is no good reason to believe that Obama had judicial activism in mind when he promoted the importance of empathy. Indeed, following his invocation of the notion of empathy in his remarks on the occasion of Souter's retirement, Obama went on to note the importance of the constitutional values that underlay the founding of the United States of America and, further, he noted that he would seek to appoint someone 'who is dedicated to the rule of law, who honors our constitutional traditions, who respects the integrity of the judicial process and the appropriate limits of the judicial role'.[20] Even more importantly for our purposes here, there is no good reason to believe that empathy and activism need go hand in hand. Why should the ability to share the emotions of another have anything to do with the promotion of a particular political agenda?

B. Lesson Two: Empathy Does Not Entail Action of a Particular Sort

Connected with the worry about activism is a further worry simply about action. Insofar as empathy seems to entail taking action on behalf of those with whom you empathise, one might worry that judges will automatically provide judicial relief to those with whom they empathise. We can see a clear example of this line of reasoning in a *Wall Street Journal* piece written by Steven G Calabresi, a law professor at Northwestern University who is also the co-founder of the Federalist Society. As Calabresi argued, Obama's 'emphasis on empathy in essence requires the

[16] ABC News (2009) *This Week* Transcript.
[17] McKee (2007), 1716.
[18] United States Senate Committee on the Judiciary (2010), 15.
[19] Ibid, 18.
[20] Obama (2009).

appointment of judges committed in advance to violating [their oath to administer justice]. To the traditional view of justice as a blindfolded person weighing legal claims fairly on a scale, he wants to tear the blindfold off, so the judge can rule for the party he empathizes with most.' In Calabresi's view, Obama's aim was to 'replace justice with empathy'.[21]

To spell this worry out a bit further, we might reason as follows. Judges who are empathetic will, presumably, be especially inclined to feel empathy when they encounter instances of suffering. If empathy requires taking action in support of those with whom one empathises, it would seem that empathetic judges would be likely to side with those who are suffering. But since the question about which party is suffering might come apart from the question about which party is in the legal right, empathy would then seem to lead to problematic decision-making.

We can begin to unravel this line of reasoning by first attending more closely to what is meant by empathy. Though a standard definition of empathy like the one with which we're operating understands empathy as requiring *concern* for those whose feelings we are sharing, there is no further requirement that there be any particular manifestation of this concern. One can count as having an attitude of concern towards someone else without acting on that concern. To count as having an attitude of concern, what matters is one's mental orientation, not one's actions. Thus, as a matter of definition, one individual may be empathetic towards another without exhibiting empathetic behaviour towards that other individual.[22]

Beyond this definitional point, we can also point to empirical research showing that empathy does not automatically issue in empathetic behaviour. As Henderson notes, studies have shown that 'empathetic responses do not inevitably elicit helping behavior', but rather that whether an empathiser will take action is 'contingent upon such factors as their skills, the means available to them, and their alternatives'.[23] The disconnect between empathy and behaviour can thus be seen in both theory and in practice.

But even if empathy does not require action, there might be a lingering suspicion that in cases of empathy devoid of any behavioural uptake, the empathy is somewhat empty, or lacking in full authenticity. Insofar as the empathy model sees the ideal judge not just as an empty empathiser but as a fully authentic empathiser, it might seem that at least some action must be being called for by those who call for more empathetic judges.

Importantly, however, even if this is right – ie even if the empathy model does imply that some action is called for – the action called for need not be action of a particular sort. More specifically, a proponent of the empathy model need not be implying that there must be immediate and unequivocal judicial relief for the

[21] Calabresi (2008), 17.

[22] See eg Bandes (2009), 136, in particular, her comment that empathy 'does not necessarily lead to action on behalf of its object, or the desire to take action on his behalf'. That said, studies have shown that empathy often does have motivational properties. See Hoffman 2011.

[23] Henderson (1987), 1583.

party with whom the judge is empathising. Rather, it's perfectly consistent with this model, and with the notion of empathy underlying it, that judicial empathy result in other kinds of actions. For example, empathy towards a party might incline a judge to re-examine evidence to be sure that nothing has been missed, to reconsider conflicting testimony, or to explore whether there are appropriate and allowable ways of exercising judicial discretion in the matter at hand. Empathy towards a party might also incline a judge to re-evaluate whether and how implicit bias might be operative, and whether and how there might be ways to combat it. In short, even if we think that fully authentic empathetic concern cannot be completely disassociated from behavioural affects, there is no reason to think that the empathy model mandates the kind of judicial action that would in any way compromise the fairness or objectivity of the legal process. Rather, as the partial list of actions just reviewed suggests, the kind of judicial action prompted by empathy has the promise to promote a fairer and more objective outcome.[24]

C. Lesson Three: Empathy Does Not Entail Arbitrariness

In addition to associating empathy with activism and action, opponents of the empathy model also associate empathy with a certain kind of arbitrariness in decision-making. In the same conversation with the *National Journal* in which he promoted the umpire model, Sessions made this association directly. After claiming not to know what President Obama meant by empathy, Sessions noted that the empathy model was a 'dangerous' one. He then went on to spell out the danger that he saw: 'So I'm one judge and I have empathy for you and not this party, and so I'm going to rule for the one I have empathy with? So what if the guy doesn't like your haircut, or for some reason doesn't like you, is he now free to rule one way or the other based on likes, predilections, politics, personal values?'[25] As Franks aptly describes these remarks, Sessions here took empathy to be synonymous with 'arbitrariness and caprice'.[26]

It would probably be a mistake to put too much weight on Sessions' chosen examples. In particular, the focus on haircuts seems especially silly. It's hard to see why empathy would have anything at all to do with liking or disliking someone's haircut. More importantly, it's hard to see why an empathetic person would be any more inclined to make decisions based on how much they like someone's haircut than a non-empathetic person would be.

But haircuts aside, the general point underlying Sessions' remarks seems to be something like the following: insofar as a judge's decision-making is guided by their own idiosyncratic likes and dislikes, their decisions end up being completely arbitrary. Here compare Senator Grassley's remarks during the

[24] For related discussion, see Abrams (2010).

[25] *National Journal* (2009).

[26] Franks (2011), 66.

Kagan confirmation hearings: as he put it, to endorse empathy is 'to endorse the application of personal politics and preferences'.[27] Let's just grant that any judicial decision-making that was guided in this manner would indeed be problematic. The question that remains is: what does any of this have to do with empathy? Why should we think that an empathetic judge would be especially victim to their personal predilections or political values?[28]

To see how puzzling this connection is, it will be helpful to step back a moment from the matter of empathetic *judges* and simply think more generally about empathetic *people*. Interestingly, we might naturally think that empathetic people are actually *less* likely than non-empathetic people to put their own interests at the forefront, ie that they are less likely to be guided by their own idiosyncratic and arbitrary preferences. When my interests collide with yours – when something I want to do is going to cause you some kind of pain – developing some kind of understanding of the pain that it will cause you seems to be a critical first step towards my setting my own interests aside.[29] This kind of understanding can often be gained by way of empathy. And it's precisely when I lack such an understanding that I'm more likely to let my own interests take precedence in my reasoning processes. Thus, contra Sessions, not only do we have no reason to believe that empathy leads to increased arbitrariness in decision-making, but we might well have reason to believe that empathy can help to prevent arbitrariness. As Bandes notes: 'Empathy properly employed will not move the judge to prefer one side over the other.'[30]

All that said, there might be a slightly more compelling worry in the vicinity. Perhaps what Sessions had in mind is not that empathetic people will be more guided in their decision-making by their own likes and dislikes, but rather that their own likes and dislikes will guide their empathetic reactions. The thought is that we are more inclined to empathise with people who share our values and experiences than those who don't.[31] A commitment to empathy might thus be seen as a *de facto* commitment to *selective empathy*, and selective empathy might plausibly be seen as inconsistent with good judicial decision-making.[32]

[27] US Senate Committee on the Judiciary (2010), 15.

[28] Grassley might here have meant something else: that endorsing empathy is to endorse a certain kind of politics, namely, liberal politics. For a discussion undercutting the association of empathy with liberal politics, see Bloom (2016), esp 113–27. Bloom argues both that conservatives often rely on empathy as much as liberals, but also that 'certain perspectives associated with liberal philosophies aren't that empathic at all' (Bloom, 2016, 126).

[29] In saying this, I don't mean to suggest that empathy *requires* us to set out interests aside. Here compare Franks' claim that empathy '*forces* us to consider more interests than our own' (Franks, 2011, 69; emphasis added). Depending on what she has in mind by this forced consideration, she and I might disagree on this point.

[30] Bandes (2011), 10.

[31] For a discussion of empirical studies that suggest we are subject to bias in our applications of empathy, see Bloom (2016). I return to this issue in Lesson Four below.

[32] White (2020), in chapter six in this volume, raises this kind of concern against selective empathy: 'A judge who empathised only with those claimants who they – consciously or unconsciously – understood to be part of their in-group would be in serious error'.

Though this version of the worry about arbitrariness is more compelling than the silliness about haircuts, it too fails to survive closer scrutiny, since there is no reason to identify empathy with selective empathy. On the one hand, in fairness to critics of the empathy model who have raised this worry, it's worth pointing out that President Obama was not always careful to guard against this problematic identification when advocating for the empathy model. Consider, for example, his claim in an address to Planned Parenthood in 2007: 'We need somebody who's got the heart, the empathy, to recognize what it's like to be a young teenage mom, the empathy to understand what it's like to be poor or African-American or gay or disabled or old – and that's the criterion by which I'll be selecting my judges.' As noted by Thomas Colby, remarks like this might seem to suggest that Obama meant to be promoting a kind of 'selective empathy for the downtrodden'.[33]

On the other hand, many instances of Obama's advocacy for the empathy model were devoid of any such implications. Yet even when such implications were absent, critics were eager to discover them anyway. Consider this piece of alleged paraphrasing from a column by David Limbaugh in response to Obama's remarks upon his nomination of Sotomayor:

> Obama said a Supreme Court nominee's two most important qualities are her rigorous intellect and mastery of the law and her recognition of the limits of the judicial role – that a judge's job is to interpret law, not to make it. Then came the 'but,' the exception that imperceptibly swallowed the rule. He quoted former Justice Oliver Wendell Holmes as saying, 'The life of the law has not been logic; it has been experience.' In other words: 'Forget what I just said about how judges should interpret, not make, the law. I want my judges to have empathy. And don't tell anyone, but when I say "empathy," that's code for bending the law to achieve the results I want based on the selective empathy I have for certain victimized groups.'[34]

Why we should think that a reference to experience is really a secret invocation of selective empathy, Limbaugh does not explain.

Ultimately, however, the main issue is not what President Obama has said or hasn't said, but rather, what a commitment to the empathy model entails. And on this issue, matters seem clear: the claim that judges should be empathetic does not entail that judges should be selectively empathetic. Consider this: if we had reason to dismiss the empathy model because of worries about the dangers of selective empathy, then we would also have reason to dismiss the umpire model because of worries about the dangers of selective umpiring. An umpire who uses a narrower strike zone to call balls and strikes when the team they like is at bat than they use when a team they don't like is at bat is a bad umpire, and so too for the judge who uses a narrow interpretation of the law only when it favours parties they like. But the fact that there might be judges who umpire selectively does not speak against the umpire model. Likewise, the fact that there might be judges who empathise selectively does not speak against the empathy model.

[33] Colby (2012), 1962.
[34] Limbaugh (2009).

There will be more to say about the worry about selective empathy in our discussion of Lesson Four below. For now, however, it's worth noting that we might plausibly think that the best way to guard against selective empathy would be to appoint judges who are *more* rather than less empathetic. The greater one's capacity for empathy, the more easily one will be able to extend it widely. A sufficiently empathetic judge will be able to empathise not only in cases where suffering is obvious, or where the figures involved are especially sympathetic ones, but in more difficult cases as well. The more empathetic you are, the more able you'll be to empathise with disagreeable characters rather than just with the agreeable ones. As this discussion suggests, then, even the most plausible version of the arbitrariness worry fails to have much bite.

IV. Three Harder Lessons

As I noted at the start of the previous section, I take the first three lessons about empathy to be relatively easy ones. Indeed, were it not for political gamesmanship, such lessons would perhaps not need to be learned at all. But insofar as our contemporary political discourse has made empathy seem inextricably intertwined with activism, arbitrariness and action, our goal of achieving greater clarity on our two competing pictures mandated that we started simply. Having learned these first three lessons, we are now ready to tackle slightly more difficult terrain. In this section, I thus turn to three further lessons that need to be learned. While I take these three further lessons to be on equally solid ground as our first three lessons, none of them are quite so obvious and, as we will see, it will take some more sophisticated treatment to tease them out.

One of the things that made the easy lessons easy was that they correct mistakes made by opponents to the empathy model. Correspondingly, one of the things that make the harder lessons harder is that here the relevant mistakes are made even by proponents of the empathy model. In what follows we need to overturn claims that, because they've often been championed by empathy model proponents, may seem to be presuppositions that are part and parcel of the model itself.

A. Lesson Four: Anyone Can be an Empathiser

To begin our next lesson, recall President Obama's 2007 speech to Planned Parenthood in which he expressed a desire to appoint judges who have 'the heart, the empathy, to recognize what it's like to be a young teenage mom, the empathy to understand what it's like to be poor or African-American or gay or disabled or old'. Above, we noted that these remarks might be taken to suggest a dangerous narrowing of the notion of empathy to a kind of selective empathy, empathy only for the 'downtrodden'. But even if we reject that uncharitable interpretation, and we reject the idea that a commitment to empathy requires a commitment to selective empathy, there is a different implication in these kinds of remarks that is potentially problematic.

Presumably in mentioning these groups in particular, Obama didn't mean to be suggesting that these classes of people are the *only* groups of people with whom justices should be empathising, but rather that they are *among* the groups of people with whom justices should be empathising. And presumably the reason that Obama is pointing to these groups of people in particular is that they are precisely those to whom he thinks that many past justices had been insufficiently empathetic and who have thus suffered various injustices as a result. But now here comes the potentially worrisome implication, namely, that the *only* kinds of judges who could be empathetic to these groups of people are judges who are themselves members of these groups. In other words, Obama may seem to be suggesting that in order to ensure empathy for all people, people from a diverse array of groups, we need judges who are themselves from a diverse array of groups.

We see a similar suggestion, perhaps, in some 2001 remarks by Sotomayor, then an appeals court judge. In a speech at the University of Berkeley School of Law, Sotomayor argued that 'our gender and national origins may and will make a difference in our judging'.[35] Explicitly disagreeing with the idea that 'a wise old man and wise old woman will reach the same conclusion in deciding cases' (a claim made in 1991 by Minnesota Supreme Court Justice M Jeanne Coyne), Sotomayor articulated her hope that 'a wise Latina woman with the richness of her experiences would more often than not reach a better conclusion than a white male who hasn't lived that life'.[36] Perhaps unsurprisingly, the remarks in this speech came under intense scrutiny upon her nomination to the Supreme Court in 2009. Though she did not explicitly reference empathy in the Berkeley speech, her 'wise Latina' comment was seized upon by critics as symptomatic of the bias embedded in the empathy model.[37]

Earlier we noted that opponents of the empathy model often take 'empathy' to be a code word for judicial activism. As we also noted, there seems to be almost no basis for such an interpretation – it doesn't seem to be intended, and even if it were, there is no good reason to think that empathy has anything to do with activism. But while detractors were wrong in identifying the concept for which empathy is a code, they might not have been too far off in thinking that it is a code for something. In particular, as our discussion here seems to suggest, the promotion of empathy seems sometimes to be a covert attempt to promote diversity.

There are all sorts of very strong reasons to favour diversity on the bench.[38] My point here is not meant in any way to undermine such reasons. Rather, it's simply to deny that these reasons have much to do with empathy. Some of these reasons have to do with credibility. As Paul Chen argues, the fact that courts are charged with dispensing justice fairly and with safeguarding constitutional rights,

[35] Sotomayor (2002), 92.
[36] Ibid, 92. See also Margolick (1991).
[37] See eg James (2009).
[38] See eg Chen (2003); Wynn and Mazur (2004).

including the rights of vulnerable minorities, suggests that we might question whether the public could 'have confidence and trust in such an institution if it is segregated – if the communities it is supposed to protect are excluded from its ranks'.[39] Other reasons have to do with appropriate role-modelling. As Chen also argues, a diverse judiciary sends an important 'message of inclusion'. Not only does it help dispel traditional stereotypes about intelligence or articulateness but it also 'assures students and young lawyers from historically underrepresented communities that they need not limit their aspirations'.[40]

Considerations of public credibility and role modelling clearly do not have much of anything to do with empathy. But Chen also points to a further set of reasons in favour of diversity on the bench that may seem to bring empathy into the picture, namely, that diversity improves the quality of judicial decision-making. As he notes, 'In addition to analyzing and applying the law, judges have to make determinations that draw not so much upon legal acumen, but on an understanding of people and of human experiences. Such experiences inform assumptions that affect legal decisions.'[41] Whether it's evaluating the credibility of a witness or understanding the potential impact that a decision will have, judges are often required to draw upon their own life experiences in their decision-making. And, as Chen notes, 'inevitably, one's ethnic and racial background contributes to those life experiences'.[42] This line of argument provides a way to defend considerations of judicial diversity on epistemic grounds, ie over and above matters of public credibility and role modelling, judicial diversity may be defended on the grounds that it improves judicial decision-making. Importantly, however, even this line of argument does not have much to do with empathy. Having a diverse set of life experiences on which to draw in judicial decision-making is different from having the capacity to empathise with people who have a diverse set of life experiences.

To some extent, the point I want to make here is an obvious one. *Anyone* can be an empathiser. A person doesn't have to be a wise Latina – or indeed, a member of any particular gender, race, sexual orientation, social class, etc – in order to have the capacity for empathy. But less obviously, perhaps, one also doesn't have to be a wise Latina to have empathy for Latinas. Not only can anyone be an empathiser, but anyone can empathise with anyone else. Sotomayor herself seems to recognise this point when, in the same 2001 speech containing the 'wise Latina' remark, she notes that we should refrain from being 'so myopic as to believe that others of different experiences or backgrounds are incapable of understanding the values and needs of people from a different group'.[43] As she then points out, in cases such as *Brown v Board of Education*, the nine white male justices were able to do so. Indeed, while there is empirical evidence that shows that people are more likely to

[39] Chen (2003), 1117.
[40] Ibid, 1117.
[41] Ibid, 1117.
[42] Ibid, 1120.
[43] Sotomayor (2002), 92.

empathise with people from their own racial group than with people from other racial groups, that same evidence shows that cross-racial empathy can and does occur.[44] Just as we refrain from seeing other capacities like intelligence and athleticism as being limited by experiential perspective, so too should we refrain from seeing empathy as being limited by experiential perspective.

Here, it will help to consider the model against which the empathy model is contrasted – the umpire model – and in particular to consider the relationship between umpiring and experiential perspective. Some umpires are short, and thus personally have very compact strike zones, whereas some umpires are tall, and thus personally have much wider strike zones. But we're not at all inclined to think that the experiential perspective of being short or tall, and thus having a narrow or wide strike zone, will affect the way that an umpire calls balls and strikes. Short umpires may use a more expansive strike zone and tall umpires may use a less expansive strike zone. Their own height doesn't matter.

But if one's experiential perspective doesn't constrain one's capacity to umpire, why should it constrain one's capacity for empathy? To my mind, we have no good reason to think that empathy is constrained in a way that other capacities are not – no good reason to think that, *in principle*, one's ability to feel empathy for someone else corresponds directly to the degree to which you share their experiential perspective. As this discussion suggests, then, it is a mistake to think that empathy and diversity are inextricably intertwined. We should not think that we will automatically achieve greater empathy in our legal system by aiming at greater diversity among the judiciary, and we should not think that we will automatically achieve greater diversity among the judiciary by aiming at greater empathy in our legal system.

Before closing out this lesson, it's perhaps worth returning to the quote with which we began above and attending carefully to what it actually says: The claim that we need judges who have 'the heart, the empathy, to recognize what it's like to be a young teenage mom, the empathy to understand what it's like to be poor or African-American or gay or disabled or old', is not really a claim about the need for diversity among our judicial nominees but about the need for *heart* among our judicial nominees. As I've tried to suggest in this section, whether or not someone does have this heart – whether they are a good empathiser – should be separated from the question of their gender, race, ethnicity and social class.[45]

B. Lesson Five: A Judge Can be Both Umpire and Empathiser

Our first four lessons have focused on the empathy model, and what is and is not entailed by a commitment to empathy in judging. In doing so, however, it may

[44] See eg Johnson et al (2006).

[45] As argued by Thomas Colby, given that some people are naturally more empathetic than others, 'we should seek judges who have evinced a proclivity for empathy, just as we want judges who have proven themselves to be intelligent. And given that people apparently can improve their empathic skills, we should seek judges who have expressed an interest in, and a commitment to, empathy' (Colby, 2012, 2001).

seem that we have implicitly accepted the contrast that has framed the discussion, namely, that the umpire model and the empathy model are not just alternative pictures but actually competing pictures. Such acceptance would be a mistake, as it is now time to make clear. Indeed, not only should we refrain from thinking that empathy poses a threat to being a successful umpire, but we should also work to recognise that there can actually be occasions in which empathy will be beneficial to an umpire in the process of applying the rules of the game.

In previous discussions of the umpire model, legal scholars such as Susan Bandes (2009) and judges such as Kim McLane Wardlaw have persuasively demonstrated that the umpire conception of a judge is either incomplete or inaccurate. To say that a judge should simply call the balls and strikes – that a judge should simply apply the law – ignores the fact that sometimes it is not clear what the law means or even which law to apply. Using several real-world examples to show the importance of judicial discretion, Wardlaw argues that there are various circumstances in which 'the act of judging involves the exercise of judgment, and the judge behaves extrajudiciously when he plays (or pretends to play) umpire in the face of a law requiring him to do something more'.[46] A slightly different critique emerges from other legal scholars, who argue that the umpire model depends on an unrealistic expectation that neutrality is possible.[47]

Such criticisms go a long way towards demonstrating problems implicit in the analogy between judges and umpires. But here I want to make a slightly different point. Whatever the merits of the umpire model itself, it is important to note that such a model cannot be at all plausible if it is thought to conflict irreconcilably with the empathy model. As we can see from closer attention to the nature of umpiring, there is no reason to think that empathy need get in the way of an umpire's calling a fair game, and in fact there may be some cases in which empathy facilitates it.

Being an umpire is not just about calling balls and strikes. During the course of a baseball game, umpires are called upon to make all sorts of other decisions. To take just one example, consider *Rule 8.02: Throwing at a Batter*. According to subsection d of this rule, a pitcher is prohibited from intentionally pitching directly at the batter. As the rule goes on to state:

> If, in the umpire's judgment, such a violation occurs, the umpire may elect either to:
>
> 1. Expel the pitcher, or the manager and the pitcher, from the game, or
> 2. may warn the pitcher and the manager of both teams that another such pitch will result in the immediate expulsion of that pitcher (or a replacement) and the manager.

[46] Wardlaw (2010), 1637. Similarly, Neil Siegel argues that 'The umpire analogy would have judges "just" decide constitutional cases according to "the rules." Judges, however, cannot "just" decide constitutional cases according to "the rules" because they cannot agree on what the rules are in the vast majority of the most important cases' (Siegel, 2007, 702).

[47] Though she does not discuss the umpire model, also relevant here is Linda Mulcahy's argument that neutrality is an 'empty goal' (2001), 505. For further discussion of the impossibility of neutrality, see Siegel (2007).

> If, in the umpire's judgment, circumstances warrant, both teams may be officially 'warned' prior to the game or at any time during the game. ('Rules of Interest')

This rule, like many other rules of baseball, makes essential reference to the umpire's exercise of judgment. Moreover, these judgments are non-trivial. Umpires must use their judgment to determine whether a certain action was *intentional* – and this cannot be done by some mere mechanical application of a rule.[48] Umpires must likewise determine whether circumstances warrant a warning – and here again, this cannot be done by some mere mechanical application of a rule.[49]

How might an umpire here make such determinations? Interestingly, here it seems that a capacity for empathy could at times be useful. Umpires who can empathise with a pitcher – who can *feel* the anger and frustration that the pitcher is feeling as a result of behaviour by the opposing team earlier in the game – may be in a better position to make a judgment that the pitch was an intentional one. Umpires who can empathise with the teammates of the player who was just intentionally thrown at – who can *feel* the simmering rage and resentment – may be in a better position to make the determination that the circumstances warrant a warning.

Ultimately, then, not only do umpires have to show judgment in order to adequately discharge their duties, but the proper exercise of this judgment may at times be facilitated by the exercise of empathy. Thus, far from offering conflicting pictures of judicial decision-making, the umpire model and the empathy model are better understood as complementary to one another.

C. Lesson Six: The Empathy Model's Emphasis on Empathy is Misguided

To a large extent, the previous five lessons have been concerned with the rehabilitation of empathy from mistaken presuppositions about it. We have seen that it would be a mistake to think that empathy requires either activism or even any kind of particular action, and that it would also be a mistake to associate empathy with arbitrariness or bias. Relatedly, we have also seen that empathy should not be thought to be confined to the experiential perspective of the empathiser and that empathetic judging is fully compatible with fair umpiring.

But there is one more lesson yet to be learned, and, though I hope my remarks already have laid the groundwork for it, it still might come as something of a surprise. At the end of the day, once we root out all the misconceptions about empathy, and uncover the reasons that proponents of the empathy model place such emphasis on empathetic judging, we start to see that this emphasis is somewhat misguided. Ultimately, the considerations that seem to be pointing toward

[48] The same point applies, perhaps even more strongly, to referees in other sports.

[49] For similar discussion, see Gerhardt (2012).

the importance of empathy are best seen as pointing toward the importance of developing a certain kind of understanding. But there is no real reason to think that empathy – the sharing of states – is required for the development of such an understanding.[50] I can have a genuine understanding of how you feel – and even the what-it's-likeness of what you feel – without actually *feeling what you feel*. As I will suggest in the remainder of this section, one particularly good way of achieving such understanding is via exercises of imagination.

Because empathy and imagination are sometimes conflated, this point can be hard to see. This point is also obscured by the fact that in many cases we think of empathy in terms of imaginative projections. But the imaginative projections, considered in and of themselves, need not be resonance phenomena – they do not themselves need to generate empathetically felt emotions. In general, imagining a state – be it a perceptual state, a different kind of sensory state, or an emotional state – is phenomenologically similar to that state but is not phenomenologically identical to that state. Even in cases in which we accurately and effectively imagine what it's like to have a sensation of red, for example, we are not actually coming to have the exact same phenomenology as this sensation. The same point holds for imaginings involving emotional phenomenology.

I do not have the space here to develop in more detail exactly how these imaginative projections work, but we can make some progress by considering a few simple, perhaps oversimplified, examples. When interacting with a student advisee who is dealing with the loss of a close relative, I might imagine the situation that she is in so as to better be able to provide her with advice about how to navigate the rest of the semester. By way of what we might think of as a kind of *imaginative scaffolding*, I draw on and scaffold out from experiences that I've had, adding and subtracting and modifying them in an effort to get at what her experiences are like. This imaginative projection can provide me with the kind of understanding of her situation that I need in order to advise her well, even if I don't actually come to feel her grief. Likewise, when interacting with a different student advisee who is struggling with the decision of whether to accept a less appealing job close to her family or a more appealing job farther away, I might again engage in an imaginative projection to help figure out what I can best say to help her make up her mind. In doing so, I don't need to actually come to feel her love for her family, or her passion for the different job offers, to come to a better understanding of her situation and how the various factors are tugging at her.

That's not to say these imaginative projections are easy ones. As I've argued elsewhere, imagination is a skill, and as with any skill, some people are better at it than others.[51] Developing this skill takes practice, and it can be hard work. But the

[50] As noted above in n 12, not everyone uses the word 'empathy' to refer to a resonance phenomenon. If empathy is interpreted as a cognitive phenomenon, for example, it may well reduce to this kind of understanding. In this sense, then, the empathy model would be about empathy. But it still wouldn't be about empathy *in the sense that the typical proponents of the empathy model have seemed to mean it*.

[51] Kind (manuscript a) and Kind (manuscript b).

hard work needed is the work of imagination, not the work of empathy. While an empathic resonance with someone else may sometimes facilitate our understanding, given that this understanding can be and often is achieved via imaginative projection that occurs absent the empathic resonance, it seems that the imaginative projection is what is of primary importance.

We can see this more clearly if we return to the point I was making about umpires in the previous section. The umpire may well use empathy to determine whether a certain pitch was intentionally thrown at a batter, or whether emotions are running so high that retaliation is likely. And this empathetic assessment might facilitate the umpire's ability to discharge the job. But notice that what's really facilitating the job is the understanding that empathy has enabled the umpire to achieve. Insofar as this understanding seems primarily to be generated by the imaginative projection underlying the empathetic reaction rather than the empathetic reaction itself, we can see that this understanding can be achieved even without the umpire actually having had to experience the emotional reactions undergone by the batter and/or the pitcher.

Recall again Sotomayor's 'wise Latina' remark – a sentiment that might have seemed misguided when interpreted as an expression of the importance of empathy. Suppose we put the point in terms of understanding instead of in terms of empathic resonance. Given that a Latina's experiential perspective is quite different from that of a white male's, how does this affect her capacity to understand the experiences of others? It's precisely here that imagination comes into play. Our experiences provide the material for our imaginative exercises, and so the closer an imaginative projection comes to our own experiences, the easier the imaginative projection will be. We can thus see why a 'wise Latina' might in some cases have easier access to a certain kind of understanding than a wise white male has. Importantly, that's not to say that such an understanding is in principle blocked from the white male. I don't believe that it is and, as we noted above, nor does Sotomayor.[52] But insofar as certain imaginative projections are more difficult for an individual, some kinds of understanding will be harder for that individual to achieve.

At this point, it is worth returning yet one more time to Obama's remarks expressing a desire to appoint judges who have 'the heart, the empathy, to recognize what it's like to be a young teenage mom, the empathy to understand what it's like to be poor or African-American or gay or disabled or old'. We've noted above that recognising what it's like to be a teenage mother, or an African American man, or someone gay or poor, does not require one to share those experiential perspectives. But, as the discussion in this section suggests, it also doesn't really require what he called 'heart', ie it doesn't require empathic resonance. Rather, it requires the kind of understanding that can often be best developed by way of imagination.

[52] See the discussion in Lesson Four above and also Sotomayor (2002), 92.

V. Conclusion

Ultimately, what is suggested by this last lesson, and indeed by all six of our lessons, is that the focus on umpiring vs empathy has been a misguided one. Indeed, to really get at the heart of the kinds of qualities that we admire and desire among the judiciary, we would do best to sidestep this debate entirely, and to instead focus on how judges can fairly decide the matters before them. Importantly, however, our lessons here suggest that such fairness will many times require an understanding not just of the bare facts of the matter but of the greater context in which the matter occurs. As I have here suggested, this understanding will in many cases be best achieved by the employment of a sophisticated and developed capacity for imagination.

References

ABC News (2009) '*This Week* Transcript: Sens. Leahy and Hatch' *ABC News*. ABC News Network (3 May). Web.

Abrams, K (2010) 'Empathy and Experience in the Sotomayor Hearings' 36 *Ohio Northwestern Law Review* 163.

Bandes, S (2009) 'Empathetic Judging and the Rule of Law' *Cardozo Law Review de Novo* 133.

Bandes, S (2011) 'Moral Imagination in Judging' 51(1) *Washburn Law Journal* 1.

Bloom, P (2016) *Against Empathy* (New York, HarperCollins).

Calabresi, S (2008) 'Obama's 'Redistribution' Constitution' *The Wall Street Journal*.

Chen, P (2003) 'The Judiciary, Diversity, and Justice for All' 91(4) *California Law Review* 1109.

Colby, T (2012) 'In Defense of Judicial Empathy' 96(6) *Minnesota Law Review* 1944.

Del Mar, M (2017) 'Imagining by Feeling: A Case for Compassion in Legal Reasoning' 13(2) *International Journal of Law in Context* 143.

Franks, M (2011) 'Lies, Damned Lies, and Judicial Empathy' 51(1) *Washburn Law Journal* 61.

Gerhardt, MJ (2012) 'Constitutional Branding' 40(3) *Hofstra Law Review* 655.

Hansberg, O (2020) 'Empathy and Negative Intimacy' in A Amaya and M Del Mar (eds) *Virtue, Emotion and Imagination in Law and Legal Reasoning* (Oxford, Hart Publishing).

Henderson, L (1987) 'Legality and Empathy' 85(7) *Michigan Law Review* 1574.

Hoffman, M (2011) 'Empathy, Justice, and the Law' in A Coplan and P Goldie (eds) *Empathy: Philosophical and Psychological Perspectives* (Oxford, Oxford University Press) 230.

James, F (2009) 'Sotomayor's "Wise Latina" Line Maybe Not So Wise' *NPR*. Available at https://www.npr.org/sections/thetwo-way/2009/05/sotomayors_wise_latina_line_ma.html.

Johnson, JD et al (2006) 'Rodney King and O.J. Revisited: The Impact of Race and Defendant Empathy Induction on Judicial Decisions' 32(6) *Journal of Applied Social Psychology* 1208.

Kind, A (manuscript a) 'What Imagination Teaches'.

Kind, A (manuscript b) 'The Skill of Imagination'.

Limbaugh, D (2009) 'Sotomayor: "Empathy" in Action' https://townhall.com/columnists/thomassowell/2009/05/27/sotomayor--empathy-in-action-n749441.

National Journal (2009). 'Sessions Says He's Looking For Judicial Restraint' (6 May). Available at https://web.archive.org/web/20090515133825/http://www.nationaljournal.com/njonline/no_20090507_5499.php.

Margolick, D (1991) 'Women's Milestone: Majority on Minnesota Court', *The New York Times* (21 February).

McKee, TA (2007) 'Judges as Umpires' 35(4) *Hofstra Law Review* 1709.

Morton, A (2017) 'Empathy and Imagination' in H Maibom (ed) *Routledge Handbook of Empathy* (London, Routledge) 180.

Mulcahy, L (2001) 'The Possibility and Desirability of Mediator Neutrality: Towards an Ethic of Partiality' 10(4) *Social and Legal Studies* 505.

Obama, B (2006) *The Audacity of Hope: Thoughts on Reclaiming the American Dream* (Crown).

Obama, B (2009) *The President's Remarks on Justice Souter.*

'Rules of Interest' (n.d.) *MLB.com*. Major League Baseball. Web.

Siegel, N (2007) 'Umpires at Bat: On Integration and Legitimation' 24 *Constitutional Commentary* 701.

Sotomayor, S (2002) 'A Latina Judge's Voice' 13(1) *Berkeley La Raza Law Journal* 87.

Stueber, K (2016) 'Empathy and the Imagination' in A Kind (ed) *Routledge Handbook of the Philosophy of Imagination* (London, Routledge) 368.

United States Senate Committee on the Judiciary. *Confirmation Hearing on the Nomination of John G. Roberts, Jr. To Be Chief Justice of the United States. Hearings, Sept. 12–15, 2005.* 109th Cong 1st sess Washington: GPO, 2005.

United States Senate Committee on the Judiciary. *The Nomination of Elena Kagan To Be an Associate Justice of the Supreme Court of the United States. Hearings, Jun. 28–30, Jul. 1, 2005.* 111th Cong 2nd sess Washington: GPO, 2010.

Wardlaw, K (2010) 'Umpires, Empathy, and Activism: Lessons from Judge Cardozo' 85 *Notre Dame Law Review* 1629.

White, EK (2020) 'On Emotions and the Politics of Attention in Judicial Reasoning' in A Amaya and M Del Mar (eds) *Virtue, Emotion and Imagination in Law and Legal Reasoning* (Oxford, Hart Publishing).

Wynn, J and Mazur, E (2004) 'Judicial Diversity: Where Independence and Accountability Meet' 67 *Albany Law Review* 775.

Zelinsky, A (2010) 'The Justice as Commissioner: Benching the Judge-Umpire Analogy' 119 *The Yale Law Journal* 113.

11

Imagining Motives

ADAM MORTON

I. Introduction

This chapter explores a tension in legal procedures between two ideals. One is *impartiality*; people should be treated 'the same', in accordance with general principles expressed in terms of morally and legally relevant objective impartial concepts. The other is *accuracy*; people should be treated 'differently', in accordance with real and relevant differences between their situations, rather than differences or commonalities that are ascribed to them in error or from prejudice. Both are aspects of the ideal of fairness. I am not going to state these principles in a careful or sophisticated way. My concern is with the application of the concepts involved, and in particular with the ascription of states of mind, including motives and emotions. Can we grasp the minds of others, for example by a kind of imagination, well enough to see at once how they fall under the same principles and how the details of each person are different? I shall be defending a sceptical attitude to this task. I shall argue that in a number of legal contexts our capacities to describe general attributes of people and our capacities to grasp what is individual about them do not mesh. In some of these contexts the form that this takes is that we are just not capable of applying the relevant concepts, the ones that would link a particular individual with a general principle, accurately enough. We are not equipped to live up to both of these ideals at once.

A regime of strict liability, where individual motives and constraints are ignored because a bare description of the legally relevant aspects of your act is all that counts, is wonderfully impersonal, but in many cases unfair for reasons of inaccuracy. A regime that takes the slightest differences between people as bases for differing ways of excusing apparent culpability *may* be wonderfully fair, but imposes a need for accurate assessment onto its participants. It is easy for people to claim that their situation is special, and tempting for those who identify with them to suppose that it really is. One might think that the tension was easily resolved: accurate attributions of legally relevant differences should allow equal treatment of people who are alike in legally relevant ways, ignoring irrelevant differences. But this easy resolution is complicated by my second theme. Our usual ways of attributing states of mind to people and anticipating their actions are very imperfect. They form a loosely connected bundle of disparate resources which we tie together with wide labels of 'empathy' and 'imagination'. But each strand in the bundle gives accurate results only under very particular circumstances. It is far from clear that these include many of the circumstances where they could be legally useful. So the difficulty of getting any guarantee of the accuracy of ways of attributing states of mind to people makes it harder to find a compromise between impartiality and fairness. The conclusion is that the competing demands on our resources produce a grave and intractable difficulty in legal procedure, which we should not gloss over. Schematically, a scepticism about the accuracy of imagination leads to a pessimism about the fairness of our practices.[1]

II. Imagination and Attribution

Since human beings are profoundly social creatures, we incorporate routines for anticipating one another's actions and their tendencies to play various roles in various shared projects. Given a normal human upbringing, normal humans tend to know pretty accurately when others are sad or angry, and whether they are likely to cooperate or obstruct many-person activities. It is not obvious in detail how we do this, and there was a lively interdisciplinary discussion between philosophers, developmental psychologists and anthropologists about this in the last quarter of the twentieth century. But all parties agree that the innate human capacities that develop in children as they master the social routines of their cultures allow them to attribute states of mind to others in the same cultures.[2] Beyond that point there is less agreement.

There is an optimistic and a pessimistic way of interpreting these developments. The optimistic way focuses on our innate but tunable capacities to make sense of one another. On this picture we have in our heads software that meets the needs of human social life.

The pessimistic way also stresses our pre-equipped nature. But it expresses doubts about how fitted for the task, especially for the contemporary form of the task, our innate equipment – biologically recent but formed by ways of life that no longer exist – might be. As background to this, note that until the last quarter of the twentieth century and in some circles much later, it was generally accepted that humans understand other humans by putting them on a grid of rational thought and behaviour. Humans are most intelligible when they are being rational. This relic of the older view, that there is a discrete faculty of rationality whose presence

[1] Zipursky (2020) (chapter four in this volume), endorses a tension between empathy and objectivity. A lot depends on whether one counts as empathy a strongly felt but mistaken take on the feelings of the other person.

[2] I have written a handbook article surveying the field (Morton, 2009). I do not there discuss my less consensual suggestions, which are found in Morton (2002) and Morton (2007). See also Gopnik and Meltzoff (1997).

marks humanity, had been sublimated in philosophy to a view that by treating people *as if* they were fully rational – whatever that means – we get our best predictive grasp over them.[3] This assumption was common to a lot of economics and philosophy of mind and social theory. The central reason for its failure is the awareness of ubiquitous sub-rational behaviour in human beings, which might have been evident from the psychoanalytic tradition but became mainline with the work of Kahneman and Tversky.[4] Doubts about the exact content of the rationality claim also took their toll. Is it rational, for example, to be risk-averse, or does rational choice for every person consist in maximising the expectation of each action according to her probability and utility functions? That would result in predictions very different from what we actually do, and might be socially disastrous. The claim is also unhelpful about the effect of our limited power. Nearly all people at nearly all times are in situations where a vastly more intelligent creature would do something very different. Is nearly all of our behaviour thus inexplicable?[5]

With this in mind, consider the competing approaches to inbuilt behaviour-predicting capacities. Nichols and Stich (2003) contrast information-rich and information-poor accounts of folk psychology. Information-rich accounts postulate a source of articulated principles to guide attribution, understanding and prediction. The principles may not be formulated in spoken language or available to conscious reflection, but they guide our more explicit judgements. They may originate in innate information-processing routines, reflection on the actions of others, or innate constraints on explanations. According to information-poor accounts, on the other hand, the fundamental features of our thinking about mind are determined by routines and capacities which do not embody any assumptions about how one state of mind leads to another.

Earlier versions of these two kinds of account referred to information-rich accounts as the 'theory theory'. The idea was that children readily develop an implicit psychological theory from which they can derive predictions as they need them. Although six-year-old children cannot do astronomy – they can hardly articulate a description of the passage of the sun through the sky – on this account they possess something from which they derive predictions and explanations of human actions in a way that is analogous to the easier task of getting a prediction of an eclipse from an astronomical theory. Some of the arguments in defence of this account emphasise how it can include specifications of innate cognitive and motivational biases. The alternative is to make the theory in question one of perfect rationality, which is a nonstarter for predicting the individual behaviour of one's neighbours, or for that matter of oneself.[6]

[3] Davidson (1982).

[4] Kahneman and Tversky (1979), Tversky (2013).

[5] See ch 2 of Morton (2002).

[6] 'Individual' because sometimes the differences between different people cancel or compensate out so that anticipating the average behaviour of large numbers of people is easier than predicting particular acts of particular people. Perhaps this is a factor that makes classical economics possible.

Information-poor accounts, on the other hand, were referred to as simulation theories. Their characteristic assumption was that faced with another person's actions, one experiments to discover what settings in one's own mind would result in similar actions, and then attributes them to the other. It is tempting to label these procedures as imagination: one imagines getting oneself to do the action and takes the other to be in the state that one has imagined for oneself. At this point, the contrast between two versions of this approach becomes relevant. The first is that of Heal,[7] which applies best to predictions of other people's intellectual output. The idea here is that when you want to know how someone else would solve a problem, you solve it yourself and predict that they would do what you would do. I have no doubt that this is a strategy that we sometimes use, though its limitations are fairly clear. The other is my own approach, on which people are hardwired to enter into small-scale cooperative activity, and will act on the assumption that others will do the mutually advantageous thing.[8] (Of course there are uncooperative and downright malign actions that this says nothing about.) And its direct application is limited to prediction of behaviour rather than prediction of thought or feeling.

While these lines were being developed and refined, experimental work on children's acquisition of adult concepts proceeded fruitfully. The central strand of this work – which stems from papers by Perner in the dying days of explanation as making rational – concerns small children's attribution of beliefs, and to some extent desires, to others.[9] The famous false belief task plays a big role here. As a result we do have a fairly good timetable of how the capacity to attribute central cognitive concepts develops.

So different theories of our grasp of one another emphasise different capacities – different *kinds* of capacities – which are directed at different mental states: thoughts, emotions, actions. That suggests a deep question. How are these different parts of 'folk psychology' tied together? Are they fragments of a comprehensive predisposition in people for interpreting one another's actions, or are they independent of each other? We do not know the answer. I have defended the second position, which I suspect is the minority view, in a paper arguing that people learn to improvise connections between a number of innate capacities.[10] It is not at all clear that this view is correct but it needs to be explored. (Though not to the present point, such a view would allow more room for individual and cultural variation.)

Two themes from this history will be particularly relevant in what follows. The first is the tribulations of the concept of rationality. In philosophy, psychology and economics, it is much less foundational than it once was. The other concerns the imaginative capacities involved, the ability to produce in one's own mind

[7] Heal (1989).
[8] Morton (2002), especially chapters 3 and 5.
[9] Perner (1991).
[10] Morton (2007).

what is going through someone else's. Since the days when theory of mind/folk psychology/mind-attribution was a new and hot topic, there has been a flowering of interest in imagination, empathy and sympathy.[11] I take it that the earlier interest has led to the present one. But the ambiguities and uncertainties remain. There is no consensus about the nature of the imaginative capacities, or about their importance in our understanding of one another, and a widespread doubt that rationality can play the role that was once given, without any confidence about what if anything can replace it.

Legal systems rely on the ability of judges, barristers and jurors to attribute motives, assess contributions to shared projects, distribute blame and negotiate matters of common concern. Without the ability to do these things, the application of law and judicial judgement, from earlier times to its current versions, would be crippled. We may be at point of transition, though. In the past we had a simpleminded trust in everyday capacities for attributing states of mind, at any rate as used by reflective reasonable people. Now, however, we are becoming aware of how problematic they can be.[12] An analogy is the naïve reliance that until recently was placed on eyewitness testimony. We thought that the only reason such testimony can be false is deliberate dishonesty or self-preservation. But the work of Loftus and others has convinced many that context and deliberate manipulation can influence beliefs that present themselves as simple direct recollection.[13] I strongly suspect that something similar is true of the imaginative attribution of motive and emotion. I do not have solid psychological evidence for this. So what I shall do is to describe some ways that the law, as seen by this particular outsider, has a problematic dependence on these skills. To the extent that they are unreliable, the institutions in question have a problem they should face.

Throughout their history legal institutions have relied on everyday capacities to do these things, in deliberate reflective form aided by specific devices, for example to encourage people to tell the truth by threatening them. So the connection between law and 'folk psychology' ought to be an important and central topic. I shall assume that all people interacting through legal systems apply the mind-attributing skills they have acquired through normal social life to those they interact with. I shall assume that the skills can be described not too misleadingly as exercises of the imagination. And I shall assume that legal procedures have the use of explicit evidence-based psychological theories to the extent that these are seen as relevant (which I am told is largely confined to cases where there is a mental

[11] Two comprehensive anthologies are Maibom (2017) and Coplan and Goldie (2011). Hansberg (2020) (chapter nine in this volume) describes a particular species of empathy, where shared emotion is central. Empathy is of course a very broad term used to cover a variety of states and a variety of relations between people. Kind (2020) (chapter ten in this volume) argues for the distinction between empathy and imagination, which is also a broad concept, and for the greater objectivity of imagination.

[12] See Levesque (2006) which argues for the relevance of experimental psychology to legal practice. I owe this reference to Maksymilian Del Mar and Amalia Amaya.

[13] Loftus (1979).

health element to a defence, or the like). The crucial facts are, first, that we have no substitute for these skills of psychological imagination – for the capacity to represent states of other people's minds in one's own intuitively and more or less vividly, when faced with a large range of puzzling behaviour. It is a flawed capacity in obvious ways but it is often the best we have, and scientific substitutes for it may be generations away (or may never be usable by human beings in an informal practical way). Second, what we get from everyday psychological imagination – this informal imaginative capacity – generally does not combine well with what we get from psychology, neurology or other sciences. Generally speaking, when we begin with an intuitive grasp of someone's action we continue it in the same intuitive terms.

We do not do a lot of conscious reasoning about these things, even in the law. We get very quickly to the judgement that someone acted out of jealousy (an emotion that is typically based on a thought – that someone has gained what is rightfully one's own – which is itself based on a standing character trait or an occurrent emotion), or malevolent lust (an emotion, inasmuch as it has an object, otherwise a very controlling mood), or desire for profit (a traditional motivating state), and then we move on to judging the moral quality of the action. Once we have done this, we can backtrack a little and consider excuses or exculpating facts, which typically retain the moral judgement of the act and qualify its implications as a judgement of the person. When we do this we normally do not consider *what* the person has done or even *why* they have done it, but *how* they could have done it – how they overcame various obstacles to heeding the motive in question. For example, it might be obvious that someone poisoned their grandmother in order to inherit a fortune, but far from obvious how they managed to overcome their affection and family feeling. This gives an explicit focus for imagination. There are many motives available to most people in most situations, and we have very little beyond platitudes to tell us which motive a person will be seized by, and how they will choose the means to the ends that it dangles before them – why the murderous grandchild acted in accordance with the chance of gain rather than respect for someone familiar from childhood.[14] So we approach this task with an improvised variety of techniques, sometimes by trying to imagine ourselves into a similar position.

Excuses are then an important context for imagination, including neglected excuses – ones that it never occurs to us to apply in particular cases. For our purposes questions of accuracy are important: whether the excuse that we are inclined to apply when things are presented in a particular way does in fact connect with the psychology of the person concerned. This takes us into largely unexplored territory. Most work on our capacities to attribute states of mind focuses on their

[14] These are issues discussed in the literature on evil, especially with authors concerned to avoid the image of mysteriously irredeemable villains nearly all of whose actions are terrible. See Card (2002) or Morton (2004).

effectiveness. This is not surprising given that the background in philosophy traces to 'other minds' problems; sceptical doubts that we have adequate evidence for taking people to have the beliefs, desires, emotions, and the like, that are normally attributed to them. And in the culture in general during these decades scientists were reconsidering the naïve empiricism of earlier generations in the light of the psychological possibility that much of the way we think is shaped by our genetic inheritance. But talking about excuses, and the attribution of motive in a legal context more generally, possibilities of misattribution – getting things wrong – are at least as relevant.

But attention to this side of attribution is not much studied.[15] The importance of issues about accuracy seems to have been missed, probably to a large extent because accuracy is so hard to assess.[16] As I note in the concluding section of this chapter, there is a common sense way of gauging accuracy in everyday life. It consists in interacting with the person and seeing whether one's expectations are fulfilled. But such interaction is not only not available but explicitly forbidden in many legal procedures, for the sake of fairness.

The conclusion of this section is that what we have learned about human capacities to attribute states of mind is rather fragmented. We have competing accounts, each of which focuses on some particular class of states of mind, and very little guidance about how to glue these together. We also have a very rough concept of imagination without much assurance of its accuracy or the conditions under which what we imaginatively ascribe to someone does capture the way they actually are. This gappy patchwork invites a sceptical response.

III. The Legal Connection

The problem of accuracy arises when we need something analogous to an everyday grasp of another person, but also need judgements that can stand up to the scepticism that fairness and impartiality require. Here is a list. I will not discuss any of them in detail, let alone engage with the vast specialised literature on each.[17]

[15] There is a literature on scientific substitutes for intuitive judgement on these topics. See Goldstein, Morse and Shapiro (2003) and Levesque (2006). However, there is not much on the (in)accuracy of pre-scientific judgement on them. Undermining this point slightly, there is a precedent for studies of attributional error in influential work on infants, associated with the false belief task, where toddlers have surprising difficulty grasping the fact that people operate on the basis of wrong information (Gopnik and Meltzoff, 1997).

[16] Intuitive imaginative judgements about what people generally think or feel are easier to test. For example, people generally expect that victims of violent crimes or their families will feel retributive emotions, but surveys suggest that this expectation is based on faulty imagination.

[17] I am not pretending to have more legal knowledge than the average informed citizen. So I shall not provide faked references to hastily digested legal works. I shall illustrate this below by the out-of-date reference to Holmes (1882).

A. Provocation

Acts are more culpable if premeditated, on standard doctrine.[18] There are situations that we can easily imagine to produce rage or vindictiveness, and the actions that result are not taken to indicate a standing intention to do harm. Husbands discovering their wives with a lover are no longer excused from culpability for actions taken in a murderous rage. But some degree of annoyance or upset would hardly be surprising. Suppose H comes upon W in the arms of L, and as a result slaps L or W, or scratches L's car, or writes a damning letter of unrecommendation in connection with a job application. As a result, H finds himself in court, charged with assault or criminal damage or professional misconduct. He is likely to be found guilty, but the sentence is likely to be minimal. In this case the decision is in the hands (mind) of a judge. (There is no law against writing vicious letters about a job candidate. But it is easy enough to imagine a situation where there is a legal aspect to a professional misconduct or harassment case. Some letters of 'recommendation' might result in libel suits.)

It may seem that there is no problem here. We can all think ourselves into these shoes and can imagine losing our tempers. But. What we imagine ourselves into may not resemble H's state at all closely. Perhaps instead of rage he felt calm, or sadness, or relief, and perhaps he acted out of professional rivalry, a calculated strategy for some other purpose, or just plain nastiness.[19] These things can be discovered, and given enough other evidence of a familiar psychological sort, they would be likely to undermine the plea. But this further evidence is unlikely to emerge in court, and would require anecdotes and descriptions of behaviour patterns, which would have an air both of irrelevance and of inadmissibility.

B. Irresistible Impulse

The idea is that some people have a lesser capacity to deny the urges that are common in the rest of us to strike out at enemies, take retribution for old injuries, or react to provocations that are not really that extreme. The reason is usually that the impulsive person is in some way damaged: some specific insanity, a deeply flawed personality, or diminished intelligence. The desired result is not full exculpation but a lesser guilt: manslaughter instead of murder in the most dramatic

[18] Is this intuitively correct in all cases? Contrast two killers. One person has for decades mused about ways of killing her abuser, and, when the opportunity presents itself, although she is a gentle soul she steels herself and takes it. The other person knows nothing of the victim, but sees a similar sudden opportunity for undetected destruction and takes it because the thought of a crushed skull appeals so evocatively. I think I would be more appalled by the second.

[19] This is a theme of Sartre's play *Les mains sales*. Sartre's suggestion is that there is no answer to the question of why his protagonist killed his rival. It is all determined retrospectively, Sartre implicitly argues. There is a subtle germ of truth here, but most of us are determined to resist the line.

cases.[20] So if you are foolish enough to tease a slow and inarticulate giant about her infantile clothes, you should not be surprised at the result but will find your hospital rest disturbed by news of her negligible penalty.

This is one of the less problematic cases under this heading. Expert testimony from a social worker or psychologist should be able to clarify whether the giant was able to restrain her impulse, and the court is likely to defer to a better informed view where common sense gives little guidance. The expert is in effect translating between scientific knowledge, or at any rate a position backed up by some thought and evidence, and what ordinary folk are likely to say given an ordinary description. Other cases are more worrying.

Consider a 'normal' person under the influence of drugs or alcohol, which we can take to be administered surreptitiously so that the person bears no responsibility for being in a diminished state. The charge is assault or rape, and the defence is that this person could not be expected to resist the provocation involved. Some people would have resisted it well, so the defence has to be that the offender is a somewhat impulsive person of strong instantaneous feelings. The hope is not acquittal but a verdict of guilt followed by a reduced sentence. For this defence to succeed the person's character and history has to be presented in just the right way. So we can expect character witnesses and we can expect the defence to struggle to introduce anecdotal material from the mouths of suitable witnesses. All going well, though perhaps unjustly, the result will be an impression of the person as basically non-malevolent but prone not to weigh all the options and their consequences.

This was a more problematic case, and it really is. It is easy to present a personality under a variety of aspects, because we are complicated inconsistent creatures who respond more to circumstances than we like to think, and as a result a little careful selection from the wide-ranging precedents in anyone's history will produce whatever impression is convenient.

C. Testamentary Capacity

A rich old woman falls under the influence of a charming but unscrupulous young man, who in her eyes makes her see life completely differently, and in the eyes of her family deludes her about her attachments and values. She dies, leaving him a fortune. The will is contested, on the grounds that she was subject to influences that made her incapable of understanding her actions, especially given her advanced age. This is a rough civil law analogue of the irresistible impulse defence to a criminal charge. The young man's lawyer is likely to produce witnesses to show that the older woman had entered into serious argumentative conversations, so she was still thinking for herself, and that she had made responsible decisions during the relevant time period. The family's lawyer is likely to produce witnesses that she was

[20] Murder is the topic for most of the examples. Perhaps this is because the crime is particularly abhorrent and the penalties particularly extreme. Insanity defences against parking tickets are rare.

unreasonably indulgent of her lover and had made gifts that no responsible person would have accepted. And that he had boasted that he was onto a good thing.

It could work out either way. The important point is that the judge, as it most likely will be, will have to get a grasp of what it was like for this aging woman to feel overwhelming affection later in her life than she would have thought possible. And a grasp of what the young man's motives might have been, and whether there was a deliberate plan to diminish her capacity for judgement or alienate her from her family. I do not envy the judge's task. Both sides are likely to have intuitive appeal, and there is no expert opinion available.[21]

D. The Reasonable Person

According to an indispensable legal device, there is a normal standard of rationality which adequately functioning citizens can live up to without superhuman effort and which it is in the public interest for everyone to hold others to. (I suspect it is also widely supposed that this, whatever it is, is a normal mode of operation for most people, and deviations from it are a matter of momentary impulse, bad character, or incompetence.) It involves seeing consequences of actions and developments and understanding the implications of information received. Attributions of negligence as well as many other determinations depend on this. But of course no one sees or understands *everything* that has a necessary connection with what they know. A superhuman genius may just take it as obvious that if you use your credit card four times in this one store this particular morning, then the Yuan will have a catastrophic slide three days later. And in a society of such creatures, not to take this into account would be considered highly irresponsible. (If, with such an elevated grasp of things, they used concepts at all like this.) But not among twenty-first century humans with our history and our limits.

It is a puzzling though indispensable concept. It becomes even more puzzling when we consider limitations of reasoning and imagination in even intelligent people, let alone the whole human race. (There is a philosophically problematic 'should' attached to reasoning, perhaps built into our culture from days when we thought that our species was just a couple of steps down from divinity rather than a couple of steps up from other primates, to use a very tendentious sense of up and down. But it is worth noting that a concept can be objective although it is relative.[22]) I gather that juries are not supposed to judge what a reasonable person would think or do by reflecting on their own reactions. (Judges are perhaps taken to be nearer the postulated target in this respect!) Instead, they are supposed to

[21] If the young man was sensible he would have ensured that the will was made in his absence but in the presence of a lawyer, and, ideally, that this was videotaped. I do not have the impression that the failure to do this would fatally undermine the case for leaving the will in force.

[22] What is right and left given a direction is objective on the surface of the earth because there is a privileged sense of 'us'; in space it needs to be relative to both a direction and to an up/down axis.

apply the standards that people normally expect other people to meet. As Holmes puts it:

> If, for instance, a man is born hasty and awkward, is always having accidents and hurting himself or his neighbors, no doubt his congenital defects will be allowed for in the courts of Heaven, but his slips are no less troublesome to his neighbors than if they sprang from guilty neglect. His neighbors accordingly require him, at his proper peril, to come up to their standard, and the courts which they establish decline to take his personal equation into account.[23] The rule that the law does, in general, determine liability by blameworthiness, is subject to the limitation that minute differences of character are not allowed for. The law considers, in other words, what would be blameworthy in the average man, the man of ordinary intelligence and prudence, and determines liability by that.[24]

But there is no codification of what these standards are. No one has ever made precise sense of what ideal rationality would consist in, or how near to ideal rationality an acceptably imperfect person would expect other acceptably imperfect people to be, let alone which deviations from such a standard would be irresponsible dangers to the public interest. But we do in some improvised, shifting way hold people to standards of thinking about the consequences of their actions. And this is reflected in the legal reliance on the concept of the reasonable person. Judges and juries are often required to consider what they would expect a reasonable person to have done in the position of some participant in a trial. Though it is not usually put this way, my take on the issue is that juries are supposed to *imagine* what people would on reflection expect or find startling in other people's actions and considerations, on the assumption that the other person knows the law and is trying conscientiously to abide by it.[25] (This raises the troubling possibility that someone might suffer for being too farsighted and too subtle to be easily intelligible to the mass of humanity, especially if she happened to have arrived at a false conclusion in this particular case, as can happen to anyone whatever their skills.[26]) If this is right, the judge or juror is asked to do something very delicate: to imagine not what they would expect of themselves but what they would expect of someone else, or even what they would expect a well informed and reflective other person to expect another well-informed affected further person to do. They have to imagine what other people would imagine under rather special circumstances that are not found in their regular lives.

[23] 'Personal equation'. Not relevant for present purposes but curious: the term comes from the astronomy of his time, where the timing and accuracy of a particular person's use of a telescope was noted and included in calculations based on their observations.

[24] Holmes (1882), Lecture 3.

[25] Stern (2020) (chapter twelve in this volume) discusses the reasonable person as an artefact of imagination, emphasising the artefactuality but awarding a degree of objectivity.

[26] The only real case at all like this that occurs to me is that of the great logician Kurt Goedel, whose claim to have discovered an inconsistency in the US Constitution almost scuppered his American citizenship hearing. Luckily he had brought along his best friend, Albert Einstein, who was able to defuse things.

It is (somewhat) supportive of this reading that the law also uses conceptions of what a reasonable child of a given age, or a reasonable person of a particular degree of intellectual disability, or for that matter a reasonable expert, would consider and do. For these can be paraphrased as what people would as a matter of fact normally expect of others in these categories. If someone in the category concerned understands what the law expects and is trying their best to live up to it, how will they usually think and act? Understanding the concept this way makes it somewhat clear what its extension is – what the characteristics of someone it applies to are. But it does not tell us how anyone, from experienced judges to jurors thrown into the situation, can reliably tell when it applies in particular cases.[27]

It is a delicate and tricky concept, but what are the deeper roots of its slipperiness? There is a connection, at any rate, with the contrast between the imaginative capacities nurtured by everyday life and those based on largely unintuitive scientific evidence. When a jury is asked to consider whether someone should have been expected to have paid attention to certain considerations, all they can do is to imagine themselves into the situation as a dispassionate observer and note their imagined reactions when the person ignored the considerations. If their imagined reaction would be that something was amiss and the person would not have been acting with care, then they are distinguishing that person from the hypothetical standard. The question is not whether the juror would personally ignore the considerations, since she may know that she is personally hasty and sloppy – a negligence charge waiting to happen. It is not whether on imagining herself observing the situation of the person in question she imagines approval or acceptance. For she may know that she would, in fact, be too permissive or too condemning. And it is not whether given just the conclusion the accused person arrived at she would consider it reasonable, careful, dutiful or whatever, since that amounts just to the full question of whether it is a matter of negligence (or whatever). More probing than this into possible thought processes is required. The jury is proposing to itself a hypothetical person who operated in the reported way and reacting through the eyes of a hypothetical thoughtful human observer. I do not see how they can do this except by imagining they are faced with such a person and asking what they would conclude of her. And the only plausible way I can come up with for them to do *this* is by imagining a constrained imagination of the person. The jurors ask themselves what conclusion someone of a vaguely specified kind would form about someone else committed to satisfying certain norms and performing the act in question. The question is whether they can succeed.

It is a hard task – hard both to follow the instructions and to do so in such a way that gets an accurate answer, one that does say whether a legally conscientious person could have operated in this way. It is hard not to be cynical about how well typical juries can do it. It will depend a lot on how the jury is instructed, and thus on the skill of the judge in setting the jury to do this psychologically

[27] See King (2017) for a better informed view about why it is not realistic to expect jurors to simulate the reactions that a reasonable person would have in given circumstances.

delicate thing rather than any of the other tasks they might suppose. I would guess that judges often approach their task by considering how they would tackle the jury's assignment were they on it, and then turning their reflection on this into instructions.[28] We might then ask how often judges and juries negotiate all these obstacles successfully. But how would we even begin to answer this? Success is rarely given by a straightforward fact such as whether or not a defendant performed some act. More often it is a question of whether someone *should* have been more careful, or the like, presupposing something close to the very concept concerned.

Everyday social/psychological capacity combined with guided introspection is thus a very fragile tool here. (The connections between capacities for social life and capacities for attributing states of mind are controversial. On the consensus view social capacities draw on independent capacities to attribute states of mind. A more radical view, to which I subscribe, puts the needs of social life at the heart of our mind-to-mind thinking. This would further encourage scepticism about our accuracy in imagined cases, especially if not mediated by an imagined social or practical connection.) But scientific psychology is no more promising. There are no experts and there is no experimental data on what people of normal intelligence trying hard to abide by the law and their responsibilities will do. How could there be? The selection of experimental subjects would depend on the result of the inquiry, what a reasonable person would do.

In the previous section I invited scepticism about the accuracy of our mind-ascribing capacities. In this section I have suggested that legal procedures give a lot of ground for such scepticism.

IV. Problems with Imagination: A Case

We tend to trust our imagination of people when we can identify with them, or otherwise think of them as people rather like us, and we trust it much less with people we find less familiar. Part of this is a matter of moving the goalposts: when we have been in a situation we often think that reactions that came easily to us do not need much explanation; when the situation is outside our experience we find it harder to grasp. This is largely a matter of being able to summon corroborating details in familiar situations, and knowing what details to look for to establish a plausible conclusion.

In recent years in English-speaking countries, and probably elsewhere, there has been a spate of episodes in which middle-aged male judges have showed

[28] As far as I know expert witnesses are never brought in at this stage. And in fact no existing expertise would fit it. Perhaps the reactions of a judge with a knowledge of the precedents and experience in managing cases where the distinction is relevant are the best kind of expertise. But there is a potential speciality here, for someone with a background combining philosophy of mind, psychology and law. If only there were people with the right combinations of skills and if only courts had the remotest inclination to make use of them.

remarkable naivety in discussing the motives of men accused of rape (and other similar offences) and their accusers.[29] In a typical case the judge criticises the accuser for foolishly allowing the man opportunity or expectation, and expresses some sympathy with the man for succumbing to what would naturally have seemed like an invitation (or so the judge thinks). So the judge ends up by saying either 'under these conditions, it wasn't a crime' or 'well, technically you broke the law, but your situation was so understandable that I'm giving you a minimal sentence'.

The judge in these cases is citing what seems to him the easy imaginability of a relatively innocent or ordinary motive as a mitigating factor. In effect he is saying 'if you are to be punished severely then so should almost everyone'. There is obviously a big topic here on imagining ordinary motives as mitigating factors in cases where there is judicial latitude in sentencing (which I realise varies a lot from one jurisdiction to another). I am not going to discuss it because it requires knowledge I do not have. It also requires a sophistication about the philosophy and psychology of motive attribution, for which I am only a little better equipped. Quite likely there is no single person who is perfectly equipped. This is an important topic waiting for an interdisciplinary approach.

But the imagination is asymmetrical. The judge imagines the man's motives and not the woman's. It is not plausible that many of the self-aware, sophisticated and responsible people who become judges are simply acting from crude prejudice. I suspect that something less obvious is going on, and that it connects with the failures of imagination I mentioned just above. Sexual attraction is a mysterious thing in cases where you are not yourself subject to it. It is hard for exclusively straight people to imagine same-sex attraction, and I take it that exclusively gay people think of other-sex attraction as just one of those peculiar things that happens with much of the human race. (This is too formal and pretend precise. We can retreat to 'we all find it hard to get a good grasp on who other people fancy'. And add that six-year-olds faced with all adult sexuality just say: yuck.) The reason is that these motives are not continuous with or well integrated with our other motives, at least not with the ones that we can easily simulate in others. So the enterprise of putting yourself in another person's shoes is difficult when the other person is in this respect not like you. In this way it is like neurology or academic psychology rather than the everyday grasp we have of everyday motives.

Can one learn to imagine across such differences? There certainly is an abstract virtue here, a description of a valuable capacity. What people can actually learn, though, is usually more specific. One overcomes an inability to grasp the motives of one kind of person in one kind of situation. If one is interacting with people of this kind on a regular basis then one gains evidence about the accuracy of the procedure. Without this interaction there is very little available from everyday

[29] The examples I have particularly in mind are well-publicised and controversial lenient sentences in rape cases in Calgary Alberta in 2011, in Stanford California in 2016, and in Winnipeg Manitoba in 2016. But there is no shortage of cases where middle-aged male judges have suggested that victims could and should have prevented the events by dressing differently and physically resisting more.

social resources to give assurance about accuracy. The danger, then, is just that the vividness of imagination will make them think that the process has captured the other person's motivation when in fact it has not. The list of *attainable* virtues and how they are acquired is not a matter of obvious common sense, and not given by philosophical reflection, but a matter of hard serious psychology.[30] And unfortunately much of the psychology does not exist.

V. A General Pattern

In all of the cases I have discussed there is a tension, to put it mildly, between what we need in order to get a sense of individual motives and what we need in order to get conclusions that will apply equally and accurately to a large range of people. Fairness-as-accuracy versus impartiality. There is a fundamental reason for the tension. Our everyday grasp of other people depends on innate routines, refined but not essentially altered by growing up in particular human cultures, which have evolved to serve us in the human ecological niche of thought-out cooperative activity. We are fairly accurate about whether someone is inclined to help, or likely to be indifferent or aggressive, what information is available to them, and which aims will appeal to them. We are much less good at predicting what specific means people will take to their ends. And we are even less good at matching combinations and compromises between all the potential motives that are lurking in any person with the actions they have in fact performed. (How they could have done it rather than why they did.) Still, the methods we learn as children work fairly well among people set on getting things done together, and one reason is that when we operate socially we are able constantly to check and reconsider the meaning of what others are doing, and – a generally neglected point – to fine-tune our side of the cooperation, or even explicitly to intervene, in order to test hypotheses (suspicions, fantasies) of what the other person may be up to.

This applies to much of our knowledge of individuals, and a lot of it takes the form of shallowly conceptualised expectations of what a person will do and how they might react to what one oneself does. (The point is reinforced when we consider the role of informal experimentation – fine-tuning, intervention – in assessing people we are interacting with.) It does not yield many nontrivial generalisations about human action and motivation in general.

Moreover, there are whole areas of human life where any thinking directed at cooperative activity, whether or not based on capacities that we can think of as

[30] Virtue ethics, from Hursthouse to Swanton via Nussbaum, while capturing important points about the accessibility to humans of their values always runs the risk of running together our terms of praise with the qualities that actually describe our capacities. See Harmon (2009). Imaginative capacities surely can be educated – see Del Mar (2020) (chapter thirteen in this volume) – but that should not make us overconfident in their educability on particular topics. As Kind (2020) (chapter ten in this volume) says, we should put more trust in people's ability to learn the delicate skill of imagining a whole situation than that of engaging with the details of one personality.

imaginative, fails. It misleads us about depression and other mental vulnerabilities, social panic and other interactive styles, the long-term effects of damaging experiences, and the ways that a person's history affects their performance. It is tempting to say that these are areas for neurology, or psychology taken in a narrowly scientific sense, rather than every day psychological acuteness. But there is a circularity in saying this: we need further resources here because this is where our inbuilt capacities fail.

So what about the alternative, evidence based psychology and the like? That does not tell you much about why individual people did particular things at particular moments. It focuses on general human motivation and cognition. Perhaps in the future we will know enough that we can feed individual differences into general theories to get predictions and diagnoses about particular people. Perhaps. (I referred above to how work such as that of Loftus (1979) of how false memories can be implanted have had an impact on legal procedures.[31]) We certainly cannot get such useful information very often at the moment. And if we could very hard issues about tensions between it and long-established routines for assessing motives would arise. The difficulty of reconciling impartiality with accuracy remains.

References

Card, C (2002) *The Atrocity Paradigm: A Theory of Evil* (New York, Oxford University Press).

Davidson, D (1982) 'Rational Animals' 36(4) *Dialectica* 317.

Del Mar, M (2020) 'The Legal Imagination: Individual, Interactive, Communal' in A Amaya and M Del Mar (eds) *Virtue, Emotion and Imagination in Law and Legal Reasoning* (Oxford, Hart Publishing).

Coplan, A and Goldie, P (eds) (2011) *Empathy: Philosophical and Psychological Perspectives* (Oxford, Oxford University Press).

Gopnik, A and Meltzoff, G (1997) *Words Thoughts and Theories* (Cambridge MA Mass, MIT Press).

Hansberg, O (2020) 'Empathy and Negative Intimacy' in A Amaya and M Del Mar (eds) *Virtue, Emotion and Imagination in Law and Legal Reasoning* (Oxford, Hart Publishing).

Harman, G (2009) 'Scepticism About Character Traits' 13 *Journal of Ethics* 235.

Heal, J (1989) 'Co-Cognition and Off-Line Simulation' 13 *Mind and Language* 348.

Holmes, Jr, OW (1882) *The Common Law* (London, Macmillan).

Kahneman, D and Tversky, A (1979) 'Prospect Theory: An Analysis of Decision Under Uncertainty' 48 *Econometrica* 263.

Kind, A (2020) 'Empathy, Imagination and the Law' in A Amaya and M Del Mar (eds) *Virtue, Emotion and Imagination in Law and Legal Reasoning* (Oxford, Hart Publishing).

King, M (2017) 'Against Personifying the Reasonable Person' 4(11) *Criminal Law and Philosophy* 725.

[31] Psychiatric testimony might be adduced here. One reason I am not considering it is that it does not compete with everyday routines of motive attribution. The domains are too different.

Levesque, R (2006) *The Psychology and Law of Criminal Justice Processes* (New York, Nova).
Loftus, EF (1979) *Eyewitness Testimony* (Cambridge MA, Harvard University Press).
Maibom, H (ed) (2017) *The Routledge Handbook of Philosophy of Empathy* (London, Routledge).
Morton, A (2002) *The Importance of Being Understood: Folk Psychology as Ethics* (London, Routledge).
Morton, A (2004) *On Evil* (London, Routledge).
Morton, A (2007) 'Folk Psychology Does Not Exist' in M Ratcliffe and D Hutto (eds), *Folk Psychology Re-assessed* (Dordrecht, Kluwer/Springer) 211.
Morton, A (2009) 'Folk Psychology' in B McLaughlin and A Beckermann (eds) *The Oxford Handbook of Philosophy of Mind* (Oxford, Oxford University Press) 713.
Nichols, S and Stich, S (2003) *Mindreading* (Oxford, Oxford University Press).
Perner, J (1991) *Understanding the Representational Mind* (Cambridge MA, MIT Press).
Stern, S (2020) 'The Legal Imagination in Historical Perspective' in A Amaya and M Del Mar (eds) *Virtue, Emotion and Imagination in Law and Legal Reasoning* (Oxford, Hart Publishing).
Zipursky, BC (2020) 'Austerity, Compassion and the Rule of Law' in A Amaya and M Del Mar (eds) *Virtue, Emotion and Imagination in Law and Legal Reasoning* (Oxford, Hart Publishing).

12

The Legal Imagination in Historical Perspective

SIMON STERN

I. Introduction

Just as, according to some estate agents, a new coat of paint covers a multitude of sins, so 'the legal imagination' has been invoked to cover a variety of proposals for bringing imaginative resources to bear on the practices of judges, lawyers and litigants – involving, for example, the need for judges to cultivate their empathetic capacities; the skill of thinking outside the doctrinal box to develop novel litigation theories and strategies; the adaptation, for legal use, of creative techniques recruited from other intellectual and artistic endeavours; and the importance, for lawyers, of using literature to understand people from other backgrounds, so as to become more proficient in effectively representing clients from all walks of life.

Evidently, what is legal about the legal imagination, and what is imaginative about it, are both questions that vary significantly depending on the problem being diagnosed. In most of these formulations, imagination proves to be a remedy, imported from outside the law, to solve problems resulting from the law's imaginative failures.[1] The law itself turns out be a barren and arid domain, replete with ossified, regimented, hidebound abstractions, and characterised by devices like balancing tests, burdens of proof, standards of review, bright-line rules, and similar bureaucratic tools. What's required is an antidote – a balm that will rejuvenate this desolate landscape and help life to flourish there again. This view of the legal imagination emphasises imaginative capacities that (according to their exponent) are rarely found within the legal domain; the prescription includes a wide array of creative techniques that have no particular habitation – they might come from any intellectual, artistic or practical field, to give lawyers the same skills that others have cultivated. This is, in short, a conception of what the legal imagination *could* be, if only it would avail itself of various resources that legal thinkers have ignored.

[1] For an excellent, but rather different, exploration of what this might entail, see Watson (1988).

But what if, instead, we asked what kinds of imaginative devices we do encounter in the law? That is, what kinds of techniques, tools and constructs do we find in the legal discourse of problem-solving, whose application invites lawyers and judges to use their imaginative capacities? One way to answer this question would involve looking to the art of advocate, and exploring the ways that advising clients, and arguing in court, draw on a range of imaginative techniques, such as creating workarounds that help to achieve the client's goals, positioning oneself in the client's story to think about how to search for evidence, inventing hypotheticals, using figurative language to help a judge understand a dilemma, and envisioning concrete situations that vividly illustrate the issues in dispute. A burgeoning literature on the theory and practice of the lawyer's imaginative craft has taken up this approach;[2] this chapter will explore a different aspect of the question: namely, what kinds of imaginative devices do we find in the judicial development and elaboration of legal doctrine? The lawyer's capacities for speculation and counterfactual thinking are almost always at work in any interpretive exercise. Occasionally they appear to play a central role, as in the case of 'imaginative reconstruction', which seeks to give effect to legislation, in a context that the legislature failed to address.[3] Despite the name, however, when engaged in this exercise courts draw on the conventional methods of statutory interpretation – which is to say that the imaginative efforts involved here are no more salient than elsewhere. In what follows, I consider some instances that do seem to afford a distinctive role for speculation and counterfactual thinking, focusing in particular on the 'reasonable man'.

II. The Constrained Imagination

According to Giambattista Vico, 'all ancient Roman law was a serious poem … and ancient jurisprudence was a severe poetry', emblematised by its use of legal fictions – 'empty masks without subjects, *iura imaginaria*, rights invented by imagination'.[4] For Vico, the poetry lay in the law's capacity for treating actual events as if they had not occurred, and vice versa: by the fictions of Roman law, 'what had happened was taken as not having happened, and what had not happened as having happened; those not yet born as already born, the living as dead; and the dead as still living in the estates pending acceptance'.[5] In modern legal parlance, these examples would all be characterised as deeming provisions: for certain purposes involving the distribution of a decedent's estate, a fetus might

[2] See eg Bankowski and Del Mar (2016); Del Mar (2017); Del Mar (2018); Rakoff and Minow (2007); Sherwin (2008).

[3] See eg *United States v Logan* 453 F.3d 804, 807-08 (7th Cir. 2006).

[4] Vico (1968), 390, paras 1037, 1036.

[5] Vico (2000), 164.

be counted as (deemed to be) alive when the father died. For similar purposes, a citizen who was captured by the enemy, in war, might be regarded as having died (the fiction of 'civil death').

Modern law abounds in deeming provisions, which exhibit a similar form. For certain purposes relating to environmental regulation, an underground pipe will be treated as a river; in some instances, the ability to control an asset is sufficient to count as possession of it. What all these provisions share is an understanding of the limited-purpose use of the proposition. The civilly dead citizen is not treated as dead for all purposes, but only for the specific purpose of distributing the assets of the estate. The pipe which 'is not a pipe' but a river, for certain regulatory purposes, nevertheless remains a pipe for other purposes.

One way to characterise the imaginative impulses at work, in the case of deeming provisions, depends on Vico's suggestion that the law is busy imagining things to be otherwise, knowing the facts but energetically revising them, exercising a kind of poetic licence by which a legal speech act brings the dead back to life and repopulates the world according to law's own conceits. This has remained a common theme in the writing on legal fictions, which often places them among the law's most inventive – and most literary – devices.[6] But another way to understand what is both legal and imaginative about these fictions is to inquire into their limited-purpose aspect. In many areas of intellectual life, we use stipulations, conditional provisions, and hypothetical assumptions to explore the implications of an idea, but in law these devices are omnipresent. As an imaginative technique, the habit of *constraining* the implications that flow from a premise may be one of the essential features of legal thought.

The same pattern we have observed in deeming provisions appears, in various guises, throughout the law. Testimony about an out-of-court utterance may be admissible for one purpose, but inadmissible hearsay if used to treat the statement as expressing the truth about the speaker's plans or intentions; one who counts as an independent agent for purposes of labour law might be an employee for tax purposes; what constitutes consent in health law, so as to protect doctors from liability for assault when performing an operation, may be insufficient to achieve the same result in criminal law, for participants in a fist fight. More generally, any given doctrine is open to being extended or limited, according to a court's view of the doctrine's rationale and pliability, and the corresponding capacities of the proposed transposition. To recognise the role these restrictions play is to see how legal thinking alters one of the central constraints that Amy Kind has examined, in her treatment of 'imagining under constraints': Kind discusses the condition, in certain types of science fiction, that 'imagin[ing] a change to the world' carries with it the requirement of being 'guided by the logical consequences of that change'.[7] To be sure, what counts as a 'logical consequence' may leave significant room for

[6] See Stern (2017a).
[7] Kind (2016).

debate; in the legal context, however, imagining changes frequently means rejecting, or at least holding in abeyance, many of the logical consequences that would seem to follow. The effect is not to afford a freer rein for the legal imagination, but a more limited one: instead of permitting the change to blossom into various results beyond the logical ones, the law restricts the array of results even more severely than Kind's account proposes.

The Harvard law professor Thomas Reed Powell famously said that 'if you think you can think about something which is attached to something else without thinking about what it is attached to, then you have what is called a legal mind'.[8] The statement is often interpreted cynically, and it seems to invite this interpretation: 'if you *think*' you can undertake that operation, then you have a legal mind (or at least what passes for one), because you believe yourself capable of the impossible. Even if this kind of compartmentalisation is possible, it may sound so strained and artificial as to reflect precisely the kind of arid and purely analytical mindset described at the outset of this chapter. But the statement is also open to a more positive interpretation: the ability to divide and separate implications and consequences in this fashion opens up other ways of thinking, encourages a kind of lateral thinking that becomes possible just because the results can be hedged about. If there is indeed a characteristically *legal* means of exercising the imagination, it may have to do with the devices by which lawyers turn constraint into possibility.

Baudelaire's essay 'The Painter of Modern Life' similarly offers a glimmer of this idea – that the imagination, acting under the pressure of constraint, may produce a certain kind of insight. In seeking to account for the kind of genius he finds in the work of Constantin Guys, Baudelaire begins with a narrow conception of the artist as an accomplished artisan, with training in a craft, but then realises that what he actually seeks is 'not precisely an artist but rather *a man of the world*'. He continues, 'I ask you to understand the word *artist* in a very restricted sense and *man of the world* in a very broad one. By the second I mean a man of the whole world, a man who understands the world and the mysterious and lawful reasons for all its uses [*homme qui comprend le monde et les raisons mystérieuses et légitimes de tous ses usages*]; by the first, a specialist, a man wedded to his palette like the serf to the soil.'[9] *Légitimes* need not be translated as 'lawful', but even 'legitimate' carries a whiff of authorisation: some reasons – even if beguiling – would be spurious and unwarranted, and consequently some person or standard must decide which ones are valid. Baudelaire evidently considered this a useful qualification, since he might have contented himself with 'mysterious' and stopped there. He offers no criterion for assessing a reason's legitimacy (that is the poet's prerogative), but to mark the distinction at all is to imply that even if an active imagination is a vital ingredient in the disposition of this worldly figure, it cannot, by itself, handle the task: what is needed, Baudelaire suggests, is a *regulated* imagination. The man of

[8] Quoted in Arnold (1930), 58.

[9] Baudelaire (1964), 6–7; Baudelaire (1885), 60. The essay originally appeared in *Le Figaro* in 1863. For discussion, see also Gogröf-Voorhees (2004), 42–49.

the world sees in this buzzing, blooming confusion an order, a consistency built on rules and processes – whether based in logic, science or some other system. Recognising these patterns requires a certain kind of discipline. The lawyer is certainly not the only one with these talents, but the professional skill of inducing order out of the mass of particulars makes those trained in the law admirably suited for the task.[10]

The idea that lawyers are capable of perceiving abstruse and otherwise invisible connections goes back at least to the time of Sir Edward Coke's musings on 'artificial reason' and William Fulbecke's insistence that a law student must be prepared to enter 'into the suruey of … intricate and hidden pointes, must [have the] abilitie to compound thinges, and to resolue them by imagination, to builde and destroy'.[11] Fulbecke sees the legal imagination as an active force, concerned not only with perception but also with the creation and destruction of the objects it contemplates. The law's artificial creations are not simply given, but made – and made anew by its practitioners. Thus the lawyer's role is not limited to observing, or refining, the coherence that abides in the legal system. That is the kind of exercise that Blackstone would propose, at the outset of the *Commentaries*, when he speaks of 'improving [the law's] methods, retrenching its superfluities, and reconciling the little contrarieties, which the practice of many centuries will necessarily create in any human system' – a comparative exercise that does not require imagination so much as methodical care and precision.[12] Fulbecke gives the lawyer a more dramatic role, encompassing the imaginative revision of facts and doctrines, to be newly parsed and combined as the lawyer's speculative efforts require.[13]

These active powers of the legal imagination would gain even more force during the nineteenth century, in ways that Fulbecke probably did not anticipate, even though in retrospect, they may seem the logical extension of the abilities he describes. In Britain and the United States, the nineteenth century marked an especially productive era of legal development, witnessing the creation of new forms, such as the limited liability company; the reconceptualisation of whole fields, such as torts; and an increasingly sophisticated concern with technical and procedural matters, such as burdens of proof, standards of review, and

[10] The point might appear to have less purchase in the civil law context in which Baudelaire was writing; however, civilian accounts of legal method often treat induction as an essential skill for practising lawyers and particularly for *juristes*. See eg Belleau (1997).

[11] *Case of Prohibitions* (1607) 12 Co. Rep. 63, 64; Fulbecke (1600) 52.

[12] Blackstone (2016) 1:30.

[13] Because of his interest in compounding and resolving intricate points, Fulbecke appears less interested in the facts of a given case than in the way that doctrines operate to recast facts in a certain light; however, he quickly adds that 'there is no case which accidents may not alter', suggesting that the lawyer's skill also involves the manipulation and reinterpretation of specific facts in a dispute (Fulbecke, 1600, 52). Consequently, his understanding of the lawyer's imaginative role may find some kinship with Catherine Elgin's (2020) observations (chapter three in this volume, p 57), about how a judge might 'use her imagination to reconfigure the facts of the case'.

permissible methods of statutory construction.[14] Each of these developed by means of the 'hidden points' and 'mysterious and lawful reasons' that Fulbecke and Baudelaire discuss, and insofar as they made the law more coherent, it was a coherence that was fashioned rather than found. It was by borrowing methods, concepts and devices from one field of law – or from fields entirely outside of the law – and trying them out in another field, that lawyers were able to bring about such significant change.

III. Modelling the Reasonable Man

The 'reasonable man' is one of the most famous legal contributions of this era.[15] A personified standard was an unusual device in the common law, with very few examples before the nineteenth century, but once this figure came onto the scene, it rapidly spread across numerous areas, including criminal law, employment law, torts, contracts, property, family law, and many others. To be sure, the law uses personifications in various ways – in representing ideals such as justice, and in attributing personhood to entities such as corporations. The reasonable man is unlike these, because it requires the fact-finder to engage cognitively with a notional person in a concrete setting (the time, place and events in the dispute), thus importing a human figure into the process of determining the facts. One may find a personified corporation liable (or not) without ever needing to depict it to oneself in human form, but the reasonable man, by virtue of its application as a standard, entails precisely that kind of depiction. To know what the reasonable man would do is to imagine a human agent in the relevant circumstances. At a time when lawyers were searching for ways to express and enact their newfound concern with objectivity, the reasonable man proved to be an ideal vehicle, albeit a paradoxical one, because the abstractions that were already familiar as legal standards (such as 'due measure' and 'sufficient care') would appear more objective than a personification that, by virtue of its human form, seems to invite questions about individual capacities and abilities, thereby undermining the standard's generic ambitions. Even as the standard strives for uniformity and regularity through its appeal to the reasonable, that aim is complicated by the introduction of a human element – unlike already existing uses of the reasonable, in which it designates a quality of an act or entity, not of an actor (eg 'reasonable doubt' or 'a reasonable time').

As an imaginative device, the reasonable man and the cognates accompanying its development – the man of ordinary caution, the man of average

[14] The scholarship on these issues is vast; among the recent discussions, Siraganian (2020) and Williams (2019) offer particular valuable treatments of the limited liability company and tort law, respectively.

[15] I use the male form when writing about its use in the nineteenth century, because it was not transformed into the 'reasonable person' until the 1970s.

prudence – exhibit two significant features.[16] First, the selective transposition of such a standard across various doctrinal domains exemplifies the kind of lateral thinking, operating under constraint, on which legal creativity often depends, and second, the mode of cognitive engagement that a personified standard solicits from its user includes imaginative dimensions that are lacking from abstract standards.[17] Speak of 'due care', and you will elicit the same kind of disengaged, analytical response as a demand that means and end must be 'proportional' or that causation must be 'proximate'. Speak of a 'reasonable person' and (no matter how emphatically you insist that it is a construct with no reference to any individual) you will elicit a more direct and personal response, involving some measure of self-reflection and self-application as part of the exercise. When using the standard, people almost invariably place themselves in the situation in question, even if it is only a step on the way to envisioning another figure, with the appropriate qualifications, in the scenario. Although this effect does not necessarily make for a richer or more elaborate imaginative form (since various legal devices make different kinds of imaginative demands on their users), it carries the potential to do so. Because of the reflective and engaged imaginative qualities that the personification elicits, it may create opportunities for emotional and sensual responses that few other legal devices invite. That people reliability and consistently consult their own experience and perceptions, when applying a personified standard, helps to account both for its remarkable success and also its shortcomings.

An early effort at legal innovation, through the use of a personified standard, occurred in the law of negotiable instruments in the 1820s. Since the latter part of the eighteenth century, British courts had been increasingly confronted with problems involving bills of exchange. These often took the form of bank drafts, drawn on a bank by a named individual and specifying a payee, who could endorse it and pass it on, writing a new recipient's name in the line below.[18] When the notes were stolen, the thief would typically endorse them in his or her own name (or pose as the most recent endorsee) and use them to pay for commercial goods or take them to a bill broker. If the theft had been reported, the issuing bank might refuse to honour the note, and the question arose whether the holder or the bank should bear the loss. Traditionally, British courts had asked whether the current holder had given consideration in exchange for the note. If it had been acquired 'in the course of trade', the holder was entitled to have the bill honoured, and the bank had to bear the loss. What 'in the course of trade' entailed is not entirely clear, but it appears to have meant 'in a legitimate commercial transaction'. In *Miller v. Race* (1758), Lord Mansfield spelt out the logic of these judgements when he explained that the bank could delay payment long enough to find out 'whether the bearer of

[16] These various personifications had begun to circulate in the late eighteenth century, and with increasing frequency in the early nineteenth century. One of the earliest texts to promote the technique was Jones (1781).

[17] Its function is thus akin to that of the 'inherently interactive devices' that Del Mar (2020) examines.

[18] Rogers (1995) 173–77.

the note came fairly by it'; Mansfield reasoned that the bank should honour the bill so long as the bearer received it for a 'full and valuable consideration in the usual course and way of his business and without any notice or knowledge of its being taken from the mail'.[19] When, as in *Miller*, the holder had taken it 'bonâ fide',[20] that was sufficient to make the bank liable. What constituted notice or knowledge of theft, and what burden lay on the recipient to investigate this question, would become matters for further dispute. Over the next sixty years, counsel for the defendant banks argued that holders should be required to show that they had actively inquired into the circumstances by which the endorser had obtained the bill, but the courts rejected this proposal and continued to emphasise that holders should prevail so long as they had been unaware of the theft and had given consideration for the bill.

In 1824, however, the courts changed course, imposing a requirement of prudence and care on the holder – and including a personified standard among the means of effecting this change. *Gill v Cubitt*[21] is known to students of the Uniform Commercial Code as the origin (quickly repudiated) of an objective standard of care for the holder in due course. By contrast with the 'bonâ fide' standard, which denies recovery only if the holder exhibits bad faith, the objective standard requires the holder to inquire sufficiently into the bill's history; it turns on what steps the holder took, rather than the holder's personal knowledge at the time of receipt. In its facts, *Gill* resembled many of the cases that preceded it. A parcel was stolen from a mail coach, and the next day, the thief presented one of the stolen bills to a clerk at Gill and Co (a bill broker), who paid full value after satisfying himself as to the credit of the previous endorsees, but without asking any questions of the bearer. The bank refused to pay when the bill was presented, and Gill sued to recover its value. At trial, Lord Chief Justice Abbott asked the jury to consider whether the broker had shown a 'want of proper and reasonable caution' in failing to probe the bearer's antecedents before accepting the bill; the jury found for the bank.[22]

Gill moved for a new trial, and at the hearing on the motion, before a panel of three judges in the King's Bench, he argued unsuccessfully that the jury should have been asked only whether he gave consideration in exchange for the bill. Abbott LCJ reaffirmed his earlier view, reasoning that unless the broker was required to use 'reasonable caution', mail thieves would be encouraged to continue their depredations, secure in the knowledge that no one would ask where their bills came from. Whereas Abbot LCJ formulated these requirements without resort to any personification, Justice Bayley explained the standard of care at greater length, using both abstract and personified forms. In his view, asking whether the broker used 'due caution' was the same as asking 'whether he took it

[19] *Miller v Race* (1758) 1 Burr. 452, 460, 452.
[20] Ibid, 457.
[21] *Gill v Cubitt* (1824) 3 B. & C. 466.
[22] *Gill v Cubitts* (1824) 1 Car. & P. 163, 166.

in the usual course of business; for the course of business must require, in the usual and ordinary manner of conducting it, a proper and reasonable degree of caution', which is to say, 'that degree of caution which, in the ordinary course of trade, a prudent trader ought to use'.[23] Agreeing with these views, Justice Holroyd also used both forms, observing that the broker should use 'due caution' and that otherwise 'he takes a risk (or what ought, in the contemplation of a reasonable man, to be a risk)'.[24]

That the judges expressed the newly adopted standard in both ways – as abstractions and personifications – suggests that they did not see any significant difference between the two. In light of the ready and unselfconscious movement between the two modes of expression, the judges probably assumed they were following an already established path. Their innovation, as they understood it, consisted in changing the 'bonâ fide' standard to one requiring appropriate prudence and caution, which could refer either to the nature of the broker's inquiry, or to the broker himself. The judges said nothing about the source of the standard, apparently taking it for granted that if any duty rested on the broker, it must be the duty to use ordinary prudence. Seemingly, this idea had already gained enough currency in contemporary jurisprudence to be available as a default, and the very explicit policy-based reasoning in *Gill* simply transposes it into a new arena: only by placing some burden on the recipient (whatever burden might readily be slotted in) could the law discourage theft and forgery.

From which other legal areas, then, did the judges borrow this standard? The source was almost certainly the law of bailments. Sir William Jones's *Essay on the Law of Bailments* (1781), which has been described as 'the first English monograph that can properly be called a legal treatise', carefully and extensively explored various standards of care that might be required of a bailee, examined through the lens of *Coggs v Bernard* (1703) and its antecedents.[25] In the course of his *Essay*, Jones expressed these standards not only in abstract terms, but also, frequently, in personified forms – for example, 'that care, *which every man of common sense* … applies to his own affairs'; 'that care, *which every prudent man takes of his own property*'; the care that 'any man of *common discretion* would [use]'.[26] *Coggs* itself used the personified standard only implicitly, speaking at one point of the difference between 'a diligent man [who] is not so liable as a careless man', and observing (with great prescience) that 'to oblige all men, that take goods to keep … that they will keep them as safe as they would do their own, … is a thing no man living that is not a lawyer could think of'.[27] Nevertheless, *Coggs* did have some effect on the use of personified standards in eighteenth-century law, because its

[23] *Gill v Cubitt* (1824) 3 B. & C. 466, 475.

[24] Ibid, 477 (per Holroyd, J).

[25] Jones (1781); Zimmerman (1996) 570; see also Ibbetson (1999) 164; *Coggs v Bernard* (1703), 2 Ld Raym 909.

[26] Jones (1781), 6, 7 88.

[27] *Coggs v Bernard* (1703), 2 Ld Raym 909, 909–10.

analysis was borrowed and reformulated a few months later in a dispute involving allegations of criminal fraud. There, the court held that a deceit was criminal only if it was too sophisticated for 'a Person of an ordinary Capacity' to detect, and that doctrine enjoyed a fair amount of currency up until the early nineteenth century.[28] This confluence of sources, but particularly Jones's widely commended and highly influential treatment (which had gone through four British editions by the time of *Gill*),[29] helped to illustrate the virtues of a negligence-oriented scale, contrasting 'ordinary' negligence (or prudence, or care) with greater and lesser degrees, and also broadcasting the possibility of conveying the standard by means of a personification.

One might seek, in the professional roles and qualifications of the bailee and the bill broker, the similarities that explain the transposition of the standard from one domain to the other; however, the likelier explanation is that the judges were looking to impose the burden of care on the broker, and without giving the matter much thought, they simply assumed that the burden should be neither too low nor too high. A personification (even if repeatedly described as 'idealised', as in modern parlance) is a useful means of striking that balance, precisely because the human figure dampens the idealising effect of a pure abstraction. An 'average' person is a poor vehicle for conveying legal norms, and 'reasonableness' may be too heavily freighted with legal norms; the combination ('reasonable person') steers between the two.[30] That appears to account for many of the uses of the reasonable person; for instance, after the US law of search and seizure was altered in *Katz v United States* (1967), turning the inquiry from one oriented around specific places to one based on 'a reasonable expectation of privacy' in the material acquired by the police, the lawyer who proposed this approach explained how it came about: '[D]uring my preparation for oral argument … I experienced a mind changing event. I had graduated from law school a little more than three years [earlier] … [and] [a]s I ruminated about the *Katz* case, I reflected on my Torts class, especially the tort of negligence.'[31] This account of the episode is particularly intriguing because it refers to an explicitly personified example (the one in torts) to account for a version in which the standard is only implicitly personified. An 'expectation of privacy' cannot exist independently of the person who holds it, and hence any application of the standard necessarily carries with it some understanding of a concrete situation in which individuals have these perceptions; at the same time, because the personification is only implicit, courts have sometimes allowed themselves to apply the test from a detached perspective that conflicts

[28] Stern (2017b); *Anonymous* (1703) 6 Mod. 105.

[29] Cannon (1979) 10–11.

[30] For a helpful recent discussion that pursues this line of thought, see Tobia (2018); similarly, Morton (2020) (chapter eleven in this volume) considers the compromises and imaginative limits that apply to the 'reasonable person' standard (see section III.D).

[31] Schneider (2009) 377–78.

jarringly with most citizens' views on the issue.[32] *Gill* and *Katz* are both typical examples of the legal imagination, which often operates not by methodically searching out nearly parallel doctrines from closely related areas of law, but by proceeding in a fashion that is at once more pragmatic and more creative, seeking inspiration from any source and testing the results.

That the *Gill* standard was chosen without much reflection is evident from its later fortunes. Ten years later, in *Crook v Jadis* (1834), the court ruled that it was asking too much of the broker to use 'ordinary' negligence, and that payment should be refused only if the broker had used 'gross negligence'.[33] At trial, the parties argued the case according to the 'due caution' standard, but Denman CJ instructed the jury that the plaintiff broker should win so long as 'he had not been guilty of gross negligence'. The defendant's counsel moved for a new trial, arguing that a properly instructed jury would have been asked whether the plaintiff had taken the efforts that 'a prudent man' would take.[34] On the hearing on the motion, the court not only insisted that the 'gross negligence' standard was correct, but more generally cast doubt on the meaning of the standard in *Gill*. Taunton J found the higher standard incomprehensible: 'I cannot estimate the degree of care which a prudent man should take. The question … whether the plaintiff was guilty of gross negligence, was more definite and appropriate.'[35] Patteson J took precisely the same view: 'I could never understand what is meant by a party's taking a bill under circumstances which ought to have excited the suspicions of a prudent man.'[36]

It may be significant that when rejecting the higher standard, both of these judges expressed it in a personified form, even though the usual formulations, when setting it out, were indifferent as between the personified and abstract versions. Doubtless, all the judges considered the higher standard unacceptable, likely because they had come to understand that when a burden was imposed on the broker to ascertain the bill's validity, the result was to delay the flow of commerce, and to make brokers generally more reluctant to accept bills – including perfectly legitimate ones. In fact, this understates the problem, because so long as the duty attached to the bill's recipient, it applied equally to all recipients, including anyone, professional or not, who took the bill as payment for a debt. What might count as ordinarily prudent, for such a person, could easily yield an answer that 'no man living that is not a lawyer could think of'. From a policy perspective, *Gill* was proving to be ill-advised, and lowering the standard could help to remedy the problem. But the judges did not simply object to the standard; they also took issue with the duties imposed on 'a prudent man', as if they were having trouble envisioning this creature. They did not attack the personification as such,

[32] See eg Slobogin and Schumacher (1993).
[33] *Crook v Jadis* (1834) 5 B. & Ad. 909.
[34] Ibid.
[35] Ibid.
[36] Ibid.

but that form seems to have helped them to specify their concerns with the standard, perhaps because it encouraged them to think more concretely about the efforts supposedly required of a such figure, and that was precisely their difficulty. To modern legal thinkers, it would be obvious that there is no single way to be sufficiently 'prudent', and this is a virtue of a standard that can be satisfied in various ways. These judges, however, seem to have regarded it as a problem: what would be required of 'a prudent man' in these circumstances is not sufficiently 'definite'. The lower standard of 'gross negligence' is at once more 'appropriate' for the issue at hand and clearer in the demands it imposes on the broker.

However, even 'gross negligence' proved to be too much, and two years later, the King's Bench completely abandoned this approach, returning to the *bona fide* standard. In *Goodman v. Harvey* (1836), Denman LCJ explained that even if the broker had exhibited 'gross negligence', that was 'not a sufficient answer, where the party has given consideration for the bill' – a condition that applied in all of the cases litigated in this area.[37] Gross negligence, he held, was relevant only insofar as it might be 'evidence of mala fides, but is not the same thing'.[38] The result? 'We have shaken off the last remnant of the contrary doctrine. Where the bill has passed to the plaintiff without any proof of bad faith in him, there is no objection to his title.'[39] In twelve short years, the prudent man had replaced the *bona fide* standard, only to be replaced by a (non-personified) standard of gross negligence, which in turn was abolished in favour of the original *bona fide* standard.

IV. The Reasonable Man is Dead. Long Live the Reasonable Man!

This brief episode, involving a precursor of the reasonable man, shows how legal creativity, when it transposes devices from one area of law to another, does not necessarily produce lasting results. The 'mind changing event' that proved so influential in US search and seizure law, produced disastrous results in the law of negotiable instruments. By imposing a burden on bill brokers, the courts interrupted the flow of commerce to an unforeseen extent, and at the end of the day, the only solution they found acceptable was to eliminate the burden entirely. At the same time, this episode conveys something of the energy and dynamism of the legal imagination in an era when it appeared that this new personified standard could suit various longstanding needs and could alter the law in significant ways, if only its proper uses could be sorted out.

As is now well known, one of those uses would begin to come into visibility the year after *Goodman* was decided. In *Vaughan v Menlove* (1837), the Court of

[37] *Goodman v Harvey* (1836) 4 Ad. & E. 870, 876.
[38] Ibid.
[39] Ibid.

Common Pleas tried a personified standard, this time testing out the prospects for objectivity in the law of torts. Despite warnings about his badly constructed hayrick, Menlove did not prevent it from igniting and causing damage to Vaughan's property. At trial, the jury was asked whether Menlove had used 'gross negligence' – an instruction that was accompanied with the explanation that 'he was bound to proceed with such reasonable caution as a prudent man would have exercised under such circumstances'.[40] Found liable, Menlove moved for a new trial, contending that the proper question was neither 'whether [he] had been guilty of gross negligence', nor whether he had used 'ordinary prudence, a standard too uncertain to afford any criterion', but rather 'whether he had acted bonâ fide to the best of his judgment'.[41] On the hearing on the motion, Tindal CJ explained that 'liability for negligence should [not] be co-extensive with the judgement of each individual, which would be as variable as the length of the foot of each individual', but instead should proceed according to 'the rule which requires in all cases a regard to caution such as a man of ordinary prudence would observe'.[42] Similarly, Vaughan J observed that '[i]t was, if any thing, too favourable to the Defendant to leave it to the jury whether he had been guilty of gross negligence', because '[t]he conduct of a prudent man' was 'the criterion for the jury in such cases'.[43] Although *Vaughan* was hardly sufficient, by itself, to set the law of torts on a new footing, based on a personified standard, it represented an important shift in that direction.

A careful reader of *Vaughan* would notice that the bailment jurisprudence and the recent experiment with negotiable instruments both figured significantly. The defendant's counsel attempted to distinguish the case at hand from those involving bailees who acted 'under an implied contract', contending that no such relationship or obligation could obtain between these neighbours; moreover, he cited *Crook v. Jadis* to show that ordinary prudence was too vague and indefinite to furnish a practicable standard.[44] His reference to the law of bailments backfired: according to Vaughan CJ, *Coggs v Bernard* usefully showed that 'the care which a prudent man would take' is perfectly intelligible: '[A] jury has always been able to say, whether, taking that rule as their guide, there has been negligence on the occasion in question.'[45] Notably, the court had no doctrinal rejoinder to the proposition that a duty could not be imposed in the absence of an express or implied contract; instead, as in *Gill*, the court opted to change the law on policy grounds – albeit with less elaboration than in *Gill*, which had been far more explicit about the harms resulting from the existing approach. Having satisfied themselves that the 'prudent man' standard could be reliably applied, the judges asked if it was

[40] *Vaughan v Menlove* (1837) 3 Bing (NC) 468, 471.
[41] Ibid.
[42] Ibid, 475.
[43] Ibid, 477.
[44] Ibid, 472–73.
[45] Ibid, 475.

preferable to leave matters up to 'the judgement of each individual', and opted emphatically for the objective standard.

Here, then, was a viable use for the kind of personification that the courts had been exploring. Whereas the courts had been dismayed by the consequences of the 'prudent man' standard, when applied to bill brokers – and despite the very recent evidence of this difficulty – the standard appeared plausible when applied to persons whose actions result in harm to their neighbours. What explains the success of this approach, in the law of bailments and then in torts, but not in the law of negotiable instruments? Notably, when consulting the bailment cases to show how readily the personified standard could be applied, the *Vaughan* court pointed to the common experience of ordinary people. Jones's *Essay*, which the court did not cite, but which lay in the background, repeatedly described the bailee's duty of care in terms that appeal to an individual's personal experience – as, for instance, when specifying the care that an ordinarily prudent man 'applies to his own affairs'.[46] That last phrase is implicit when Tindal CJ speaks of the 'caution such as a man of ordinary prudence would observe'. That person's own knowledge and experience furnish the very conditions that facilitate the use of the standard. The court dismissed the 'supposed difficulty of applying' this standard because 'a jury has always been able to say' what it would entail in a given case. Again, a jury could easily apply the standard because the jurors knew how much care they would take of their 'own affairs'; the case at hand would impose some imaginative demands on them, but none that would require them to transpose their experience into a completely unfamiliar realm.

By contrast, the difficulty with *Gill* and its progeny was that, except for those already familiar with the procedures involving the transfer of bearer bills, it would be hard to say how much care an 'ordinarily prudent' bill broker would take. In the days before the penny post, let alone the telegraph, the solution of communicating with the bank before accepting the bill was not available, and it was unclear what other measures would be effective, nor how much effort they would require. Recall the assertion, in *Crook v Jadis*, that it was impossible to 'estimate the degree of care which a prudent man should take'; in retrospect, this statement makes sense if we substitute 'a prudent bill broker' for 'a prudent man', and most likely, that is precisely what the court meant. The problem lay not in the standard, but in its application to an area in which few jurors could have any personal experience.

The analysis in *Vaughan* hints at the difference in 'fit' between the recent bill broker cases, and the older bailment cases. The judges insisted that jurors inquiring into a bailee's conduct had always been capable of applying the standard, and that consequently the jury in a tort case would be equally adept. Evidently, the court sensed that torts would be a more appropriate locale for the standard than the recently abandoned effort with negotiable instruments. What this set of

[46] Jones (1781), 6, 31, 83.

cases documents, then, is an emerging understanding about where the personified standard could work. Rather than developing the standard in a methodical, fully deliberate fashion, first establishing that the transposition was warranted, and then proceeding by enumerating all the grounds that would justify the extension, the courts proceeded haltingly, most explicitly in *Gill*, but also, to some extent, in *Vaughan*, where the reasons for adopting the personification may be evident on a close reading, but were hardly spelt out in a manner that identified the differences between tortfeasors and bill brokers. The lawyers' and judges' analogical efforts ranged imaginatively across various legal domains in search of a device that would answer the present need, and it is perhaps worth observing that *Gill* was no less confident than *Vaughan*, in adopting the new approach.

Just as these cases allow us to observe the imaginative use of a particular kind of legal device, they also show us a slowly growing awareness of the different affordances of rules and standards. Before the nineteenth century, British law made great use of rules, even if the result was a complex and byzantine tangle that few could view comprehensively. The law of torts, before the onset of the reasonable man, offers an excellent illustration of this tendency, but the same pattern may be seen in numerous other areas. The brief detour that *Gill* inaugurated involved a turn towards standards, in a field that ultimately proved more amenable to a rule-based approach. Unless the jury were to hear expert evidence from professional bill brokers, or to be instructed by the judge on what kinds of measures would satisfy the broker's duty, they would find it too challenging to undertake the imaginative exercise demanded by the standard. A more rule-like approach, leaving much less scope for the imagination, was far more effective. The question of 'bad faith' does not eliminate any room for speculation and perspective-taking on the juror's part, but in this context, it cabins those opportunities more narrowly than the question of ordinary prudence (or gross negligence), by restricting the array of relevant details. 'Bad faith' is concerned with what the broker actually knew; 'ordinary prudence' opens the door to numerous considerations that vary from case to case. Conversely, in torts, it seemed desirable and effective to allow for the wider latitude for judgement, which accompanied the invitation to consult personal experience and to position oneself in the defendant's place. This does not necessarily mean that the fact-finder will look solely to personal experience (although the standard's use is notoriously difficult to control); at a minimum, however, the standard encourages a kind of perspective-taking that makes one's own knowledge a valid yardstick.[47] Torts was only one of many areas that would embrace this shift – towards the use of personified standards and the substitution of standards for rules – but given the relative frequency of tort disputes, as against those involving bailments, the innovation in *Vaughan* was probably a significant factor in the broader trend in nineteenth-century jurisprudence.

[47] On the ways in which judges generally must 'draw upon their own life experiences in their decision-making', see Kind (2020) (chapter ten in this volume, p 190).

V. Conclusion

In considering how legal devices move from one domain to another, it is often helpful to examine the unsuccessful efforts alongside the better-known successes. Doing so can give us a better appreciation of the ways in which the legal imagination is constrained. The law is replete with conditions that delimit the scope of doctrines, ascriptions, presumptions and conclusions, in a fashion that lawyers often take for granted but that seems extremely artificial to laypersons. By the same token, a new doctrinal extension, or the transposition of a test or standard into a new area, may ultimately fail because of unanticipated constraints on its operation. Nineteenth-century lawyers displayed an almost unbridled enthusiasm for the 'reasonable man', which continued well into the twentieth century. Although the *Katz* test has long appeared to represent one of the standard's more successful applications, it too has recently come into question. In 2014, Justice Sotomayor observed that 'it may be necessary to reconsider the premise that an individual has no reasonable expectation of privacy in information voluntarily disclosed to third parties'.[48] Even more recently, Justice Thomas criticised the test as lacking any 'basis in the text or history of the Fourth Amendment' and requiring courts to render decisions that 'distort Fourth Amendment jurisprudence'.[49] Although it has lasted significantly longer than the effort in *Gill* (perhaps in part because of its implicit personification, noted earlier), this formulation of the standard may now be approaching the end of its use. Precisely because the legal imagination is so thoroughly pragmatic, it is always open to recognising constraints and to seeking new adaptations.

References

Cases

Anonymous (1703) 6 Mod. 105
Carpenter v United States 138 S Ct 2206 (2018)
Case of Prohibitions (1607) 12 Co. Rep. 63
Coggs v Bernard (1703) 2 Ld Raym 909
Crook v. Jadis (1834) 5 B. & Ad. 909
Gill v Cubitt (1824) 3 B. & C. 466
Gill v Cubitts (1824) 1 Car. & P. 163
Goodman v Harvey (1836) 4 Ad. & E. 870
Jones v United States 565 US 400 (2014)

[48] *Jones v United States* 565 US 400, 417 (2014).
[49] *Carpenter v United States* 138 S Ct 2206, 2236 (2018).

Miller v Race (1758) 1 Burr. 452
United States v Logan 453 F.3d 804 (7th Cir. 2006)
Vaughan v Menlove (1837) 3 Bing (NC) 468

Articles and Books

Arnold, TW (1930) 'Criminal Attempts – The Rise and Fall of an Abstraction' 40 *Yale Law Journal* 53.

Bankowski, Z and Del Mar, M (eds) (2016) *The Moral Imagination and the Legal Life: Beyond Text in Legal Education* (Abingdon, Routledge).

Baudelaire, C (1885) 'Le Peintre de la vie moderne' in *Œuvres complètes de Charles Baudelaire*, tome III (Paris, Calmann Lévy) 51.

Baudelaire, C (1964) 'The Painter of Modern Life' in *The Painter of Modern Life and Other Essays*, J Mayne (trans and ed) (London, Phaidon) 3.

Belleau, M-C (1997) 'The "*Juristes Inquiets*": Legal Classicism and Criticism in Early Twentieth-Century France' *Utah Law Review* 379.

Blackstone, W (2016) *Commentaries on the Laws of England*, Book I, D Lemmings (ed) (Oxford, Oxford University Press).

Cannon, G (1979) Sir William Jones: A Bibliography of Primary and Secondary Sources (Amsterdam: John Benjamins).

Del Mar, M (2017) 'Legal Reasoning in Pluralist Jurisprudence: The Practice of the Relational Imagination' in N Roughan and H Haplin (eds) *In Pursuit of Pluralist Jurisprudence* (Cambridge, Cambridge University Press) 40.

Del Mar, M (2018) 'Emotion Experiments in Legal Thought' 5 *Critical Analysis of Law* 9.

Del Mar, M (2020) 'The Legal Imagination: Individual, Interactive and Communal' in A Amaya and M Del Mar (eds) *Virtue, Emotion and Imagination in Law and Legal Reasoning* (Oxford, Hart Publishing).

Elgin, CZ (2020) 'Impartiality and Legal Reasoning' in A Amaya and M Del Mar (eds) *Virtue, Emotion and Imagination in Law and Legal Reasoning* (Oxford, Hart Publishing) 47.

Fulbecke, W (1600) A Direction or Preparatiue to the Study of the Lawe (London, Thomas Wright).

Gogröf-Voorhees, A (2004) Defining Modernism: Baudelaire and Nietzsche on Romanticism, Modernity, Decadence, and Wagner (New York, Peter Lang).

Ibbetson, D (1999) *A Historical Introduction to the Law of Obligations* (Oxford, Oxford University Press).

Jones, W (1781) *An Essay on the Law of Bailments* (London, J Nichols for Charles Dilly).

Kind, A (2016) 'Imagining under Constraints' in A Kind and P King (eds) *Knowledge Through Imagination* (Oxford, Oxford University Press) 145.

Kind, A (2020) 'Empathy, Imagination, and the Law' in A Amaya and M Del Mar (eds) *Virtue, Emotion and Imagination in Law and Legal Reasoning* (Oxford, Hart Publishing) 179.

Morton, A (2020) 'Imagining Motives' in A Amaya and M Del Mar (eds) *Virtue, Emotion and Imagination in Law and Legal Reasoning* (Oxford, Hart Publishing) 199.

Rakoff, TD and Minow, M (2007) 'A Case for Another Case Method' 60 *Vanderbilt Law Review* 597.

Rogers, JS (1995) *The Early History of the Law of Bills and Notes: A Study of the Origins of Anglo-American Commercial Law* (Cambridge, Cambridge University Press).

Schneider, HA (2009) '*Katz v. United States*: The Untold Story' 40 *McGeorge Law Review* 13.

Sherwin, RK (2008) 'Sublime Jurisprudence: On the Ethical Education of the Legal Imagination in Our Time' 83 *Chicago-Kent Law Review* 1157.

Siraganian, L (2020) *Corporate Form: Personhood, Politics, and Meaning in Legal and Literary Modernism* (Oxford, Oxford University Press).

Slobogin, C and Schumacher, JE (1993) 'Reasonable Expectations of Privacy and Autonomy in Fourth Amendment Cases: An Empirical Look at Understandings Recognized and Permitted by Society' 42 *Duke Law Journal* 727.

Stern, S (2017a) 'Legal and Literary Fictions' in B Meyler and E Anker (eds) *New Directions in Law and Literature* (Oxford, Oxford University Press) 313.

Stern, S (2017b) '*R. v. Jones* (1703): The Origins of the Reasonable Person' in P Handler, H Mares, and I Williams (eds) *Landmark Cases in Criminal Law* (Oxford, Hart Publishing) 59.

Tobia, K (2018) 'How People Judge What is Reasonable' 70 *Alabama Law Review* 293.

Vico, G (1968) *The New Science of Giambattista Vico*, TG Bergin and MH Fisch (eds) (Ithaca, Cornell University Press).

Vico, G (2000) *Universal Right*, G Pinton and M Diehl (trans and eds) (Amsterdam, Rodopi).

Watson, A (1988) *Failures of the Legal Imagination* (Philadelphia: University of Pennsylvania Press).

Williams, D (2019) 'Accident' in S Stern, M Del Mar, and B Meyler (eds) *The Oxford Handbook of Law and Humanities* (Oxford, Oxford University Press) 335.

Zimmerman, R (1996) *The Law of Obligations: Roman Foundations of the Civilian Tradition* (Oxford, Oxford University Press).

13

The Legal Imagination: Individual, Interactive and Communal

MAKSYMILIAN DEL MAR*

I. Introduction

Theories of legal reasoning – including those on imagination, emotion and virtue in legal adjudication – often focus on individuals. Typically, this means an emphasis on individual judges, and their processes of reasoning, imagining or feeling, or on virtues appropriate to a single judge. A spectacular instance of this focus in contemporary legal theory is of course the Dworkinian figure of Hercules – the ideal, super-human judge. The level of the individual is undoubtedly important – and this is no less so when we are interested in the role and value of imagination, emotion and virtue. And yet, if we focus exclusively on the individual level, we risk obscuring from view a great deal that is important about legal reasoning and its methods and devices – including about the role and value of imagination, emotion and virtue. In order to avoid this, we ought to theorise – or so this chapter argues – in a multi-level way, that is, with attention to the individual level, the interactive level, and the communal level.

To work in this multi-level way is also to be sensitive to the different temporalities at which legal reasoning operates: for instance, individual judges seek to balance doing justice in the instant case with caring for the quality of the law in the future; and whereas interaction typically occurs in the relatively short duration of a trial, the level of communal practice (and its forms of expression) is spread out temporally over long periods of time (years, decades or even centuries).

My focus in this chapter is on the practice – and ultimately also the role and value – of imagination at the three levels and with sensitivity to the different temporalities at play. Given the themes of this volume, I seek also to pay some (though inevitably inadequate) attention to the relations between imagination, emotion and virtue. If there is a great deal more work that can and ought to be done on

*I am grateful to my co-editor, Amalia Amaya, for her characteristically insightful and helpful comments on an earlier version of this chapter.

imagination at the level of interaction and community (and, with respect to the latter, over time), then this also applies to emotion and virtue: for example, what are the affective interactive dynamics within courtrooms? What kinds of emotions are shared (enabling, say, joint attention), and how do they persist over time in particular communities of legal practice? Can we speak of some legal institutions as constituted by particular communities of feeling? Further, what institutional virtues are appropriate to the legal context – might we speak, for instance, of virtuous courts?

The last decade has seen a flurry of activity on imagination – though the term and concept has a long history, stretching back at least to Plato and Aristotle (and especially the latter's treatment of phantasia in *De Anima*).[1] This interest has included not only the philosophers,[2] but also a wide variety of scholars from the social sciences,[3] the humanities,[4] and psychology.[5] Within this growing literature, there is increasing awareness of the vital role of imagination as a method of inquiry – for instance, in philosophy (where the status of thought experiments has long been discussed, but has intensified of late)[6] and in the sciences.[7] Some of the new interest in imagination is covering old ground, but under a new label; for example, consider the long-standing tradition of rhetorical studies of the languages of philosophy, history, science and law,[8] or recall the analysis of fictionality in some of these domains.[9] Some scholars are now also beginning to speak of 'simulated experience'.[10] Within legal scholarship, too, there have been explicit studies of imagination,[11] and related (though not often seen as related) studies on the role of fictions in law.[12] If one adds to this list the literature on the specific devices associated with imagination – for example, just to mention two, metaphor[13] and figure[14] – then this literature is almost unmanageably large, if not entirely overwhelming.

[1] On phantasia, see Watson (1988). For sweeping histories of imagination, see eg Brann (2017) [1991]; Kearney (1988); Cocking (1984); and Ferraris (1996).

[2] To give just two recent examples, see the chapters and references in Kind (2016), and in Kind and Klug (2016).

[3] For a recent collection, see Zittoun and Glaveanu (2018).

[4] This is especially so among literary theorists, many of whom are recently turning to the intersection between literature and cognitive science: eg see Cave (2016), Spolsky (2015) and the chapters in Zunshine (2014).

[5] See eg Byrne (2016) on the counterfactual imagination. This includes developmental psychology – see eg Harris (2000). See also Markman, Klein and Suhr (2008).

[6] See eg Camp (2009); and Stuart, Fehige and Brown (2017).

[7] See Elgin (1996); Stuart (2014); Godfrey-Smith and Levy (forthcoming).

[8] For science, see eg Fahnestock (1999); for law, see Goodrich (1987) and Shaw (2017); for history, see Hayden White (1973); for philosophy, see La Caze (2002), and Le Doeuff (1989).

[9] See, classically, Vaihinger (1924) [1911], and more recently, Appiah (2017). See also Gallagher (2006); and Walsh (2007).

[10] See Silcox (2018).

[11] See, famously, James Boyd White (1973); and Winter (2001).

[12] See Del Mar and Twining (2015), and Stern (2017).

[13] See, most recently, the chapters and references in Hanne and Weisberg (2018).

[14] See eg Moran (2003).

This chapter is not the moment for an overview of the principal themes and disagreements in this literature, though I shall be touching on some of these below. Instead, my aim in this chapter is to propose a basic model of imagination (in section II), and then flesh out its role and value at the three levels mentioned above (in sections III to V).[15]

II. The Basic Model – Artefacts and Related Processes of Imagination

To imagine on the model I here propose is to combine two processes (this dual or double consciousness is key to the model): first, having been made aware of an artefact, we enter into a distinct epistemic frame, in which we take epistemic distance, suspending certain epistemic commitments and norms while retaining others; and, second, we simultaneously actively participate, by doing things with and thanks to those artefacts. Clearly, important to this model is the concept of an artefact. I model artefacts as fabricated forms that (1) capture our attention by signalling their own artifice; and (2) call on us to do something with them.

In broad terms, the above model of imagining is one that understands it as an epistemic activity – a particular distinctive way of engaging epistemically (rather than, say, withdrawing from the world, or being epistemically disinterested or irresponsible). It is also a model that is purposefully skeletal, allowing for multiple variations. Imagination can be exercised in a number of different ways, and there are different kinds of artefacts.

With respect to imagination, we enter into a distinct epistemic frame in different ways, regulating epistemic distance differently, and suspending different kinds of epistemic norms and commitments (we can, eg, suspend norms and commitment relating to reference, relevance, coherence, etc); and we can participate actively in different ways, along a spectrum of affective, sensory and kinetic involvement (eg we can suppose without mental imagery or affective involvement, or we can enact an imaginary perspective, experiencing it affectively and simulating it kinetically).

With regard to artefacts, these can signal their own artifice in different ways (some explicitly, eg as when we say 'Let us suppose X', and some implicitly, as when something appears overly stylised or patterned, eg alliteration); and they can call on us to participate in different ways, appealing to a range of affective, sensory and kinetic abilities (eg, artefacts can be under-specified and thus invite us to complete them – as in an ellipsis – or they can be incongruous, and ask us to resolve a tension – as in metaphor and its semantic clashes, which require work to make coherent).

[15] The model I provide is a much shorterned version of the fuller treatment in Del Mar (forthcoming).

Modelled in this way, there are many examples of artefacts in legal discourse and related processes of imagination. Here are four examples:

(1) *Legal fictions*: on the model I have proposed elsewhere,[16] fictions involve a temporary suspension of an operative fact while allowing for the imposition of the same normative consequence. For example, when a court treats it as if material contribution to injury has been proved when the evidence only shows material increase in risk, then it temporarily suspends the operative requirement of proof of causation (as material contribution), nevertheless allowing the plaintiff to succeed (see *McGhee v National Coal Board* (1972)). It thereby tolerates contradiction: again, it treats something as if it was proven when it knows it not to have been. Legal fictions are artefacts because they involve signalling of artifice, sometimes explicitly (eg 'let us treat this operative fact as having been proved when we know it has not been'), and sometimes implicitly (eg ignoring evidence to the contrary), and they invite us to do something (here, to search, even if this search is deferred, for some way to resolve the contradiction, and thus de-fictionalise the justification). As artefacts, they invite us to imagine because we take epistemic distance (we tolerate contradiction), and we simultaneously actively participate (we search for ways to resolve the contradiction, even if not immediately – eg by introducing a new explicit rule or exception, which no longer requires the fictionalisation of the operative fact);

(2) *Metaphors*: metaphors are strewn throughout legal discourse, and are commonly utilised in legal judgements and the submission of advocates. They are artefacts because they involve explicit (eg 'X is Y') or implicit signalling of artifice – we are put on epistemic alert by the semantic clash involved in relating two seemingly distant terms – and we are invited to do something, ie precisely to resolve the semantic incongruity by relating the terms (and their imagistic associations) in some way (or, more accurately, in multiple ways). They involve imagination because we take epistemic distance by, say, suspending the otherwise-operative epistemic norm of referentiality (not taking constitutions to really be living trees, as in the famous constitutional metaphor in *Edwards v Attorney-General for Canada* (1930)), and we simultaneously actively participate (we relate the two images in various ways – eg considering how constitutions change and grow, and thus require evolving and progressive interpretation).[17]

(3) *Figures*: the use of imaginary perspectives is frequent in law, for example as in the well recognised figure of the Reasonable Person, but involving a whole cast of imaginary characters deployed for a wide range of reasons.[18] Figures

[16] See Del Mar (2015).

[17] For more details on my own take on metaphor in legal thought, see Del Mar (2017a).

[18] See Moran (2003); and Del Mar (2018a). See also Morton (2020) and Stern (2020) (chapters eleven and twelve in this volume).

are artefacts because they implicitly or explicitly involve signalling artifice (eg by capitalisation of the Reasonable Person), and, in being under-specified (their qualities or characteristics left to be determined in any specific case), they invite and call on us to do something (precisely to construct mental imagery, eg run the film of what the Reasonable Person would have done in the circumstances of the case). This requires imagination, for it means we need to take epistemic distance (eg from certain of our own biases and proclivities, as well as our knowledge base, which may not be shared by the Reasonable Person), and we participate actively, ie we simulate an imaginary perspective, experience it, and reflect on our experience of it.

(4) *Scenarios*: these typically involve imagining the possible (but also sometimes fanciful) implications or consequences of adopting some proposed ruling or justification. They are common features of legal reasoning, featuring often in submissions of advocates and in interactions between advocates and judges. They are artefacts because they involve the implicit or explicit signalling of artifice (implicit, when, for example they are caricatures or involve hyperbole or exaggerated facts), and they invite us to do something by being under-specified (typically, scenarios are short, pithy narratives), ie they require us to construct mental imagery, playing out the scenarios in our minds. They involve the exercise of imagination because we take epistemic distance (we suppose such-and-such a scenario, and suspend certain norms, eg probability or likelihood), while participating actively (eg constructing mental imagery, experiencing the scenarios we imagine affectively, and reflecting on our affective responses to them).[19]

The above is, of course, but a thumbnail sketch of the complex domain of artefacts and related processes of imagination. Much of the devil, as always, is in the detailed analysis of each of these artefacts, and the different ways in which they involve imagination. To do this is outside the scope of this chapter, but what has been sketched above does I hope provide at least a taste sufficient to go on now to examine the role and value of artefacts and related processes of imagination at three different levels of practice: individual, interactive and communal, and with sensitivity to the different temporalities at play.

III. The Individual

When we analyse legal reasoning at the level of the individual, it is useful to model that practice as one engaged in by epistemically limited, institutionally constrained and affectively embodied agents. Thus, the first step in unpacking the role and value of imagination at the level of the individual is explaining this

[19] For some more details, see Del Mar (2018b).

rather dense proposition. This cannot be done in any real detail here, but a few words need to be said, as they provide the backdrop to much that follows.

At first blush, to assert that individuals are epistemically limited is to state something so obvious it goes without saying. However, there is more to this acknowledgement than meets the eye. That is because at stake here is the kind of attitude we take to the individuals whose processes of reasoning we study. To model those individuals as epistemically limited already excludes certain approaches that idealise the figure of the individual, typically the judge. The obvious example, already referred to at the outset of this chapter, is Dworkin's Hercules.[20] I would argue, though cannot properly do so here, that Dworkin's approach is misleading, as it obscures from view precisely those processes of reasoning that judges engage in because they are limited in what they know and what they can discern on any one occasion (especially on their own, without assistance from others). In other words, there are distinct processes that individuals engage in under conditions of uncertainty – including normative uncertainty (ie uncertainty about what values and interests may be at stake in a certain case or cases of that kind) – and these will be obscured from view if we begin with and anchor our account of reasoning in an idealised figure (eg with infinite knowledge, acumen and patience, as with Dworkin's Hercules).

It is, then, important not to idealise individuals when theorising about legal reasoning. However, it is also important not to be too cynical about legal reasoning. When we approach the study of legal reasoning with too much of an attitude of suspicion – of judges hiding their real intentions, said to be informed or determined by their political sensibilities – then we miss those processes of genuine cognitive effort and struggle under conditions of uncertainty. Judges often simply do not know how best to decide a case – and thus it is misleading to represent them as already knowing where they want to go, and then merely manipulating language to persuade others of the appropriateness of their decision. To conceive of judges as so thoroughly strategic will, once again, miss the distinct processes (including of imagination and emotion), and the distinct virtues, exercised under conditions of uncertainty, where a judge will grapple and struggle with the best way to proceed.

To say all this is not to deny that these approaches – idealistic and cynical alike – contain important insights, but it is to say that we ought to make room for a middle path: one that seeks to understand what processes individuals (judges especially, but also advocates) engage in, in good faith and under conditions of epistemic and normative uncertainty. This means situating oneself as a theorist as much as possible in the circumstances of an individual judge who does not yet know, and who may not come to know in the near future, what is most normatively relevant to deciding this case and cases of this kind. Thus, rather than positing (in hindsight) what the theorist already takes to be the right answer, and then either praising or criticising the processes of the judge, theorists ought to try,

[20] See Dworkin (1986); and see the critique by Fish (1982).

as much as possible, to see how judges grasp for – how they reach out to explore – what may be normatively relevant (ie what values and interests may be at stake). Indeed, as I shall discuss in the next sections, what may seem like bugs or failures at the level of an individual modelled idealistically or cynically – or with the benefit of hindsight – may in fact be features or benefits that contribute to the vitality and resourcefulness of a legal tradition – for instance because they require interactive and collective (rather than individual, Herculean) effort.

In addition to being epistemically limited, individuals engaged in legal reasoning are also institutionally constrained. Depending on the exact institutional context, judges rely, for instance, on the submissions of advocates to frame the case and its issues and facts (at least initially) and to bring forward the proposed relevant legal materials. Judges also rely on the character and state of related knowledge practices, for example their assistants and clerks, and the library and its methods of storing and finding potentially relevant materials.[21] Judges and advocates are limited by time, sometimes quite drastically (in the US context, advocates only have 30 minutes each to present their arguments), but always to some degree (some courts are more overburdened by their case load than others). And specific institutions have specific habits and rituals, for example as to relations between judges (eg how much dialogue there is, what the process of exchanging drafts is like), and between judges and advocates (the climate of such exchanges – how formal, how open to humour), as well as a whole host of other factors (whether the proceedings are filmed and televised, whether the judiciary is a career one or taken from the Bar, and so on). Theories of legal reasoning only rarely take such institutional constraints seriously,[22] and yet they have an enormous impact on the kinds of processes individuals engage in (including the manner in which their imagination is exercised).

Finally, individuals – judges and advocates – are also affectively embodied beings. As demonstrated by other chapters in this volume[23] there is now growing recognition of the historical[24] and contemporary[25] pervasiveness and importance of emotions in legal environments generally, including in legal reasoning. A great deal more work needs to be done here, especially in terms of recognising the wide variety of emotions experienced by individuals in processes of legal reasoning, including, for instance, satisfaction at summarising a complex set of facts, disgust or indignation at some testimony, emotional experience of counsel

[21] See eg Halliday (2014).

[22] There are important exceptions, of course, see eg Bell (2006) who lists further institutional constraints. I do not mean here to list all the possible constraints – and I emphasise in particular institutional constraints. Theorists of legal reasoning have of course extensively examined constraints on reasoning in legal contexts, eg the constraints imposed by authority reasons.

[23] See especially the chapters by Zipursky (2020), van Domselaar (2020), Brady (2020), White (2020), Hansberg (2020), Blum (2020) and Kind (2020) in this volume (chapters four, five, eight, six, nine, seven, and ten respectively).

[24] See, recently, Bailey and Knight (2017); and Holmes and Johnson (2018).

[25] See eg recently Sellers (2017); and the papers in Feenan (2017), which includes my take on the role of compassion in legal reasoning (see Del Mar (2017b)).

narratives, the pride taken in certain legal traditions or concepts (eg common law constitutionalism), or the importance of epistemic emotions like certainty, doubt, wonder or curiosity.[26] There are many ways in which aesthetics and emotion intersect in legal reasoning, but although there is important work on each, they are rarely put in dialogue.[27] There is also some – though not as much – work on the embodied and kinetic dimensions of legal reasoning. Individuals are, of course, embodied creatures, and if we are to take the experiences of individuals seriously, then we cannot ignore the role of the body. This has been recognised by some legal theorists, mostly inspired by the work of contemporary cognitive theory,[28] and there is also important work done by feminist theories on legal reasoning that foregrounds the related, but specific, issues of gender and sexuality.[29]

For present purposes, what is key to this recognition of the affectively embodied character of individuals is that we acknowledge that processes of inquiry into what may be normatively relevant (what values and interests may be at stake in a case and in cases of this kind) cannot operate in an affective and disembodied vacuum. This is a thesis that, of course, requires a proper well-worked account – as has been done in the case of moral reasoning[30] – and that is outside the scope of this chapter. What I will refer to below, however, are how processes of imagination involve and relate in complex ways to affective and kinetic processes. For now, I simply assert that an important part of the background of the study of the role and value of imagination in legal reasoning has to be an acknowledgement that normative judgement is impossible without the affective and kinetic involvement of individuals.

Proceeding, then, with these background assumptions about individuals engaged in processes of legal reasoning in mind, I will, in what follows in this section, explore three further themes: first, how imagination is valuable for individuals conceived in the above way; second, how imagination is valuable for individuals balancing the need to make a decision in the instance case with a concern for the quality of the law; and, third, how imagination relates to virtue-based approaches to legal reasoning.

A. Imagination and the Inquiry into Normative Relevance

When engaged in searching for what may be normatively relevant – what values and interests may be at stake in the case before them and in cases of that kind

[26] Here, we can draw on affectively-sensitive pragmatist epistemologies, which recognise the role of a variety of epistemic emotions. For a taste of these approaches, see Brun, Doguoglu and Kuenzle (2016).

[27] On the aesthetics of legal thought, see eg Schlag (2002) and Shaw (2017).

[28] See Winter (2001).

[29] See especially the various manifestations of the Feminist Judgments Project, eg Hunter, McGlynn and Rackley (2010).

[30] See eg Fesmire (2003); Prinz (2009); and Johnson (2018).

(the latter of course being a judgement the individual must make) – an individual will often be uncertain (in part also because of the institutional pressures of time and resources) as to how to conceive and articulate what is normatively relevant. Some guidance and assistance may, of course, be gleaned from the submission of advocates. The judge(s) may also be more or less experienced in this area of the law, having more or less recent knowledge of potentially past relevant cases and scholarship on the issues. However, in many instances, these materials will be inadequate – and even if they are perceived to be adequate, they will require (re-) interpretation in light of the present facts and possible consequences of the decision. In such circumstances – which, as I say, will be common – a judge will feel a need for, and will grasp for, devices that will enable non-committal exploration and experimentation as to what may be normatively relevant. We can think of these as little artificial shelters for inquiry – ways of creating space and time to generate possibilities and evaluate them. Artefacts and related processes of imagination are precisely that: they fulfil the role of, and are valuable because they enable, searching tentatively for what may be normatively relevant. In addition, such artefacts and related processes of imagination often require affective and kinetic involvement, and so they connect to us as affectively embodied beings. They are also fun and pleasurable to engage in.

The examples provided earlier in this chapter illustrate this well. Faced with a case where a plaintiff has proved everything but causation (at least in accordance with the test requiring material contribution), a court searches tentatively for how differently causation may need to be conceived of in cases of harm where scientific uncertainty prevails (where there is just not enough scientific certainty about what causes some harm, eg dermatitis from exposure to brick dust).[31] Enabling that search in the instant case – but also deferring to it a later stage – is the artefact of a legal fiction. The judges treat causation – still understood in the traditional sense of material contribution – as if it was proved, when they know it has not, thereby making a decision in the case, and signalling that the law may need to change (eg to material increase in risk, and for cases of this kind – it being left open what the scope of that kind will be). The point here is that a fiction is precisely a little shelter of inquiry: it opens a space, and creates time, for further reflection on whether, and how, it may be appropriate to change the requirements of causation in this area. Metaphors, scenarios and figures also perform this role, and are valuable because of it. Grasping for the appropriate approach to interpreting the Canadian constitution as an imperial court (the Privy Council), the judges deploy a metaphor of the constitution as a living tree – living, that is, in Canadian soil (rather than in England), and thus allowing for a more progressive interpretation than an English-based test would allow, but also raising the general question (to be examined in further cases, precisely by reference to the metaphor) of the

[31] See *McGhee v National Coal Board* (1972), and in the cases that followed.

appropriateness of certain methods of constitutional interpretation (especially in relations between empires and colonies).[32]

Notice that in these two examples, the degree of affective and kinetic involvement by the individual judge varies. It is relatively high in the case of the metaphor – the judge grapples here with the abstract articulation of a method of constitutional interpretation by exploring kinetically the concrete image of a tree, with all of its affective overtones of pride in the health and progress of a distinct legal order (for the imperialists, a colony). It is relatively low in the case of the fiction, which requires only a thin supposition, deferring resolution of the contradiction for a later occasion. Even in the case of the fiction, however, and especially if we take a gregarious approach to emotion, there may be frustration (a certain kind of aesthetic annoyance) experienced at having to tolerate such a contradiction (asserting proof without the evidence supporting it) in the absence of a satisfactory alternative test of causation.[33] This can be valuable in signalling to future courts that a change is needed (a value that already points us towards the social character of legal reasoning, explored in subsequent sections).

The role for affective and kinetic involvement is high also in the case of scenarios and figures. In the former case, a judge will play out the scenario in her mind (constructing mental imagery) and make normative judgements about the appropriateness of the behaviour of the imaginary characters in the scenarios based, at least in part, on whether she sympathises with one or other of those characters. Similarly so with figures: simulating a film of what the Reasonable Person would have done, a judge compares their feelings about the reasonableness of the actions of the Reasonable Person with the actions of the victims/accused or the plaintiff/defendant.[34] In all these cases, artefacts and related processes of imagination enable a tentative, non-committal search and exploration of what may be normatively relevant for the case at hand and cases of this kind.

B. Imagination and the Quality of the Law

The second theme that impinges upon the role and value of imagination for individuals – and one to which allusion has already been made immediately above – is that of balancing the need to make a decision in the instance case with a concern for the quality of the law. Judges are mindful of deciding not only the instant case, but also of the potential impact of the decision they make on future cases, and, in that respect, on the quality of the law in general in this area (whatever 'area' may

[32] See *Edwards v Attorney-General for Canada* (1930).

[33] For an argument that supposition connects (even if indirectly) to the affect system, see Arcangeli (2018).

[34] I give some more details of this process, inspired by Adam Smith's model of the impartial spectator, in Del Mar (2018a).

mean for them). Thus, at the individual level, too, there are multiple temporalities at play: for instance, there is the temporarily of the instant case and the temporality of the future (in which potentially alike cases may arise). Artefacts and related processes of imagination are valuable in part because they assist judges to keep one eye on the instant case and one eye on the future:

- A judge can use an artefact to decide the case, while not changing the law, and not offering many resources to future courts, but nevertheless signalling the need for change in the future. The clearest artefact that judges can use for this purpose is that of a legal fiction – a fiction does not change the law,[35] but does allow for a decision in the case, all the while suggesting to future courts that something may need to be introduced here (a new rule or a new exception to the rule).
- A judge can use an artefact to decide the case, while not changing the law, but offering some concrete resources to future courts. Some uses of figures and scenarios allow for this. Thus, the use of a scenario in obiter by a judge – mentioning the scenario, but distinguishing it from the facts of the present case (it thus not being strictly speaking necessary to deciding the case) – can introduce resources for future courts (whose facts may be closer to the scenario than the actual facts in the case). This does not change the law, but it does offer (optional) resources for future courts. It may also signal that the law is creaking under the pressure of the facts of new cases, and that further distinctions are called for, or that more is at stake than the current law recognises.[36]
- A judge can use an artefact to decide the case, while changing the law but doing so (more or less tentatively). Thus, although changing the law, the manner in which this is done is unlike that of introducing a new explicit rule or exception – it retains its subjunctive-like (rather than assertive or indicative) character. Some uses of metaphor, scenario and figure fulfil this role. For instance, stating that a constitution is a living tree does change the law – in this case, on what is the appropriate way for an imperial court to interpret the constitution of a former colony – and it also introduces concrete resources for future courts that will also be tasked with interpreting such constitutions. But it does so quite tentatively, leaving much that is open: given certain cultural associations with trees (as living organisms – an association strengthened by referring to a 'living' tree) – the metaphor certainly has a progressive flavour; nevertheless, the metaphor itself could be interpreted in a more conservative manner, eg emphasising the roots of the tree.

Exercising imagination, then, can allow judges to balance doing justice in the instant case with caring for the quality of the law in the future.

[35] This is controversial – see Del Mar (2015).

[36] For some further details, see Del Mar (2018b).

C. Imagination and Virtue

Finally, let me mention some ways in which the role and value of imagination, as conceived above for individuals, may intersect with some of the work on virtue in legal reasoning. Other chapters in this collection focus more squarely on virtues[37] – and I acknowledge the risks involved in addressing virtues as briefly as I do here. I therefore make the remarks below tentatively, and in the spirit of suggestion.

If one thinks of virtues as acquired character traits, and one further extends virtue theory to the domain of epistemology, one then opens up the prospect of epistemic virtues, ie acquired character traits that are beneficial for epistemic inquiry. Of course, there is much disagreement in the literature on just what ought to count as a virtue (some, for instance, resist the idea of acquired character traits, preferring to think of faculties, such as memory, as virtues). There is just as much disagreement on what is meant by beneficial, ie is it the internal qualities of the person with the virtue (their motivations, etc.) or is it the external qualities (eg the consequences of the virtue being exercised), or some mixture? Furthermore, there is considerable disagreement on which virtues are beneficial for epistemic inquiry, even if one does define them as acquired character traits. How might we relate all this to imagination?

If one is sympathetic to the idea of imagination as a faculty, one might be tempted to draw on the theories supporting 'faculty virtues'.[38] If one is further minded to see imagination as a faculty, one could suggest imagination is a faculty virtue. I myself resist such a move, preferring to see imagination as a mental process or activity. If one does resist that move, then another possibility is to translate imagination into an acquired character trait, such as imaginativeness (akin, for instance, to creativity). I resist this too. The danger I see in speaking of imaginativeness, and tying imagination too close to creativity, is that it will push one's account of imagination into the realm of a rarefied exercise of genius, dependent on some account of what it means to be creative. I prefer, instead, to see imagination as an ordinary, everyday process (although also one that takes on specific qualities in particular contexts, such as adjudication), which we exercise often, and often without creativity.

There remains one further option, however, for connecting imagination to virtue theory. And that is to consider the links between artefacts and imagination on the one hand, and the development and flourishing of certain epistemic virtues on the other hand.

Some of the epistemic virtues that scholars have defended have included: open-mindedness, intellectual courage, intellectual caution, intellectual humility, intellectual generosity, epistemic temperance, intellectual perseverance, inquisitiveness and curiosity.[39] Some of these virtues – as well as others – have also been

[37] See especially the chapters by Amaya (2020) and Elgin (2020) in this volume (chapters two and three, respectively).

[38] See eg Goldman (2006).

[39] The literature is large; for a helpful overview, see Alfano, Greco and Turri (2017).

applied to the adjudicatory context.[40] Further, in some accounts of these virtues – perhaps most obviously open-mindedness, inquisitiveness and curiosity – appeals are made to the role and value of imagination. For instance, Jason Baehr, in his account of open-mindedness,[41] speaks of the importance of detaching oneself from one's commitments, considering alternatives to one's view, and imagining or conceiving ways of thinking where no data is available. It would not be difficult to connect open-mindedness to the above model of artefacts and related processes of imagination. Where, for instance, we imagine figurally – participating affectively, sensorily and kinetically from an imaginary perspective – then we are indeed detaching ourselves from some of our commitments and personal knowledge, not only considering (or conceiving) but indeed experiencing alternatives to our own view.

Even, however, where imagination is not appealed to directly, we may nevertheless want to claim that artefacts and imagination contribute to the development and flourishing of a whole variety of epistemic virtues. Constructing and processing a metaphor, for instance, takes time: we first attend to a piece of language that signals its own artifice to us, and we do something with it, for example, we enter into a distinct epistemic frame in which we suspend, say, the epistemic norms of reference or coherence, and we explore and seek to resolve the (for instance) kinetic discordance set up by a metaphorical relation. Insofar as this is a process that takes time, as well as effort, it can contribute, for example, to the epistemic virtues of caution and perseverance.

Further, given the invitational character of artefacts (as above, how they are often used to signal to others the need for change, generating resources for future readers, and thus involving deference to the views of others), one could argue that they contribute to the epistemic virtues of intellectual humility and intellectual generosity. Imagining a metaphor together, and seeing how differently others do so, or being witness to the many different ways that others construct imaginary perspectives, or observing the manifold variations others can invent for scenarios, we come to attend to the limits and finitude of our own cognitive dispositions or affective associations, and we come to see the benefits of inviting and including the views of others.

Part of the value of artefacts and imagination, then, may consist in how they contribute to the emergence and nourishment of certain epistemic virtues.

IV. The Interactive Level

I have spent considerable time here on the level of the individual – in part because of the very clear and important relations between imagination, emotion and virtue at this level. However, already in the elaboration of the role and value of

[40] See the chapters in Part I of this volume, and Amaya and Ho (2012).
[41] See Baehr (2011).

imagination at that level, it became quickly necessary to appeal to its social dimensions, for example in various signalling, invitational or communicative functions of artefacts. Indeed, an important part of the point of studying the role and value of imagination in legal reasoning is that it helps us see the social dimensions of it. This is so at two distinct, but related, levels: the level of interaction (most typically, in a courtroom, and thus between judges and judges, and judges and advocates); and the level of the community (especially over time), and particularly in terms of its language, which can be conceived of as the resource of a community composed of past, present and future generations. In this section I explore the former; in the next section, the latter.

The individualistic bias is well entrenched, both in general philosophical theories of reasoning, as well as in theories of legal reasoning (an emblematic example of which is Dworkin's Hercules, already mentioned above). As Anthony Laden explains, in his excellent book, *Reasoning: A Social Picture* (2012), the standard view of reasoning is that of an:

> … activity of reflectively arriving at judgement through the alignment of the progress of our thoughts with certain formal structures in order to better navigate the world, to solve particular problems and, perhaps, seek out the truth or the good. I am reasoning according to this picture when I am working out the implications of a moral commitment, or figuring out whether the evidence in front of me is sufficient to justify my belief in the truth of a proposition, or figuring out how best to accomplish my aims given the obstacles I face.[42]

Laden proposes a different, social picture of reasoning. A paradigmatic analogy for him is of reasoning as a (casual) conversation. The analogy is significant for various reasons – for instance, in conversation, unlike in one-way communication, surprise is a feature, not a bug: 'conversation thrives on a certain degree of surprise', whereas 'surprises in one-way communication are a sign of failure'.[43] Further, conversation is an open-ended activity, and does not have 'a natural end':

> … casual conversation is an activity … which is structured as on-going … [it] leaves room for playfulness, for offering new ways of seeing or occupying or shaping spaces of reasons we inhabit which can be rejected without offence or a disruption of our relationships … It affords low-cost opportunities to attempt to re-shape those spaces and low-cost opportunities for others to either accept or reject our suggested changes. At the same time, it provides us opportunity to take responsibility for our positions, and thus to fully engage in the reciprocal and open-ended offering of invitations that my alternative [social] picture says is definitive of the act of reasoning.[44]

The reference to the issuing of invitations is important – and echoes what was said about artefacts above (ie that they are precisely invitations to others to do something with them). It allows Laden to characterise the following acts as typical in a

[42] Laden (2012), 9.
[43] Ibid, 119.
[44] Ibid, 101.

social account of reasoning: 'proposing, engaging, conversing, and other activities of mutual attunement' – as distinct from 'calculating, deducing, problem-solving and judging', which are typical in monadic pictures of reasoning.[45] For Laden, then, 'I am reasoning' on the social account 'when I am listening to your response to what I have said and taking it seriously', or 'when I am telling a story in response to something you have said'.[46] Indeed, more strongly, reason in the social sense 'requires that we are not commanding or ordering, ignoring or manipulating, blindly obeying or deferring'.[47] When you take 'my words as potential reasons … you leave some space for them to make a difference in what you do' and, similarly, 'offering you what I take to be a reason and not a command, means that I leave space for you to rebut or criticise it'.[48] A good reasoner, on this account, is much like 'a good listener: someone who is able to hear others' words as invitations, and be affected or moved by them, and someone who is able to hear and appropriately react to the responses her own invitations prompt'.[49] Good reasoning builds, develops and shapes relationships.[50]

Laden's account, and its implications for the study of legal reasoning, call out for further study, but already this barebones sketch allows us to locate the role and value of imagination in an important way. An essential part of reasoning in a legal context is the constant exchange of views – sometimes in an institutionally adversarial (and competitive) setting, and sometimes in a less adversarial manner (as in dialogues between judges). This interaction, occurring in real time, is vital – not only because it provides each party with an opportunity to be heard, and to try to persuade the judges of the merits of their position – but also because it allows for the investigation of the issues and values at stake in the case and in cases of this kind. Some of the language in these interactions will be assertive – it will claim this or that, it will express belief and conviction, or it will make predictions; it will, in short, be very close to a language driven by belief. However, not all of it will be like that – I venture to suggest that much of it will be considerably less assertive, more suggestive, and more tentative – indeed, much more like invitations to others in the course of a conversation.

Recall the examples of artefacts given above: fictions, metaphors, scenarios and figures. Inquiry into what may be normatively relevant often proceeds by way of these artefacts and – here is the suggestion – it also often proceeds interactively. We typically suppose something together – we suggest to another, 'Let us suppose X' or 'Let us say X, for the sake of argument', as part of an interactive inquiry into some issue. Or, one of us proposes a metaphor, and this proposal is directed at someone or a group of persons, as an invitation to them to explore the metaphor

[45] Ibid, 8.
[46] Ibid, 8–9.
[47] Ibid, 13.
[48] Ibid, 28.
[49] Ibid, 46.
[50] See ibid, 101.

together. Indeed, insofar as artefacts invite us to do something – because, say, they are incongruous (as with the semantic clash in metaphor) – then they are inherently interactive devices, or devices that are made for interaction. It might be even said that they – amongst other things of course – enable interaction, and are themselves dependent on interaction. Importantly, metaphors enable interaction in a way that preserves and protects difference and disagreement: people can, and often do, have very different associations with a certain metaphor, and thus explore the relations between the images in a metaphor differently, often starkly differently. Metaphors, then, contribute to the quality of interaction, preserving the possibility of multiple voices (including tension between them).

What goes for fictions or metaphors goes also for scenarios and figures: an advocate offers a scenario, a judge reacts by proposing a variation, or perhaps the advocate for the other side offers a counter-example, and then the other advocate responds, and so on. The conversation is ongoing; the interactive inquiry into what may be normatively relevant, whis is being explored through the scenario, does not appear to have a natural end. It is structured as an interaction – it is not one-way communication, designed by one side to persuade the other (though of course it may sometimes be intended to also, or even mainly, have this effect).[51] In the case of figures too – we exchange (sometimes very different) views on what the Reasonable Person would or might have done, and explore variations or contrasting accounts of that simulation together. Artefacts, then, can be understood to be invitations to participate together, interactively, in an imaginative space – the space of metaphor, for instance, or of a scenario or of the doings and sayings of an invented character. Again, to speak of interaction here is not to say the encounters must be friendly and devoid of strategic maneovuering: indeed, what often matters (to the quality of interaction) is the exchange of different (including opposing) views.

To give some more flavour to these abstract claims, consider the following exchange between judge and advocate, in the case of *California v Carney* (1985).[52] The issue in the case was whether a motor home fell within the definition of a vehicle (if it did, then the police did not need a warrant to search it):

> **Judge:** What would you do with a houseboat?
>
> **Lawyer:** A houseboat? I think that would be covered, and I think that the –
>
> **Judge:** It has wheels?
>
> **Lawyer:** No, it's a vessel, and it is covered by the same rule. …
>
> **Judge:** Well, I want to be more specific. There is a houseboat. It's tied up to a dock that's got no motor on it at all. It's just sitting there. And it's hooked up to the sewage, electricity, etc, and it's right beside a house. The house is covered, and the boat is not?

[51] Part of the point here is that artefacts are not in the control of any one party, including the party that creates them and may intend them not as an invitation but as a means of persuasion. Further, there is nothing that suggests that some artefact cannot have dual functions: intended as a means of persuasion (and sometimes successfully so) and serving as an invitation to interact in an imaginative space.

[52] See *California v Carney* (1985).

Lawyer: That's correct. It's sort of like an automobile that is parked right next to the house in the driveway. The automobile might not be covered, and the house is.

Judge: But the automobile has a motor in it –

Lawyer: That's correct.

Judge: – and the houseboat does not.

Lawyer: No. There may be oars. There may be some way to move that from one place to another.

Judge: There 'may be'. May be. I've seen houses moved, too.

[Laughter]

Lawyer: As have I. I've passed a few of them on the beltway.

Judge: You've got to get more than that.

Lawyer: Certainly. Again, the objective indicia of mobility would be what the officers are looking to. Perhaps in Your Honour's example, they would be looking to see if there's oars there. There's no motor. There's no way to move that thing.

Judge: Well, let me add one more thing. It's been tied up there for the last 36 years.

[Laughter]

Lawyer: If the officer doesn't know that, I don't see why he should be called to that particular knowledge. One thing he does know about when he is dealing with a house –

Judge: The moral is, don't live in a houseboat.[53]

In this case, the scenario is introduced by the judge – but often enough advocates also offer scenarios, typically in an attempt to discredit an argument from the opposing side. My point here is this: exchanges like this may be seen to be more or less successful attempts at persuasion, but they can also be understood as interactive explorations of what may be normatively relevant to not only the case at hand, but to cases of this kind.

The above exchange also illustrates the pleasurable and fun character of these interactions, which often involve humour and wit. This is also part of their role and value: humour has important cognitive and political values. It can diffuse tension, and it can help build or re-build relationships, despite disagreement. Indeed, the role and value of humour in the legal contexts deserves more study, and can draw on the literature that explores relations between the genre of comedy and politics.[54]

At the level of interaction, these artefacts and related process of imagination, are important for other reasons too. They are often indirect ways of interacting, ie rather than direct confrontation of assertions as to what ought to be done, we explore what may be normatively relevant through, say, a scenario or by imagining the film of an imaginary figure. In that sense, one could argue that these artefacts and related processes of imagination spark conversations (enabling a form of joint

[53] The transcript of the oral proceedings is available online: https://www.oyez.org/cases/1984/83-859.

[54] See eg Fletcher (2016). There is a need for more scholarship on the relations between comedy and legal reasoning.

attention, in this case, on an imaginary object), and sustain them. And, they enable the sharing of, or at least exchange of, (sometimes quite different) affective and kinetic experience: we may laugh together at the absurdity of some scenario, or we can exchange affective reactions to, for instance, the behaviour of some invented character in a scenario or to some metaphor. In short, artefacts and imagination can enable and enhance the quality of interaction, which itself is such an important part of the adjudicatory process.[55]

V. The Communal Level

In addition to the individual and interactive levels at which we can study imagination, we also have the level of the community. There are many ways of approaching this communal level – and the role and value (though no doubt also danger) of collective or communal imagination. Indeed, one might argue that twentieth century philosophies of imagination have been split along the lines of approaches that are focused either on individuals or on communities. This latter focus was, in part, inspired by the influence of psychoanalysis and structuralism (and of course the key figures of Marx and Freud). Thus, theorists have spoken of 'social imaginaries', which tend to be conceived of as shared and sub-conscious forms (eg myths, fables, etc) that are more or less determinative of individual cognition. This is important work – and it suffices to mention Jacques Lacan, Cornelius Castoriadis, Benedict Anderson and Charles Taylor – to get a sense of that importance. Some of this work, too, has found its way into legal scholarship.[56] Nevertheless, it remains the case that in this work individual consciousness is depicted as overly passive, and too determined by the social or collective level.[57] Can we examine the communal level without making it overly determinative – and thus allow the communal level to co-exist alongside the individual and the interactive? I think we can, though we need to proceed with care.

It is also important to pay attention to the temporalities of the communal level, especially the sense in which we might speak of the value of legal language for a community over time.[58] This also helps us see that at the communal level, the range of persons included is much wider, and refers not only to judges and

[55] It would be fascinating, in future work, to connect the importance of interaction in adjudication to the recent emergence of interactive science: see eg Tylen et al (2010).

[56] Attention to the collective level of imagination has been paid mainly by constitutional scholars: see Loughlin (2015) and Oklopcic (2018); as well as some legal historians: Ando (2015) and Stacey (2018). There are a number of current research projects suggesting this is a dynamic, emerging, area of legal scholarship: eg see the recently funded project run by Jan Komarek on 'European Constitutional Imaginaries' (https://jura.ku.dk/icourts/research/imagine/), and Neil Walker's Leverhulme project on 'Law, Community and Utopia'.

[57] For a discussion of this problem, and an interesting attempt to overcome it, see Biotti (2014).

[58] There have of course been important studies of the communal character of legal reasoning, eg in the context of common law theory: one need only mention Karl Llewellyn, AWB Simpson, and, more recently, Gerald Postema and John Bell, all of whom have explored aspects of common law reasoning as a communal practice, held together and constrained by communal norms and values, which

advocates, but also to legal officers in other institutions (the Parliament, Law Reform Commissions), scholars and citizens. Thus, the question we might ask is: what forms of language enable inquiry at the communal level (with its wide range of participants) over extended periods of time?

My suggestion will not come as a surprise: the forms of language that will enable collective inquiry over time, and thus be generative of resources for future readers, will be artefacts, and thus forms that invite future readers to imagine. This will be, in other words, a language that contains within it legal fictions, metaphors, scenarios and figures – as well as other examples of forms of language that signal their own artifice and invite us (ie future readers) to do things with them.

What might be some of the general characteristics of language that makes room for artefacts of that kind? We might surmise it will be a language in a subjunctive mood (including 'maybe', 'perhaps', 'one could say'), which allows for and encourages the use of tentative modes of expression, of transitional phrases (like 'quasi', 'not yet', 'something like', 'close to'), and for confessional and speculative expressions ('I confess to the difficulty of this …', 'I'm not sure about this'). Furthermore, and in keeping with the examples of the artefacts I have given above, this is a language that is more concrete than abstract – more imagistic and exemplary than it is formal, structured and universalised. None of this, of course, is to decry the value of universalisation, of the use of general and more abstract concepts, of attempts at rational reconstruction and systematisation. It is, however, to say that legal language that contains only such statements might be less generative for future readers, and thus less able to stimulate and sustain communal inquiry into normative relevance over time.

If we return to some of the examples of artefacts above: the inclusion of metaphor into legal discourse, for example, allows future readers to pick the inquiry where it last left off, and to renew the conversation by re-examining the metaphor, and perhaps emphasising different aspects of it. Or, the inclusion of a scenario might – as it has on countless occasions in the common law – be picked up on by an advocate in a future case, and offered as a resource for framing and characterising the facts of that future case, or by the judge in that future case when considering what values and interests are at stake in it and in cases of that kind. A metaphor might also enter more widespread cultural circulation, and in that sense extend the conversation to citizens (eg novelists, playrights, journalists, but also citizens in their everyday conversations). The point is that artefactual language generates such resources over time because it invites future readers to do things with those artefacts – to engage, that is, in processes of imagination.

A related value of artefactual legal language is that it does not allow language to become too automatic, too ready-to-hand. In part, this is because it surprises future readers – for example, at least as long as they remain alive, metaphors continue to tap us on our shoulders, making us sit upright. Surprise, we might say,

develop and change over time. Nevertheless, these important contributions have not explored the more specific question that interests me here: namely, what kinds of legal language are beneficial for enabling communal inquiry over time?

is an important epistemic emotion – or an emotion with much epistemic value. In another sense, artefacts de-instrumentalise legal language. Artefacts, as noted above, signal their own artifice: they thereby foreground their own form. Language of this kind suddenly ceases to be transparent. It becomes a mirror to ourselves, and thereby helps us to reflect on the words we draw on in thinking about and articulating our values.

Further, artefactual language affords collective memory. Fictions, metaphors, scenarios and figures are memorable – some for different reasons (say, because they give us aesthetic annoyance, as with fictions, or because they are so strikingly incongruous, as with many metaphors, or so exaggerated, as with some scenarios). Just as there is an economy of attention, so there is an economy of memory – there is too much to attend to and too much to remember, and artefactual language is a way of marking significance, of signalling where more work may need to be done, but also that it needs to be done (and needs to be remembered that it ought to be done).

Earlier, at the level of the individual, I mentioned that we could draw on the literature on epistemic virtues in bringing out the epistemic significance of artefacts and related processes of imagination. It may be that we could do the same at the communal level, though this time by reference to collective epistemic virtues. Just as there was at the individual level, here too there is plenty of disagreement within this literature on how to connect collectivity to virtue, for example whether to think of social groups as themselves somehow acquiring and possessing virtues (in ways that are not reducible to the sum of all the individual virtues), or whether to think of how certain collective arrangements (eg institutions, with their rules, habits and rituals) enable the fostering and flourishing of virtues that could not be pursued either by individuals on their own or by individuals acting independently (rather than jointly and collectively). As Miranda Fricker, one of the key voices in this debate, has pointed out, we often colloquially refer to a jury as being 'fair-minded', or a research team as being 'tenacious', or an appointments committee as being 'scrupulous', and so on.[59] Is this just loose talk which ought not to be taken too seriously,[60] or is there more to it? Might there be collective virtues or collective arrangements that enable particular kinds of virtues? And how might such virtues be related to epistemic activity? Recalling some of the virtues mentioned at the individual level: can we – and how can we – speak of, say, open-minded, humble, courageous, generous or inquisitive collectives (eg courts, or communities of legally-trained persons or the broader polity with respect to, say, criminal matters)?

This is a large question, and I cannot examine it in detail here. Perhaps one could argue, for example, that in order for an epistemic community to enable and enhance the flourishing of collective open-mindedness and inquisitiveness, which

[59] See Fricker (2010); see also Lahroodi (2007).
[60] See eg Cordell (2017).

would be of value to collective inquiry, such an epistemic community might need an appropriate language. This would need to be a language that would allow the community as a whole to detach itself from its commitments and consider alternatives to its views (to recall Baehr's interpretation of open-mindedness). A language like this would need to have the capacity to surprise, to pull members of the community out of their ordinary run of communication with each other, to enable them to pause and hesitate together – to make, in short, language less automatic, less ready to hand, and something in itself strange or requiring attention and care. Arguably, artefactual language does precisely that: when an epistemic community includes within its collective resources (eg written judgements available on accessible databases) language that is, say, metaphorical, or language that involves the construction of imaginary figures or absurd scenarios, then this is a language that maintains the capacity to surprise, allowing members to detach themselves from otherwise automatic uses of language, and to generate alternatives (eg through different possible extrapolations of a metaphor, or in terms of variations on a scenario). The point here is that artefactual language may create conditions for the emergence of a particular kind of collective dynamics – one in which we imagine together, collectively, over a period of time. Further, artefactual language – and perhaps especially metaphors, figures and scenarios, which connect so readily to us as affectively-embodied creatures – is highly accessible to a wide range of participants (including not only lawyers, but also scholars and citizens), and in that respect too artefactual language, and its related processes of imagination, can contribute to the open-mindedness (or the democratic quality) of an epistemic community.[61]

Of course, these claims would need more analysis and refinement. I offer them here in the spirit of inquiry into a question I find as difficult as I do fascinating: what kind of legal language is beneficial for collective inquiry over time? In future examinations of this question, we would do well to draw not only on the literature on collective epistemic virtues[62] and the epistemic life of groups in general,[63] but also on the tradition of rhetoric, including the study of the rhetorical dimension of not only legal language, but also the language of science and philosophy.[64] A good starting point for such an inquiry would be defences of the argumentative and conceptual resources of poetry and poetic language[65] – of the cognitive benefits of lyric, for instance, or of the cognitive effect of associational or condensed language, of symbols and blank spaces, of rhythms and melodies, and of the affectivity of such linguistic devices and forms.[66]

[61] For an interesting argument as to the importance of the participation of the citizenry in the making of legal meaning, see Levenbook (2000).

[62] See Green (2019).

[63] See Brady and Fricker (2016).

[64] See Goodrich (1987) and Fahnestock (1999).

[65] Famously, of course, Sidney's *An Apology for Poetry* (1868) [1595]; see also Kertzer (1988).

[66] See eg Vickers (1970); and, more recently, Spolsky (2015).

VI. Conclusion

In this chapter, I have pleaded for a multi-level and multi-temporal account of the legal imagination. The level of the individual is certainly very important: it shows us how individuals draw on artefacts and related processes of imagination when they find themselves, as they often do, in conditions of normative uncertainty and operating under a wide range of epistemic and institutional limitations. This level also shows us how artefacts and related processes of imagination connect to us as affectively embodied creatures, drawing as we do on our affects and bodies to search for what may be normatively relevant. Further, this level also reveals to us how artefacts and imagination help individual judges balance doing justice in the instant case with caring for the quality of the law in the future.

All this is important, but there is much more to be said about the role and value of artefacts and imagination. To do that we need to turn, as I have urged in this chapter, to two social levels: the level of interaction (typically, in the coutroom for the duration of a trial) and the level of the community (especially over time). In each level, or so I sought to argue here, we can see the role and value of artefacts and imagination. Artefacts, such as fictions, metaphors, figures and scenarios enable and enhance the quality of interaction, for example by leaving room for multiple (including competing) versions and variations of the artefact in question. At the level of the community, artefacts are memorable over time, while also remaining pliable and transformative, contributing to making legal language resourceful (rather than automatic or too-ready-to-hand), and involving a wider range of participants in the conversation.

Although I have not been able to devote it the time and space it deserves, I have also tried to point to some of the relations between imagination, emotion and virtue in the context of adjudication. At both the individual and collective levels, I have referred to the possibility of connecting imagination to individual and collective epistemic virtues. And in all levels – individual, interactive and collective – part of the case for the role and value of imagination is undoubtedly reliant on the vital epistemic significance of the emotions. As always, so much further remains to be explored.

References

Cases

California v Carney 471 U.S. 386 (1985)
Edwards v Attorney-General for Canada (1930) AC 124
McGhee v National Coal Board [1972] 3 All ER 1008

Articles and Books

Alfano, M, Greco, J and Turri, J (2017) 'Virtue Epistemology', *Stanford Encylopedia of Philosophy*. Available at https://plato.stanford.edu/entries/epistemology-virtue/.

Amaya, A and Ho, HL (2012) *Law, Virtue and Justice* (Oxford, Hart Publishing).
Amaya, A (2020) 'Admiration and the Development of Judicial Virtue' in A Amaya and M Del Mar (eds) *Virtue, Emotion and Imagination in Law and Legal Reasoning* (Oxford, Hart Publishing).
Ando, C (2015) *Roman Social Imaginaries* (Toronto, University of Toronto Press).
Appiah, A (2017) *As If: Idealisation and Ideals* (Cambridge Mass, Harvard University Press).
Arcangeli, M (2018) *Supposition and the Imaginative Realm: A Philosophical Inquiry* (London, Routledge).
Baehr, J (2011) *The Inquiring Mind: On Intellectual Virtues and Virtue Epistemology* (Oxford, Oxford University Press).
Bailey, M and Knight, K-J (eds) (2017) 'Writing Histories of Law and Emotion', Special Issue, 38(2) *The Journal of Legal History*.
Bell, J (2006) *Judiciaries within Europe* (Cambridge, Cambridge University Press).
Biotti, C (2014) *Imaginal Politics: Images Beyond Imagination and the Imaginary* (New York, Columbia University Press).
Blum, L (2020) '"Black Lives Matter": Moral Frames for Understanding the Police Killings of Black Males' in A Amaya and M Del Mar (eds) *Virtue, Emotion and Imagination in Law and Legal Reasoning* (Oxford, Hart Publishing).
Brady, M and Fricker, M (eds) (2016) *The Epistemic Life of Groups: Essays in the Epistemology of Collectives* (Oxford, Oxford University Press).
Brady, M (2020) 'Suffering and Punishment' in A Amaya and M Del Mar (eds) *Virtue, Emotion and Imagination in Law and Legal Reasoning* (Oxford, Hart Publishing).
Brann, E (2017) [1991] *The World of the Imagination: Sum and Substance* (Lanham, Rowman & Littlefield Publishers).
Brun, G, Doguoglu, U, and Kuenzle, D (eds) (2016) *Epistemology and Emotions* (Abingdale, Routledge).
Byrne, R (2016) 'Counterfactual Thought' 67 *Annual Review of Psychology* 135.
Camp, E (2009) 'Two Varieties of Literary Imagination: Metaphor, Fiction, and Thought Experiments' *Midwest Studies in Philosophy: Poetry and Philosophy* 107.
Cave, T (2016) *Thinking with Literature: Towards a Cognitive Criticism* (Oxford, Oxford University Press).
Cocking, JM (1984) *Imagination: A Study in the History of Ideas* (London, Routledge)
Cordell, S (2017) 'Group Virtues: No Great Leap Forward with Collectivism' 23(1) *Res Publica* 43.
Del Mar, M (2015) 'Legal Fictions and Legal Change in the Common Law Tradition' in M Del Mar and W Twining (eds) *Legal Fictions in Theory and Practice* (Dordrecht, Springer) 225.
Del Mar, M (2017a) 'Metaphor in International Law: Language, Imagination and Normative Inquiry' 86(2) *Nordic Journal of International Law* 170.
Del Mar, M (2017b) 'Imagining by Feeling: A Case for Compassion in Legal Reasoning' 13(2) *International Journal of Law in Context* 143.
Del Mar, M (2018a) 'Common Virtue and the Perspectival Imagination: Adam Smith and Common Law Reasoning' 9(1) *Jurisprudence* 58.
Del Mar, M (2018b) 'Emotion Experiments in Legal Thought' 5(2) *Critical Analysis of Law* 9.
Del Mar, M (forthcoming), *Artefacts of Legal Inquiry: The Value of Imagination in Adjudication* (Oxford, Hart Publishing).
Del Mar, M and Twining, W (eds) (2015) *Legal Fictions in Theory and Practice* (Dordrecht, Springer).

Domselaar, van, I (2020) 'All Judges on the Couch? On Iris Murdoch and Legal Decision-Making' in A Amaya and M Del Mar (eds) *Virtue, Emotion and Imagination in Law and Legal Reasoning* (Oxford, Hart Publishing).

Dworkin, R (1986) *Law's Empire* (Cambridge Mass, Harvard University Press).

Elgin, C (1996) *Considered Judgment* (Princeton, Princeton University Press).

Elgin, C (2020) 'Impartiality and Legal Reasoning' in A Amaya and M Del Mar (eds) *Virtue, Emotion and Imagination in Law and Legal Reasoning* (Oxford, Hart Publishing).

Fahnestock, J (1999) *Rhetorical Figures in Science* (New York, Oxford University Press).

Feenan, D (ed) (2017) 'Law and Compassion', Special Issue, 13(2) *International Journal of Law in Context*.

Fesmire, S (2003) *John Dewey and Moral Imagination* (Bloomington, Indiana University Press).

Ferraris, M (1996) *L'immaginazione* (Bologna, Il Mulino).

Fish, S (1982) 'Working on the Chain Gang: Interpretation in the Law and in Literary Criticism' 9 *Critical Inquiry* 201.

Fletcher, A (2016) *Comic Democracies* (Baltimore, Johns Hopkins University Press).

Fricker, M (2010) 'Can There Be Institutional Virtues?' in TS Gendler and J Hawthorne (eds) *Oxford Studies in Epistemology*, Vol 3, 235.

Gallagher, C (2006) 'The Rise of Fictionality' in F Moretti (ed) *The Novel* (Princeton, Princeton University Press) 336.

Godfrey-Smith, P and Levy, A (eds) (forthcoming) *The Scientific Imagination* (Oxford, Oxford University Press).

Goldman, A (2006) 'Imagination in Responses to Fiction' in S Nichols (ed), *The Architecture of the Imagination* (Oxford, Oxford University Press) 41.

Goodrich, P (1987) *Legal Discourse: Studies in Linguistics, Rhetoric and Legal Analysis* (Houndmills, Palgrave Macmillan).

Green, A (2019) *The Social Contexts of Intellectual Virtue* (London: Routledge).

Halliday, P (2014) 'Authority in the Archives' 1 *Critical Analysis of Law* 1.

Hanne, M and Weisberg, R (eds) (2018) *Narrative and Metaphor in the Law* (Cambridge, Cambridge University Press).

Hansberg, O (2020) 'Empathy and Negative Intimacy' in A Amaya and M Del Mar (eds) *Virtue, Emotion and Imagination in Law and Legal Reasoning* (Oxford, Hart Publishing).

Harris, P (2000) *The Work of the Imagination* (Oxford, Blackwell).

Holmes, R and Johnson, T (eds) (2018) 'In Pursuit of Truth: Law and Emotion in Early Modern Europe' 54(1) *Forum for Modern Language Studies*.

Hunter, R, McGlynn, C and Rackley, E (eds) (2010) *Feminist Judgments: From Theory to Practice* (Oxford, Hart Publishing).

Johnson, M (2018) *The Aesthetics of Meaning and Thought: The Bodily Roots of Philosophy, Science, Morality, and Art* (Chicago, Chicago University Press).

Kearney, R (1988), *The Wake of Imagination: Towards a Postmodern Culture* (London, Routledge).

Kertzer, J (1988) *Poetic Argument: Studies in Modern Poetry* (Kingston, McGill-Queen's University Press).

Kind, A (ed) (2016) *The Routledge Handbook of the Philosophy of Imagination* (London, Routledge).

Kind, A and Kung, P (eds) (2016) *Knowledge Through Imagination* (Oxford, Oxford University Press).

Kind, A (2020) 'Empathy, Imagination, and the Law' in A Amaya and M Del Mar (eds) *Virtue, Emotion and Imagination in Law and Legal Reasoning* (Oxford, Hart).
Laden, A (2012) *Reasoning: A Social Picture* (Oxford, Oxford University Press).
Lahroodi, R (2007) 'Collective Epistemic Virtues' 21(3) *Social Epistemology* 281.
La Caze, M (2002) *The Analytic Imaginary* (Ithaca, Cornell University Press).
Le Doeuff, M (1989) *The Philosophical Imaginary* (London, The Continuum Press).
Levenbook, B (2000) 'The Meaning of a Precedent' 6(2) *Legal Theory* 185.
Loughlin, M (2015) 'The Constitutional Imagination' 78(1) *Modern Law Review* 1.
Markman, W, Klein, MP and Suhr, JA (eds) (2008) *Handbook of Imagination and Mental Simulation* (New York, Psychology Press).
Moran, M (2003) *Rethinking the Reasonable Person: An Egalitarian Reconstruction of the Objective Standard* (Oxford, Oxford University Press).
Morton, A (2020) 'Imagining Motives' in A Amaya and M Del Mar (eds) *Virtue, Emotion and Imagination in Law and Legal Reasoning* (Oxford, Hart Publishing).
Oklopcic, Z (2018) *Beyond the People: Social Imaginary and Constituent Imagination* (Oxford, Oxford University Press).
Prinz, J (2009) *The Emotional Construction of Morals* (Oxford, Oxford University Press).
Schlag, P (2002) 'The Aesthetics of American Law' 115 *Harvard Law Review* 1047.
Sellers, M (ed) (2017) *Law, Reason and Emotion* (Cambridge, Cambridge University Press).
Shaw, J (2017) 'Aesthetics of Law and Literary License: An Anatomy of the Legal Imagination' 38(1) *Liverpool Law Review* 83.
Sidney, P (2002) [1595] *Apology for Poetry (Or the Defence of Poesy)* (Manchester, Manchester University Press).
Silcox, M (2018) *A Defense of Simulated Experience* (London, Routledge).
Spolsky, E (2015) *Contracts of Fiction: Cognition, Culture, Community* (Oxford, Oxford University Press).
Stacey, R (2018) *Law and the Imagination in Medieval Wales* (Philadelphia, Pennsylvania University Press).
Stern, S (2017) 'Legal and Literary Fictions' in B Meyler and E Anker (eds) *New Directions in Law and Literature* (Oxford, Oxford University Press), 313.
Stern, S (2020) 'The Legal Imagination in Historical Perspective' in A Amaya and M Del Mar (eds) *Virtue, Emotion and Imagination in Law and Legal Reasoning* (Oxford, Hart Publishing).
Stuart, M (2014) 'Imagination: A Sine Qua Non of Science' 17(49) *Croatian Journal of Philosophy* 9.
Stuart, M, Fehige, Y and Brown, J (eds) (2017) *The Routledge Companion to Thought Experiments* (London, Routledge).
Tylen, K, Weed, E, Wallentin, W, Roepstorff, A and Frith, C (2010) 'Language as a Tool for Interacting Minds' 25(1) *Mind & Language* 3.
Vaihinger, H (1924) [1911] *The Philosophy of 'As If'* (Abingdon, Routledge and Kegan Paul).
Vickers, B (1970) *Classical Rhetoric in English Poetry* (Carbondale, Southern Illinois University Press).
Walsh, R (2007) *The Rhetoric of Fictionality* (Ohio, Ohio State University Press).
Watson, G (1988) *Phantasia in Classical Thought* (Galway, Galway University Press).
White, H (1973) *Metahistory: The Historical Imagination in Nineteenth-Century Europe* (Baltimore, The Johns Hopkins University Press).
White, JB (1973) *The Legal Imagination* (Chicago, Chicago University Press).

White, EK (2020) 'On Emotions and the Politics of Attention in Legal Reasoning' in A Amaya and M Del Mar (eds) *Virtue, Emotion and Imagination in Law and Legal Reasoning* (Oxford, Hart Publishing).

Winter, S (2001) *A Clearing in the Forest: Law, Life and Mind* (Chicago, Chicago University Press).

Zipursky, B (2020) 'Austerity, Compassion, and the Rule of Law' in A Amaya and M Del Mar (eds) *Virtue, Emotion and Imagination in Law and Legal Reasoning* (Oxford, Hart Publishing).

Zittoun, T, and Glaveanu, V (eds) (2018) *Handbook of Imagination and Culture* (Oxford, Oxford University Press).

Zunshine, L (eds) (2014) *The Oxford Handbook of Cognitive Literary Studies* (Oxford, Oxford University Press).

INDEX

A

Abbott LCJ 224
Abrams, L and Keren, H 5
accuracy
  fairness and 205
  imagination and 199–200, 203–211, 214
admiration 159
  acquired talent, for 28–29, 41
  affective component 26–27
  attainability of model 32, 38, 40, 42
  character development, role in 34, 40
  conferring authority 35
  conscious and unconscious imitation 30, 39
  cultivating in legal education 37–41
  cultural transmission 34–35, 41
  epistemic virtue, for 41
  exemplarity and 25–27, 29, 34–42
  fetishism 33, 38, 42
  identity formation, role in 36–37
  imitation and 13, 15, 25–26, 27, 29–34, 38, 39
  intentional object 26
  judicial virtue and 13, 25–26
  misguided 31–32, 42
  moral excellence, for 28, 41
  motivation for 38
  motivational role 26, 27, 29, 41
  other praising emotion, as 27
  positive emotion, as 17, 25–26, 27, 41
  regulating hierarchy 35–36, 41
  self-image, shaping 36–37
  social functions 26, 27, 34–37
  social learning and cultural transmission 34–35, 41
  social relationships and 36
  unproductive 33–34, 42
  virtue, for 26–29
  virtuous disposition to admire 37–42
advocacy
  audience and 7
  judgement and 7
affective sciences
  impact on law 4–6
Algoe, SB and Haidt, J 27
Amaya, Amalia 13, 17, 18, 49–50, 52
Anderson, Benedict 252
anger
  contagion 161
  emotion-centred approach 5, 154
appeal system 54
arbitrariness
  empathy and 185–188, 193
Arcangeli, Margherita 20
Aristotle
  on empathy 110–111
  phronimos 50, 52
  role of imagination 6, 110–111, 236
  virtue theory 2, 3, 4, 50
arrogance 17, 37, 41, 42
artefacts of language 237–239, 243
  communal level, at 252–256
  communicative functions 247–256
  effect on future cases 244–245
  enabling collective inquiry 253–255
  epistemic significance 246–247, 254
  humour, use of 251
  indirect interactions 251–252
  individual imagination 235, 239–247, 256
  interactive and social dimension 9, 10, 16–17, 235–239, 247–256
  invitational character 247, 250
  memorability 254, 256
  signalling functions 248, 254
  value in legal reasoning 245
aspect-seeing 81
attention, role of
  distribution of attention, principled 102
  emotions and politics of attention 14, 101–117
  empathy and 6, 79, 103, 106–109, 110
  error recognition and 106
  errors of application 110–113
  errors of attention 102, 104–113
  false or anti-attention 105–109, 116–117
  fixing and sustaining judicial attention 14, 101–117
  imagination, engaging 146

intersubjective focus of emotions 105–109
legal reasons for paying attention 103–104, 116–117
Murdochian moral philosophy 14, 79, 81, 88, 91, 102
punishment's attention-directing role 145–147
rule of law requirements and 113–116
suffering's attention-directing role 145–147
Weil's concept of 79, 104–105

austerity
compassion and 14, 61, 71
judicial 14, 61
rule of law and 14, 59–75
virtue theory and 2–3, 17

authority
admiration conferring 35
judicial hierarchy 35–36, 41

awe 18, 41

B

Baehr, Jason 247, 255

bailments
personified standards 225–226, 229, 230

Baker, Ella 128

Bandes, S 181, 186, 192

Baudelaire, Charles
'The Painter of Modern Life' 220–221, 222

Bayley J 224–225

Bedau, Hugo and Kelly, Erin 141

Berger, John 105–106

Berger, Linda 8

bias
biased or idiosyncratic judgments 52–53, 55, 94
empathy and 185–186, 193
imagination and 9
implicit 129–130, 136, 185
socially or conventionally constructed 94
umpire model of judiciary 191–196

Bishop, Elizabeth
'Man-Moth' 101, 102

Black Lives Matter movement
affective dimension 14–15
criticism of 130
generally 121–122, 125, 128
as moral framework 128–129
stereotyping, moral understanding of 125

black males, US police killings of
affective dimension 14–15
aggressive mindset problem 131–132
black police officers 135–136
case studies 122–123, 125–128, 129
failure of compassion 128
implicit bias 129–130, 136
inadequate emotional attitude 15, 121–122
internalised racism 136
killings of white males compared 133–135
leniency of the legal system 136
moral frames for understanding 121–136
police behaviour after killing 125–128
public deference to police 136
stereotypes and stereotyping 15, 123–125, 128–129
stigmatising of black people 136
Zack's rights-based approach 130

Blackstone, Sir William
Commentaries 221

Bloom, Paul 111

Blum, Lawrence 14–15, 17, 19

Brady, Michael 8, 15, 18

Breyer J 65, 68

Brown, Michael 122–123, 124, 127–128, 129, 131, 135

Brown v Board of Education 190–191

Bruner, Jerome 8

C

Calabresi, Steven G 183–184

California v Brock Allen Turner 55–56

California v Carney 250–251

capacity
irresistible impulse 206–207, 298
testamentary 207–208

Castoriadis, Cornelius 252

change-being effected (CBE) procedure 68

character
development, role of admiration 34, 40
relevance in virtue theory 2
traits, intimacy and 170–173

Chen, Paul 189–190

Coggs v Bernard 225–226, 229

cognitive imagination 20

cognitive legal studies
theorising imagination 7–8

Coke, Sir Edward 221

Colby, Thomas 187

community service as punishment 145, 147, 148

compassion
austerity and 14, 61, 71
dangers of 111–113
dispassionate reasoning as a virtue 61, 62
empathy distinguished 6, 15, 162–165, 168, 169, 173
judicial 14, 47, 59–75

motivating force, as 163, 168, 169
rule of law and 14, 59–75
stereotyping and 128
suffering and 60
virtue theory and 2
Confucius
on virtue 3
connoisseurship model of virtue 50–52
consistency, principle of
affective dimensions of crime 14–15
ascribing motivation 199–200
bias and 52–53, 94
emotion constrained by 14, 47, 57–58, 199
imagination constrained by 14, 47, 57–58, 199
impartiality and 14, 47–50, 57–58, 199
judicial discretion and 48–54
in legal reasoning 14, 47–53, 199
principle of legality 72
as requirement for viable legal systems 14, 48
rule-based legal systems 48–50, 53–54
rule of law and 47–53, 62, 66
virtuous judgement and 50–53, 57–58
constitutional rights
judicial scrutiny 103–104, 110
contempt 28, 41
contract law
reasonable person concept 222, 229
Coplan, A 160, 164, 165
counterfactual narrative
use in legal reasoning 10
Court, Robert 73
Coyne J 189
criminal law 219, 254
affective dimensions of crime 14–15
legal doctrine approach 6
reasonable person concept 10, 222, 226
sentencing *see* punishment
Crook v Jadis 227, 229, 230
cultural transmission
admiration and 34–35, 41
Cuomo v Clearing House Ass'n 66
curiosity 5, 18
attention and 107, 110, 117
epistemic virtue, as 246–247
morality and 117

D
de Blasio, Bill 124
deeming provisions *see* **legal fictions**
Del Mar, Maksymilian 12, 16–17, 18
Demahy v Actavis, Inc. 64–65, 66, 69–71
Denman LCJ 227, 228
determination/perseverance 29, 40, 42
deterrence
punishment as 143, 154
discernment
connoisseurship and 51–53
discovery, context of 47
discretion, judicial 48–54
disdain 28
disgust 5, 28, 41
doctor-patient relationship
emotional engagement 6
dramatic imagination 20
Duff, Antony 141
communicative theory of punishment 15, 142–148, 155
Dworkin, Ronald
Judge Hercules metaphor 235, 240–241, 248
Dylan, Bob 105

E
education *see* **legal education**
Edwards v Attorney-General for Canada 238
egalitarianism
humility and 41
elevation
as other praising emotion 27, 28–29
Elgin, Catherine 8, 9, 13–14
emotion
admiration *see* admiration
affective aspect of social structures 157
affective dimensions of crime and punishment 14–15, 139
affective imitation 161–162
aggressive mindset problem 131–132
appropriate, absence of 133
awe 18, 41
behavioural expression of 154
censure and condemnation, role in 149–155
communicative theory of punishment 15, 139–140
compassion *see* compassion
consistency should constrain 14, 47, 57–58
constraints on role in legal reasoning 14, 47
contempt 28, 41
dangers of 111–112
deep-rooted assumptions about 4–5
disdain 28
dissenting judicial opinions 115–116
doctrinal revision of scholarship on 5
education of the emotions 39–40, 42

elevation of others 27, 28–29
emotion-centred approach 5
emotion-theory approach 5, 6
emotional communication 158–159, 169, 173
emotional contagion 15, 161
emotional matching 15, 161, 163
emotional motivation 117
emotional openness 62
emotional phenomenon approach 5–6
empathy and 5–6, 102, 103, 106–109
epistemic 6, 18, 41, 113–116, 254
errors of attention, precipitating 104–113
expressive role 6
focus on behaviour 132–133
gratitude 27, 41
historical perspective 4
imagination and, generally 8, 11–13, 194, 241–242
imitation and 15, 27
impartiality and 55–58, 199–200
inadequate emotional attitude 121–122
indifference 14–15, 17, 112, 133
individuals, affectively embodied 241–242, 243–244
inspiration 28, 40
interactive and communal 9, 10, 16–17, 18, 235–236
internal and external viewpoints 114
intersubjective focus 105–109
intimacy relationships *see* intimacy
judge, emotional disposition of 2, 102
judicial attention, fixing and sustaining 101–117
judicial reasoning and 103
law and emotion movement 4–6
legal actor approach 5, 6
legal doctrine approach 5, 6
in legal reasoning, generally 1, 2, 4–6, 47, 55–58, 102, 241
legal training 6
motivational role 6, 26, 27, 29
Murdochian approach to legal decision-making 14, 87–90
narcissistic 105–106
negative 5, 17–18, 40, 41
optimism 28
other praising 27
perception and 11, 14, 52
perspective and 27
philosophy of 102
pity 105
positive 5, 17–18, 27, 41
pride 18
proportionality in reasoning 103
proposed normative goals 5
psychological dependency 159
publicity should constrain 14, 48, 57–58
punishment, affective dimensions 6, 15, 139, 143, 149–155
reason and 5
rhetorical tradition and 7
salience, emotions are sources of 56–57
satisfaction 18
scorn 28
self-indulgent 105–106
state expressions of 152–153
suffering *see* suffering
sympathy 6, 15, 67, 162–165, 168, 169
theory-of-law approach 5, 6
upward assimilative emotions 28
vice and 12
virtue and 6, 11, 12–13
virtuous judgement and 12

empathy

actions generated by 183–185, 193
activism, connection with 182–183, 188, 189, 193
affective imitation 161–162
affective state 163, 165, 169–170
arbitrariness and 185–188, 193
ascribing motivation 163, 168, 169, 182–183, 200
attention and 6, 79, 103, 106–109, 110, 112–113
benefits 111
bias and 185–186, 193
characteristics of 160–161, 162–165, 169, 173, 180–182
cognitive aspect 163
compassion distinguished 6, 15, 67, 162–165, 168, 173
criminal law sentencing 103
cross-racial 190–191
dangers of 55–56, 111–113, 166, 168–169
disposition to feel 170–173
emotional aspect of legal reasoning 5–6, 102, 103, 106–109
emotional contagion 15, 161
emotional phenomenon approach 5–6, 163–164, 169–170
empathy model of judicial role 16, 66–67, 179, 180, 182–196, 217
episodes of empathy 170

experiential perspective of empathiser 188–191, 193, 195
imagination and 6, 15–16, 110–111, 160, 163–164, 180, 194–196, 217
imitation and 15, 181
impartiality and 55–58, 111–112
'in his shoes' form 106–108
inference and 160
intimacy and 6, 15, 111, 157–160, 165–173
judicial reasoning and 103, 180, 182
limitations of 164–165
morality and 160
Murdochian moral philosophy 14, 79, 86–87, 90
perspective-shifting form 106–108, 163–170, 173, 180–181
pseudo-empathy 164
resonance phenomenon, as 181–182
selective 110, 186–189
subjectivity and 12, 163–164
sympathy distinguished 6, 15, 162–165, 168, 169, 173, 181
triggering 110–111
umpire model and 191–196

emulation *see* **imitation**

epistemic emotions 6, 18, 41, 113–116, 254

Erasmus 37

Escola v Coca-Cola Bottling Co. of Fresno 73

evenhandedness, principle of 47, 62, 66, 74–75

evidence
eyewitness testimony 203
hearsay 219

exemplarity
admiration and 25–27, 29, 34–42
books of *exempla* 38, 42
exemplarist ethics 3
imitation of exemplars 13, 25–27
moral excellence and non-moral excellence 28
virtue exemplarism 25–26

exemplars
see also exemplarity
acquired talent 28–29, 41
admiration and imitation 29–34, 39, 41–42
conferring authority 35
destructive mimicry 31, 40
identity formation, role in 36–37
imagination and 30, 33–34
imitation of 13, 25–27, 29–34
judicial 13, 25–26, 34–41
narratives of 39
natural talent 28
negative 31, 40
sub-conscious imitation 30–31
virtuous disposition to admire 37–42

eyewitness testimony
fallibility 203

F

facts
counterfactual thinking 10, 80, 218
descriptions of 88, 92, 115, 241
determining 222, 231
disagreements as to 84–85
imaginative revision 10, 219, 221
legal fictions and 238, 245, 253
patterns of 12, 55, 57, 213–214
relevance 12, 77, 88, 115, 204

fairness
accuracy and 205
imagination and 199–200, 205, 213
preemption doctrine and 72
principle of 48, 74
punishment and 142–143, 148–149, 153–154
strict liability regimes 199

false belief task 202

fear
contagion 161
emotion-centred approach 5

fetishism
imitation and 33, 38, 42

fictions *see* **legal fictions**

figures, use in legal reasoning
artefacts, as 239
effect on future cases 245
enabling collective inquiry 253–254
enquiry into normative relevance 243–244, 249–250
generally 7, 8, 16, 17, 238–239, 249–250, 254–256
idealised figures 240
memorability 254, 256
open-mindedness and 247
reasonable person 8, 9, 10–11, 16, 208–211, 218, 222–232, 238–239, 244
value 243

Frank, Jerome 85–86, 89, 91

Franks, Mary 181, 182, 185

Fredrickson, Barbara 27

Freud, Sigmund 79, 252

Fricker, Miranda 254

Fulbecke, William 221–222
Fuller, Lon 72

G
Garcia, Jorge 133
Garner, Eric 122–123, 125–126, 129, 131
Geier v American Honda Motor Co. 68
gender and sexuality 10, 48, 113, 189, 190, 242
Giddens, A 158
Gill v Cubitt 224–225, 227, 229–230, 231, 232
Ginsburg J 36, 52, 65
Goldie, Peter 106–107, 114, 165
Goldie, Peter and Coplan, A 164
Goodman v Harvey 228
Grassley, Charles 183, 185–186
gratitude
as other praising emotion 27, 41
Gray, Freddie 122–123
guilt
imposition of punishment 142
value of feeling 140
Gurley, Akai 122–123, 126–127, 131
Guys, Constantin 220

H
Haidt, J 26–27, 28
Hansberg, Olbeth 15, 18
Hart, HLA
on punishment 140–141
Hatch, Orrin 183
Hatch-Waxman Amendments 65, 68, 69, 70, 74
Heal, J 202
Heidegger, Martin 78
Henderson, L 181, 184
hierarchy
admiration regulating 35–36, 41
historical perspective
emotions and legal reasoning 4
legal imagination, on 9, 10–11, 16, 217–232
on personification 16, 222–232
Roman law 218
Hobbes, Thomas
on punishment 140
Holmes, Oliver Wendell 187, 209
Holroyd J 225
human dignity
concept of 103
human person
normative conception of 103–104
Hume, David
role of imagaination 6
humility
empathy and 107
epistemic virtue, as 246
necessity for 2, 40–41, 42
humour
role in legal reasoning 251
Hunt, Lynn 111
hypothetical narrative
imagination, generally 12, 20
use in legal reasoning 9, 10

I
identity formation
role of admiration 36–37
idiosyncratic judgments
controlling 52–53, 55
ill-will
indifference and 133
imagination
absence of 17
accuracy and 199–200, 203–211, 214
acquired character trait, as 246
anticipating actions of others 200–205, 213
artefacts *see* artefacts of imagination
asymmetrical 212–213
bias and 9
cognitive 7–8, 20
collective 18, 254
communal level 252–256
consistency should constrain 14, 47, 57–58
constraints on, in legal reasoning 14, 47, 219–222, 223, 241
constructing counter-factual alternatives 10
creativity 246
dangers of 9, 16, 55–56, 211–214
deeming provisions 218–219
dramatic 20
dual consciousness 237
education of the imagination 39–40, 42
emotion and, generally 8, 11–13, 194, 241–242
empathy and 6, 15–16, 110–111, 160, 163–164, 180, 194–196, 217
enquiry into normative relevance 243–244, 249–250
epistemic nature 237, 240, 254
excuses or exculpating facts 204–205
exemplars and 30, 33–34
experiential perspective 78–85, 188–191, 193, 195
fairness and 199–200, 205, 213
fantasy 79–80
figures *see* figures, use in legal reasoning

historical perspective on legal imagination 9, 10–11, 16, 217–232
hypothetical narratives 9, 10, 12, 20
idealised figures 240
imaginative scaffolding 194
imitation, imagination necessary for 30
impartiality 199–200, 213, 214
individual 235, 239–247, 256
innate faculty for 246
interactive and social dimension 9, 10, 16–17, 235–239, 247–256
judge's imaginative capacity 2
justification and 9
language and 7, 8, 17, 18, 237–239
legal doctrine, judicial development 218
legal reasoning, generally 1, 47, 55–58, 217
limitation 208
mental imagery, role 7
metaphor *see* metaphor in legal reasoning
metonymy and 7
moral 7, 79–80
motivation, ascribing 16, 199–214
narrative and 8
normative relevance, inquiry into 242–244, 249–250
open-mindedness and 247, 254–255
parable and 7
personification 7, 8, 9, 10, 16, 222–232
perspective-shifting form 10, 12, 30, 163–170, 173, 180–181, 237, 238–239, 247
philosophical view of 9
politics of 10
process of imagining as moral discipline 102
projections, imaginative 16, 194–195
propositional imagining 10, 20
Prudent Man in legal thought 10
psychological view of 9
publicity should constrain 14, 48, 57–58
quality of the law and 244–245
reason and 6–11
reasonable person concept 8, 9, 10–11, 16, 208–211, 218, 222–232, 238–239, 244
reconstruction, imaginative 218
regulated 220–221
resistance to 17
in Roman law 218
scenarios *see* scenarios in legal reasoning
self-involvement 20
sensory 20
simulation theories 202
social imaginaries 252
statutory interpretation and 218
suffering facilitating imaginative engagement 146
supposition 10, 20, 70, 193, 211, 237–239, 244, 249–252
surprise 248–249, 253–254
synecdoche and 7
value in legal reasoning 9, 242, 243, 245
virtue and 12–13, 246–247
virtuous judgement and 12, 91

imitation
acquired talent, of 28–29, 41
admiration and 13, 15, 25–26, 27, 29–34, 38, 39–42
affective 161–162
attainability of model 32, 38, 40, 42
blind copying 33–34, 38, 39, 40
conscious and unconscious 30, 39
critical engagement, necessity for 40
destructive mimicry 31, 40
emotion and 15, 27
emotional contagion 15, 161
empathy and 15, 161–162
emulation of natural talent 28
of exemplars 13, 25–27, 29–42
fetishism and 33, 38, 42
imagination necessary for 30
misguided admiration 31–32, 42
moral and intellectual autonomy and 40, 42
transformation of the self 30–31
unproductive 33–34, 38, 39, 40
virtue 25–42
when appropriate response 38

impartiality
consistency, principle of 14, 47–53, 57–58, 199–200
imagination and 199, 213, 214
impartial procedure 53–54
in legal reasoning *see* impartiality in legal reasoning
publicity and 14, 50–53, 57–58
virtue theory and 2

impartiality in legal reasoning
emotions and 55–58, 199
empathy and 55–58, 111–112
generally 2, 13–14, 16, 47
impartial judgments 13, 16, 53–55, 199
impersonal judgments 13–14, 48–50, 53
requirements for 48
virtuous judgments 50–53

impersonality
in judicial decision-making 13–14, 48–50, 53
objectivity distinguished 83–84, 88
impulsive acts
attributing motivation to 206–207, 208
testamentary capacity and 207–208
indifference
ill-will and 133
moral life, in 112
vice of 14–15, 17, 133
inference
empathy and 160
inquisitiveness
epistemic virtue, as 246–247, 254–255
inspiration
admiration as motivating force 27, 29, 40, 41
as upward assimilative emotion 28
institutional structures
impact on decision-making 19
intentionality of criminal action
determining 193
intimacy
affective imitation 161–162
affective matching 15, 161, 163
among equals 159, 173
asymmetric 159, 173
character traits and 170–173
components characteristic of 158
emotional communication 158–159, 169, 173
emotional engagement 6, 157–158
empathy and 6, 15, 111, 157–160, 165–173
negative 15, 159, 160, 166–173
positive 159, 166, 169, 170, 173
psychological dependency 159
victim-victimiser relationships 6, 159, 166–169, 171

J
Jarrell, Randall 108–109
Joas, Hans 111
Johnson, Mark and Lakoff, George 8
Jones, Sir William
Essay on the Law of Bailments 225, 226, 230
judgment
accessibility of reasoning 57–58, 92–93
advocacy and 7
biased or idiosyncratic 52–53, 55, 94
consistency, principle of 14, 47–53, 57–58
dissenting opinions 115–116
impartial 53–55
impersonal 13–14, 48–49, 53
judicial discretion 48–54
judicial perception 85–88
judicial review 57
moral 204–205
Murdochian moral philosophy 85–86
requirements for viable legal systems 48
rule-based 48–50, 53–54, 85, 87–88
transparency, principle of 48
virtuous judgments 13, 50–53, 91
judicial reasoning
see also legal reasoning
accessibility 57–58, 92–93
role of understanding in 16
virtue-based analysis 2
judicial virtues
admiration, positive emotion of 5, 25–26, 27
development 3–4, 13
emotional involvement 12
imaginative engagement 12
imitation of exemplars 13, 25–26, 27
impartiality *see* impartiality; impartiality in legal reasoning
Murdochian moral philosophy 14, 85–86
social learning and cultural transmission 34–35, 41
judiciary
see also judicial reasoning; judicial virtues
activist 182–183
compassion *see* compassion
dispassionate reasoning 61, 62
diversity 189–190
Dworkin's Hercules metaphor 235, 240–241, 248
emotions of 6, 55
empathy model 16, 66–67, 179, 180, 182–196, 217
exemplarity 13, 25–26, 34–41
hierarchy of authority 35–36, 41
imaginative projection by 16, 55, 194–195
judicial perception 85–88
moral/intellectual character 14, 50, 86, 88–90, 180
Murdochian moral philosophy 85–92
organisational cohesion 34
pedagogical functions 41, 42
results-oriented judging 183
role of, conception 61
self-image 34, 37
umpire model 15–16, 179–180, 182–183, 187, 191–196

'unselfing' 91
virtuous judge, concept of 14, 50, 86, 88–90, 180
jury
emotions of 6
justice
consistency, principle of 14, 47–53, 57–58
transparency, principle of 48
justification
discovery and 9, 47
imagination and 9
legal decision-making, in 16, 47–58, 60, 90, 92–93
proportionality reasoning 103, 153
punishment, of 6, 140–147, 148–149, 153
value concepts and 84

K
Kagan J 65, 183, 186
Kahneman, D and Tversky, A 201
Kant, Immanuel 78
role of imagaination 6
Katz v United States 226–227, 232
Kind, Amy 8, 12, 15–16, 219
Kirby J 36
Kyl, Jon 183

L
Lacan, Jacques 252
Laden, Anthony
Reasoning: A Social Picture 248–249
language
artefactual 253–255
collective memory and 254
ellipsis 237
enabling collective inquiry 252–254
figures *see* figures, use in legal reasoning
imagination and 7, 8, 17, 18, 237–239
legal 17
metaphor *see* metaphor in legal reasoning
moral perception and 82–83
poetic 255
rhetorical 7, 236
lawyer-client relationship
emotional engagement 6
legal culture
impact on decision-making 19
legal doctrine
emotions and 5, 6
imaginative devices used judicial development 218
legal education
cultivating virtuous disposition to admire 37–42
education of the emotions 39–40, 42
education of moral and intellectual autonomy 40, 42
exemplary judges 13, 25–26
generally 19
of the imagination 39–40, 42
judiciary, pedagogical functions of 41, 42
personal transformation as goal 92
professional ethics 4
social learning and cultural transmission 34–35, 41
training emotions 6
virtue education 3–4, 11, 13, 19, 37–41, 42
legal fictions
artefacts, as 238, 245
constraints on role of 219–222
effect on future cases 245
enabling collective inquiry 253–254
enquiry into normative relevance 243–244, 249–250
imaginative nature 218–219, 238
limited-purpose aspect 219
memorability 254, 256
role 17, 236, 238, 245, 249, 256
value 243, 245
legal institutions
impact on decision-making 19
legal realism 85–86
legal reasoning
affectively embodied individuals 239, 241–242
cognitive engagement 223
compassion in 47
consistency, principle of 14, 47–53, 57–58
constraints on 14, 47, 48, 219–222, 223, 239, 241
effect on future cases 244–245
epistemic limitation 239–241
foreseeability of decisions 93
hypothetical narratives 9, 10, 12, 20
idealism and cynicism towards 240
imagination in, generally 1, 47, 55–58, 217
impartiality in *see* impartiality in legal reasoning
individual experience and 239–247
interactive and social dimensions 247–256
justification in 16
language 17

Murdochian approach 14, 51, 52, 77–78, 85–92
quality of the law, concern for 244–245
requirements for viable legal systems 48
rules and standards compared 231
subjectivity 52
viewed as cognitive enterprise 5

liberal legal order
legal decisions must be foreseeable 93
Murdochian approach to legal decision-making and 14, 92–95
virtue jurisprudence and 4

Limbaugh, David 187
Loftus, EF 203, 214

M

McDowell, J 50
McGhee v National Coal Board 238
McKee, Theodore 183
magnanimity
virtue theory and 2

Mansfield LJ 223–224
Margalit, A 112
Maroney, Terry 5, 115
Marx, Karl 252
Matravers, Matt 15, 140, 142, 147–149, 151, 153, 155
mental imagery, role 7
metaphor in legal reasoning 7, 8, 9, 10, 17, 18, 236, 237, 238, 247, 256
artefacts, metaphors as 238
effect on future cases 245
enabling collective inquiry 253–254
enquiry into normative relevance 243–244, 249–250
imagination and 238
memorability 254, 256
semantic clash 18, 237, 238, 250
value 243–244

metonymy
in legal reasoning 7

Miller v Race 223–224
moral excellence
admiration for 28, 41

moral imagination 7, 79–80
moral judgement 204–205
moral philosophy
aspect-seeing 81
concept of attention 79, 81, 88, 91
imagination, role of 79–80
moral freedom 80–81
moral perception 80–84
Murdoch 3, 77, 78–85, 102
phenomenological approach 78
society as 93

morality, empathy and 160
Moran, Richard 20
Morton, Adam 8, 9, 10, 16, 181, 182
motivation
admiration as motivating force 26, 27, 29, 41
anticipating actions of others 200–205, 213
ascribing 199–214
determining intentionality 193
excuses or exculpating facts 204–205
imagining motives of others 16, 199–214
information-rich and information-poor accounts of 201–202
irresistible impulse 206–207, 208
premeditated actions 206
provocation as factor 206
rational analysis of 200–201, 202–203, 208–211
simulation theories 202
strict liability regimes 199
testamentary capacity and ascribing motivation 207–208
virtuous disposition to admire 38, 41

Murdoch, Iris
see also Murdochian approach to legal decision-making
art and morality 80, 91
concept of attention 14, 79, 81, 88, 91
curiosity as matter of morality 117
imagination, role in moral life 79–80, 102
language and perception 82–83
moral freedom 80–81
moral perception 14, 80–85
moral philosophy 3, 77, 78–85
phenomenological approach to morality 78
process of imagining as moral discipline 102

Murdochian approach to legal decision-making 14, 51, 52, 77–78, 85–92
biased or idiosyncratic judgments 94
demarcating private and public life 87
empathy, requirement for 14, 79, 86–87
key role of judge's perception 14, 85–91
legal objectivity 83–84, 88
liberal rule of law and 14, 92–95
objections to 78, 92–95
personal transformation 92
role of emotion 14, 87–90

role of empathy 14, 79, 86–87, 90
virtuous judge concept 14, 86, 88–92

N

Nagel, Thomas 109, 116
narcissistic emotion 105–106
narrative
counterfactual 10
emotional experience of 241–242
exemplars, of 39
hypothetical 9, 10, 12, 20
imagination and, generally 8, 12, 20
pre-conceived 109, 134
natural law
virtue theory and 3
negligence-scale
personification and 226–230
negotiable instruments
objective standard of care 223–225, 226–228, 229–230
Nelson, Caleb 70–71
Nichols, S and Stich, S 201
normative relevance
imagination in search for 242–244, 249–250
Nussbaum, Martha 7, 56, 57, 94, 111
Poetic Justice 112

O

Obama, Barack
advocacy for empathy model 66–67, 179, 180, 183–184, 185, 187–189, 195
Task Force on Policing 132, 134
objectivity
impersonal approach distinguished 83–84, 88
obsequiousness
vice of 17, 37, 42
open-mindedness
epistemic virtue, as 246–247, 254–255
optimism
as upward assimilative emotion 28
Ortony, A et al 28

P

parable in legal reasoning 7
partiality, emotional 55–58, 112, 199
Patteson J 227
perception, role of
connoisseurship model of virtue 50–52
emotion and perception 11, 52
individual and social epistemology 51–52
judicial perception 85–87
language and 82–83
Murdochian moral philosophy 14, 82–91
perceptual account of virtue 3, 11, 50–51
Perner, J 202
Persky J 55–56
personification
cognitive engagement 223
dangers of 228
historical perspective on legal imagination 16, 222–232
legal reasoning, in 7, 8, 9, 10, 16, 222–228
negligence-scale and 226–230
personified standards 223–226, 231
reasonable person 222–232
tort law 226, 229–231
value of 226, 231
perspective/perception
Eastern 3
emotions and 27, 56–57
empathy and 106–108, 163–170, 173, 180–181
experiential 56, 78–85, 188–191, 193, 195
imagination and 10, 12, 30, 163–170, 173, 180–181, 237, 238–239, 247
pre-conceived narratives 109
reasonable person concept 231
Western 3
phronesis 50–53
phronimos 50, 52
pity
dangers of 111–113
intersubjective focus 105
Plato
concept of imagination 236
moral psychology 79
virtue theory 3
PLIVA v Mensing 14, 47, 63–75
Police
emotional outlook 6
Powell, Thomas Reed 220
precedent
quality of the law, concern for 244–245
requirement of respect for 54, 55, 57
preemption
express 67
federal preemption doctrine 63–65, 67–75
field 67
frustration 68, 70
implied (conflict) 67–68, 70, 74
impossibility 68–70, 72–74

legislative purpose 67
presumption against 69–71
premeditation 206
pride 18
principle of legality
principle-of-legality virtues 4, 14, 62, 66
rule of law and 72, 74
private law *see* **contract law; tort law**
probation as verbal censure 145, 147, 148
professional ethics
virtue education 3–4, 11, 13, 19
proportionality
emotion in judicial reasoning 103
justification and 103, 153
propositional imagination 10, 20
see also supposition
provocation
motivating factor, as 206
prudent man
in legal thought 10
psychoanalysis, influence 252
publicity
accessibility of judicial reasoning 57–58, 92–93
impartiality and 14, 50–53, 57–58
judicial discretion and 48–54
legal reasoning constrained by 14, 48
principle-of-legality virtue, as 4, 62, 66, 72
as requirement for viable legal systems 14, 48
transparency 48, 62
virtuous judgement and 50–53, 57–58
punishment
appropriate 139, 142, 154
attention-directing role of 145–147
communicative theory of 15, 139–155
community service 145, 147, 148
consequentialist account 142
definitions of 140–141
deterrent effect 143, 154
differential treatment for the same crime 148–149, 153–154
emotional censure 6, 15, 139, 142, 149–155
empathy and criminal law sentencing 103
fairness and 142–143, 148–149, 153–154
guilt and 142
hard treatment 140–147, 149, 153–155
just/justified 6, 140–147, 148–149, 153
probation 145, 147, 148
proportionate 153
reforming offenders, aiming at 144
repentance and remorse, engendering 144–147, 153
retributivist 142, 143–144
suffering and 15, 139–155
verbal censure 145, 147–149, 150–153

Q
quality of the law, concern for 244–245

R
race
see also Black Lives Matter movement; black males, US police killings of; racism
cross-racial empathy 190–191
emotions and politics of attention 113
legal relevance 48
sentencing affected by 52
racism
see also Black Lives Matter movement
internalised 136
stigmatised groups 136
Rae J 143
rationality
anticipating actions of others 200–201, 202–203
ascribing motivation and 208–211
limitation 208
reasonable person norm 8, 9, 10–11, 16, 208–211, 218, 222–228
Raz, Joseph 59
reason, artificial 221
reasonable person
imaginary figure in legal thought 8, 9, 10–11, 16, 208–211, 218, 222–232, 238–239, 244
personification and cognitive engagement 223
reconstruction
imaginative 218
rational 253
repentance and remorse 153
punishment engendering 144–147
resilience 29, 40, 42
retribution, punishment and 142, 143–144
retroactivity
rule of law and 72
rhetoric
emotion in rhetorical tradition 7
legal theory 7
rhetorical language theory 7, 236
virtue in rhetorical tradition 7
Rice, Tamir 122–123, 124, 126–127, 129, 131, 135
Roberts J 179

role models
see also admiration; exemplarity; exemplars
attainability of model 32, 38, 40
books of *exempla* 38, 42
negative 31–32, 42
social proximity 38
Rossi, M and Tappolet 172
rule of law
austerity and 14, 59–75
compassion and 14, 59–75
consistency, principle of 47–53, 62, 66, 72
institutional role 66, 67–72
liberal legal order 4, 95
PLIVA v Mensing 14, 65–75
respect for 59–62
transparency, principle if 48, 62
Rylands v Fletcher 73

S
satisfaction as positive emotion 18
Scalia J 62, 70
scenarios in legal reasoning 17, 236, 239, 249–250, 254–255, 256
artefacts, as 239
effect on future cases 245
enabling collective inquiry 253–254
enquiry into normative relevance 243–244, 249–250
memorability 254, 256
value 243–244
Schadenfreude 166, 167
scorn 28
self-affirmation 33
self-aggrandisement 41, 42
self-delusion 33
self-image, role models and 36–37
self-indulgent emotion 105–106
self-involvement 20
sensory imagination 20
sentimentalist virtue theory 3
servility 41, 42
Sessions, Jeff 179, 185–186
shame
emotion-centred approach 5
value of feeling 140
Smith, Adam 56
Smith, Angela 121
Smith, RH 28
social learning
admiration facilitating 34–35
social relationships
admiration and 36
social structures
affective aspect 157
impact on decision-making 19
social hierarchies 35–36, 41
Solomon, Robert 105, 106
Solum, LB 92
Sotomayor J 182–183, 187, 189, 195, 232
PLIVA v Mensing 14, 47, 63, 65–67, 74, 75
Souter J 179, 182, 183
Spolsky, Ellen 8
standard of care, objective 223–225
standards, personified 231
statutory interpretation
imagination and 218
stereotypes and stereotyping
exaggerating differences 123–124
failure of compassion 128
implicit bias compared 129–130, 136
masking group's internal diversity 123
moral distance and 124
moral framework, as 128–129
moral understanding of 125
subconscious 124
US police killings of black males 15, 123–125, 128–129
Stern, Simon 10, 16
Stevens, Wallace 108–109
Stevens J 68, 70
strict liability regimes
fairness 199
structuralism, influence 252
Stueber, Karsten 181, 182
subjective
empathy and 12, 163–164
fetishism and subjectivity 33
intersubjective focus of emotions 105–109
legal reasoning and subjectivity 52
pity and 105
politics of attention and 104–105, 113–115
punishment, accounts of 148
sentencing and subjectivity 52–53
thick value concepts 83
suffering
attention-directing role of 145–147
communicative theory of punishment 15, 139–155
compassion and 60
emotion, role in censure 149–155
emotional response to 104–105
empathy with *see* empathy
imaginative engagement facilitated by 146
punishment and 15, 139–155

repentance and remorse, engendering 144–147
sympathy for 163
verbal censure engendering 145, 147–149
supposition 10, 20, 70, 193, 211, 237–239, 244, 249–252
surprise in interactive communication 248–249, 253–254
sympathy 67
empathy distinguished 6, 15, 162–165, 168, 169, 173, 181
motivating force, as 163, 168, 169
synecdoche in legal reasoning 7

T
Taunton J 227
Taylor, Charles 252
Thomas J 232
PLIVA v Mensing 47, 62–63, 65–73, 75
Tindal CJ 229, 230
Tomasello, M 35
tort law 63–64, 70–73, 221
personification and objectivity 226, 229–231
reasonable person concept 222
transparency
see also publicity
principle of 48, 62

U
understanding, role in judicial reasoning 16
unpredictability, rule of law and 72
utilitarianism 78

V
value pluralism 4
van Domselaar, Iris 14, 18, 51, 52, 62
Vaughan CJ 229
Vaughan J 229
Vaughan v Menlove 228–230, 231
vices
absence of appropriate emotions 133
arrogance 17, 37, 41, 42
austerity 17
destructive mimicry 31, 40
emotion and 12
future research into role of 17
indifference 14–15, 17, 133
obsequiousness 17, 37, 42
vices generally 172
Vico, Giambattista 218, 219
victim-victimiser relationship
negative intimacy 6, 159, 166–169, 171
Vincent v Lake Erie Transportation Co. 73
virtue
see also virtue jurisprudence; virtue theory
acquired character traits, virtues as 246
admiration and 26–29
collective connection to 254
connoisseurship model 50–52
constraints on role in legal reasoning 47, 48
dispassionate reasoning 61, 62
emotion and 11, 12–13
emulation 29–41
epistemic 41, 246–247, 254, 256
exemplarist virtue ethics 3, 25–26
imagination and 12–13, 246–247
imitation 25–42
impartial and virtuous judgements 13–14
individual 18
innate faculty and 246
institutional 236
intellectual 28–29
judicial discretion and 50–53
in legal reasoning, generally 55–58
models of 3
moral 28–29, 41
perceptual account of 3, 11, 50–51
principle-of-legality virtues 4, 14, 62, 66
rhetorical tradition and 7
social dimension 18, 235–236
structure 3
virtues generally 172, 246
virtuous disposition to admire 37–42
virtuous judgments 13, 50–53, 91
virtue jurisprudence
direction of analysis 2
generally 1, 2–4, 13–14
law and emotion movement 6
liberal legal orders and 4
virtue theory
Aristotelian 2, 3, 4, 50
Confucian 3
Eastern perspectives 3
epistemology 246
generally 2
interactive and social dimensions of virtue 18
judicial reasoning 2
natural law approach 3
Plato 3

relevance of character 2
sentimentalist 3
virtue education 3–4, 11, 13, 19, 37–41, 42

W

Wallace, R 50
Wardlaw, K 192
Weil, Simone 79, 104–105
White, Emily Kidd 14, 18
White, James Boyd 7
Williams, Bernard 93
Winnicott, Donald 92
Winter, Steven 8
Wittgenstein, Ludwig 78, 81, 82–83
Wyeth v Levine 64, 65, 67–68, 69–70

Z

Zack, Naomi
White Privilege and Black Rights 130
Zagzebski, Linda 25, 28
Zipursky, Benjamin 14, 17, 47

Z